AF776092

Leap into Modernity – Political Economy of Growth on the Periphery, 1943-1980

GESCHICHTE - ERINNERUNG - POLITIK

POSENER STUDIEN ZUR GESCHICHTS-, KULTUR-
UND POLITIKWISSENSCHAFT

Herausgegeben von Anna Wolff-Powęska und Piotr Forecki

BAND 16

PETER LANG
EDITION

Adam Leszczyński

Leap into Modernity – Political Economy of Growth on the Periphery, 1943-1980

PETER LANG
EDITION

Bibliographic Information published by the Deutsche Nationalbibliothek
The Deutsche Nationalbibliothek lists this publication in the Deutsche Nationalbibliografie; detailed bibliographic data is available in the internet at http://dnb.d-nb.de.

Library of Congress Cataloging-in-Publication Data
Names: Leszczyński, Adam, 1975- author.
Title: Leap into modernity : political economy of growth on the periphery, 1943-1980 / Adam Leszczyński.
Description: Frankfurt am Main ; New York : Peter Lang, [2017] | Series: Geschichte, Erinnerung, Politik, ISSN 2191-3528 ; Vol. 16 | Includes bibliographical references.
Identifiers: LCCN 2016054980 | ISBN 9783631656365
Subjects: LCSH: Economic history–20th century. | Economic development–History–20th century. | Economics–Political aspects–History–20th century.
Classification: LCC HC54 .L395 2017 | DDC 338.9009/045–dc23 LC record available at https://lccn.loc.gov/2016054980

This publication was financially supported by the
Institute of Political Studies of the Polish Academy of Sciences.

Cover illustration: © liuzishan / Fotolia.com

ISSN 2191-3528
ISBN 978-3-631-65636-5 (Print)
E-ISBN 978-3-653-04886-5 (E-PDF)
E-ISBN 978-3-631-71000-5 (EPUB)
E-ISBN 978-3-631-71001-2 (MOBI)
DOI 10.3726/b10801

© Peter Lang GmbH
Internationaler Verlag der Wissenschaften
Frankfurt am Main 2017
All rights reserved.
Peter Lang Edition is an Imprint of Peter Lang GmbH.

Peter Lang – Frankfurt am Main · Bern · Bruxelles · New York ·
Oxford · Warszawa · Wien

All parts of this publication are protected by copyright. Any utilisation outside the strict limits of the copyright law, without the permission of the publisher, is forbidden and liable to prosecution. This applies in particular to reproductions, translations, microfilming, and storage and processing in electronic retrieval systems.

This publication has been peer reviewed.

www.peterlang.com

Table of contents

Chapter 1. A brief history of backwardness

1. Malthus was right

In 1825 on orders from the British government, Englishman William Jacob travelled the length and breadth of what was then Congress Poland, Galicia and the Baltic provinces of Russia. His journey had a very practical purpose. The United Kingdom needed grain to feed the workers in its rapidly expanding industrial cities. Jacob had been instructed to determine how much grain could be supplied by the lands of "ancient Poland", and at what prices. He was also to assess the possibilities for exporting grain through Gdańsk, East Prussia and Riga. He fulfilled these tasks brilliantly. After returning to England, he issued a comprehensive report in which he also characterized – in the style of travel narratives of the day – the inhabitants of the Polish lands.[1] He noted the reluctance of the nobility to involve themselves professionally in anything outside of military service, the dominant position of Jews in commerce, and of the Germans in the skilled trades. (Germans, he noted, felt ill at ease in Poland and dreamt only of returning to their homeland once they had made their fortune.) He also devoted much attention to the Polish peasantry:

> In general, this Peasantry is in a condition of great distress, and involved in debt to their lord. They are no longer slaves, or *adstricti glebae*. [...] These people live in Wooden Huts, covered with thatch or shingles, consisting of one room with a stove, around which the inhabitants and their cattle crowd together, and where the most disgusting kinds of filthiness are to be seen. Their common Food is cabbage, potatoes sometimes, but not generally, pease, black bread, and soup, or rather gruel, without the addition of butter or meat. Their chief Drink is water, or the cheap whiskey of the country, which is the only luxury of the peasants; and is drunk, whenever they can obtain it, in enormous quantities. [...] In their houses they have little that merits the name of furniture; and their clothing is coarse, ragged, and filthy, even to disgust [...] Very little attention has been paid to their Education, and they are generally ignorant, superstitious, and fanatical [...] All the Operations of Husbandry struck me to be very ill performed.[2]

---

1 W. Jacob, *Report on the Trade in Foreign Corn: And on the Agriculture of the North of Europe*, London, 1826. Descriptions of Polish backwardness and poverty had been a permanent element of travel literature since at least the seventeenth century: cf. J. Kochanowicz, "Polska w epoce nowoczesnego wzrostu gospodarczego", [in:] *Modernizacja Polski. Struktury, agencje, instytucje*, ed. W. Morawski, Warszawa, 2010.

2 Jacob, *Report*..., pp. 65–66.

Jacob's account is all the more telling if we consider its context. The reference point for the author was England – then the richest country in the world, but one with rapidly growing expanses of abject poverty. According to estimates by historians today, in 1820 the wages of workers in England were only 10 percent higher than in 1770. At the same time, we have good reason to believe that living and working conditions for most of these workers were in many respects worse than a few decades earlier.[3] Soon after Jacob's report on the Polish lands, several widely-discussed books depicting the misery of British workers were published in London; this included the publication in 1833 of a book by Peter Gaskell about English workers that provided the inspiration for Engels' writing *The Condition of the Working Class in England.*[4] Jacob had visited the Polish lands at an important historical moment; never before and never again during the English Industrial Revolution was there a greater contrast between the rapidly growing economy and stagnant wages (and even of deepening poverty, in the opinion of many). Both Jacob and his readers still had fresh in their memory the times of the French Revolution and the Napoleonic wars, when sudden and dramatic rises in food prices left many British workers with too little income to avoid starvation. Every few years, the country was shaken by waves of revolts by the working classes; English society, at least according to contemporary opinions, was like a volcano ready to explode. It is from such an England – the one described by Dickens, Gaskell and Engels – that Jacob travelled to Congress Poland. And once there he was struck by its poverty and backwardness.

Jacob also noted that Polish peasants worked much less efficiently than English agricultural labourers. The Englishman attributed this laziness not to any innate features found in the Polish peasantry, but to a "system of duty work" in which they had no personal investment.

> [...] labour is performed in the most negligent and slovenly manner possible. No manager of a large estate can have his eye constantly on every workman; and when no advantage is gained by care in the work, it will naturally be very imperfectly executed. [...]

---

3 For the most commonly cited estimate of wages in Great Britain during the Industrial Revolution, see C. Feinstein, 'Pessimism Perpetuated: Real Wages and the Standard of Living in Britain During and After the Industrial Revolution', *Journal of Economic History* 1998, no. 58.

4 P. Gaskell, *The Manufacturing Population of England. Its Moral, Social and Physical Conditions, and the Changes which Have Arisen from the Use of Steam Machinery; with an Examination of Infant Labour*, London 1833.

> it appeared to me that a much greater proportion of the grain was left among the straw, than in that which has passed under an English flail.[5]

This brief description of the Polish countryside contains all the elements that can be found in different images of social, cultural and economic backwardness. We thus have here an inefficient and anachronistic social order (in the Polish case this was actually still a feudal system of forced labour, although the peasants had been formally freed); a rural and agricultural society, rather than an urban and industrial society divided into fixed and impermeable classes; a low level of labour productivity, outdated technology, economic stagnation and an uneven distribution of income; and finally, a low level of formal education, consumption and material culture, so low, in fact, that the filth, ignorance and misery of the peasantry aroused disgust in an observer who harkened from the centre of European civilization. Jacob was a generally dispassionate observer – as dispassionate as only the author of a thick tome on grain prices and transport costs could be. In spite of this, he could not hide his disgust. He was overpowered by it – despite being an intelligent traveller and being fully aware that the people he was describing were not to blame for their misery.

His description of the civilizational gap between the centre and periphery contains so many historical, social and economic dimensions that it is hard to encompass them all in a single definition. The eminent historian Eric Hobsbawm once said it all boils down to finding an answer to the question: "why is Switzerland richer than Albania?"[6] This question only seems to be unreasonable: the two countries share similarities – both are small, mountainous, and lack natural resources and fertile soil; over the centuries, both have also experienced extreme poverty, fiercely defended their independence, and sent their young to serve as mercenaries in foreign armies out of economic need. (Switzerland does not even have access to the sea!) To answer to the above question, we have to refer back to a number of historical, religious and economic causes; the story of the evolution of both countries is a long and complicated one, which cannot be summed up in a single sentence or encompassed in a single set of numbers.

Notwithstanding, it is impossible to discuss notions of accelerated development without attempting to describe backwardness. How large was the distance that separated the centre of European civilization and those countries that were

---

5 Jacob, *Report…*, p. 67.

6 Hobsbawm's question is cited by Daniel Chirot in the Introduction to: *The Origins of Backwardness in Eastern Europe: Economics and Politics From the Middle Ages Until the Early Twentieth Century*, ed. D. Chirot, Berkeley–Los Angeles 1991, p. 3.

peripheral and backward? How can this distance be measured? How was it shaped by history?

Statistics do not provide answers to these questions. They do not reach sufficiently deep into the past – rarely further than the nineteenth century – and, moreover, they often cannot be trusted. They were not even trusted in their own time. Jerzy Jedlicki quotes the Director of the Government Commission for Internal Affairs in the Kingdom of Poland (and therefore a high official who had a good idea of how the administration under him operated), who wrote in 1860 that the data provided by the local authorities was completely unreliable. In response to a question from another office, which had doubts as to whether the data provided to it by the local administration were accurate, one dignitary he wrote: "Purely administrative centralised statistics yield accurate results only where they relate to receipts or expenditures of public money, only where they are strictly controlled and where there is accountability for falsehoods."[7] Given such thinking among contemporaries, historians should be all the more cautious about quoting these numbers.

This leaves us with indirect methods. Using sophisticated statistical methods, economists attempt to assess the gross domestic product of various countries in the past, up to the beginning of our present era.[8] By means of archival research, we can attempt to determine what factors influenced earnings in different periods and in different countries: when they rose, when they fell, and what this money could buy – and this provides us with an idea of the standard of living. We can also describe the level of material culture: counting how much furniture and how many spoons, pots and other objects were listed in wills or court documents. On the basis of field work in cemeteries, we can determine the average height of people in different historical periods, with the assumption that these

---

7 J. Jedlicki, *Nieudana próba kapitalistycznej industrializacji: analiza państwowego gospodarstwa przemysłowego w Królestwie Polskim XIX w.*, Warszawa 1964, p. 20.

8 Among these, the most complete (and most often cited) estimates are those of A. Maddison (*The World Economy,* vol. 1: *A Millenial Perspective,* vol. 2: *Historical Statistics*, Paris 2006). Often cited are the early estimates found in P. Bairoch (P. Bairoch, M. Levy-Leboyer, *Disparities in Economic Development Since the Industrial Revolution,* London 1981); P. Bairoch, "Europe's Gross National Product: 1800–1975", *Journal of European Economic History*, 1976, no. 3. Maddison speaks critically of Bairoch: "Bairoch's source notes were frequently cryptic and often cited "personal estimates" he did not publish." (*The World Economy,* vol. 1, p. 628). In practice, many economic historians use their own estimates, the sources of which are not always clear, and the differences between individual authors remain considerable. Maddison devotes a large chapter to this issue.

changes correspond roughly to changes in the level of nutrition and living conditions (although this relationship is not always straightforward). We can also look at wills, parish registers, and other documents, attempting to determine the average lifespan. Still, these methods provide us with few definitive answers. All of them are imperfect, and they sometimes lead to seemingly conflicting conclusions. Taken together, however, they give us an approximate image of the past.

About what is there any certainty? That Malthus was right when he described the logic of economic life in the centuries before the industrial revolution (and in many countries, perhaps still today). In *An Essay on the Principle of Population*, first published in 1798, Pastor Thomas Robert Malthus argued that the human economy was governed by the same rules as the "natural economy" of animals; the same criterion – the availability of food – defined the living conditions of both animals and humans.[9] People, like animals, multiply as long as have enough to eat; an increase in food production, Malthus argued, will always lead to an increase in population. Therefore, an influx of new workers will cause wages, according to the law of supply and demand, to move toward a minimum, subsistence level. Sometimes this can take time – and a generation or two can enjoy a slightly greater level of prosperity. However, in a Malthusian world, a steady increase in the standard of living is impossible: technological progress only leads to population growth (assuming, as Malthus wrote, that "the passion between the sexes" is constant and the population always increases faster than food production).[10]

The consequences of this principle lead to interesting paradoxes. As the historian Gregory Clark How put it – perhaps with some exaggeration – the Malthusian world is from today's perspective turned on its head: what today is an obstacle to increased prosperity, then promoted it:

> In the Malthusian economy before 1800, economic policy was turned on its head: vice now was virtue then, and virtue vice. Those scourges of failed modern states—war, violence, disorder, harvest failures, collapsed public infrastructures, bad sanitation—were the friends of mankind before 1800. They reduced population pressures and increased material living standards. In contrast policies beloved of the World Bank and the United

9 T. Malthus, *An Essay on the Principle of Population, as It Affects the Future Improvement of Society, with Remarks on the Speculations of Mr. Godwin, M. Condorcet, and Other Writers*, London 1798.

10 Cf. also C. K. Maisels, *The Emergence of Civilization: From Hunting and Gathering to Agriculture, Cities, and the State in the Near East*, London–New York 1993, p. 20 ff.

Nations today—peace, stability, order, public health, transfers to the poor—were the enemies of prosperity. They generated the population growth that impoverished.[11]

In the Malthusian world, a second paradox – social differences – also had a different meaning than today. Effectively raising the standard of living of the majority was impossible in the long run. Therefore, regardless of how much land and wealth was held by the ruling class, the standard of living of their subjects changed very little: their numbers merely rose or declined. A rise in the standard of living of the masses was always temporary, and the vast majority of humanity always lived on the brink of starvation. The biblical description of the exile from Eden, where God says to Adam: "Cursed is the ground because of you / through painful toil you will eat food from it / all the days of your life / It will produce thorns and thistles for you, / and you will eat the plants of the field" (Genesis 3: 17–18), was until very recently a good metaphor for the fate of the common man: there was no escape from it.

The key to freeing oneself from the Malthusian trap was technological progress. For real incomes to rise, food production had to increase faster than the population. For many centuries, however, technological change occurred too slowly. If we assume that the population grew at a rate equal to the pace of technological development (according to the logic of the Malthusian world), it turns out that the increase in productivity from 1000 to 1820 did not exceed an average of 0.05 percent per annum – that is, it reached only one-thirtieth of its current level.[12] Differences in productivity associated with the culture of work – for example, that described by Jacob in his comparison of Polish peasants to English agricultural labourers – were most likely real, though not measurable (especially by historians today). However, they translated into only minor differences in living standards. If, for example, in the seventeenth century productivity on the Vistula was lower than on the Thames, in practice this meant only that the Polish lands were much less densely populated than those in England.[13] The fact that Jacob was so deeply moved by what he saw indicated that he had travelled from a country that was already on the road to the industrial revolution, in which real wages – although still at starvation levels from today's point of view – had

11 G. Clark, *Farewell to Alms: A Brief Economic History of the World*, Princeton–Oxford 2007, p. 5.

12 Cf. A. Maddison, *Growth and Interaction in the World Economy. The Roots of Modernity*, Washington 2005, p. 5 ff.; A. Maddison, "The West and the Rest in the World Economy: 1000–2030, Maddisonian and Malthusian Interpretations", *World Economics*, 2008, no. 4.

13 G. Clark, *Farewell...*, op. cit., pp. 14, 366–367.

already risen significantly.[14] They would soon begin to grow at a rate previously unimaginable.[15]

Although a constant increase in prosperity in the Malthusian world was impossible, differences in standards of living between different countries and eras could be considerable. Experts explain these through culturally imposed restrictions on fertility – for example, a later age of marriage in northern Europe than in southern Europe or infanticide in China (according to a universal principle: the fewer the people, the greater the prosperity). There were also differences in the culture of everyday life that cannot easily be made to fit Malthusian principles. The Romans, for example, mass-produced very cheap items for daily use, and developed an extensive trade network, which meant that these items were also available to the poor in many parts of the empire.[16] The study of Roman pots may seem not a very inspiring pastime, but it says a lot about the lifestyles of their users. At excavation sites from Roman times, one can find an abundance of functional kitchenware used to prepare food; elegant tableware for display and use; and amphorae, large vessels used in the Mediterranean to transport and store wine and olive oil. An outstanding archaeologist described it thus:

> Three features of Roman pottery are remarkable, and not to be found again for many centuries in the West: its excellent quality and considerable standardization; the massive quantities in which it was produced; and its widespread diffusion, not only geographically (sometimes being transported over many hundreds of miles), but also socially (so it reached not just the rich, but also the poor). In the areas of the Roman world that I know best, central and northern Italy, after the end of the Roman world, this level of sophistication is not seen again until perhaps the fourteenth century, some 800 years later. […] When people today are shown a very ordinary Roman pot, and, in particular, are allowed to handle it, they often comment on how 'modern' it looks and feels, and need to be convinced of its true age.[17]

This organised world of mass production disappeared along with the invasion of the barbarians; starting from the fifth century, the items used in everyday life in Europe became more primitive, and evidence provided by archaeologists shows

14 The difference in income levels (and domestic comfort) between Eastern and Western Europe goes back much further than the Industrial Revolution, but it started to increase rapidly at that time.

15 C. K. Harley, "Reassessing the Industrial Revolution: A Macro View", [in:] *The British Industrial Revolution. An Economic Perspective,* ed. J. Mokyr, Boulder–Oxford 1999, p. 161.

16 B. Ward-Perkins, *The Fall of Rome and the End of Civilization,* Oxford 2005, p. 88 ff.

17 Ibid., p. 89.

the gradual dying off of trade routes from ancient times. Meaningful evidence is also provided by Monte Testaccio in Rome, a fifty-metre high heap of amphorae shards from the second and third century A.D. According to estimates by archaeologists, the 53 million amphorae contained there are the remnants of 6 billion litres of oil imported to the imperial capital. Goods were also imported in the sixth and seventh centuries, but the quantities were minimal. "This was a society with similarities to our own—moving goods on a gigantic scale, manufacturing high-quality containers to do so, and occasionally, as here, even discarding them on delivery. Like us, the Romans enjoy the dubious distinction of creating a mountain of good-quality rubbish", archaeologist Bryan Ward-Perkins wrote about ancient Rome.[18] Researchers studying arctic ice have also recorded high levels of air pollution, produced by the smelting of lead and copper in Roman times, which immediately after the fall of the empire dropped to levels recorded in prehistoric times. These metals were not produced again on a scale similar to that in Roman times until the sixteenth and seventeenth centuries.[19]

Despite the well-developed organization of production and trade, and the mass production of items for daily use, Roman society continued to operate under the rules of the Malthusian economy.[20] Historical estimates of per capita income show a decline between the fall of the Empire and the late Middle Ages, associated with the collapse of the imperial economic system and a decline in labour productivity.[21] The population decreased even more drastically: in comparison with the days of ancient Rome, the European continent in the early Middle Ages was not only rural but empty. Since productivity had fallen, population density had declined, as well.

The paradoxes of the Malthusian economy mean that economic historians today can write seriously about what a great boon the Black Death was for Europe – the plague epidemic in 1346–1347 killed, according to various estimates,

---

18 Ibid., p. 92.

19 Ibid., p. 95.

20 A. Bowman, A. Wilson, "Quantifying the Roman Economy: Integration, Growth, Decline?", [in:] *Quantifying the Roman Economy. Methods and Problems*, eds. A. Bowman, A. Wilson, Oxford 2009, p. 28.

21 The most popular and most widely cited statistical data on income per capita are the estimates of A. Maddison, *The World Economy. A Millennial Perspective*, Paris 2006. See also A. A. Avakov, *Two Thousand Years of Economic Statistics. World Population, GDP and PPP*, New York 2010.

between a third and half of the inhabitants of the West.[22] The population loss resulted in a rapid increase in wages and in the standard of living – which lasted until the population increased once again (in the case of England, this occurred only around the year 1600; the population had dropped from six to less than three million in the fifteenth century, and had reached seven million in the times of Queen Elizabeth).[23] While some died because of war or plague, the income of the remaining population increased, because in practice this meant that agricultural production per capita was higher – and that was what really mattered in an economy in which more than 90 percent of the people lived in the countryside, and 70 percent made their living directly from farming.

Some historians, such as Nico Voigtländer, even believe that the plague provided the first impetus for the accumulation of capital. Since the number of people who could work the land had declined, it was necessary to come up with ways to take better advantage of those who were available, for example, by investing in improved agricultural technologies – capital had to compensate for the deficit in labour. This is only a step from the idea that the plague was one of the root causes of the Industrial Revolution, which first occurred in those areas most affected by the epidemic four hundred years earlier.[24] Even the jump in income caused by the Black Death looks today like a tiny twitch of the seismograph compared to that brought about by the industrial revolution.

Yet Malthus still has something to say about the modern world. As modern-day economists have estimated, the poorest countries in the world – despite international aid, low-cost transport enabling the delivery of food to any place on earth, and giant food surpluses in rich countries – we are still unable to break out of the closed circle that he described.[25]

---

22 The decline in agricultural production in Europe was less than the decline in population: income increased. The opposite was true in Egypt, which also had not yet undergone a proto-capitalist structural transformation along the lines of that in Western Europe. S. J. Borsch, *The Black Death in Egypt and England*, Austin 2005, p. 15 ff.

23 J. Hatcher, J. Bailey, *Modelling the Middle Ages. The History and Theory of England's Economic Development*, Oxford 2001, p. 31.

24 Cf. e.g. N. Voigtländer, H.-J. Voth, "Malthusian Dynamism and the Rise of Europe: Make War, Not Love", *American Economic Review*, 2009, no. 2.

25 After analyzing the relationship between economic growth, per capita income and population, this is the conclusion reached by scholars such as D. N. Weil and J. Wilde, "How Relevant is Malthus For Economic Development Today?", *American Economic Review*, 2009, no. 2

In around 1640, there was probably only one place on Earth – England – where the rules described by Malthus were beginning no longer to hold true.[26] This breakthrough occurred slowly. By 1800, the population had grown from six to seven million to ten million, while the standard of living had not fallen, but risen (though only very slightly: average income had increased by 0.2 percent annually, or 10 percent per generation). At the beginning of the nineteenth century, the income of the working class in England was twice as high as in 1250, and three times higher than in 1600, but only slightly higher than in the decades following the Black Death.

2. Wealth and poverty in the past

On April 20, 1697, an advertisement appeared in the newspaper *Amsterdamsche Courant* for a new gadget, the *Zak-aardebol*, or pocket globe. As advertised by its manufacturers, cartographers Abraham van Ceulen and Gerrit Drogenham, it was "very appropriate for all devotees of astronomy and other sciences, as well as [all those] who would customarily carry a pocket watch with them." The globe was five centimetres long in diameter and was sold in a decorative leather case, in the centre of which was a tastefully and stylishly painted sky with constellations of stars – it was, according to one modern-day historian, one of the earliest geocentric representations of the heavens.[27]

Not without reason, the producers were looking for customers among the devotees of pocket watches (and therefore gadget lovers: like their globe, watches were then a technical novelty). The mini-globe's ability to indicate its owner's position in space was meant, according to its producers, to supplement a watch's ability to indicate the time. It did not catch on, perhaps because – in contrast to the very practical watch – it remained an expensive toy. (It is known that Tsar Peter the Great bought one while visiting Holland, but he did not have to concern

26 Cf. G. Clark, *Farewell…*, op. cit., p. 30. Clark's conclusions are based on meticulous, long-term archival research on income in England from the Middle Ages to the nineteenth century; however, debate continues over when England freed itself from Malthus' vicious circle, the shape this process took, and the extent to which it had been trapped within it earlier; cf. e.g. M. Kremer, "Population Growth and Technological Change: One Million B.C. to 1990", *Quarterly Journal of Economics*, 1993, no. 3 or O. Galor, D. N. Weil, "Population, Technology and Growth: From the Malthusian Regime to the Demographic Transition and Beyond", *American Economic Review*, 2000, no. 4

27 The story of the *zak-aardebol* is told by J. de Vries, *The Industrious Revolution. Consumer Behavior and the Household Economy, 1650 to the Present*, Cambridge 2008, pp. 1–4. Data on the production of watches in Europe were also taken from this book.

himself with costs). At the end of the eighteenth century, European watchmakers were producing 400,000 pocket watches per year. Although they became cheaper as production methods improved, they remained expensive from today's point of view: they cost an artisan the equivalent of several weeks' work, and served the owner – according to various estimates – for an average of four to twelve years, and thus, not very long. Nevertheless, people bought them willingly. In 1780, 70 percent of the servants in Paris had them, as did one in three workers, traders and artisans. Watches were bought during good times by many families who had nothing to put into the pot in harder times when prices were high.

The history of the *zak-aardebol* and pocket watches shows how difficult it is to compare the standard of living in the past with that of today. Economists can estimate per capita income and write that GDP per capita in Africa today is lower than in Western Europe in 1820 or in England in 1700, but the cognitive value of such rankings is limited: both the structure of expenses and the goods you could buy with this money vary too greatly.[28]

This seems obvious, but it is worth recalling for two reasons. First, it is easy to forget about the distance that separates us from the past, even the most recent past. Secondly, even today, comparisons between the standard of living in the poorest and richest countries are difficult for very similar reasons. Differences in price structures and available goods – whether these are between the past and present, or between developed and developing countries – mean that simple statements of income are misleading. Hiring a servant costs tens of dollars per month in Nairobi, a few hundred in Rio de Janeiro, and several thousand in London. These differences have grown sharper since the era of the industrial revolution. Since the industrial revolution, the disparities have increased between the rich industrial countries and the poorest countries of Africa and Asia, where some goods – for example, expert medical care – are very expensive or unavailable, while others, particularly services that do not require qualifications, such as, the work of a janitor, are cheap. Of course, Africans and Asians today do not live in medieval conditions: in 2009, every second Nigerian had a cell phone, even though his income estimated in U.S. dollars was significantly lower than that of a British citizen two hundred years ago. Nor can the difference in living standards between Lagos and London today be easily converted into monetary terms – just like the differences between Warsaw during the Gomulka era and Paris during the times of Pompidou.

---

28 Cf. A. Wyczański, "Czy można porównywać poziom życia gospodarczego krajów w epoce przedstatystycznej?", [in:] *Badania nad historią gospodarczo-społeczną w Polsce. Problemy i metody*, Warszawa–Poznań 1978, p. 53 ff.

A significant part of this difference can be reduced to technology. This is how the apartment of an intellectual in Warsaw was described two hundred years ago in one diary:

> He lived in a small flat with a porch facing the street. The vestibule led directly into the living room, which was also the dining room, the room where guests were entertained, the library and the bedroom, because in an open niche stood his narrow bed, neatly made, and above it, beneath a picture of Our Lady of Czestochowa, hung a scimitar in a shagreen scabbard. The front and side walls were covered by a high wall of books.[29]

What does the homeowner lack? A telephone, automobile, electric lighting, central heating, air conditioning, gas cooker, washing machine, refrigerator, dishwasher, private bathroom with hot running water and a toilet – not to mention a computer, Internet access, mobile phone, television and a music system. This list could easily be extended. Many modern comforts were unavailable at any price; others, such as in-home music on demand, could be afforded by only a few (the emperor of Austria had his own personal opera).[30] In times when doing the laundry required a day of tiring labour, maintaining a life of relative comfort demanded hard work from full-time domestic workers. The level of medical care was incomparable to that of today.

It is also difficult to compare differences in the lifestyles of the rich and the poor in the past, and not only due to a lack of data. Although we know that until the mid-nineteenth century, the average worker spent 80 percent of his income on food – roughly the same as in the Middle Ages – the consumption patterns of those even slightly wealthier underwent a much greater change. Modern-day research shows slow but steady economic growth in Europe in the two centuries leading up to the Industrial Revolution: in Western Europe the proportion of city-dwellers among the population increased from 5.6 percent in 1500 to 10 percent in 1800.[31]

---

29 K. W. Wójcicki, *Pamiętniki dziecka Warszawy i inne wspomnienia warszawskie*, vol. 1, eds. J. W. Gomulicki, Z. Lewinówna, M. Grabowska, Warszawa 1974, quoted in M. Janowski, *Narodziny inteligencji, 1750–1831*, Warszawa 2008, p. 163.

30 This comparison comes from Prof. J. Bradford DeLong from Berkeley, who was kind enough to provide me with a chapter from a book he is working on (*Slouching Towards Utopia. Economic History of the World in the Long Twentieth Century, 1870–2010*, unpublished).

31 E. Horlings, "Pre-industrial Economic Growth and the Transition to an Industrial Economy", [in:] *Early Modern Capitalism. Economic and Social Change in Europe 1400–1800*, ed. M. Prak, London–New York 2001, p. 89; J. L. van Zanden, "Early Modern Economic Growth: A Survey of the European Economy, 1500–1800", Ibid., p. 67 ff.

Since the beginning of the modern era, more and more exotic spices, coffee and tea had been consumed in wealthier homes. In Western Europe, beginning in the seventeenth century, even in poor homes, the number of everyday household objects rapidly increased. According to a study conducted on wills and judicial acts, in one rural province in the Netherlands, between 1630 and 1670, the average household owned 241 items (divided in 47 categories); the average for the period 1700–1795 was 538 items (divided into 71 categories).[32] This is telling testimony of a revolution in consumption. Studies in England and France have yielded similar results. In these countries, the increase mainly represents imported and luxury goods: ornamented furniture (bureaus, commodes, desks, stylish sofas and chairs), luxurious tableware (often made from Chinese porcelain), clocks, paintings, curtains, and, of course, coffee and tea services. At the end of the eighteenth century, all of these items were in 80 percent of Dutch homes, although according to the estimates of economists from that century, the average earnings in the Netherlands had either decreased or remained flat. (This is further proof that statistics on income do not tell the whole story.)

Yet, a different story of how Europeans freed themselves from the Malthusian trap is told by studies on their height over the centuries. The average change in height reflects both the quality of nutrition and the degree of social inequality: in simple terms, it can be assumed that the greater the disparity in living standards between the rich and the poor, the greater the differences in height among the people of a given country and time.[33] The average inhabitant of the Roman Empire measured about 169–170 cm in height. The barbarians who settled on the former Roman lands in the fifth and sixth centuries were markedly taller, which experts attribute to a diet richer in protein and the fact that the barbarians did not live in unhealthy cities – as well as, perhaps, to certain genetic differences and less distinct social differences among the Germanic tribes. Again, this information still does not tell everything about the standard of living: "A Northern barbarian living in the sixth century was tall and certainly lived relatively long, [...] but in the event that he was amusement-loving and fond of consumer goods, he would most probably have preferred to live in second century Rome, write the authors of one recent study."[34] By the early seventh century, however, the Germans who had

32 J. A. Kamermans, *Materieele cultuur in de Krimpenerwaard in de zeventiende en achttiende eeuw*, Wageningen 1999. Quoted in J. de Vries, The Industrious Revolution..., op. cit., p. 124.

33 N. Koepke, J. Baten, "The Biological Standard of Living in Europe During the Last Two Millennia", *European Review of Economic History*, 2005, no. 1.

34 Ibid, p. 88.

settled on the former Roman territories were shorter than the Romans – shorter even than those born during the collapse of the empire.

Judging from the average height of Europeans, the quality of their food varied little between 1000 and 1800, even if their lifestyle and the availability of consumer goods had changed significantly. According to the rules of the Malthusian economy, the greater the population density, the poorer the quality of nutrition, and thus, the lower the average height; these variations are noticeable, but they are not large. However, the data show a clear difference in the quality of nutrition in modern times: while almost all the Romans examined were of roughly the same height (which seems to contradict the view that there were enormous social differences in Rome), height differences among men in modern times reached 6 cm, which according to specialists reflects growing social distances and progressive urbanization, as the sanitation and general quality of nutrition in cities were terrible.[35] The workers living in British industrial centres began to grow progressively taller only in the latter half of the nineteenth century, when the Industrial Revolution was already at least eighty years old.[36]

A decline in living standards was accompanying economic expansion on the other end of the continent, in Russia, as well, though for different reasons. New studies of lists of Russian recruits from the eighteenth century show the effects of a different but likewise interesting mechanism: in the eighteenth century – a period of unprecedented economic growth and military power in Russia – the average height of a twenty-year-old decreased by 5 cm. The economy grew, but all the benefits from increased productivity went to the state; empire-building necessitated an increase in taxes and a reduction in the standard of living of ordinary people. In this respect, Stalin was to be heir to a Russian tradition: in the eighteenth century, the shortest generation of recruits were born in the times of Peter the Great and Catherine the Great.[37]

---

35 Cf. J. Boulton, "'Turned into the Street with My Children Destitute of Every Thing': The Payment of Rent and the London Poor, 1600–1850", [in:] *Accommodating Poverty. The Housing and Living Arrangements of the English Poor, c. 1600–1850,* eds. J. McEwan, P. Sharpe, Houndmills–New York 2011; and: P. King, "The Residential and Familial Arrangements of English Pauper Letter Writers, 1800–1840s", Ibid., p. 145 ff.

36 See R. W. Fogel, *An Overview of the Changing Body: Health, Nutrition and Human Development in the Western World since 1700*, NBER Working Paper 16938, April 2011, http://www.nber.org/papers/w16938.

37 B. Mironov, The Burden of Grandeur. Physical and Economic Well-being of the Russian Population in the Eighteenth Century", [in:] *Living Standards in the Past. New*

In the story of ideas about accelerated development after 1943, this distant historical background is important for two reasons. First of all, it shows that the relationship between expansion of the economy and production and a rise in living standards is by no means directly proportional: in the past, there have been many examples of countries where economic growth has been coupled with a decrease in the average standard of living. Secondly, it appears to show that the only path from backwardness to development (or from a "traditional" to "modern" society) is through blood, sweat and tears. This was well known long before Marx, and the authors of the concept of accelerated development after World War II also seemed well aware of this issue, although they did not have at their disposal such precise historical research as is available today.[38] Widely cited was a well-known article published in 1955 by future Nobel laureate Simon Kuznets, a pioneer in research on national income, which showed a decline in average earnings in the first phase of industrialization.[39] This observation had political consequences. It was easier to justify a decline in living standards during periods of state-led planned industrialization. If even England had to pass through a purgatory of working-class indigence on the way to achieving industrial might and bourgeois prosperity, then perhaps we were dealing with a regular pattern in economic development. There was simply no other path. This was an important argument, which – as we shall see – continues to return in various forms, providing justification for the growing social disparities in China and other rapidly developing countries of the developing world.

The purgatory through which England passed looks today more like a hell – an inescapable abyss. For many decades, up until the mid-nineteenth century, the wages of workers in British cities grew only slightly, while the wages of agricultural workers fell.[40] Even the best-paid workers in most industries, the employees of some textile factories, for example, had to resign themselves to a drastic decline in living standards following a move from the countryside to the city. The mortality rate in cities was extremely high: in times of epidemics, which recurred regularly every few years, diseases such as typhoid and cholera were responsible for nearly every second death. In London, even in years in which there was no such pestilence, at least a third of all deaths were caused by tuberculosis. An infant born in

---

Perspectives on Well-Being in Asia and Europe, eds. R. Allen, T. Bengtsson, M. Dribe, Oxford 2005, pp. 255–277.

38 See Chapter 2.

39 P. Kuznets, "Growth and Income Inequality", *American Economic Review*, 1955, no. 1.

40 See e.g. R. C. Allen, *Engel's Pause: Pessimist's Guide to the British Industrial Revolution*, University of Oxford Department of Economics Discussion Paper 315, April 2007.

the 1840s in Liverpool to parents from the upper or middle classes – a businessman, lawyer or doctor – could expect to live to the age of 35; the child of a small merchant or a shopkeeper, to age 22; the child of a mechanic or worker, to age 15, due to a very high rate of mortality not only in childhood, but at every stage of life. (In Liverpool, most workers lived in cellars. In the 1830s, as one journalist of that day noted without surprise, the "fluid matter of the court privies" flowed into several such cellars, carving out a one-metre deep channel under one family's bed.) In addition to descriptions from the period, a range of data confirms the dreadful living conditions in cities at that time: for example, the average height of British-born recruits during this period was shorter by 5 cm than that of previous and later generations (they began to grow taller only after 1870).

In the eyes of first-hand observers, the large industrial cities of England in the first half of the nineteenth century were a chaotic maze of brothels, gin shops, beer halls, thieves' dens, dirty courtyards, communal bathrooms, puddles, piles of garbage, cheap, crowded working-class housing made of red brick and badly lit, dangerous streets, where you could run across wild dogs, rats and – posing the greatest threat to pedestrians – bands of homeless children. Cities were noisy, dirty, and smoky; full of flies and dust in the summer and mud in the autumn and spring; there was no way to protect oneself from the ever-present fleas and lice. Even the cemeteries were overcrowded: the Church of England blocked plans to build large municipal cemeteries outside the city because of the money it earned from burials.[41] Crime rose to record levels, and the police were hardly visible outside the capital. Commentators of the time wrung their hands over the prevalence of sexual promiscuity and alcoholism among the working class. When in 1830 the British Parliament allowed beer to be sold without a permit in the hope that this would reduce the consumption of whiskey and spirits, within six months 24,000 new taverns and pubs opened in urban areas. Revolts and riots were the order of the day, and the social order seemed perpetually fragile.[42] Conflicts between rich and poor were brutal, and among the propertied classes, it was a commonly-held view that poverty motivated people to work and entrepreneurship, and thus had a beneficial moral influence on workers.[43] Child labour became a source of moral protest quite late – even at the end of the eighteenth century, many enlightened authors still believed that children should

41 B. Hilton, *A Mad, Bad, and Dangerous People? England, 1783–1846*, Oxford 2006, pp. 574–575; I owe my descriptions of early industrial England primarily to this book.

42 J. E. Archer, *Social Unrest and Popular Protest in England*, Cambridge 2000, p. 40; J. Foster, *Class Struggle and the Industrial Revolution*, London 2005, p. 36 ff.

43 E. P. Thompson, *The Making of the English Working* Class, New York 1963, p. 277.

work.[44] According to recent studies, it is very likely that more children worked during the Industrial Revolution than before or after it.[45]

Peter Gaskell, author of one of the most famous books published then on the situation of the working poor, compared the appearance of factory workers with that of their parents, "ruddy and healthy" farm workers. A wide gulf can clearly be seen between an idealized image of merry rural life and that of workers vegetating in dark factories. There was a general longing for an alleged lost rural idyll.[46] "Any man who has stood at twelve o'clock at the single narrow door-way, which serves as the place of exit for the hands employed in the great cotton-mills, must acknowledge, that an uglier set of men and women [...] would be impossible to congregate," Gaskell writes. He also writes at length about their short, frail build, thin hair, and unhealthy pale complexion, and even about the prevalence of flat-foot and a lurching gait; he saw their uncertain, slouching manner of walking as a sign of anxiety and feelings of rejection.[47] He viewed poor living conditions as the source of what he described as widespread and, worse yet, unabashed, drunkenness and debauchery: a crowded home "in which all the decencies and moral observances of domestic life are constantly violated, reduces its inmates to a condition in nowise elevated above that of the savage." The profanity-filled language spoken by working-class families filled him with dread. Progress, viewed up close, did not look very appealing, and, in any case, it was clear that the social price for it was extremely high.

Even if industrialization in the long term also benefitted workers, according to historian Boyd Hilton, in its early stage, it was a demographic and social disaster.[48] Machines were expensive, so they needed to have as little downtime as possible in order to yield a profit. In many industries, factories operated from six in the morning until eight at night, six days a week, with short breaks for meals. The tempo of work, set by factory bells and measured by the clock, was totally unlike the rhythm of field work, regulated by nature; making the shift from one to the other was not easy.[49]

---

44 K. Honeyman, *Child Workers in England, 1780–1820*, Aldershot-Burlington 2007, p. 4.

45 J. Humphries, "Childhood and Child Labour in the British Industrial Revolution", *The Economic History Review*, 2013, No. 2.

46 J. Burchardt, *Paradise Lost. Rural Idyll and Social Change Since 1800*, London–New York 2002, p. 21 ff.

47 P. Gaskell, *Manufacturing Population...*, op. cit., pp. 161–162.

48 B. Hilton, *A Mad, Bad, Dangerous People...*, op. cit., p. 582.

49 P. Pollard, "Factory Discipline in the Industrial Revolution", *The Economic History Review*, 1963, no. 2.

The more advanced the technology, the more outrageous the contrast seemed to many observers between the technical capabilities of industrial society and the poverty that stubbornly refused to disappear from social life. Gaskell wrote about workers that:

> When it is borne in mind that the class which is so little elevated in its social instincts and domestic habits and intelligence, lives in the nineteenth century, in a country, which has long been freed from hostile aggression, in the midst of a nation pre-eminent for its cultivation of the arts and sciences – celebrated for its benevolence, and its unceasing efforts to extend the blessings of religion and moral instruction over the whole habitable globe – famed for the general extent of its education – its enjoyments of political rights – its charitable institutions – the numbers of its clergy – the wealth and splendour of its church – its degraded condition becomes the more remarkable.[50]

This voice of moral outrage is noteworthy, even though it concerns the internal affairs of the West, which are not the topic of this book.[51] The same argument, however, returned in the twentieth century (and continues to return) in discussions on development in the least developed countries, and in recent debates on development aid. In its modern incarnation, it claims that the situation today, in which a small fraction of the world enjoys a level of wealth and technological advancement that was until recently unimaginable, is a moral scandal, something that no compassionate individual could find acceptable.

In the times of the industrial revolution, poverty ceased to be a painful, manifest reality to which people had to reconcile themselves because there were no technical means for eliminating even its most drastic symptoms from social life. It became – first in the West, and after 1945, throughout the world – a disease, a moral and political problem. As a political problem, it demanded a political solution.[52]

---

50 P. Gaskell, *Manufacturing population…*, op. cit., p. 132.

51 It is worth noting that the wages of British workers were still the highest in the world. Compared to the rates paid in the textile factories of Manchester, a city that invoked horror in its day (one contemporary historian called it a "world shock city") the hourly wages offered in factories abroad were only a fraction of what British workers earned: in Mulhouse in the Alsace region – 37 percent; in Zurich – 28 percent, in Rouen – 47 percent, in Vienna – 36 percent, and in Prussia – just 25 percent; see G. Clark, "Why Isn't the Whole World Developed? Lessons From the Cotton Mills", *Journal of Economic History*, 1987, no. 1.

52 Perhaps the most convincing argument on this point has been offered by philosopher and ethicist Peter Singer in *The Life You Can Save. Acting Now to End World Poverty*, Melbourne 2009. Cf. also L. Weinar, "Responsibility and Severe Poverty", [in:] *Freedom from Poverty as a Human Right. Who Owes What to the Very Poor?*, Oxford–New York 2007, p. 259.

3. Empire and its colonies

The history of the industrial revolution in England is important to this book's considerations for another reason: in its civilizational success – because, despite the horrors of Manchester and Liverpool, breaking out of the Malthusian "perpetual struggle for room and food"[53] was a civilizational success – perhaps England was just the first on this road to development, with other societies to follow naturally in its footsteps. If this is true, the best thing a good government in a poor country can do is to follow the advice of Adam Smith: create stable, impartial institutions, and patiently await the inevitable progress of civilization. It will surely come.

But if we consider the transformation of England to have been for some reason exceptional, then the government of a country in the developing world aspiring to modernization and prosperity, has a much wider field of action. That government then has two roads before it, both of which require the wide-scale use of costly social engineering. It should either create a situation based, at least in part, on local conditions, but modelled on countries that have been successful, or it should it take the matter of modernization and industrialization into its own hands, treating England's success as, at best, an inspiration (or a historical curiosity, since the world has changed, and history does not repeat itself). The position one takes in this matter generally coincides with his or her answer to a question that is fundamental to telling the story of theories of accelerated development: is a spontaneous escape from backwardness possible?

A review of the literature on the origins of the British industrial revolution would be longer than this book; moreover, this is not our primary concern. It is worth noting, however, the basic points in this dispute as it looks today, because attempts made in the Third World to "leap into modernity" cannot be understood without this historical context.

A textbook narrative of the origins of industry in England begins in the seventeenth century, when a rapidly growing middle class and the aristocracy associated with it became strong enough to defeat their ruler on the battlefield.[54] During the Civil War in the 1640s and the glorious revolution of 1688, there was a change in England's political institutions, with the monarchy losing a significant share of its power to parliament. The victors carried out changes in the country's economic institutions that benefitted them – above all, stronger guarantees on property

53 T. R. Malthus, *Essay…*, op. cit., p. 48.

54 This view is most often represented in school textbooks: E.g., D. Acemoglu, *Introduction to Modern Economic Growth*, Princeton 2008, p. 1060 and F. Crouzet, *The History of the European Economy, 1000–2000*, Charlottesville–London 2001, p. 110.

rights for owners of land and capital, to encourage them to invest. In the eighteenth century, the English state guaranteed (perhaps not fully, but more than others) the enforcement of contracts and public order, refrained from imposing high taxes, invested in the country's infrastructure, and removed social barriers that prevented talented individuals from all classes from achieving success in business and social advancement (which does not mean that it was not easier for some than for others). The result was easy to predict; this led to a rise in private investment in factory buildings and equipment (and later in railroads and telegraph lines) and in "human capital" (i.e., education), and to the development of new technologies that increased productivity. The culmination of the expansion that this sparked was the industrial revolution. "That's how it was" – this is how Daron Acemoglu, one of today's most prominent economists specializing in economic development, summed up this story.[55] You can place emphasis on different aspects of this story: recently, for example, historians have tended to emphasize the role of institutions – especially those responsible for protecting property rights and enforcing contracts and for defending citizens against arbitrary power. Economic growth, and especially the industrial revolution, as Daron Acemoglu and James Robinson note in a recently published book, was against the interests of the elites in many countries, and therefore they tried to prevent it. Institutions of power could either be "inclusive", incorporating as many people as possible into the decision-making process, which promoted economic growth (because it was in the general interest); or "extractive", that is, facilitating the acquisition of wealth by a narrow elite that was not interested in growth because it could weaken their power. From this relative perspective (compared to other European monarchies), the inclusiveness of England's institutions was critical to its success.[56]

Other historians, such as Charles I. Jones, underscore the importance of institutions in protecting inventors, especially patent law, which guaranteed they would derive profits from their work.[57] Others write about the role of capital markets, which developed in the eighteenth century, first in Amsterdam and then in London, which facilitated the financing of investments – primarily trade

---

55 D. Acemoglu, *Introduction to*…, op. cit., s. 1031.

56 D. Acemoglu, J. Robinson, *Why Nations Fail? The Origins of Power, Prosperity and Poverty*, New York 2012; cf. also D. Acemoglu, J. Robinson, *Economic Origins of Dictatorship and Democracy*, Cambridge 2006, p. 350 ff.

57 Cf. e.g. C. I. Jones, "Was an Industrial Revolution Inevitable? Economic Growth Over the Very Long Run", *Advances in Macroeconomics*, 2001, no. 2; in his opinion, this institutional change had a decisive impact.

and war, but later industry, as well.[58] Many authors find the roots of Britain's growth in the Middle Ages, for example, in weaker social barriers (in comparison to those in countries on the continent) separating the aristocracy and the middle class, both of whom, generally without conflict, profited from overseas trading. Scientific rationalism, capital markets, property rights, the idea of economic freedom (invented in the eighteenth century), lower barriers between the classes than existed on the continent: all of these could have contributed to Britain's success.[59] These, in turn, were accompanied by new ideas about the sources of wealth, and the nature and role of money: the West changed its thinking about usury, and began to venerate capital.[60] Technological advances and investments in education brought rapid – compared to other eras – increases in productivity in Europe, which slowly began spreading beyond its borders.[61] The eminent economic historian Joel Mokyr believes that Enlightenment rationalism was of the greatest importance, because it led the British to make use of recent scientific discoveries as a means of achieving greater prosperity, and encouraged them to make new finds.[62]

Yet, perhaps the "English miracle" was about something completely different? There is no lack of alternative hypotheses. "By 1200 societies such as England already had all the institutional prerequisites for economic growth emphasized today by the World Bank and the International Monetary Fund. These were indeed societies more highly incentivized than modern high-income economies: medieval citizens had more to gain from work and investment than their modern counterparts did. [...] The institutions necessary for growth existed long before growth itself began," says the author of one of the most talked-about recent

---

58 L. Allen, *The Global Financial System, 1750–2000*, London 2001, p. 56, 108; cf. also *The Origins and Development of Financial Markets and Institutions*, eds. J. Atack, L. Neal, Cambridge 2009; cf. also C. Wennerlind, *Casualties of Credit. The English Financial Revolution 1620–1720*, Cambridge–London 2011.

59 W. J. Bernstein, *The Birth of Plenty. How the Prosperity of the Modern World Was Created*, New York 2010, p. 192; cf. also J. Goldstone, *Why Europe? The Rise of the West in World History, 1500–1850*, New York 2009. On the rise of the concept of economic freedom, see E. MacGilvray, *The Invention of Market Freedom*, Cambridge 2011.

60 F. Boldizzoni, *Means and End. The Idea of Capital in the West, 1500–1970*, Houndmills–New York 2008, p. 50 ff.

61 R. A. Easterlin, "Why Isn't the Whole World Developed?", *The Journal of Economic History*, 1981, no. 1.

62 J. Mokyr, *The Enlightened Economy. Britain and Industrial Revolution*, London–New York 2011.

books on England's economic success, historian Gregory Clark.[63] According to his interpretation, the most important factors were work ethic and demography, in that order. In the Middle Ages, he argues, the children of the upper classes had a greater chance of survival than the children of peasants; this led to a steady "migration downward" of the habits and cultural norms prevalent in the upper classes. Peasants "from time immemorial" had been lazy and disinclined to work (they had little to gain); the children of parents from the upper strata of society, even if they did not have the social position of their parents, inherited good habits concerning work, saving and investing. Important causal factors behind Britain's leading role in the industrial revolution should therefore be sought in the British system of inheritance, in which the eldest male heir received the entire estate. This accelerated the social degradation of his brothers and sisters, and thus disseminated among the poor masses attitudes conducive to economic development. Although studies by the same author on wages in England have been highly praised and widely quoted (here, as well), this Darwinian theory has not gained many followers.[64]

Robert Fogel, another noted historian, considers the most important cause of industrialization to have been a change in diet.[65] Researchers of the industrial revolution agree that in the years 1760–1830 the workday for a citizen of the West was lengthened by an average of at least one-quarter. On the basis of years of detailed research on menus in France and England, the historian came to the conclusion that this success was possible thanks to better nutrition – people earlier were simply too weak and malnourished to work efficiently. The bottom 20 percent of the population was simply not suitable for factory work – food provided them with "on average, only enough energy for a few hours of slow walking." That changed in the mid-eighteenth century, when agricultural productivity in the West suddenly increased, and colonial trade led to a fall in the price of sugar and other commodities (we should note that this view seems hard to reconcile with knowledge about the decline in height among people at that time, which seems to suggest a deterioration in the quality of their diet; Fogel attributes this to urbanization). Another historian, Nathan Nunn, using sophisticated statistical procedures, calculated the impact of the production of potatoes,

---

63 G. Clark, *Farewell to Alms…*, op. cit., p. 10.

64 Other historians are cited by the reviewer in *The New York Times Review of Books*; cf. B. N. Friedman, "Industrial Evolution", *The New York Times*, 9 December 2007. A bourgeois work ethic is also credited with having a decisive impact by D. N. McCloskey, *The Bourgeois Dignity. Why Economics Can't Explain the Modern World*, Chicago 2010

65 R. Fogel, *The Escape from Hunger and Premature Death, 1700–2100*, Cambridge 2004.

which started to become widely available in the West in the eighteenth century, on urbanization, and consequently, on industrialization (workers in the city, even if they were malnourished, had to have something to eat).[66] He concluded that the potato led to a 12 percent rise in the population in the West, and a 47 percent increase in the urban population, and therefore, that the potato contributed significantly to the industrial revolution.

Longer working hours could have also resulted, as proposed by yet another famous scholar, Jan de Vries, in a change in consumption patterns in the West.[67] A growing handicraft sector was supplying the market with an expanding assortment of more and less necessary items (such as the *zak-aardebol*). De Vries argues that the desire to own such goods prompted first the Dutch and English, and then the Belgians, French and Germans, to work longer and more efficiently. This yielded a prototype of today's consumer society, in which manufacturers use fashion and advertising to create needs in their customers: spiralling growth in consumption fuelled economic growth. Neither Marx, who attributed changes in work culture to the demands of the factory's production rhythm ("the needs of capital") and saw them as an objectification of work and the worker, nor Weber, who saw the source of this new diligence in Protestantism, were correct, according to de Vries, because: it was really about consumption. "Did people who valued leisure and autonomy find themselves forced to work harder and longer forced to abandon an ancient material culture with regret? Or did they actively participate – in their own messy, inefficient ways – in the pursuit of goals of their own that helped bring about something not fully foreseen, a new sort of economy and society?" de Vries asks.[68] The answer to this question is of importance to our story because many plans for dynamic development created in the twentieth century assumed a reduction – at least in theory, temporary – in private consumption (we will return to this). Changes in work culture in modern times, however, were a fact and, in the general opinion of specialists, led to the creation of modern industrial society, first in England and then in the West.

All of these explanations assume, however, the uniqueness of England (or more broadly of the West), regardless of whether a fundamental role is attributed to religion, politics or geography. It was the unique availability of coal in the British Isles that played a decisive role, says another prominent specialist, Robert C. Allen, in

66 N. Nunn, N. Qian, "The Potato's Contribution to Population and Urbanization: Evidence from an Historical Experiment", National Bureau Of Economic Research Working Paper no. 15157 from 2009.

67 J. de Vries, *Industrious…*, op. cit.

68 Ibid., p. 114.

a recently published book.[69] Colonial trade in the eighteenth century in England, helped make earnings there the highest in the world; high earnings combined with "the cheapest energy in the world" sparked demand for machines, that is, technology that was energy- and capital-intensive, and which required the employment of a smaller number of expensive workers. This geo-political difference between England and the rest of the world that provided the motivation for technological advancement was fraught with consequences and shaped the lowest rungs of economic life. Allen describes the main difference in the construction of kilns in China and in England: the English kilns were cheap to build, but required large amounts of fuel and a small number of employees. The Chinese were much more complex, expensive to build and required the employment of a much larger number of people. However, they had the advantage that they wasted less energy than the English ones, because in China energy was much more expensive. In England, it was simply not profitable to build energy-efficient stoves.

Different cost calculations costs were among the key reasons for the very slow adoption abroad of English industrial inventions. In the 1860s, Englishman James Hargreaves invented a new spinning machine; "Spinning Jenny" brought huge gains in efficiency to British industry. In 1771 the first models were exported to France. However, they were installed there only in large, state-supported factories. Twenty years later, in England there were 20,000 such spinners, while in France, only 900. Why? Allen writes that in France, human labour was cheaper and energy more expensive, and therefore, the British inventions were not profitable there. A smelter modelled on a British unit, built at the request of the French government, met with a similar fate. The French did not lack raw materials or capital; they spent large sums of money hiring the best, most experienced British engineers. Production, however, was not profitable – despite the lower earnings of the workers – and the production plants failed. At the same time, in England ever-newer technical innovations were being introduced at a pace never before seen in history.[70] France began to catch up with Britain effectively only in the latter half of the nineteenth century.[71]

---

69 R. C. Allen, *The British Industrial Revolution in Global Perspective*, Cambridge 2009; Another author considers the availability of energy to have been "a necessary condition for the industrial revolution but it was not in itself a sufficient cause." – E. A. Wrigley, *Energy and the English Industrial Revolution*, Cambridge 2010, p. 23.

70 M. Berg, *The Age of Manufactures, 1700–1820. Industry, Innovation and Work in Britain*, London–New York 2004, p. 23.

71 J. Horn, *The Path Not Taken. French Industrialization in the Age of Revolution, 1750–1830*, Cambridge–London 2006, p. 3.

Similar situations will reappear repeatedly in this book. The engineers of industrial policy in countries whose economies lagged behind often learned the hard way that importing technology and offering lower – sometime several times lower – labour costs was not sufficient to build profitable industries (not to mention ones that could compete on global markets with firms from developed countries). Other costs – transport, energy, capital, differences in labour productivity – could easily compensate for the difference in the "price of a worker". This lesson was learned by the authors of industrial policies in countries as diverse as the Kingdom of Poland in the days of prince Drucki-Lubecki, the Polish People's Republic under Edward Gierek, and Ghana during the times of Kwame Nkrumah.

Allen argues that high wages in the cities of England were a product of colonial trade, and thus colonies played an enormous, albeit indirect, role in the British "leap into modernity". We need to look more closely at this piece of the puzzle of the industrial revolution: it concerns a question that will return repeatedly – the moral responsibility of the West for its civilizational success. For if the wealth and industry of the West were built on slave labour and the domination of foreign peoples, this means that its civilization as a whole is morally tainted at its roots. The West has in this case an important and quite practical commitment to those on whose backs it climbed to build its power and prosperity. Moreover, in such a situation, the West's success is not only impossible to emulate – because times have changed – but that it should not even be considered because it was attained by means that are unacceptable from a moral point of view. For this reason, countries that remain under-developed today – such a conclusion often flows from this line of reasoning – should seek their own path to development, one other than that taken by the West, at most graciously offering to accept its assistance; this is, after all, not really assistance, but redress for past wrongs.

Until at least the 1960s, the most widespread view among western (non-Marxist) historians was that, as historian François Crouzet put it, "the role of the 'periphery' was peripheral."[72] To the question "Why are the rich countries so rich and the poor countries so poor?", the answer usually given was summed up by another historian as follows: "Europeans were smarter, better organized, harder working; the others were ignorant, arrogant, lazy, backward, superstitious" In the 1960s, a different answer to the same question began to appear more often: "Europeans, they say, were aggressive, ruthless, greedy, unscrupulous,

72 F. Crouzet, *The History…*, op. cit., p. 54 ff.

hypocritical [...] and willing to exploit others; they also had favourable geographical conditions.[73]

The thesis that the capital being invested in English factories derived largely from the slave trade was formulated clearly and unequivocally by economist Eric Williams in his book *Capitalism and Slavery*, published in 1944, though in Britain not until 1964. It was not without reason that its publication was delayed in the UK; nevertheless, it still caused a scandal: the "Williams thesis", as it was called, became an issue of hot debate. Although Williams earned his doctorate in history at Oxford, he was black, and, in addition, came from Trinidad, a Caribbean island with a long history of slave labour; in 1956 he also became the Prime Minister of Trinidad and Tobago, and therefore a politician, which did not arouse confidence among academics; in addition, his last book, written in the 1960s, was a long indictment of the greatest nineteenth-century British historians, accusing them of being ideologists of imperialism. His emotional language also did not earn him sympathy among scholars, especially those in Britain, many of whom had been raised in the Victorian faith in the beneficial effects of the liberal empire's reign over conquered peoples: "Negroes therefore were stolen in Africa to work the lands stolen from the Indians in America" – this sentence is a good example of his style.[74]

Among specialists, it was widely accepted at the time that for many European countries, their colonies had been an unprofitable enterprise. Spain and Portugal in the eighteenth century grew poorer as a result of their colonial empires, due to spending on wars overseas – which did not generate the revenues anticipated – and actually contributed significantly to the bankruptcy of France in the period preceding the revolution. Only the United Kingdom, the most aggressive and most efficient of the imperial powers, managed to turn a profit from its colonies, though in the end, these sums were not as large as previously thought. It has also been calculated that the slave trade was not extremely profitable. Revenue from this business was highly unstable, and the average return on capital did not exceed 10 percent per annum, which was only slightly higher than that which could be earned from other, safer investments.

Yet, how much – in hard currency – did England earn from this trade? Critics quickly pointed out to Williams that he relied heavily on anecdote: he cited examples of individuals or families linked to the slave trade, who later invested

73 This question and the two main responses were discussed by David Landes in his classic work on economic history *The Wealth and Poverty of Nations: Why Some are So Rich and Some So Poor*, New York 1998, p. xxi.

74 E. Williams, *Capitalism and Slavery*, Chapel Hill 1944, p. 9.

capital in industry.[75] Polemicists reached for statistically grounded arguments, which revealed that profits from the slave trade accounted for only a small part of Britain's national income; it therefore did not affect the way in which the United Kingdom marched into modernity. According to one such estimate, the slave trade in 1770 accounted for 0.54 percent of British GDP, and 7.8 percent of investment (while trade and industry comprised 38.9 percent). In 1700 the then well-known economist Malachy Postlethwayt called the slave trade "an inexhaustible source of wealth."[76]

In an attempt to disprove the "Williams thesis", another contemporary author, H.V. Bowen, came to the conclusion that income from colonial trade (including the slave trade) from 1784 to 1786 amounted to no more than 5.66 million pounds. According to his estimates, during that same period, 10.3 million pounds were invested in the overall British economy (and Britain's GDP amounted to 140–150 million pounds). A sum equal to half of total capital investment was thus earned from the colonial trade! But not only slavery generated income: the revenues of the East India Company in Bengal from duties, taxes and trade in the eighteenth century totalled from 2 to 4 million pounds per year, though, of course, the net profit was much lower.[77]

Nevertheless, Patrick O'Brien, who calculated the profits derived from the slave trade, found that if slavery had hypothetically been abolished by the British in 1607, the resulting decline in real income would not have greatly impacted the level of wealth and income in Western Europe in 1807. He adds, however, that the decline in consumption would certainly have been greater than the drop in production.[78] Discourse about the slave trade in the 1970s and 1980s was directly tied to the popular world-system theory expounded by Immanuel Wallerstein,

75 The debate over William's book is described in depth in R. Findlay and K. O'Rourke, *Power and Plenty. Trade, War, and the World Economy in the Second Millennium*, Princeton–Oxford 2007, pp. 335–338.

76 D. B. Davis, *Inhuman Bondage. The Rise and Fall of Slavery in the New World*, Oxford 2006, p. 80.

77 H. V. Bowen, *The Business of Empire. The East India Company and Imperial Britain, 1756–1833*, New York 2006, p. 3.

78 P. O'Brien, "European Economic Development: The Contribution of the Periphery", *The Economic History Review*, 1982, no. 1. His argument was, roughly speaking, as follows: colonies provided primarily consumer goods (tobacco, coffee, tea, sugar, etc.); therefore, they had a greater impact on standard of living than on economic development. The demand for such goods was very flexible: if tea was expensive, the English simply drank less – and the rest of the economy would have followed approximately the same course with little change.

Andre Gunder Frank and Samir Amin (they are even explicitly mentioned in Obrien's article). It is not hard to guess the reason for interest in these technical debates and – if I may say so – their ideological stakes. If the prosperity of the West in the past depended on the exploitation of foreign peoples, in accordance with the thesis of theorists of the world systems, then a necessary condition for wealth and power of the civilizational centre is the permanent underdevelopment of the periphery.

It is also possible, as claimed by some contemporary authors, that the slave trade contributed to the British "leap into modernity" in an indirect but very important way.[79] New World plantations provided cheap cotton to factories in England. England then exported its industrial products to Africa, where payment was made in slaves slated for sale in the New World, where they would work on plantations. This created the closed economic cycle of the "Atlantic Triangle", from which not all benefited equally.[80] Because the numbers of slaves working on plantations constantly diminished (the birth rate was lower than the mortality rate), the systematic import of Africans to the New World was necessary to keep the factories of Manchester running.[81] Cheap cotton – which was cheap thanks to slave labour – gave British industrialists a competitive advantage over producers from the continent and the Far East. The existence of such a mechanism seems to have been confirmed in recent years by fragmentary research on changes in the prices of slaves during the eighteenth century and the structure of exports in the Caribbean; according to one study, in the crucial, initial period of the industrial revolution, up to 80 percent of exports from the Americas to Europe were produced by the work of black slaves.[82]

The slave trade had a devastating impact on local communities. African societies became caught up in destructive conflicts, selling captured prisoners to western traffickers.[83] Mortality was high in all phases of the slave trade – from the

79 D. Acemoglu, P. Johnson, J. Robinson, "The Rise of Europe: Atlantic Trade, Institutional Change and Economic Growth", *American Economic Review*, 2005, no. 2.

80 See e.g. R. Findlay and K. O'Rourke, *Power and Plenty…*, op. cit.

81 Cf. *Slavery and the Rise of the Atlantic System*, ed. B. Solow, Cambridge 1991.

82 J. Inikori, Africans and the Industrial Revolution in England: A Study in International Trade and Economic Development, Cambridge 2002, p. 197; see also J. E. Inikori, "Transatlantic Slavery and Economic Development in the Atlantic World, West Africa, 1450–1850", [in:] *The Cambridge World History of Slavery*, vol. 3, eds. D. Eltis, P. L. Engerman, Cambridge 2011, p. 650 ff.

83 The case of Senegambia is described in B. Barry, *Senegambia and the Atlantic Slave Trade*, Cambridge 1998, p. 107 ff.

moment they were caught by African brokers and transported to the coast, to the journey across the Atlantic and work on the plantation. Historians can say little about the first two legs of this journey; it is estimated that between 10 and 50 percent of the Africans captured died on the way to the coast (the longer the march, the greater the numbers who perished along the way). Statistics on mortality during transport across the Atlantic are more accurate: depending on the historical period (in the eighteenth century slaves grew steadily more expensive, so they were treated with more care) and the length of the journey, the rate ranged from 7 to 20 percent.[84] The later the stage of the journey, the fewer slaves died, not only because the weakest had perished earlier, but also because, as the distance from Africa grew, they became an increasingly expensive commodity, so it was only fitting that they would receive somewhat better treatment. These are the conclusions of modern-day specialists, not merely the speculations of politically engaged intellectuals from the 1960s: through painstaking research carried out in archives around the world in the late twentieth century, historians have compiled detailed information on 34,584 slave transports between 1514 and 1866; historians estimate that this provides us today with information on more than 80 percent of all such shipments, in many cases, including the travel route, the origin of the slaves, and, of course, the mortality rate (which was meticulously recorded because settlement had to made for dead slaves; the sums involved were considerable).[85] Plantation owners were incredibly rich: John Tharp from Jamaica, who died in 1805, earned revenues of 362,000 pounds annually and owned 2900 slaves.[86]

On Caribbean plantations, an average of 2 percent of slaves died each year. Inventories of movable assets left by planters indicate that the rest suffered from ill health as a result of exhausting work and malnutrition. In the register of slaves from plantations belonging to the Beckford estate in Jamaica, drawn up at the end of the eighteenth century, 188 of 604 young (under forty) women were described as unfit to work; the others were usually described as "weak" or "unhealthy". Slaves also stubbornly refused to procreate. In 1780, on one plantation belonging to the same owner, only 19 live newborns were brought into the world

84 N. Nunn, "The Long-term Effects of Africa's Slave Trade", *Quarterly Journal of Economics*, 2008, no. 1; R. H. Steckel, R. A. Jensen, "Determinants of Slave and Crew Mortality in the Atlantic Slave Trade", NBER Working Paper no. 1540, 1985.

85 D. Eltis, P. D. Behrendt, D. Richardson, H. P. Klein, *The Trans-Atlantic Slave Trade: A Database on CD-Rom*, New York 1999.

86 T. Burnard, "The Planter Class", [in:] *The Routledge History of Slavery*, eds. G. Heuman, T. Burnard, London–New York 2011, p. 191.

by the 274 young women working there.[87] The owners tried various methods to increase the birth rate among slaves; one, for example, offered a silver dollar to every mother whose baby survived its first week of life, but the results were meagre.[88] Plantation owners and their agents complained that women would prolong the nursing period as long as possible in order to avoid becoming pregnant, and when this failed, they used home remedies to cause their foetus to abort.

Even if the industrial revolution could have taken place without slave labour, there are good reasons to believe that slavery had a significant impact on the subsequent fate of both the countries that exported slaves and those in which plantations were established, leaving behind a social and economic structure that perpetuated backwardness. "Institutions for exploitation are hard to change once they arise" – this is the painful lesson learned by specialists in development after World War II, as summed up by economist and historian Nathan Nunn.[89] Already in 1526, Congo's first Christian king, Alfonso I, complained in letters to Lisbon that "each day the traders are kidnapping our people," and that "our land is entirely depopulated".[90]

The harms were much greater than simple demographic losses (11 to 14 million Africans were transported to America). The slave trade favoured the disintegration of indigenous African countries and the degeneration of local social institutions: the initial suppliers of slaves were usually local rulers. The demand for slaves led to devastating wars and hostility between tribes that was remembered by later generations. When kings did not have other people's subjects to sell, they often invented creative ways to sell their own. One Western traveller described a system of the justice invented by the chief of the Kassanga tribe in what is now Guinea-Bissau in West Africa. The king ordered people accused of crimes to undergo the "red water ordeal". They were forced to drink a poisonous red liquid. If they wretch threw up, they were considered guilty and sold into slavery. If they did not vomit, they usually died of poisoning. The king then took control of the deceased's property and sold his family into slavery; the ruler therefore benefited regardless of the outcome of the ordeal.[91]

The system of slave labour also shaped the institutions of the countries in which plantations operated. It left them with the legacy of an economy specialized in

87 L. Mathurin Mair, "Women Field Workers…", op. cit., p. 192.

88 B. W. Higman, *Plantation Jamaica 1750–1850. Capital and Control in a Colonial Economy*, Jamaica–Barbados–Trinidad and Tobago 2008, p. 220.

89 N. Nunn, "The long-term effects…", op. cit.

90 Quoted in A. Hochschild, *King Leopold's Ghost,* Boston–New York 1999, p. 13.

91 Ibid.

the export of only a few agricultural products, such as cocoa, sugar and tobacco. After independence, long after the abolition of slavery, a small elite ruled in these countries over masses living in misery with whom they shared little or nothing (starting with the colour of their skin) – certainly not any sense of a common destiny. The interests of both groups were often divergent, and the elite saw no reason to invest in improving the quality of life, which only fed feelings of fear, superiority and contempt.

Although the legacy of colonial institutions was not the same everywhere, and its balance-sheet is not clear (we will return to this issue), the verdict of historians today is merciless: countries drawn into the closed circle of the slave economy were condemned to a fate on the periphery long before people they started to think about emancipation.[92]

4. Slaves to barbaric superstitions

What is probably the most interesting question in the history of the "great divergence" (as one contemporary historian has somewhat awkwardly labelled it) concerns neither Africa nor the Caribbean, but rather China and India, and to a lesser extent the Arab world: Why did Europe overtake these ancient civilizations on the road to the industrial revolution?[93]

Such an outcome was neither obvious nor a foregone conclusion. In the year 1000, any rational observer would have placed odds on China succeeding rather than Europe, which was still poor, peripheral, and divided into dozens (if not hundreds) of rival political bodies. When Europeans were just beginning to discover in monastic libraries remnants of the knowledge of the ancient Greeks and Romans, the Chinese were inventing paper, gunpowder and the compass, as well as introducing paper money and trading on credit. China was densely populated and had a strong, centralized state that provided stability and order, a professional administration run by personnel selected on the basis of examinations (while offices in Europe were often inherited or bought), a better network of roads, and cultural norms emphasizing the value of hard work. The relations of European travellers, beginning with Marco Polo, left no doubt: they were poor guests from the backward provinces. The first European explorers risked their

---

92 W. Easterly, R. Levine, "The European Origins of Economic Development, NBER Working Paper 18162", June 2012.

93 K. Pomeranz, *The Great Divergence. China, Europe, and the Making of the Modern World Economy*, Princeton 2000.

lives and health on a quest for the riches of China and India, not in the name of disinterested geographical discoveries.

In the eighteenth century, the image in Europe of the Far East – and the Arab world – changed radically: images of wealth and power were replaced by scenes of backwardness, oriental despotism and economic stagnation. While the West was becoming rich and growing in power, China[94] and India seemed – up until almost the end of the twentieth century – doomed to widespread poverty. Admiration was replaced by contempt and a sense of civilizational superiority.[95]

Experts tried to explain this surprising reversal by means of various theories: differences in the organization of production (contrasting dynamic capitalism in Europe with the conservative, "Asian system of production"), guarantees on property rights (they were said to be stronger in Europe, which encouraged Europeans to invest), the influence of the State (either decentralised or absolutist and enlightened in Europe, and therefore not interfering in private interests; despotic and arbitrarily imposing its will on the most trivial matters in Asia), and finally, differences in religion and "the presence of the scientific spirit" (and its alleged lack among Asians). The classic form of this theory came from Max Weber, who believed that capitalism was rooted in Protestantism, and Chinese stagnation in the Buddhist and Confucian ethics that shaped that country's rigid institutions.[96] A similar diagnosis was made in regard to India.[97] Institutional explanations remain popular today: the dominant view on the source of backwardness in the Arab world points to religion, which stifles the formation of scientific rationality along the lines of that in the west, and despotism, which is not conducive to the safe conduct of business.[98] The same holds true for the differences between the

94 Cf. e.g. E. H. Mielants, *The Origins of Capitalism and the Rise of the West*, Philadelphia 2007, p. 60 ff.

95 P. K. Khan Khattak, *Islam and the Victorians. Nineteenth Century Perceptions of Muslim Practices and Beliefs*, London–New York 2008, p. 61 ff.

96 M. Weber, *The Religion of China*, Detroit 1968, p. 152.

97 German edition 1916–1917, revised in 1920; English edition 1958 (M. Weber, *The Religion of India: The Sociology of Hinduism and Buddhism,* Glencoe 1958). Cf. also R. Swedberg, *Max Weber and the Idea of Economic Sociology,* Princeton 2000, p. 140.

98 The most well-known analyst of the reasons why Arab countries "lagged behind" Europe is T. Kuran, "Institutional Causes of Economic Underdevelopment in the Middle East: A Historical Perspective", [in:] *Institutional Change and Economic Behaviour*, eds. J. Kornai, L. Maytyas, G. Roland, Houndmills–New York 2008, p. 63 ff.; cf. also T. Kuran, *The Long Divergence: How Islamic Law Held Back the Middle East*, Princeton 2010; as well as T. Kuran, *Islam and Mammon: the Economic Predicaments of Islamism*, Princeton 2005.

United States and Latin America and the Caribbean islands. While in 1700 per capita income in Mexico and the American colonies was similar, and Haiti was probably the richest country in the world, in 1800 the United States was already clearly in the lead: its social structure and institutions were said to account for the difference in growth rates.[99] Science, property rights, medicine, a rigorous work ethic: all this was said to secure the West an advantage.[100]

These theories, writes Robert C. Allen, were impressive in their range, but they were based on poor quality source materials. In the case of Asia, studies carried out in recent years in China raise doubts – as we will see – about most of them.[101] Generally speaking, there are two clashing trends in the literature today: one tells us to look for the sources of Europe's exceptionality and civilizational success in an increasingly distant past, for example, in the revolution in trade during the thirteenth and fourteenth centuries, which opened the West up to the world.[102] The second trend emphasizes the narrow gap dividing European technology and Asian wealth in the eighteenth century: we were more alike then than we think.

The image of Asian stagnation and backwardness appeared in modern times, and – until the successes achieved by Japan, and later, China – remained present in Europeans' image of the East. This perception was widely held, and such diverse thinkers as Adam Smith and Karl Marx shared this view of Asia. "The difference between the money price of labour in China and in Europe is still greater than that between the money price of subsistence; because the real recompence of labour is higher in Europe than in China, the greater part of Europe being in an improving state, while China seems to be standing still", wrote Smith in *The Wealth of Nations*, in which he devoted a great deal of space to explaining the reasons for Europe's superiority.[103] He noted the large difference in earnings calculated in silver: "Half an ounce of silver at Canton in China may command a greater quantity both of labour and of the necessaries and conveniences of life, than an ounce at London."[104]

---

99 K. L. Sokoloff, P. L. Engerman, "History Lessons: Institutions, Factor Endowments, and Paths of Development in the New World", op. cit. Cf. also D. Acemoglu, J. Robinson, *Why Nations Fail: The Origins of Power, Prosperity, and Poverty*, New York 2012.

100 For a conservative variant of this theory see N. Ferguson, *Civilization. The West and the Rest*, New York 2011.

101 R. C. Allen, "Real Wages in Europe and Asia: A first Look at the Long-term Patterns", [in:] *Living Standards in the Past...*, op. cit., p. 111.

102 J. L. Abu-Lughod, *Before European Hegemony*, New York–Oxford 1989, p. 22 ff.

103 A. Smith, *The Wealth of Nations: An Inquiry into the Nature and Causes of the Wealth of Nations*, Petersfield 2007, p. 123.

104 Ibid., p. 24.

However, the Chinese could survive on lower wages, because "China is a much richer country than any part of Europe, and the difference between the price of subsistence in China and in Europe is very great."[105] Smith painted a dramatic picture of the average living conditions in China:

> The accounts of all travellers, inconsistent in many other respects, agree in the low wages of labour, and in the difficulty which a labourer finds in bringing up a family in China. If by digging the ground a whole day he can get what will purchase a small quantity of rice in the evening, he is contented. The condition of artificers is, if possible, still worse. Instead of waiting indolently in their workhouses for the calls of their customers, as in Europe, they are continually running about the streets with the tools of their respective trades, offering their service, and, as it were, begging employment. The poverty of the lower ranks of people in China far surpasses that of the most beggarly nations in Europe. In the neighbourhood of Canton many hundred, it is commonly said, many thousand families have no habitation on the land, but live constantly in little fishing boats upon the rivers and canals. The subsistence which they find there is so scanty, that they are eager to fish up the nastiest garbage thrown overboard from any European ship. Any carrion, the carcase of a dead dog or cat, for example, though half putrid and stinking, is as welcome to them as the most wholesome food to the people of other countries. Marriage is encouraged in China, not by the profitableness of children, but by the liberty of destroying them. In all great towns, several are every night exposed in the street, or drowned like puppies in the water. The performance of this horrid office is even said to be the avowed business by which some people earn their subsistence.[106]

Turning to the economy, he admits that although China seemed to have become stuck in the doldrums on its path to riches, it did not appear to be slipping backward.

Smith attributed stagnation in China to its institutions, in particular the prohibition of free trade with foreigners, and weak guarantees on property rights, which meant that at any time and under any pretext one's property could be confiscated by an official. The same mechanism which in the eyes of classical economics explained Europe's wealth, also explained China's backwardness.

Marx attributed Asian backwardness to its social structures. The real theatre of history for Marx was Europe; Asia, closed in an "Asian system of production", remained only a static decoration. In his famous articles about India (especially his article "The British Rule in India", published in 1853), he described Hindustan society as an atomized accumulation of villages whose fate and prosperity depend entirely on the whims of a despotic administration. This had, he added, a certain justification in geography: the need to maintain complex irrigation

105 Ibid., p. 123.
106 Ibid., pp. 85–86.

systems in Asia was conducive to the emergence of a strong, centralized government. The main reason for backwardness, however, was the structure of production. Indian villages, where the cultivation of soil was combined with cottage textile production, did not allow for the development of the modern division of labour and the rise of capitalism, which thereby halted the wheel of history. According to Marx, India was wrenched from its lethargy by British imperialism, which broke up its anachronistic social structures.

Few believed in the transformative power of capitalism more than Marx. His angry tirade, full of contempt and feelings of superiority, directed at Indian traditions, though long, is also worth remembering because these ideas of Marx, as we shall see, caused trouble later for Marxists plotting the way forward for the developing world:

> Now, sickening as it must be to human feeling to witness those myriads of industrious patriarchal and inoffensive social organizations disorganized and dissolved into their units, thrown into a sea of woes, and their individual members losing at the same time their ancient form of civilization, and their hereditary means of subsistence, we must not forget that these idyllic village-communities, inoffensive though they may appear, had always been the solid foundation of Oriental despotism, that they restrained the human mind within the smallest possible compass, making it the unresisting tool of superstition, enslaving it beneath traditional rules, depriving it of all grandeur and historical energies. We must not forget the barbarian egotism which, concentrating on some miserable patch of land, had quietly witnessed the ruin of empires, the perpetration of unspeakable cruelties, the massacre of the population of large towns, with no other consideration bestowed upon them than on natural events, itself the helpless prey of any aggressor who deigned to notice it at all. We must not forget that this undignified, stagnatory, and vegetative life, that this passive sort of existence evoked on the other part, in contradistinction, wild, aimless, unbounded forces of destruction and rendered murder itself a religious rite in Hindostan. We must not forget that these little communities were contaminated by distinctions of caste and by slavery, that they subjugated man to external circumstances instead of elevating man the sovereign of circumstances, that they transformed a self-developing social state into never changing natural destiny, and thus brought about a brutalizing worship of nature, exhibiting its degradation in the fact that man, the sovereign of nature, fell down on his knees in adoration of Kanuman, the monkey, and Sabbala, the cow.[107]

Since British imperialism is what brought capitalism to India, it was therefore a tool for progress and – in the long run – for emancipation. It would free Indians from degrading conditions which "have subjugated man to external circumstances instead of elevating man the sovereign of circumstances." What strikes today's

107 K. Marx, *The British Rule in India* https://www.marxistp.org/archive/marx/works/1853/06/25.htm.

reader is how strongly this keen critic of capitalism believed in the civilizing power of the British empire; any past (or present) apologist of the Empire could have in good conscience signed his name to this passage, though many of them would probably have expressed it in a less straightforward manner. The British had used the Chinese and Indians, but, according to Marx, in the final analysis, this served to promote progress. Imperialism was an "unconscious tool of history".[108] Engels similarly praised French imperialism in North Africa, writing about the "barbarian state of its society".[109]

Marx's opinion about China was equally tainted by Eurocentrism. In a series of articles about the Taiping Rebellion, a social uprising that lasted 15 years and left 20 million dead, he wrote about both China itself and the insurgents in manner that was openly hostile and full of prejudices. He called China a "living fossil", and said the Taipings were interested only in replacing one dynasty with another. According to Marx, they had no social programme; they were merely a brute force bent on destruction. He wrote that rule by the Taipings, who for years controlled a large part of China, had been more disastrous for the civilian population than the governments of the imperial bureaucracy. Although Marx saw emancipatory aspirations in virtually every European rebellion or revolution, in the case of the Taipings, he did not even look for them.[110]

The notion of "Asian stagnation" has it supporters to this day; the eminent contemporary historian David Landes formulates it so:

> The one civilization that might have surpassed the European achievement was China. At least that is what the record seems to show. [...] The specialists tell us, for example, that Chinese industry long anticipated European [...] in iron manufacture, where the Chinese early learned to use coal and coke in blast furnaces for smelting iron (or so we are told) and were turning out as many as 125,000 tons of pig iron by the later eleventh century—a figure reached by Britain seven hundred years later. The mystery lies in China's

---

108 P. Avineri, *Karl Marx on Colonialism and Modernization*, Garden City 1968, p. 125 ff.

109 Z. Lockman, *Contending Visions of the Middle East. The History and Politics of Orientalism,* Cambridge–New York 2004, pp. 85–86.

110 Similar opinions about India were expressed by both Marx, Engels many times; there is neither the space nor the need to quote them extensively. Modern Marxists are sometimes inclined to say that in his writings about the "Asian production system", Marx was influenced by contemporary historians and apologists of the British Empire, especially James Mill's *History of India*, and by this fact that few knew the realities of the two countries; another argument says that he described and ideal political system, and not really an existing regime (see e.g. M. Curtis, "The Asiatic Mode of Production and Oriental Despotism", [in:] *Marxism: The Inner Dialogues*, ed. M. Curtis, New Brunswick 1997, p. 350 ff.) Perhaps they are right, but he still wrote what he wrote.

> failure to realize its potential. One generally assumes that knowledge and know-how are cumulative; surely a superior technique, once known, will replace older methods. But Chinese industrial history offers examples of technological oblivion and regression. […] It would seem that none of the conventional explanations tells us in convincing fashion why technical progress was absent in the Chinese economy […][111]

Landes ultimately arrives at the conclusion that the causes of stagnation lie in cultural norms, or, as he writes, "the larger values of society." Restrictions on individual liberty, and the pressures imposed by customs, consensus and tradition that "passed for higher wisdom" were what slowed economic growth.[112] The lower social status of women also played a role. Landes writes that women were not permitted to operate as freely within the public sphere as they did in Europe or Japan, where they often worked outside the home. These differences made it difficult, for example, to put newly developed machinery for textile production into use in Chinese factories due to a lack of manpower. The greed and the arbitrary decision-making of the bureaucracy also made it difficult to conduct business. In his explanation of the situation, Chinese historian Deng Gang also refers to cultural norms – and similar issues – but his conclusions are different: between two values, stability and progress, China chose the first. As it turned out, this was only an apparent choice because, ultimately, they achieved neither progress nor stability.[113]

Research conducted over the last twenty years in China has radically challenged this image. China in the seventeenth and eighteenth centuries was supposed to have developed in a very similar direction – and as quickly – as Europe; it was right on the doorstep of the industrial revolution. To prove this point, historians, among other things, calculated the calorific value of the food eaten by Chinese workers in the Yangtze River delta and the functioning of the cereal markets in southern China.[114] In the eighteenth century, a Chinese agricultural worker (and his family) consumed roughly the same number of calories as a British labourer at that time – 2386 in China, compared with 2349 calories in Britain; the level of detail in this technical discussion is noteworthy (historians can write long papers on the nutritional value contained in one *shi* of rice and how this can be compared to a European grain-based diet). Experts

111 D. Landes, *The Wealth and Poverty of Nations…*, op. cit., p. 55.

112 Ibid., p. 56.

113 G. Deng, *The Premodern Chinese Economy. Structural Equilibrium And Capitalist Sterility*, London–New York 1999.

114 K. Pomeranz, "Standards of Living in Eighteenth-century China: Regional Differences, Temporal trends, and Incomplete Evidence", [in:] *Living Standards in the Past…*, op. cit., p. 22 ff.

have calculated the amount of protein in the average diet of a Chinese pauper (22 grams per day throughout the year) and come to the conclusion that they ate as well as poor Europeans at that time. This meant that the level of earnings was similar – in both England and China the poor spent 80 percent of their earnings on food. The populations were also similar in size, with some 31 million people living on the Yangtze River delta, roughly the same number as in Western Europe. Revisionist historians also claim that property rights in China were in practice protected at least as well as in Europe, and that commodity markets were at similar levels of development and integration. Agricultural productivity and the average level of education rose just as rapidly in China in the seventeenth and eighteenth centuries as in the West.

Where, then, does the source of China's stagnation and Europe's success lie? In comparing the economic history of China and Europe, Kenneth Pomeranz, the author of one of the most talked-about books in recent years, *The Great Divergence: China, Europe, and the Making of the Modern World Economy*, writes:

> For instance, western Europe may well have had more effective institutions for mobilizing large sums of capital willing to wait a relatively long time for returns—but until the nineteenth century, the corporate form found few uses other than for armed long distance trade and colonization, and long-term syndicated debt was primarily used within Europe to finance wars. More important, western Europe had by the eighteenth century moved ahead of the rest of the world in the use of various labor-saving technologies. However, because it continued to lag behind in various land-saving technologies, rapid population growth and resource demands might, in the absence of overseas resources, have forced it back onto a path of much more labor-intensive growth. In that case it would have diverged far less from China and Japan. The book thus calls upon the fruits of overseas coercion to help explain the difference between European development and what we see in certain other parts of Eurasia (primarily China and Japan).[115]

Left to their own fate, both China and Japan in their own time would have experienced their own industrial revolution; they were on the same road as England, they merely followed it more slowly – this is the clear message here. These studies not surprisingly were subjected to harsh critique: critics argued that wages in China may have been similar to those in Britain in terms of calories, but their lower value in silver meant that a Chinese worker could buy much less than a British one. This reflected differences in non-farm productivity that were already significant in the eighteenth century, and the fact that that the Chinese economy more closely resembled the stagnant economies of eastern and southern Europe

115 K. Pomeranz, *The Great Divergence…*, op. cit., p. 4.

than those in Britain or the Netherlands.[116] Similar limitations applied to the Arab world: according to recent studies, differences in the pace of urban development were already growing in the Middle Ages, when Europe was underdeveloped and Baghdad was the capital of the world.[117] Growing intolerance towards religious diversity in the Islamic world was also not conducive to development.[118]

However, there is greater consensus on another, perhaps more important issue: if Asian countries had any chances of avoiding the Malthusian trap, these were ruined by their contact with Europeans. The fate of India provides the most telling example of this. Up until the eighteenth century, the British imported fabric from India. Some experts believe that in some parts of the subcontinent, the beginnings of industry were already present – with competitive labour markets, productivity and wages on a level similar to those in Britain (as in the case of China, wages were much lower when converted to their calorific value calculated in silver, which is why buyers profited from exports to Europe).[119]

In Britain, the import of cotton fabric from India was banned in 1700 by an Act of Parliament; in 1721 even the wearing of such cloth was forbidden. In spite of the efforts of British manufacturers, there were many loopholes in these laws, which still allowed domestic producers to dominate the home market. The ban on imports was abolished only in 1774, when British industry, now equipped with the latest machinery, no longer had to fear outside competition, and the ideas of Adam Smith were winning minds among the British elite. It is also of relevance that over the course of this half century, Indian producers fell into decline. In 1701 the French market was also closed off to Asian fabrics. Similar examples, as well as the successful cases provided in the nineteenth century by Germany and the United States of using high tariffs to protect industry, were later cited by many politicians and economists from the developing world as arguments in favour of economic protectionism.

---

116 Cf. e.g. P. Broadberry, B. Gupta, "The Early Modern Great Divergence: Wages, Prices and Economic Development in Europe and Asia, 1500–1800", *Economic History Review*, 2006, no. 1; This discussion is noteworthy, although there is no space to discuss it in detail her.

117 M. Bosker, E. Buringh, J. L. Van Zanden, "From Baghdad to London. The Dynamics of Urban Growth in Europe and the Arab World, 800–1800", Utrecht University/IISH working paper, 2008.

118 Cf. e.g. E. Chaney, "Tolerance, Religious Competition and the Rise and Fall of Muslim Science", working paper, Harvard University, November 2008.

119 P. Parthasarathi, "Agriculture, Labour, and the Standard of Living in Eighteenth-century India", [in:] *Living Standards in the Past…*, op. cit., p. 90.

The collapse of Indian industry was closely connected with British domination, although this was not necessarily the result of policies consciously adopted (or at least was not their main aim). Critics of the day, such as Edmund Burke, estimated that the 400,000 pounds in taxes paid by Bengal annually placed an enormous burden on the Indian economy. To this were added the costs of a corruption and incompetent administration, whose aim was to extract as much wealth from India as possible.

Administrators in the East Indian Company frequently rotated. They had enormous power over the "natives", to whom they did not feel in any way bound. Control was exercised from a distance; the chances of detecting corruption – small; the likelihood that someone would be punished – even smaller. Colonial administrators were also perfectly aware that they had a good chance of dying from one of a number of tropical diseases before returning to their homeland. It is thus not surprising – nor incompatible with the laws of human nature – that for risking their lives working in the Company for several years, everyone – from top to bottom – wanted to earn some extra money, *fas et nefas*. The Company might have been generating losses on paper, but the administrators were amassing fortunes. According to contemporary estimates, Britain exported 1.5 million pounds from Bengal per year – including official taxes, profits from its trading monopoly (which the company owned) and private income; according to one Indian historian today, this sum could have totalled as much as 9 percent of GDP, enough to have a ruinous effect on any economy.[120] Indian handicrafts, or, as some historians prefer to say, nascent industries, according to other estimates in 1750 could have provided even a quarter of the world's production of industrial products. One hundred years later, it was dying. In the modern factories that were built in India in the late nineteenth century, nearly everything was British – the capital, engineers and machines. Only the workers were locals.

5. "Our little peasant, overburdened with work"

Several years after the publication in London of William Jacob's description of his trip through the Polish lands, with its quite unfavourable description of the customs and standard of living there, another book was published in Warsaw about the customs of the Polish people written by Łukasz Gołębiowski, one of the first Polish ethnographers. The book, *The Polish People, Their Customs and Superstitions* (Pol. *Lud polski, jego zwyczaje i zabobony*), which featured the work

120 Quoted in N. B. Dirks, *The Scandal of Empire. India and the Creation of Imperial Britain*, Cambridge–London 2006, p. 145.

of a number of ethnographers, opened with a description of the history and customs of Polish peasants:

> He who calls the state of our peasants slavery, or deems them most unhappy, or accuses our fathers or us of savagery is either mistaken or claims this only for appearances (in line with what the foreign press proclaims) [...] That the clothing of the peasant seemed shabby in the eyes of a foreigner, that his food was coarse and unrefined, that his cottage, compared with those abroad, was wretched, and therefore he lived in pure misery. Local circumstances and needs caused the former to grow accustomed to the latter; he maintained his health, and in his modest cottage, virtue, vigour and happiness resided with him and his family. The very goodness of the character of the Poles made that each peasant's Master hardly threatened him, but was more a father and guardian, who built him a cottage, gave him horses, oxen and needed allowances, gave him a measure of soil, provided him with access to the forests, the fruits of his fishing, and the mushrooms and berries he collected, and accepted as modest payment for all these benefits a mild form of serfdom and small tribute to be paid regularly. [...] If the peasant found himself wanting, the Master provided assistance; when ill he found solace; he received protection from any harm that someone else or an army might inflict. [...] If the Master was at all moral, and the Polish peasant possesses virtue, he can rightly boast before the eyes of the whole world: that he is bound to the faith of his fathers, faithful to his Monarchs; righteousness, nobility and honesty, it seems, he drank with his mother's milk.[121]

Gołębiowski admitted, though not directly, the accuracy of foreign descriptions, whose the authors looked down at Polish backwardness. In part, the origins of his idealization of patriarchal rural life can be traced to a romantic response to the social ills brought about by progress – a response that was widespread both in the West and in Poland.[122] Decades later, equally lofty descriptions would issue from the pens of intellectuals in other underdeveloped countries. The belief that we may be poorer, but we are more noble and morally superior, and moreover, live in greater harmony with nature, not only served as an excuse for their own backwardness, but also as an instrument for defending national pride. In addition, it was used to justify the choice of a different path of development than the West (which was often associated with a very slow increase in overall prosperity). Convictions about the intrinsic and autonomous value of local traditions also served as a symbolic barrier against an "invasion" by the West. In the wake of technology and abundance, came a western lifestyle, and western norms and values, which many intellectuals in the developing world no longer felt was desirable: they saw it as a threat to the identity of the people to which they belonged and in whose name they wanted to speak.

121 Ł. Gołębiowski, *Lud Polski. Jego zwyczaje, zabobony*, Warszawa 1830, pp. 7–8.

122 J. Jedlicki, *Świat zwyrodniały. Lęki i wyroki krytyków nowoczesności*, Warszawa 2000.

In praising the "righteousness, nobility and honesty" that peasants sucked from their mothers' breast milk, the Polish ethnographer admits that in the past not everything in this patriarchal idyll always went so well. At the time of the "elective kings" bad policies meant that "our peasant could be overburdened with work": "when a nobleman sighed and, without dismounting from his horse, began to tend to his increasingly profitable farm, either the closer and more befitting the ensuing relations with the peasants became, or the heavier and swifter their subjugation."[123] In writing these words nearly two hundred years ago, Gołębiowski summed up the issue well: economics textbooks today speak of this "refeudalization" or "second serfdom" as one of the primary causes of civilizational backwardness, or, to use more neutral terms, the social and political dissimilarity of the region.[124]

Its initial cause was primarily economic in nature. Beginning in the late fifteenth century, the nobility profited from the export of grain (but also of other goods, such as wood and tar) to the West. However, they had trouble securing for themselves a sufficiently inexpensive, accessible and obedient workforce; the nobility therefore used its political leverage to tie peasants to the land, making their situation little better – if at all better – than that of slaves on plantations in the Caribbean. A desire to maintain access to consumer goods and the fear of losing their privileged social position also encouraged them to maximize their profits.[125]

Geography, politics and earlier historical events also played a role. The country had an extensive network of navigable rivers and vast amounts of land suitable for growing crops. The new feudal economy first began to appear on estates along the banks of major rivers; only later did it spread to Poland and Lithuania's vast open spaces. Exports of cereals began to increase after the victorious conclusion to the Thirteen Years' War (1466), after which Royal Prussia and Gdańsk were incorporated into Poland; this allowed for the safe export of goods along the Vistula river basin to the West. Polish cities were poor, and the handicrafts

---

123 Ł. Gołębiowski, *Lud Polski…*, op. cit., p. 5.

124 F. Crouzet, *The History of the European Economy…*, op. cit., pp. 77–78; see also e.g. Z. Wójcik, *Historia powszechna XVI–XVII w.*, Warszawa 1991, p. 15 ff. A recent survey of these theories was carried out in J. Kochanowicz, "The Polish Economy and the Evolution of Dependency", [in:] *The Origins of Backwardness in Eastern Europe: Economics and Politics From the Middle Ages Until the Early Twentieth Century*, ed. D. Chirot, Berkeley–Los Angeles 1991, p. 92 ff.

125 J. Topolski, "The Manorial-Serf Economy in Central and Eastern Europe in the 16th and 17th Centuries", *Agricultural History*, 1974, no. 3.

they produced were generally of low quality in comparison with those of the West; they also had limited access to markets, which hampered development. The townspeople's goods could not compete with products imported from England or the Netherlands. They also could not impose limits on imports because their political influence was too weak. They quickly took to peddling imported goods; those who could afford to do so, strove for ennoblement. "Eastern Europe became for a long time a region complementary to the expanding West" – this is how this process was summed up in the 1960s by Marian Małowist, the specialist who is probably most often quoted by western historians in relation to the economic specificities of the region.[126]

By the seventeenth century, the Polish Republic found itself in a – to some extent self-imposed – "colonial situation" (as writes late Jacek Kochanowicz, an expert on the subject; the term he uses comes from the title of a much-talked about book edited by Wallerstein,[127] the foremost theorist of the world system).[128] Another prominent Polish historian, Jerzy Topolski, also wrote about "colonial theory" in his history of the Polish Republic.[129] Not only was its entire economy oriented toward the export of a few agricultural products, the Republic's trade had also slipped out of the hands of its subjects, and was now controlled by traders, first from Antwerp, and then from Amsterdam.[130]

Moreover, although the Polish manor estate (Pol. folwark) produced goods for the market, it was not really a capitalist enterprise – this is how we could sum up a long discussion that took place among Polish historians on this issue.[131] What the

126 M. Małowist, "The Problem of the Inequality of Economic Development in Europe in the Later Middle Ages", *Economic History Review*, 1966, no. 1, p. 28.

127 *Social Change in the Colonial Situation*, ed. J. Wallerstein, New York 1966.

128 J. Kochanowicz, "The Polish Economy...", op. cit., pp. 95–96.

129 J. Topolski, *Gospodarka polska a europejska w XVI–XVIII wieku,* Poznań 1977, p. 23.

130 A. Mączak, *Między Gdańskiem a Sundem*, Warszawa 1972, p. 155.

131 W której brali udział m.in. Witold Kula, Marian Małowist and Antoni Mączak. Cf. e.g. J. Topolski, "Economic Decline in Poland from the Sixteenth to the Eighteenth Centuries", [in:] *Essays in European Economic History,* ed. P. Earle, Oxford 1974; J. Topolski, "Sixteenth Century Poland and the Turning Point in European Economic Development", [in:] *A Republic of Nobles. Studies in Polish History to 1864,* ed. J. K. Fedorowicz, Cambridge 1982; M. Małowist, "Poland, Russia and Western Trade in the Fifteenth to the Seventeenth Centuries", *Past & Present*, 1958, no. 13; M. Małowist, "Problem nierówności rozwoju gospodarczego Europy późnym średniowieczu", [in:] *Europa i jej ekspansja XVI–XVII w.*, ed. H. Zaremska, Warszawa 1993; M. Małowist, *Wschód a Zachód Europy w XIII–XVII wieku. Konfrontacja struktur społeczno – gospodarczych,* Warszawa 1973; A. Mączak, "The Social Distribution of Landed Property

manor estate produced was generally used to meet the needs of the owner, and it was in many ways a self-sufficient entity; it usually did not hire workers, and when it did hire them, it paid them more often in kind than in cash. Cash from the sale of grain and other products was spent primarily on the consumption of luxury goods, rather than on investments in the farm, which frequently did not require cash outlays. And the level of production was determined by the harvests, rather than by market needs. The Polish economy at that time can thus be described, as Kochanowicz recognized, as "an agglomeration of atomized, independent noble domains."[132] Poland was an "extreme case" of a country in which nothing, from the economic structure, to the norms of social life, was conducive to the development of entrepreneurship in the modern sense of the word. It was not fitting for a noble to engage in trade; an external dependence on colonial exports to the West was accompanied by a feudal mentality, and the "spirit of capitalism" was completely alien. This was nonetheless a rational situation: until at least the beginning of the seventeenth century, rising prices had led the nobility to earn more and more.[133]

Let me make here a brief digression: looking at Polish backwardness from this perspective, there is nothing surprising in the fact that Polish reformers often considered the state to be the key to overcoming it. What else could they do? There was no other force – neither internal nor external – on which to base change. The middle-class was too weak, and the nobility showed little interest in economic progress; industry, where it existed, was often founded and run by foreigners with foreign capital (which in the nineteenth century began to be an issue of growing importance in public debates). Regardless, there was very little industry on the scale of that in the West.

Efforts to carry out "top-down industrialization" in Poland have a long history – and it is mostly a history of failures. Witold Kula, probably the most prominent analyst of Poland's backwardness, once wrote that industrialization in Poland was carried out in waves. It lacked continuity and new projects were rarely built on the achievements of previous ventures because, ultimately, little remained to show for them. In his monumental two-volume *Sketches on Manufacturing* [Pol. *Szkicach o manufakturach*, 1956], Kula analyzes some two dozen factories set up by the king

---

in Poland from the 16th to the 18th Century", [in:] *Third International Conference of Economic History*, vol. 1, Paris 1968; A. Mączak, *U źródeł nowożytnej gospodarki europejskiej*, Warszawa 1967.

132 J. Kochanowicz, "Could a Polish Noble Became an Entrepreneur? Mentality, Market and Capital", [in:] idem, *Backwardness and Modernization. Poland and Eastern Europe in the 16th–20th Centuries*, Aldershot 2006, p. 935.

133 J. Topolski, *Gospodarka polska...*, op. cit., p. 24.

and magnates in the late eighteenth century. The vast majority of these ventures quickly failed. They faced difficulties in terms of employees, sales, production quality, and transport; the agrarian country seemed to reject with its very essence the transplant of industry. "New forces are on the rise", Kula wrote. "But they have failed to learn their history".[134]

And while Kula writes that the role of "commercial capital" in the financing of these investments was greater than he had anticipated, the most ambitious of these ventures – a project by court treasurer Anthony Tyzenhauz to build factories on the royal estates in Lithuania – was based on unpaid, forced peasant labour. Tyzenhauz planned to use such extremely (even for those days) brutal methods to "finance" a large part of the investment. According to Kula: "Extremely labour-intensive and back-breaking irrigation work, water engineering projects, and road building, the construction of handicraft and manufacturing colonies, and the associated felling and transport of trees, the servicing of factory operations (the transport of raw materials and products, provision of lumber, and maintenance of water facilities) all these additional burdens fell on the backs of peasants."[135]

Tyzenhauz's "system", despite complaints and protests, operated for 15 years, and provided the king with significant revenues. Proceeds from the Lithuanian economy accounted for one-third of the income in the royal coffers, and Stanisław August's factories enhanced his prestige – providing the court with luxury goods and earning him a reputation as a protector of industry. There were many reasons for Tyzenhauz's eventual fall – the intrigue of magnates and foreign intervention played a role – but its root cause was bankruptcy. At that time, however, this process looked different than in a capitalist economy, in which an entrepreneur is unable to repay his debts, banks refuse to loan him money, and the remaining assets of the company are eventually divided among his creditors according to rules set by law. Tyzenhauz had financial problems: he was unable to repay the loans he had taken

134 Kula writes: "Disharmony between production relations and what was needed for the development of productive forces became a brake on the development of manufacturing in Poland at the time, resulting in weakness in the first area, limited "manufacturing" in the second, and the failure of the third. In the end, this was balanced out by relatively weak growth in the ultimate marker test of economic development – growth in labour productivity"; W. Kula, *Szkice o manufakturach*, Warszawa 1956, vol. 1, p. 32. For more on the attitudes of Polish historians – Witold Kula, Marian Małowist, Jerzy Topolski and Andrzej Wyczański – towards the problems of backwardness, see A. Sosnowska, *Zrozumieć zacofanie. Spory historyków o Europę Wschodnią 1947–1994*, Warszawa 2004.

135 W. Kula, *Szkice...*, op. cit., vol. 1, p. 419.

out, and even the revenues he supplied to the king were declining and becoming increasingly irregular.[136] Stanisław's motivation to protect Tyzenhauz progressively weakened, and he finally allowed his political opponents destroy him.

Tyzenhauz had exploited his (or rather, the king's) subjects, investing in various, at times prestigious, projects: for example, he redesigned the town of Sokolka in the spirit of Enlightenment-era "urban design", which Kula summed up as: "a little parody of the rationalist urban planning of enlightened absolutism".[137] Peasants abandoned their estates. They first wrote complaints, then rebelled – and when this did not yield results, they fled en masse. Since their forced labour was the major "capital" held by feudal estates, we can say that the royal assets entrusted to Tyzenhauz underwent permanent decapitalization. This was difficult to reverse. Machines can by purchased quickly, but new people are acquired slowly over time, because they must either reproduce, or be encouraged to return. Moreover, it appears that Tyzenhauz knew this perfectly well: he long refused to supply the king with the archive and inventory of assets entrusted to his management, and when his fate was sealed, one night he packed the archive into 39 wagons (!) and "commanded his economic official to transport the goods to his estate, and in the event of pursuit, to burn or sink them."[138] A small portion of this archive has survived to the present day.

The history of this venture is worth remembering: in many twentieth-century accelerated growth projects in under-developed countries, there were attempts to make use of a similar mechanism – exercising administrative pressure to utilise capital and labour "trapped" in the countryside, as a means for providing the state with resources to undertake an ambitious modernizing investment programme. As in the case of Tyzenhauz, not only economic factors, but also issues related to politics and prestige, tended to influence investment decisions; the cost of progress achieved by these means, measured in human suffering and poverty, was frequently, as we shall see, very high.

Similarly instructive is a second attempt at industrialization in Poland – the mining companies established by Fr. Drucki-Lubecki in Congress Poland. Although in the nineteenth century capital from the state played a significant role in agriculture and forestry, as well as in light industry and, later, the construction of railways, mining consumed the lion's share of its available resources. Investments in industry were not sufficiently remunerative to attract private capital – high transport costs

136 Ibid., p. 436.
137 Ibid.
138 Ibid.

resulted in low profits and huge investment costs. It was much more profitable to be a wholesaler or to lease taxes and excise duties. One historian studying this issue writes, "it can be assumed that if this sector of the economy had remained a field for the free play of interests, the development of industrial capitalism would have been delayed for years to come."[139]

Lubecki's industrial policy from the outset assumed of a low level of profitability: real profits in relation to capital investment were to be, according to the assumptions of the plan's author, 2–2.5 percent a year, and thus very little for those times.[140] And these were optimistic calculations. In reality, his undertakings continually lost money, in part, because the state was little inclined to control costs – building, for example, magnificent and expensive factory buildings. Lübeck, who was self-taught in terms of economics, saw industrialization as a tool for the elimination of backwardness; meanwhile, industrialization was to be financed by – apart from loans (the first major foreign loan taken out by the Kingdom in 1829 was intended for investments in mining) – a reduction in consumption. When in 1823 a tariff war began with Prussia, which had placed high duties on Polish grain exports, Lubecki – despite the very difficult situation of Poland's indebted landowners – firmly refused to reduce taxes, explaining that investment needs came first. He also sought – without success – to establish a state monopoly on the trading of colonial goods, such as sugar, coffee and arrack (as well as wine).[141] This policy was not without effects, although most were in areas other than those in which the state had invested most heavily: in the years 1820–1830, for example, textile production in the Kingdom grew by 10 percent annually.[142] But these efforts were based on fragile foundations: when after the November Uprising the political conditions changed drastically, most of the projects supported by the government failed.

In 1824 Lubecki wrote in a memorandum:

> Political independence must be supplemented by economic independence. Meanwhile, the industry of foreign countries is making unfair use of its advantages and keeping our [industry] underdeveloped and dependent. It is therefore necessary to break this yoke [...]. Industry left alone would be unable to free itself, and therefore the government should remove these obstacles that hinder the development of production, should encourage private

139 J. Jedlicki, *Nieudana próba...*, op. cit., p. 32.

140 Ibid., p. 35.

141 P. Smolka, *Polityka Lubeckiego przed Powstaniem Listopadowym*, Warszawa 1983, vol. 1, p. 491.

142 J. Górski, *Polska myśl ekonomiczna a rozwój gospodarczy 1807–1830. Studia nad początkami teorii zacofania gospodarczego*, Warszawa 1963, p. 41.

individuals to make efforts and help them [...]. The government should attract suitable people to the arts and crafts, to establish some businesses and sell them later to entrepreneurs even at a discount.[143]

There can be no political independence without economic independence – this belief was common to many writers of economic development plans in underdeveloped countries. Economic nationalism (understood here in a descriptive, not evaluative sense) also provides arguments in favour of direct involvement by the state: after all, it best represented – as the authors of such theses were want to state –best represented the interests of the community. Thus, in the name of common interest you could impose high taxes on individuals – or dispossess them – arguing that progress is not made without sacrifice, and group interests outweigh those of the individual.

For a reader today, the story of Lubecki's ventures is striking not only due to their scale and ambitions, but also due to the scale of corruption and waste they produced at the intersection of the state and private economy. Government investments enriched legions of entrepreneurs, because the government commissioned private companies for provide supplies, and to build factory halls and housing for workers. These businessmen were all guided by the same principle – to engage as little capital as possible. Moreover, in some cases, they did not supply any capital, and in some questionable cases, it turned out that the entrepreneur's sole capital was the money deposited to secure the performance of the contract.

This led to scandals that would sound familiar to today's readers. In one example in 1833, two young engineers bought the village of Niwka in order to build an ironworks there. Ostensibly, the location was perfect: the village was close to both iron ore and coal deposits, and to a navigable river that could power the machinery. The investors did not have the money needed to build the factory, but they had connections – the whole venture was based on good personal contacts between the two investors and Henryk Łubieński, a rich landowner and entrepreneur, and a vice-president of the state-owned Bank of Poland, which financed the investments. The further course of events is recounted by a historian as follows:

The enterprising swindlers quickly proved, the following year, to be financially incapable of bringing construction to completion. The vice-president of the Bank took steps to "save the bank credit", but, in reality, he was bailing out his protégés and silent partners. After a somewhat inflated appraisal of the real estate was arranged, the bank repurchased the

143 Quoted in J. Górski, *Polska myśl ekonomiczna...*, op. cit., pp. 218–219.

> property, hiding the loss in the fictitious value of the purchased assets; the entrepreneurs walked away with their small capital investment along with a profit, and the Bank completed construction.[144]

It is still too early to ask whether such scandals – of which there was never a lack at any latitude or in any era – put into question the sense of top-down industrialization. Perhaps this should be considered an unavoidable cost of the "leap into modernity," which, even in the most favourable conditions, has never been achieved by the hands of saints, and the history of which fails to provide many morally inspiring stories.

In 1800 the income disparities between different parts of Europe were still small. Average wages in the West were perhaps 50 percent higher than in countries such as Poland.[145] But the cards in the game of progress had already been dealt, and the fates of east and west on the continent sealed. One side was destined to grow in power and prosperity; the other – to fall deeper and deeper into poverty and backwardness: in 1914 the distance was greater than a century earlier.[146] There was also a growing awareness that overcoming this would require radical measures.

---

144 J. Jedlicki, *Nieudana próba*..., op. cit., p. 71.

145 P. Bairoch, "Europe's Gross National Product: 1800–1975", *Journal of European Economic History*, 1976, no. 2, quoted in F. Crouzet, *The History*..., op. cit., p. 78.

146 Cf. e.g. A. P. Bénétrix, K. H. O'Rourke, J. G. Williamson, "The Spread of Manufacturing to the Periphery 1870–2007: Eight Stylized Facts", IIIS Discussion Paper no. 401, June 2012.

Chapter 2. “A task without historical precedent”

1. History

It is interesting to note that the landmark text from which the entire postwar economics of development in underdeveloped countries began was a blueprint for the future of Central Europe. This text, Paul Rosenstein-Rodan's “Problems of Industrialization of Eastern and South-eastern Europe” appeared in the prestigious *Economic Journal* in 1943 and, despite what may seem like a rather uninspiring title for today's reader, it carried an explosive ideological and political charge.[147] In it Rosenstein-Rodan wrote:

> It is generally agreed that industrialisation of “international depressed areas” like Eastern and South-Eastern Europe (or the Far East) is in the general interest not only of those countries, but of the world as a whole. It is *the* way of achieving a more equal distribution of income between different areas of the world by raising incomes in depressed areas at a higher rate than in the rich areas. [...] It is a tremendous task, almost without historical precedent. There is no analogy to the process of industrialisation in the early nineteenth century for a number of reasons.[148]

Rosenstein proposed a model of large-scale planned industrialization that was later called the “big push” (a name he himself also adopted and used). He argued that to be effective, industrialization must simultaneously encompass several complementary industries. He argued, for example, that you could not build a giant shoe factory employing 20,000 workers in a poor Eastern European country. Such a project was doomed to failure: the factory would not have anyone to sell its shoes to because there would be no market (the shoes would not be purchased by poor peasants, who constituted three-quarters of the population). And, in order to survive, factory workers would have to be paid much more than peasants living in the countryside – because, unlike the peasants, the workers would not be able to even partially feed themselves. For these reasons, the project would soon prove to be unprofitable.

The key to success lay in the overall scale of the operation. Rosenstein-Rodan wrote:

---

147 P. N. Rosenstein-Rodan, “Problems of Industrialisation of Eastern and South-Eastern Europe”, *The Economic Journal,* 1943, no. 210/211.

148 Ibid., pp. 202–204.

> If, instead, one million unemployed workers were taken from the land and put, not into one industry, but into a whole series of industries which produce the bulk of the goods on which the workers would spend their wages, what was not true in the case of one shoe factory would become true in the case of a whole system of industries: it would create its own additional market, thus realising an expansion of world output with the minimum disturbance of the world markets. The industries producing the bulk of the wage goods can therefore be said to be complementary. The planned creation of such a complementary system reduces the risk of not being able to sell, and, since risk can be considered as cost, it reduces costs.[149]

Rosenstein-Rodan was not a supporter of industrialization according to the Soviet model.[150] This was not because he believed that it had failed. On the contrary, like most economists of the day (including non-communists), he thought it had been a spectacular success. However, he thought that investing in heavy industry in the East would be inefficient, because the same industries in the West had a large surplus production capacity; it would be a pointless duplication.

The economist also pointed to humanitarian concerns. He considered the social costs of the Soviet model – which "squeezed" resources for investment out of its own citizens – to be too great. The people of Eastern European were living in such miserable conditions that it would be inhumane to worsen them further. This led Rosenstein-Rodan to indulge in the following psychological observation: "People (even Eastern Europeans!) are not as tough today as they used to be. Social conscience would not stand for as much misery in peace-time as was taken for granted in the Darwinist nineteenth century. Milder methods must be used."[151]

A number of ideas contained in Rosenstein-Rodan's concept later appeared in accelerated development projects. The first was that private capital was not what mattered. Investments as large and complex as those required by the "big push" were for him unattractive – due to both the long period of time required to realise their benefits, and political risks, such as war or nationalization. (Rosenstein-Rodan: "Political risks of international investment are very much greater today than in the nineteenth century, when it was assumed that certain things were 'not done.'"[152])

Capitalism was not also capable of undertaking such a great transformation for structural reasons: the projected future would be radically different from the

149 Ibid., p. 206.
150 Cf. S. Chakravarty, "Paul Rosenstein-Rodan: An Appreciation", *World Development*, 1983, no. 1.
151 Rosenstein-Rodan, op. cit, p. 202.
152 Ibid., p. 206.

past, and capitalism belonged to the past. Rosenstein-Rodan wrote, "Experience of the past is partly irrelevant, however, where the whole economic structure of a region is to be changed. An individual entrepreneur's knowledge of the market is bound to be insufficient in this case because he cannot have all the data that would be available to the planning board [....]."[153] Thus, if things took their natural, capitalist course, not only would the standard of living in underdeveloped Eastern Europe rise much more slowly than its untapped potential offered, its industrial structure, built in such a way, would be less than optimal from the point of view of social needs.

This difference reflected the superiority of rational planning over the chaos of the market. The capitalist financial markets which usually financed individual investments could not grasp (or support) massive, technologically and socially complex projects involving multiple sectors of the economy. A capitalist will not even create institutions for training industrial workers on a mass scale – because it would not be profitable. For-profit schools will only teach the children of parents who can pay, and from the point of view of society as a whole, this is obviously a loss, because it means that dormant human potential is left unrealized. Capitalists will also not build infrastructure: roads, electricity, railways. According to Rosenstein-Rodan, education and infrastructure will absorb 30–35 percent of the cost of a "big push", so it must therefore be steered from above by the state. "The theory of growth must be very largely a theory of investment," he wrote some years later.[154] "Natura facit saltum", he would say, in an obvious reference to a well-known saying by classical economist Alfred Marshall, who thought that leapfrogging stages of development was impossible.[155]

The entire project faced several perilous conundrums. First of all, it was not clear how to finance the "big push". Rosenstein-Rodan assumed that part of the cost, which he estimated at the time to be five billion pounds, would cover the costs of an "Eastern European Industrial Trust", which was to be established after the war, financed in part with Western loans, and in part from compensation paid by Germany (perhaps in kind, or in machines for Poland's or Romania's newly built industries). It was a purely hypothetical idea: some source of capital was simply necessary. As many as 3.6 billion pounds, however, was to come from Eastern Europe itself. With its national income estimated by Rosenstein at two

153 Ibid.

154 P. Rosenstein-Rodan, "Natura Facit Saltum: Analysis of the Disequilibrium Growth Process", [in:] *Pioneers in Development...*, op. cit., p. 211.

155 W. L. David, *The Conversation of Economic Development. Historical Voices, Interpretations, and Reality*, Armonk 1997, p. 87.

billion pounds a year, he calculated it would require committing to investment 18 percent of national income annually for a number of years, roughly as much as the USSR spent during Stalin's five-year plans. In Russia, however, it had been necessary to use police terror and drastically reduce citizens' living standards in order for the state to collect the funds required for investment. How could this be accomplished using "softer" methods?

The second problem concerned people. Rosenstein-Rodan estimated that among Central and Eastern Europe's 110 million inhabitants, up to 20–25 million were actually unemployed (he had in mind primarily disguised unemployment). These people, he claimed, were surplus labour: their work in the fields did not increase agricultural production, i.e., they could be employed in factories in cities without harming agriculture. The whole project therefore involved social engineering on a massive scale. The economist treated it as a completely natural part of the development process. The population was like pawns on the planner's chessboard: people were pieces to be "placed", "moved"," and "taken".

Thirdly, Rosenstein-Rodan in practice used interchangeably such notions as "industrialization", "growth" and "income growth". There was no hint of consideration that perhaps they were not all equivalent. He was also not interested in redistribution. He assumed that all "Eastern Europeans" would benefit from a "big push" and not merely a narrow elite.

Rosenstein-Rodan's article was more than just an academic work printed in a prestigious journal. It was a chapter from an official report of the Royal Institute for International Affairs, prepared by the Economic Group of the Committee on Reconstruction, and an expression of the allied governments' profound interest in the problems of the development of underdeveloped countries.

In 1941 a number of very different institutions in the U.K. were dealing with development planning – including the Royal Institute for International Affairs and the Oxford Institute of Statistics– as well as émigré governments and various informal (or semiformal) groups of economists and politicians meeting at seminars.[156] In 1941 Rosenstein-Rodan also became secretary of the Committee for Postwar Reconstruction at Chatham House, where he worked with Eastern European economists. As he wrote later, he chose Eastern Europe, not because he considered it to be the most interesting or characteristic example of underdevelopment, but simply because he had "at hand" émigré governments from the region and the ability to work with the numerous Eastern European economists;

156 Cf. e.g. articles in *Agenda: A Quarterly Journal of Reconstruction*, published by the London School of Economics in 1942–1944.

he maintained, for example, regular contacts with a group working at Oxford, which included, among others, Michał Kalecki.[157] Kalecki was considered the intellectual leader of the group, which also included Dudley Seers and Nicholas Kaldor.[158] In *The Economics of Full Employment*, a report published in 1944 by six young economists from this circle, we can read: "the regulation of the economic process by market forces [...] must be supplemented by conscious and deliberate regulation of public authorities."[159] It was a document written fully in the spirit of Keynes.[160] It assumed the possibility of obtaining full employment in developed economies through macroeconomic policies and remained influenced by discussions in the U.K about planning during the 1930s by the Political and Economic Planning (PEP) think tank.[161] By 1935, the PEP had already published three major reports – on construction, textiles, and metallurgy – and its journal *Planning* had a circulation of 2,000 copies and a readership that included almost a hundred members of parliament.[162]

Interest in the fate of the poorest countries had been at least partly forced upon Britain by the circumstances of war. Hitler offered countries allied with Germany a "New Order" – which in the economic sphere meant the promise that they could "eat from the German table" once the war had been won. Japan had its own "Co-Prosperity Sphere" for the peoples of Asia. Even if hiding behind platitudes about prosperity and development was the brutal exploitation of conquered peoples (and, as military defeats increased, of their allies, as well). The Allies felt obliged to present a more credible proposal.

Yet there were greater considerations involved than just politics and propaganda. The reasons for the Allies' interest in the development of poor and peripheral countries went much deeper, and were not merely utilitarian in nature. In *The Great Transformation*, a study of the formation of market economies and the modern nation state published in 1944, Karl Polanyi foresaw the coming of a socialist society that would embody a spontaneous reaction to the market's ills.[163]

---

157 Ibid., p. 124.

158 H. W. Arndt, "The Origins of Structuralism", *World Development*, 1985, no. 2

159 Ibid.

160 E. J. Berg, "Socialism and Economic Development in Tropical Africa", [in:] *Comparative Economic Systems*, ed. J. S. Prybyla, New York 1969, p. 147

161 D. Ritschel, *The Politics of Planning. The Debate on Economic Planning in Britain in the 1930s*, Oxford–New York 1997, p. 153 ff.

162 Ibid., p. 181

163 K. Polanyi, *The Great Transformation,* New York 1944; cf. G. Dale, *Karl Polanyi: The Limits of the Market*, Cambridge–Malden 2010, p. 70 ff.

"Socialism is, essentially, the tendency inherent in an industrial civilization to transcend the self-regulating market by consciously subordinating it to a democratic society," he wrote.[164] In 1942 the Beveridge Report was published in Great Britain. The document called for the creation of a welfare state, and delineated specific individual needs that should be met by society.[165] 630,000 copies of the report were sold.[166] The war had been a cataclysm from which a better world was supposed to emerge, one free of the inequalities and injustices of the past. Such was the thinking of Paul Rosenstein-Rodan, but he was not alone.[167] At almost the same time, a solution very similar to Rosenstein-Rodan's for South-Eastern Europe was being suggested by a group at Oxford associated with the economist Kurt Mandelbaum, who proposed harnessing the "hidden reservoir of manpower in the countryside" for purposes of industrialization.[168] In all of these projects, a rational, planning state was to be an instrument of social progress.[169]

This view was at least as much the fruit of experience as of ideology. Already during World War I, the Viennese philosopher and political scientist (and socialist) Otto Neurath had noted that in the realities of the wartime system of planning and control, governments had managed to eliminate many of the evils plaguing the liberal economy of the *belle epoque*, including unemployment and economic fluctuations. It turned out that the state was able to effectively mobilize resources – money, raw materials and people – and organize production on a large scale. Neurath, one of the authors of the Austro-Hungarian planning system during the war, and later an adviser and chief planner for the government of the short-lived Bavarian Council Republic, he was convinced that the state could use the same methods to effectively deal with the economy in times of peace (he also proposed the abolition of money and basing the economy on the exchange of goods, but these ideas drew far fewer supporters). The successes of German war planning during World War I had also inspired the Bolsheviks in Russia.[170]

164 K. Polanyi, *The Great Transformation*, op. cit., p. 234

165 W. Beveridge, *Social Insurance and Allied Services*, London 1942; cf. K. Williams, *From Pauperism to Poverty*, London 1981, p. 367

166 D. Kynaston, *Austerity Britain, 1945–51*, London–Berlin–New York 2007, p. 16

167 H. W. Arndt, *The Origins...*, op. cit.

168 K. Mandelbaum, *Industrialization of Backward Areas*, Oxford 1947; cf. also E. Staley, *World Economic Development: Effects on Advanced Industrial Countries*, New York 1944

169 Cf. J. Kochanowicz, "Początki planowania w Polsce po II wojnie światowej w perspektywie porównawczej", [in:] *Ekonomia i ekonomiści w czasach przełomu*, ed. E. Mączyńska, J. Wilkin, Warszawa 2010.

170 Cf. Chapter 3.

The lessons of World War II were even more explicit. The economies of the Soviet Union and Germany were completely controlled by the state. Although Germany had not murdered its capitalists, it had essentially incapacitated them, and could boast impressive results afterwards. In 1946 the well-known Marxist historian E.H. Carr wrote in his book *The Soviet Impact on the Western World*:

> The economic impact of the Soviet Union on the rest of the world may be summed up in the single word "planning". [...] President Roosevelt's enemies were never tired of claiming that the New Deal had been framed on a Soviet model.[171]

Carr added that the idea was a mixture of naivety and genius, and that the core idea was essentially correct, although the details were often utopian. We are all planners, he confessed, under the influence of the Soviet practice and Soviet achievements. He also wrote that the poorer the country, the more it is fated to planning, and therefore an impoverished postwar United Kingdom planned to a greater extent than the United States, modelling it on the Soviet Union's wartime efforts.

Germany as well, despite its defeat, provided arguments for the proponents of planning and statism. In the face of destructive bombing raids and a permanent lack of raw materials, the Reich's industrial production continued to grow in the latter half of 1944.[172]

Propaganda made an equally strong impression as hard numbers. Albert Speer, author of the German "armaments miracle," was also a master of mass persuasion: he made it possible for the regime not only to continue the war (after the defeat at Moscow in 1941 many managers of the German economy agreed that the war was unwinnable and that a political resolution had to be sought), but also persuaded the Germans that they were capable of overcoming all obstacles through their collective efforts. Total mobilization of the economy was an enterprise which lay as much in the realm of social psychology as in the economic sphere itself. Beginning in April 1942, German newsreels began to show the first views of the factories that build tanks; on May 20, 1942 at a giant public ceremony publicized in the press, radio and newsreels, Franz Hahne, a worker from the Alkett tank factory in Berlin, received a high distinction, the War Merit Cross (*Ritterkreuz zum Kriegsverdienstkreuz*). Alongside Hahne – "Germany's most efficient armaments worker" – thousands of other employees of the armaments industry were honoured with medals, with the highest-ranking Nazi dignitaries (including Goering, Speer and Keitel) all in attendance for this propaganda "show". The German newsreel showed Franz

---

171 E. H. Carr, *The Soviet Impact on the Western World*, London 1946, p. 20.

172 W. Abelhauser, "Germany: Guns, Butter and Economic Miracles", [in:] *The Economics of World War II*, ed. M. Harrison, Cambridge 2000, p. 163.

Hahne beaming with pride as he paraded before an honour guard composed of soldiers, sailors, airmen and Waffen-SS, while the narrator's voiceover proclaimed: "The best soldiers with the best weapons will defeat the enemy". In 1943 such armaments-related performances had become the daily bread of German propaganda: for example, on June 5, 1943 Speer spoke at the *Sportspalast* in Berlin to 10,000 workers of the armaments industry while rewarding their bosses for service to the German nation.[173] Germany lost the war, but the vision of the unlimited potential that could be harnesses through centrally directed, collective efforts had taken root among both the losers and the winners.

The capitalist West also quickly switched over to a centrally planned war economy. In the U.S., the state controlled prices and wages with an iron fist. A Bureau of Planning and Statistics was set up within the War Production Board to direct the economy (its chief economist and statistician was Simon Kuznets).[174] Private investors were also replaced: between 1942 and 1945, net private investment amounted to minus $ 6.2 billion, which meant that private industrial plants underwent decapitalization. Meanwhile, government investment totalled $ 99.4 billion.[175] The government's armaments investment programme was enormous in scale; from 1940 to 1943, as many factories were built (mainly for armaments, but also for other branches of industry, from steel mills to rubber and chemical plants) as in the previous two decades. Yet America did not avoid the pitfalls typical of a planned economy: already in 1944, some factories were not operating at full capacity because of poorly calculated deliveries of raw materials; excessive production in some areas was accompanied by deficits in others. But in the eyes of people who still remembered the misery and absurdities of the Great Depression, the U.S. war economy functioned with impressive efficiency.

After 1945, it quickly became apparent that many previous investments did not make sense in peacetime: for example, in 1951, shipyards built at a cost of $1.4 billion could hardly find a buyer at slightly more than 10 percent of this sum.[176] "Contemporaries greatly exaggerated the heroic achievements of wartime socialism," U.S. researcher Robert Higgs concludes in relation to the war economy, adding that the waste of funds during the war, even if you consider it to be justified

---

173 A. Tooze, *The Wages of Destruction. The Making and Breaking of The Nazi Economy*, New York 2008, pp. 554–555.

174 J. Lacey, *Keep From All Thoughtful Men. How U.S. Economists Won World War II*, Annapolis 2011, p. 74.

175 R. Higgs, *Depression, War and Cold War. Studies in Political Economy*, Oxford 2006, p. 81.

176 Ibid., p. 88.

by circumstances, was gigantic.[177] Perhaps this is true; it is hard to forget, however, that the war economy was what eventually pulled the United States out of the Great Depression.[178] In the eyes of many contemporaries, this was an argument for the idea that liberal capitalism was an inefficient and wasteful system, and the return to it after World War I had been a gross mistake of historic proportions.[179] Full employment and economic growth had been restored through state intervention, and even if consumption had not recovered to pre-Depression levels, in the eyes of many, freedom from unemployment and abject poverty was worth the price.

"Development economics – the study of how poor countries can become rich – was forever cursed by the timing of its birth after the Great Depression. That gave development economics a bias toward relying on governments, rather than markets, to create growth," wrote William Easterly, former chief economist of the World Bank and one of the most prominent critics of development aid.[180] The question of whether it was a blessing or a curse needs to be put aside for the time being; it is a fact, however, that postwar ideas about the development of underdeveloped countries drew heavily upon the means by which the West tried to cope with the Great Depression.

Many economists felt guilty: they were late in realizing the enormity of the economic collapse that followed the stock market crash in 1929, and were slow to find a way out of crisis.[181] In the latter half of the 1940s, one of the main tasks the Keynesian "new economy" had set for itself was preventing a repeat of the Great Depression. After the war, Western countries all led policies of full employment and built the institutions of a welfare state. Specialists in the development of underdeveloped countries set similar targets for themselves; they also wanted to use the same instruments, and that meant, above all, state intervention in various spheres of life, beginning with planning and ending with foreign trade. This distinguished them from Keynes, whose theory postulated controlling demand, not interfering with supply.[182] Like him, however, they did not believe in the market. This distrust of the market was deeply rooted and justified by the experience of recent past

---

177 Ibid., p. 95.

178 R. A. Rosenbaum, *Waking to Danger. Americans and Nazi Germany, 1933–1941*, Santa Barbara– Denver–Oxford 2010, p. 126.

179 R. Boyce, *The Great Interwar Crisis and the Collapse of Globalization*, London–New York 2009, p. 18.

180 W. Easterly, "Development Doesn't Require Big Government, *The Wall Street Journal*, 3 October 2008.

181 G. M. Meier, "The Formative Period", [in:] *Pioneers...*, op. cit. p. 11.

182 R. Skidelsky, *Keynes. The Return of the Master*, London 2009, p. 153.

disasters. They also thought that social evolution had led to a split between profit and economic progress.

Many future specialists in development had been followers of classical economics in their youth (the roads of two Poles active in this sphere, Oskar Lange and Michał Kalecki, who had previously ascribed to Marxism, were not typical in this respect). The famous Argentinean economist Raúl Prébisch, one of the spiritual fathers of dependence theory in the 1970s and a leading supporter of protectionist industrial policy in underdeveloped countries, recalled shortly before his death:

> When I started my life as a young economist and professor during the 1920s, I was a firm believer in neoclassical theories. However, the first great crisis of capitalism – the world Depression – prompted in me serious doubts regarding these beliefs. It was the beginning of a long period of heresies, as I tried to explore new views on development matters.[183]

Total war inclined people to think about a new beginning. It was clear that the world after this disaster could not return to its old routine. It had to be built on a better, more equitable basis. Paul Rosenstein-Rodan wrote then:

> If we were to emerge alive, we should not return to the previous status quo but… form a better world […] Not to do enough about inequality of opportunity and poverty when our world resources are sufficient to improve the situation is the real moral crisis.[184]

Another noted economist of the time, Hans Singer, wrote that his mission is simply the creation of a "global welfare state".[185] This idealism was expressed in development projects and tasks that emerged during the war, and which were placed on the agendas of then-forming international organizations.

The first political statements postulating a rise in the standard of living in peripheral and underdeveloped countries came out of the circle of leftist liberals associated in the 1930s with the World Labour Organisation (who, among other things, called for providing better nutrition in the colonies of the European empires). But it was the war that gave impetus to these ideas. Already in September 1939, just days after the outbreak of war in Europe, U.S. Secretary of State Cordel Hull appointed an advisory committee, whose job was to prepare plans for the

---

183 R. Prébisch, "Five Stages in My Thinking on Development, [in:] *Pioneers…*, op. cit. p. 175.

184 Quoted in D. Yergin, J. Stanislaw, *The Commanding Heights: The Battle Between Government and the Marketplace That Is Remaking the Modern World*, New York 1998, p. 77.

185 W.W. Rostow, *Theorists of Economic Growth from David Hume to the Present*, New York 1992, p. 413.

postwar order. The problem of the development of underdeveloped countries was taken up by the Committee in January 1941, when Roosevelt announced the "four freedoms" as the foundation of the new order: among them was "freedom from want" (next to freedom of speech, freedom of religion and freedom from fear). In the Atlantic Charter, signed in August 1941, Roosevelt and Churchill promised equal access to trade and raw materials for all countries; they wrote that "they desire to bring about the fullest collaboration between all nations in the economic field with the object of securing, for all, improved labor standards, economic advancement and social security."

Soon international organizations began to form which were designed to bring this programme into effect: the FAO (now the U.N. Food and Agriculture Organisation) in 1943, and the World Bank and International Monetary Fund in 1944. The International Labor Organization put together programmes for full employment which included colonies and dependent territories.[186] In 1945 the economic development of underdeveloped countries had already become one of the main official objectives of the domestic and foreign policies of Western countries.[187] It also had a leading place among the tasks of the emerging United Nations.

The rapid and successful postwar reconstruction of the West was a fourth – in addition to the two world wars and the Great Depression – important historical experience. Many economists later involved in development began their careers in offices of planning and reconstruction after the war. Dutchman Jan Tinbergen, later one of the most influential specialists on development (Nobel Laureate in 1969 and Chairman of the U.N.'s Committee for Development Planning from 1965 to 1972) had previously been (after 1945) the director of the Central Planning Bureau in the Netherlands. In the early 1950s, he began to advise the Government of India during the drafting of its first five-year plan ("the poverty prevailing in India – as a normal situation – was such a contrast [to living conditions in the Netherlands] that it redirected my thinking and main activities").[188] Western Europe rebuilt itself following the enormous destruction caused by the war in part through rational planning, and in part thanks to the injection of American capital.[189] (The Marshall Plan was equal to two percent of U.S. GDP; its success only strengthened the belief – then an already well-established theory – that a

---

186 D. Maul, *Human Rights, Development and Decolonization*, London–New York 2012, p. 86 ff.

187 H. W. Arndt, *Economic Development: the History of an Idea*, Chicago 1987, pp. 44–45.

188 Quoted in D. Yergin, J. Stanislaw, *The Commanding Heights*..., op. cit., p. 77.

189 M. J. Hogan, *The Marshall Plan. America, Britain and the Reconstruction of Western Europe*, Cambridge 1987, p. 431 ff.

lack of capital is the primary and most important brake on development).[190] The relative ease with which Europe and Japan rebuilt themselves out of the ruins after the war, managed to maintain full employment, and quickly become richer than before the war, inclined people to optimism.[191]

It is difficult today to understand the mix of idealism and optimism in which new development projects were undertaken. "In a sense, all the pioneers, without exception, felt they were engaged in a battle on behalf of the underdogs of the world, – i.e., the men, women, and children of countries that were latecomers", one of the most important protagonists in these events wrote in the 1990s.[192]

A look at the résumés of the economists involved helps us better understand their motivations. Tinbergen wrote, for example, that in the 1920s he abandoned physics for economics because he wanted to fight poverty.[193] Others had experienced the vicissitudes of emigration: fleeing war, they had travelled halfway around the world, eventually finding jobs at British or American universities. Rosenstein-Rodan was born in Austro-Hungarian Kraków, and studied in Vienna and London; he later worked at the World Bank, and retired at the Massachusetts Institute of Technology. Albert O. Hirschman was born in Berlin, earned his doctorate in Trieste, and served – as a German-anti-fascist – in the Allied forces during the war (first with the French, then with the Americans); he later worked in the administration supporting implementation of the Marshall Plan and spent four years in Colombia as an adviser to the World Bank.

Irma Adelman worked as an economist for the World Bank, the UN, FAO and ILO, advised the South Korean government (which was then carrying out its own five-year plans) in the 1960s, and ended her career as a professor at Berkeley. She was born in 1930 to a family of a socialist-leaning Romanian businessman. Having been born into a Jewish family, and brought up in a Catholic school

---

190 Many experts today believe that the significance of the Marshall Plan had a different meaning – it was too small of a capital injection to be of economic importance, and did nothing to help in the reconstruction of infrastructure because it had already mostly been rebuilt before the plan started; however, it supported democratic institutions in Western Europe, which threatened to slide into the Soviet sphere of influence. The result was democracy combined with a mixed economy – and one of the greatest economic success stories in history. See B. DeLong, B. Eichengreen, *The Marshall Plan: History's Most Successful Structural Adjustment Program*, National Bureau of Economic Research Working Paper no. 3899 from 1991.

191 J. M. Cypher, J. L. Dietz, *The Process of Economic Development*, London–New York 2009, pp. 73–74.

192 W.W. Rostow, *Theorists…*, op. cit., p. 413.

193 Ibid.

run by nuns, she carried within her, as she wrote, "a massive sense of primordial guilt, that was later reinforced by the guilt of the survivor of the Holocaust." Years later, she wrote that the redemption of this guilt by means of the only mechanism possible – service to humanity – was the main force pushing her through life.[194] In the late 1960s and 1970s, Adelman came to the conclusion, based on years of painstaking research, that economic growth does not translate into higher earnings for the poor masses in the countries of the developing world, because most of the benefits went to urban elites.[195] For two years, she refused to publish these studies because she was afraid that they would serve the political opponents of development aid as an argument to cut off funds. Her compassion towards the poor, excluded and marginalised is inscribed into her biography.

"[M]y mother had brought me up to believe that anything they [the white British] can do we can do. This is not a scientific proposition, but it turned out to be true", recalled years later Arthur W. Lewis, the first black winner of the Nobel Prize (in 1979).[196] "They" were, of course, not just the British, but the citizens of the white, rich world in general. He was born in St. Lucia, and his father died when he was seven years old, leaving behind a widow and five children aged five to seventeen. Lewis left school when he was 14 years old, having completed all the requirements of the curriculum, and began working as a clerk. He later recalled in the autobiography he prepared for the Nobel Committee that the job had proven valuable because it taught him how to type, take notes and keep order.[197] Lewis, a descendant of slaves, rose to the top through persistence and perseverance: he earned a government scholarship to study in Britain, and before the war became the first black lecturer at the London School of Economics. (Lewis' interest in the history of economic development was sparked by his boss at the university, the ultraliberal Friedrich von Hayek, from whose ideas he would distance himself throughout his life.) As the son of a poor black teacher from the empire's distant provinces, he had learned that success was possible even under the most unfavourable circumstances: it was only a matter of will and effort. When in the 1950s debate continued over how much capital underdeveloped countries were able to absorb – this was a key point in the wider debate over accelerated development – Lewis used the argument

194 I. Adelman, "Confessions of an Incurable Romantic", [in:] *Recollections of Eminent Economists*, ed. J. A. Kregel, Houndmills–London 1989, vol. 2, p. 129 ff.

195 I. Adelman, *Economic Growth and Social Equity in Developing Countries*, Stanford 1973.

196 W. A. Lewis, "Development Economics in the 1950s", [in:] *Pioneers…*, op. cit., p. 140.

197 *Nobel Lectures. Economic sciences 1969–1980*, ed. A. Lindbeck, Singapore 1992, p. 395.

that it was just a matter of will. As he recalled years later: "This is not a scientific proposition, but it turned out to be true."

2. Theories

Theoretical innovations also tended to be optimistic. The very term "economic development" was still fresh; before World War II it had been used rarely.

The concept, however, was older than words. In the nineteenth century, English literature commonly used the word "progress", sometimes adding "material" or "economic" (for example, in the writings of Adam Smith and John Stuart Mill). "Development" began to appear sporadically at the beginning of the twentieth century: it was used by Schumpeter in a book published in German in 1911 (but only in 1934 in English), *The Theory of Economic Development*. In the 1920s, British economic historians and colonial administrators were also beginning to write, though not so often, about "development".[198]

Polish authors wrote more frequently and eagerly about "progress". The word itself appeared late in the Polish language, towards the end of the eighteenth century, and gained popularity during the era of Napoleon and Congress Poland: it was used by, among others, Staszic, Wybicki and Szaniawski, as well as by many journalists during the times of the November Uprising and the Great Emigration. It was also used by Mickiewicz (as counted by one tenacious literary scholar, Francis Pepłowski, it occurs in his writings exactly 58 times, and thus, perhaps, not all that often).[199]

Even by then, the word had become a symbol – a banner for all radical sociopolitical ideas. "Progress is life", wrote the radical philosopher and economist, Henryk Kamieński. Another philosopher, Bronisław Trentowski, used the word repeatedly as part of the phrase "freedom, light and progress".[200]

The word "development" appears in the Polish language still later yet, in the 1840s, and originally had a clear philosophical context, appearing in discussions of Hegel's philosophy.

The economic sphere was only one part of the great, all-encompassing advancement of progress. "The material economy," wrote Kamieński, "is thus a term defining and objectifying the general progress of humanity, its scientific

---

198 H.W. Arndt, "Economic Development: A Semantic History", *Economic Development and Cultural Change*, 1981, no. 3.

199 F. Pepłowski, *Słownictwo i frazeologia polskiej publicystyki okresu oświecenia i romantyzmu*, Warszawa 1961, p. 201.

200 Ibid., p. 203.

embodiment. And this progress, scientifically defined and scientifically objectified, becomes material development."[201] The phrase "economic development" became prevalent in Poland during the interwar period: among those who used it was Ludwik Landau, who wrote in 1933 about "the link between wages in Poland and economic development", and Oskar Lange, who included it in his outline for an economic programme for Poland after the war, written in exile in 1943.[202] This change in terms was significant, because "development" has a different meaning than "progress": it presupposes hidden potential that you can only develop what already exists in a germinal state.[203]

Landau and Lange were associated with the left. The impressive career of the concept of "economic development" stemmed not only from its ties to the Hegelian-Marxist tradition. (The words "development of production" or "development of the social economy" appear on nearly every page of the last pre-war issue of the Polish annual journal *Przegląd Gospodarczy* (Eng. *Economic Review*), published by the Central Association of Polish Industry, and thus, an institution which distanced itself from the ideas of the Left.) There was something in this notion that seemed to reach to the hidden depths of modern spirituality, and that touched upon a vision of the historical process in which not only the Marxists believed - because they were not the only ones who were deeply convinced that history was governed by universal laws; that it was a process that had a beginning and an end, and, above all, was moving in a certain direction; that the future would be, *on balance*, morally *better* than the past; and that *scientific* inquiry into the path that guides it was possible. Economics was, not only for Marx, but for the spirit of modernity, a record of the historical process in a crystallized, scientific form; "economic development" was the essence of economics. Its identification with "progress" was a matter of course; in the years after World War II, few people questioned this. In general, the terms "economic development", "progress", "industrialization" and often "income growth" were simply equated with one another. The notion that economic growth did not necessarily mean

---

201 H. Kamieński, *Filozofia ekonomii materialnej ludzkiego społeczeństwa*, Warszawa 1959, p. 61.

202 L. Landau, *Płace w Polsce w związku z rozwojem gospodarczym*, [in:] idem, *Wybór pism*, Warszawa 1957, p. 221 (the first edition was published by the Institute of Social Affairs in 1933); O. Lange, *Gospodarcze podstawy demokracji w Polsce*, [in:] idem, *Dzieła*, vol. 2, Warszawa 1973, p. 469.

203 For more on Kalecki's and Lang's views, see Chapter 4.; cf. also B. Popławski, "Polska szkoła rozwoju – zapomniany paradygmat studiów nad transformacją globalnego południa", *Kultura Współczesna*, 2012, no. 3

progress, common among nineteenth-century critics of industrial civilization, would not reach the popular consciousness until the 1970s.

Marx's writings were among the first classical works on economics to use the phrase "economic development" in the sense given to it in the 1950s and 1960s. In the preface to the first German edition of *Capital*, Marx wrote:

> The physicist either observes physical phenomena where they occur in their most typical form and most free from disturbing influence, or, wherever possible, he makes experiments under conditions that assure the occurrence of the phenomenon in its normality. In this work I have to examine the capitalist mode of production [...] Up to the present time, their classic ground is England. [...] If, however, the German reader shrugs his shoulders at the condition of the English industrial and agricultural labourers, or in optimist fashion comforts himself with the thought that in Germany things are not nearly so bad; I must plainly tell him, "*De te fabula narratur!*" [...] Intrinsically, it is not a question of the higher or lower degree of development of the social antagonisms that result from the natural laws of capitalist production. It is a question of these laws themselves, of these tendencies working with iron necessity towards inevitable results. The country that is more developed industrially only shows, to the less developed, the image of its own future.[204]

In the next paragraph, in writing about the underdevelopment plaguing Germany, Marx uses the term in the same sense as Rosenstein-Rodan, Lange and Lewis did in the 1940s and 1950s: "Alongside the modern evils, a whole series of inherited evils oppress us, arising from the passive survival of antiquated modes of production, with their inevitable train of social and political anachronisms. We suffer not only from the living, but from the dead."[205]

However, it was not until the interwar period that economists developed theoretical tools which allowed them to consider providing underdeveloped countries with a prescription for bridging the gap dividing them from the affluent West. After the war, the collapse of colonial empires and widespread aspirations for emancipation in peripheral countries opened up a vast space for experimentation.

The first technical innovation was the publishing of truly global economic statistics. In the mid-1930s, the first studies on nutrition levels had been carried out in different countries (including the colonies) at the request of the League of Nations. These showed a disastrous level of malnutrition – which was common everywhere except the rich West and a number of countries in the New World dominated by European immigrants. In 1940, a groundbreaking book

---

204 K. Marx, *Capital*. Preface to the first German edition, 1867, https://www.marxists.org/archive/marx/works/1867-c1/p1.htm.

205 Ibid.

titled *The Conditions of Economic Progress* was published in England by Colin Clark, a friend of Keynes' and a participant in his seminar. In it Clark published the first global compilation of national income statistics, data that was cited for many years afterward. The gulf in income between developed countries and the developing world could now for the first time be shown in numbers – and turned out to be greater than expected.[206] Clark's book was extremely popular; as the author himself noted, illegal handwritten copies even circulated in Japan during the war.[207] By 1947, Clark had been made an adviser to the Planning Commission in India, and he spent the rest of his career dealing with problems of development in underdeveloped countries. As with all new tools, including national income statistics, they were widely used and even abused: the level of national income soon became recognized as the measure of development. This tool offered numerous advantages, the most important of which was that it provided an easy means for comparing very diverse societies (although economists realized how imperfect it was as a measuring stick).

In the 1930s, economics created a new model of economic growth, which suggested – unlike classical economics, which assumed that progress took its "natural course"– that it was possible to accelerate the rate at which national income rose. A tangible example (to which we will return shortly) was provided by the USSR, while the applicable theory was constructed by two economists, Sir Roy Harrod, a Brit, and Evsey Domar, a Russian émigré. The two men formulated their models independently of one another, a true expression of the spirit of the times. Harrod, like Colin Clark, was a member of Keynes' circle (he was even the author of a biography of him); Keynes and his theories on full employment in developed capitalist countries was the starting point for his analysis. (Keynes himself was interested mainly in developed countries, and did not express particular interest in peripheral countries, or place trust in their governments: in a confidential report on the Bretton Woods conference for the Foreign Office, he called the Third World countries participating in it "the most monstrous monkey-house assembled for years").[208]

For Domar, who was born in Łódź brought up in a Russian colony in Manchuria, from which he emmigrated in 1936 to America, the starting point was Marx, and the purpose of his analysis was political in nature: he wanted to prove theoretically the inherent instability of capitalism. The two men's conclusions,

---

206 H. W. Arndt, *Economic Development: the History…*, op. cit., p. 35.

207 C. Clark, "Development Economics: The Early Years", [in:] *Pioneers…*, op. cit., p. 60.

208 G. M. Meier, "The Formative Period…", op. cit. p. 9.

however, shared many similarities: the so-called Harrod-Domar model is a very simple equation for describing the relationship between income growth, the level of saving (which was equal to the level of investment), and the "capital-output ratio", which expresses the productivity of capital (which was associated primarily with the level of technological development and was thus relatively constant at a given period in history).[209]

The political moral to be drawn from the Harrod-Domar model was appealing simple: the key to growth (and therefore economic development) was the level of investment.[210] The more a country saves, the more it invests; the higher the level of investment, the higher the rise in economic growth, and, therefore, the future rise in standard of living. Arthur W. Lewis in his most important article on accelerated development, "Economic Development with Unlimited Supplies of Labour", published in 1954, wrote that a fundamental problem in the theory of economic development is understanding the process by which a community which had previously saved and invested 4 or 5 percent or less of its national income is transformed into a economy in which voluntary savings are at 12–15 percent of national income or more. For Lewis fundamental to economic development was the rapid accumulation of capital, and the key to explaining each industrial revolution was a sudden, sharp rise in savings.[211]

Lewis based his reasoning on an analysis of economic growth in India: in the first half of the twentieth century, 4–5 percent of national income was invested, which led to growth of 1.25 percent annually. The population grew at roughly the same pace. The level of income of an average Indian thus remained on a constant, very low level. For it to rise, concluded Lewis, investment had to at least double.

In the Harrod-Domar equation, there was no place for a number of important elements found in later, significantly more complex models of growth. It was assumed, for example, that the level of production depended on just two factors – the availability of labour and capital inputs (and not, for example, the educational level of workers). It also did not take it into consideration the possibility of large injections of capital for investment from outside; accumulation always came at

---

209 In later textbooks the theory was reduced to a simple equation: $g = s/k$, where g is the growth rate, s – the savings rate, and k – the capital-output ratio, see e.g. R. Jha, *Macroeconomics for Developing Countries*, London–New York 2003 and G. M. Meier, "The Formative Period…", op. cit. p. 29.

210 Cf. A. Łukaszewicz's introduction to J. D. Domar, *Szkice z teorii wzrostu gospodarczego*, trans. L. Niżyński, Warszawa 1962, p. 26.

211 Quoted in F. Crouzet, *Capital formation in the Industrial Revolution*, London 1972, p. 10.

the expense of local consumption. He also did not consider the possibility that one could invest wastefully – the productivity of capital was determined by the level of technological development.

It is hard to overestimate the political consequences of this simplicity. It led experts to offer politicians, many of whom had a very limited understanding of economics, a clear goal for economic policy: the need to increase the level of investment (and thus savings). Just like the petty bourgeois who saves on food and heating, investing every penny in high-yield interest-bearing securities, the governments of Third World countries likewise had to reduce consumption in order to invest. Money "consumed" today equalled a missed opportunity for prosperity tomorrow. This led politicians and economists to an interesting question: whose consumption should be reduced? Who has to pay for growth? In 1957 Oskar Lange wrote:

> First of all, let us explain what accumulation in general involves. It essentially involves – and this is true for all social systems – some portion of social income not being consumed, but instead used to create new means of production. [...] In underdeveloped countries the excess surplus product, which could serve as a source of accumulation, is rather low. This is due to the widespread poverty prevailing in these countries. At a low level of labour productivity, in relation to which the full potential of the labour force is underutilised, income is low, and so, the surplus product, which could be used for accumulation, is likewise low.[212]

Accumulation requires an appropriate social structure. In underdeveloped countries, any surplus in production – which itself is rather limited – is used by the elite on forms of conspicuous consumption. In order to change this, one needs to change society. Such thinking led development economics to assume the role of a critical social science. Lange linked this to a feudal economy:

> A significant or even predominant part of the surplus product is allocated for consumption by the feudal lords and the state apparatus associated with the feudal regime, the church, court etc. We are familiar with the lifestyle of the ruling classes and strata in a feudal regime: the maintenance of a large number of servants, an unproductive "clientele", a greatly expanded church apparatus with numerous expenses, the courts of the monarch and magnates. Surplus product was allotted to such objectives under feudalism. [...] It follows that a basic condition for the development of an underdeveloped country is to eliminate feudal relations in production and the corresponding parasitic political superstructure.[213]

---

212 O. Lange, "Dlaczego kapitalizm nie potrafi rozwiązać problemu krajów gospodarczo zacofanych", [in:] idem, *Dzieła*, vol. 1, p. 736.

213 Ibid., p. 738.

Even when such a view was not expressed in the language of Marxism, as it is in Lange, the proposals made were generally similar in practical terms: the traditional elite, often additionally burdened by the sin of collaboration with the colonial metropolis, had to pay for accumulation. Economic development had to be accompanied by the social emancipation of the masses.

The realities of political life usually complicate considerably the application of this formula. If surplus production in underdeveloped countries is small – 4–5 percent – even if it is allocated to socially useful investments, rather than to luxury consumption, it will still be insufficient. Where can we obtain the missing 10 percent? Development policy planners turned to various methods. The most radical was nationalization, which allowed governments to gain full control over the investment process (and retain the earnings in the country if the nationalized industries belonged to foreigners). More often they tried to build a system of customs duties and indirect taxes, thus, placing the burden for raising capital for investment on consumption. This was all done according to the formula: we have to tighten our belts today, in order to loosen them tomorrow.

In practice, however, it often turned out that the only possible solution was to lower the standard of living of the poor. Of course, politicians may have seen this as merely a temporary solution, and were forced to turn to this option in spite of their populist rhetoric. The old elites might have been politically unjust and corrupt, but they still possessed money and influence; it rarely paid to engage in open warfare with them, as the risks were too great. You could curse them aloud, because they tolerated populist and nationalist politics as long as they did not interfere with their true interests. The people allowed themselves – for the moment – to be won over with by words. One of the most popular mechanisms for "extracting" money for investment from a poor, rural population was the nationalized monopoly purchasing of agricultural products at prices fixed by the government significantly below those on the global market (this was the case in many postcolonial countries, such as Ghana; we will return to this case). In this way, the state obtained income from villagers, who were forced to finance an ambitious modernization programme.

In the 1950s, there was an inundation of theoretical works justifying such a policy. Their authors, without exception, were sworn democrats, and many of them had leftist sympathies; all were also supporters of the emancipation of the Third World. The paradox was that the economic prescriptions they offered during their visits to governments in Africa, Asia and Latin America implicitly required authoritarian institutions; in democratic conditions, they could often simply not be put into practice.[214] Another noted economist, Gunnar Myrdal, wrote in 1957:

> There is no other road to economic development than a compulsory rise in the share of the national income which is withheld from consumption and devoted to investment. This implies a policy of the utmost austerity quite independently of whether the increased savings are engendered by high levels of profits to be ploughed back in industrial expansion or by increased taxation.[215]

Myrdal added that planning was necessary, and that planning had to be anti-market, because only large-scale investments involving the creation of entire industries from scratch could lead to an industrial breakthrough, and these would not be profitable from a capitalist standpoint.

The government had to involve itself in the process of industrialization: the message was clear. Ragnar Nurkse, an emigrant from Estonia and professor at Columbia and Princeton Universities, was convinced, like Rosenstein-Rodan and many other colleagues, that the only remedy for poverty in the Third World was industrialization. Otherwise, they would remain trapped indefinitely in a vicious circle of low investment, a growing population and stagnant wages. This was a commonly held view: impoverished countries were caught in "low-level equilibirum traps", that is, their social and economic structure condemned them to stagnation.[216] Another noted economist, Harvey Leibenstein, wrote in 1958 that underdevelopment is a state of "quasi-stable equilibrium", which requires a "push" in order to reach a new state of equilibrium – where investment and the associated risk-taking are necessary in order to maintain a place on the market. Reaching this state would of course require both coordinated intervention by the state and international aid.[217]

---

214 We must also mention here a very influential and widely are reading the work of a historian. In 1951, he published a book A. Gerschenkron, *Economic Backwardness in Historical Perspective*. Gerschenkron's thesis was great fit at the time for the theory of accelerated development. He wrote that the farther from the economic and cultural "centre" a country is located, the more backward they are and less likely to develop spontaneously. A stronger modernization impulse must therefore come from the state. Gerschenkron also gave hope: showing that "catching up" economically could be achieved very quickly, within one or two generations.

215 G. Myrdal, *Economic Theory and Under-Developed Regions*, Gerald Duckworth & Co, 1957, p. 82.

216 W. Ascher, *Bringing in the Future. Strategies for Farsightedness and Sustainability in Developing Countries*, Chicago–London 2009, p. 40

217 H. Leibenstein, *Economic Backwardness and Economic Growth*, New York–London 1957.

Unlike Rosenstein-Rodan, Nurkse believed, however, that it was not enough to invest in a number of interrelated sectors – what was needed was sustainable growth in the overall economy: the "big push" was to encompass simultaneously the whole of the economy, as a mean of breaking the vicious circle of poverty and low investment:

> For example, a poor man may not have enough to eat; being under-fed, his health may be weak; being physically weak, his working capacity is low, which means that he is poor, which in turn means that he will not have enough to eat; and so on. A situation of this sort, relating to a country as a whole, can be summed up in the trite proposition: 'a country is poor because it is poor'. Perhaps the most important circular relationships of this kind are those that afflict the accumulation of capital in economically backward countries.[218]

But where could capital for investment be obtained? Nurkse was optimistic: he believed that poor countries did not lack capital; they were merely unable to mobilize it. This hidden capital in poor countries was the labour of their people; if we add international aid to this (Nurkse often wrote about two percent of U.S. GDP, which is equal to the cost of the Marshall Plan in Europe), this should, according to Nurkse, be sufficient for a "big push". The cheapest path to industrialization was the bring into the labour force those people living in the countryside who were *de facto* surplus, that is, their labour did not increase agricultural production. If villagers who were actively working sent their surplus relatives – cousins, brothers and nephews who lived with them – to work on large public construction projects, and continued to feed them there, then, according to the economist, the unproductive consumption of the surplus rural population would become productive consumption.[219]

The economist did not respond to questions posed to him by reviewers at the time: perhaps assigning poor villagers to new jobs would cost more than the cost of merely providing them with substinence?[220] And where could money be obtained for their accommodation on construction sites? For transport? For job training? For oversight and supervision? For building materials? Finally, the crucial point: how to encourage them to work, since currently they were, Nurkse claimed, supported by relatives, and allegedly had nothing to do? Why should they work for free? Nor was it clear how many farmers and in what seasons could actually be mobilized to work – that is, how many people were really surplus.

---

218 R. Nurkse, *Problems of Capital Formation in Underdeveloped Countries*, Oxford University Press 1966, p. 4.

219 Ibid., pp. 37–38.

220 Cf. e.g. Brofenbrenner's review in *Journal of Political Economy*, 1954, no. 2.

Nurkse also believed – like Prébisch – that exports would not help poor countries raise capital for investment. The developing world generally exports either natural resources or agricultural products. The market demand for their goods in the rich countries of the West is limited. Increasing production would only lead to lower prices, rather than to higher incomes. One can even imagine a situation in which a country through enormous effort expands its exports of cocoa and coffee, but that its income from them is lower than before.

Foreign trade could also be harmful from another point of view. In exchange for cocoa, gold and coffee, an underdeveloped country imported machinery to produce industrial and consumer goods. According to Nurkse, however, there should be as little of the latter as possible. This is because luxury is demoralising and not conducive to savings. Nurkse believed that many consumer needs were neither necessary nor essential, and thus not truly needs. The consumption of luxury goods was just part of a play for social status. Imported luxury goods are consumed by the elite and become a status symbol. In this way, they become a widespread object of desire among a poor country's poorest citizens – and any effort to meet these needs will weigh on the trade balance and lower the savings rate (and therefore investment).[221] Imports of cars or perfume were harmful, since for the same money you could buy equipment needed for the "big push". But can a democratic government permit such restrictions on consumption?

Arthur W. Lewis wrote about the potential benefits for poor countries of their surplus labour. In a famous and much-quoted 1954 article, he described the economy of a poor country that consisted of two sectors: a small industrial and a dominant agriculture sector, full of surplus people.[222] If industrialists were willing to pay workers more than they could earn in the fields – Lewis estimated that 30 percent more would suffice – this would sufficiently compensate landless villagers for the costs and inconvenience associated with a move to the city and would be adequate to support them. Industrialists in poor countries would then be in possession of two trump cards. First, they could pay workers much less than their competitors from rich countries. Second, along with the expansion of industry, more and more workers would migrate to cities, but their earnings would not have to rise because as long as a labour surplus remained in the countryside, the cost of food (on which workers spend most of their money) would remain stable. In this way, urbanization and industrialization might proceed

221 This mechanism was later labelled the "demonstration effect"; Nurkse, however, did not yet use this term.

222 W. A. Lewis, "Economic Development with Unlimited Supplies of Labour", *The Manchester School*, 1954, no. 2.

somehow "spontaneously".[223] If labour shortages began to occur in the countryside, food prices would rise, and the wages of workers in the cities would likewise have to rise; however, industry would then have become strong and competitive enough to afford these costs.

Lewis immediately faced accusations that his model assumed growing social inequality: living in cities alongside capitalists and the middle class, who were acquiring new wealth along with industrialization, would be masses of rural workers, whose salaries barely covered the costs of subsistence. Lewis thought this was painful, but inevitable: he could not see another way to accelerate growth. His research on the industrial revolution in England seemed to confirm that a temporary increase in social inequalities could not be avoided. In later books, he proposed income redistribution in the form of draconian taxes on the elites in traditional societies, namely, the landowners, but also on financial speculators and other unproductive parasites. (Lewis did not include in this category capitalists investing in industry; he had no liking for them, but he appreciated their historical role.) Although the industrialization process had to take place largely automatically, the state nevertheless had a decisive role to play. In 1952 Lewis wrote:

> Planning in backward countries imposes much bigger tasks on governments than does planning in advanced countries. The government has too many things [to do] which can in advanced countries be left to entrepreneurs. It has to create industrial centers, to put through an agricultural revolution, to control the foreign exchanges more strictly, and in addition to make up a great leeway of public services and/or ordinary economic legislation. And all this has to be done through a civil service that is usually much inferior to that of an advanced country. Why then do backward countries take more readily to planning? Because their need is also so obviously much greater. And it is also this that enables them to carry it through in spite of error and incompetence. For, if the people are on their side, nationalistic, conscious of their backwardness, and anxious to progress, they willingly bear great hardships and tolerate many mistakes, and they throw themselves with enthusiasm into the job of regenerating their country. Popular enthusiasm is both the lubricating oil of planning, and the petrol of economic development–a dynamic force that almost makes all things possible.[224]

Lewis added that development "increases the range of human choice". A list of similar statements could be extended virtually indefinitely. There were discussions about how to plan, in how many industries to invest, how far nationalization

223 J. M. Cypher, J. L. Dietz, *The Process*..., op. cit., pp. 153–156.

224 Quoted in G. M. Meier, "The Old Generation of Development Economists and the New", [in:] *Frontiers Of Development Economics. The Future In Perspective*, ed. G. M. Meier, J. E. Stiglitz, New York 2001, p. 16.

should go, and what rules to impose on foreign trade and capital flows, but nobody doubted that all this was the domain and mission of the State.

By the mid-1950s, Albert O. Hirschman had acquired a reputation as a dissident, who after his experience acting as an advisor to the Colombian government (1952–1956) began doubting the wisdom of integrated planning for the economy as a whole. In 1958 he published a book in which he announced, in contrast to Nurkse, the need for "unbalanced growth". He believed that the state should invest in one industrial sector, which through linkages would "pull along" other branches of the economy. Hirschman was much less condescending towards his clients than many of his colleagues: he wrote about the "hidden rationalities" in forms of economic life in the Third World that were seemingly irrational to an outside observer. He gave as an example Colombia, where in many regions it was more economical to invest in air transport than to build a road (seemingly less expensive) through the jungle, as advocated by experts from the World Bank and the UN. However, Hirschman (the dissident!) was likewise convinced of the need to build industry, and that the state should provide inspiration for this (or simply do it on its own). In the spirit of the era, he thought that in backward countries hidden potential lay in the people's skills and talents, but was held back by irrational and outdated institutions; this potential had to be freed up before the country could enter onto the shining path of growth. He ascribed a great deal of importance to cultural factors, which at that time was unparalleled, explaining the backwardness of Latinos as the result of a widespread belief in luck and the need to outwit others to get ahead in life.[225]

Economic development was unthinkable without political emancipation, whether this concerned the masses in underdeveloped countries, or entire nations seeking to free themselves from outside domination. This view found its fullest expression in the texts of the Argentine economist Raúl Prébisch, who would later become one of the spiritual fathers of the theory of dependency. It is no coincidence that these ideas were born in Latin America, where economic and political failure in times of independence could easily be explained as a product of imperial (and no longer colonial) domination. This was – especially from the late nineteenth to the mid-twentieth century – a very real concern. The U.S. ambassador represented not only the political but also the economic interests of his country, which did not necessarily coincide with the interests of Latinos. His

225 A. O. Hirschman, *The Strategy of Economic Development*, Westview Press, Boulder–London 1958, p. 29.

interference in local politics and business was meticulous, painful, and often carried out with a striking lack of respect for local sensitivities and pride.[226]

Even countries less subject to imperial dictates, such as Argentina, suffered badly from the collapse in world trade during the Great Depression. In Latin America, as in the West, this was a formative experience – albeit in a different way. The turn of the century had brought Argentina true prosperity. The country's standard of living was among the highest in the world, and many Argentines believed they could attain universal prosperity through the export of agricultural products. In those days, even the socialist press in Buenos Aires praised liberal free trade: in 1891, one of them attacked economic protectionism as a "tremendous capitalist barbarity" that "raises the prices of essentials and is designed to free the upper classes from paying taxes by shifting these to the shoulders of the workers."[227]

The crisis brought a painful awareness not only of their own economic backwardness, but also of their dependence on foreign export markets. When the demand for their goods vanished, Latinos found themselves trapped with no way out. Latin American countries returned to 1929 levels of income very slowly, in some cases not until after World War II, which reignited demand for their exports. In the early 1930s, the GDP of Chile and Mexico fell by more than a third. This shock led people to draw conclusions: though various forms of state control over the economy were experimented with in the 1930s, only Prébisch turned his reflections into an economic theory. In the late 1940s, in a report for the recently formed UN Economic Commission for Latin America and the Caribbean, Prébisch wrote:

> If by "the community" only the great industrial countries are meant, it is indeed true that the benefits of technical progress are gradually distributed among all social groups and classes. If, however, the concept of the community is extended to include the periphery of the world economy, a serious error is implicit in the generalization. The enormous benefits that derive from increased productivity have not reached the periphery in a measure comparable to that obtained by the peoples of the great industrial countries. [...] The industrialization of Latin America is not incompatible with the efficient development of primary production. On the contrary, the availability of the best capital equipment and the prompt adoption of new techniques are essential if the development of industry is to fulfil the social objective of raising the standard of living. The same is true of the mechanization of agriculture. Primary products must be exported to allow for the importation of the considerable quantity of capital goods needed.[228]

---

226 S. Farber, *The Origins of the Cuban Revolution Reconsidered*, Chapel Hill 2006, p. 12.

227 Quoted in H. W. Arndt, *Economic Development: the History…*, op. cit., p. 21.

228 R. Prébisch, *The Economic Development of Latin America and Its Principal Problems*, New York 1950, p. 2.

Blame for this lay in the very structure of international trade. Prébisch thought that growth in labour productivity was higher in industry than in the extraction of commodities, particularly in agricultural production. According to him, however, this difference did not lead to a decline in the prices of industrial products, as the supporters of classical economics would expect. Because workers and business owners in industrial countries had a virtual monopoly on new technology, they could also reduce the pace of its dissemination. In this way, they prevented the prices of industrial products from declining, and thereby protected their profits and living standards. Workers and entrepreneurs from peripheral countries did not have such opportunities; they had to sell their products at prices, which – thanks to this technological monopoly – were dictated by the centre.[229] The more tobacco, coffee, sugar, rubber, oil, gold or diamonds manufactured, the more prices would drop on the global market.

Prébisch had in hand fresh substantive arguments in favour of his theory – a new document produced by the United Nations, the first complete statistical data on the prices of agricultural products and commodities compiled since 1860; it proved that prices did indeed fall as production increased.[230] He also had strong historical arguments: two great industrial powers – the United States and Germany – during the period of intense industrialization in the late nineteenth century, strongly protected their markets. The political message of his theory was clear: development is unthinkable without the creation of domestic industry; however, suitable conditions for its growth need to be created, while also protecting the domestic market from an influx of imported goods. It is clear that industry in developed countries can produce better and cheaper goods than fledgling local producers: free competition would have bankrupted them. In an interview held a year before his death, Prébisch recalled how his theory was born:

> We had to industrialize in Argentina without previously building a theory, because we needed to supply more goods to the population. But we could not pay for all the imported goods, due to the fall of our exports and the deterioration in our terms of trade. That's the simple fact. Without any theory, the whole of Latin America did the same. From Mexico all the way down. […] [For instance,] import-substitution, not as a theoretical preference, but insofar as we cannot find sufficient markets for our exports. That's all.

---

229 R. Jolly, *UN Contributions to Development Thinking and Practice*, Bloomington 2004, pp. 57–58.

230 A similar thesis was formulated by Hans Singer and (somewhat later) Gunnar Myrdal; see H.W. Arndt, *Economic Development: the History….* op. cit., p. 73.

We need to increase our income. We need to import more. Insofar as we cannot import more by paying with exports, then we have to pay with our own production.[231]

In this case, as well, breaking out of a vicious cycle of poverty demanded sacrifices. Prébisch did not conceal the fact that the protection of domestic industry would come, inevitably, at the expense of the citizens, who would have to pay more for poorer quality local products. But there was no other choice; the alternative was being eternally fated to the periphery. No one had promised that the road to prosperity and national emancipation would be easy.[232]

3. Politics

The laws governing intellectual life can be very brutal. Challenging dominant intellectual currents requires courage; those who dissent often face ridicule and barely concealed contempt. In the 1940s and 1950s, such a fate was experienced by those (very few!) who believed that planning, nationalization and statism were not necessarily the best ideas for the development of underdeveloped countries.

In 1952 a prestigious economic journal printed a critical discussion of a new UN report on development written by Herbert Frankel, a well-known economist from Oxford, (where he held the Chair in Colonial Economic Affairs). The report was prepared by a group of experts (among whom was Arthur W. Lewis) and devoted to his methods, which allowed unemployment to be rapidly reduced in the poorest countries.[233] However, the report's contents revealed something more, as Frankel wrote:

[The report] is also significant because of the *unconscious* expression which it gives of the climate of economic opinion in the middle of the twentieth century. Indeed, it is in itself a very interesting case study for economists, political scientists and even for philosophers, of preconceptions which are apparently current not only in the offices of governments, but also in the more cloistered retreats of academicians – preconceptions which seem at times to be developing into something like an "Official Concept of Progress" […] The authors of the report, true to the spirit of the times, do not appear to have been troubled unduly by any inconvenient difficulties of definition. To them progress is clearly progress; if it cannot be clearly seen or sensed (and reading the report one almost

231 D. Pollock, D. Kerner, J. L. Love, "Raúl Prébisch on ECLAC's Achievements and Deficiencies: An Upublished Interview", *Cepal Review*, 2001, no. 75.

232 For more on Prébisch and his theory of dependency, cf. Chapter. 6

233 *Measures for the Economic Development of Under-Developed Countries*. Report by a Group of Experts appointed by the Secretary-General of the United Nations, New York 1951

> gets the feeling that it really can be), it can, at any rate, be *measured* in terms of national income aggregates or averages and the like, to which I refer later in this article.[234]

Frankel drew attention to the tendencies attributed to "human beings" by the report's authors, and the conclusions that followed: "human beings are experimental in their attitude to material techniques, to social institutions, and so on [...] The important point at issue, however, is the rate, and the cost – in terms of human life and suffering at which the process of 'experimentation' (in itself a very significant abstraction) is being conducted."[235]

The UN experts wrote that economic development depended primarily on the actions of governments, and therefore, according to Frankel, development was "largely a matter of social will". This was taken as a given – the economists made no effort to provide any justification for it. "It seems to me very doubtful whether a history of economic change, of innovation, or of economic growth in different societies supports this optimistic view of the role and capacities of governments," the Oxford professor commented.[236] He accused the authors of accepting authoritarian solutions and a mechanical approach. He quoted the report:

> As it is we are left with the *ex cathedra* conclusion (par. 38) that "there cannot be rapid economic progress unless the *leaders* of a country at all levels – politicians, teachers, engineers, business leaders, trade-unionists, priests, journalists – desire economic progress for the country, *and are willing to pay its price*, which is the creation of a society from which economic, political and social privileges have been eliminated. On the other hand, *given leadership* and *the public will to advance, all problems of economic development are soluble.*"[237]

But what does it mean to "pay the price"? Who had to pay it? Frankel commented: "It would have been useful to have been told more exactly what the authors meant by 'willingness to pay the price of economic progress' Is it to be paid by the masses or by the leaders, by the young or the old, by the weak or the strong?".

He also questioned the prescription for unemployment suggested by the UN experts: the state-sponsored building of industry, which would absorb surplus labour from the countryside. It is not known, wrote Frankel, how many people are truly surplus in the countryside, because nobody had ever made an exact count; it was not known who would buy the products produced by the newly-built industry

234 S. Frankel, "United Nations Primer for Development", *The Quarterly Journal of Economics*, 1952, no. 3, pp. 302–303.

235 Ibid., p. 303

236 Ibid.

237 Ibid., p. 304.

(the remaining peasants in the countryside were too poor, so there would be no market for these goods). This was not what was contained in the report; one thing was – that development should take place rapidly. The word "development" was repeated numerous times and with emphasis. Recommendation No. 4 of the report, for example, stated:

> [T]he government of an underdeveloped country *should survey the prospect* of creating new productive employment by industrialization, by bringing more land under cultivation, by developing mineral resources, or *by other means*; and announce its programmes for expanding employment.[238]

Frankel commented:

> This is about as useful advice as would be that of a doctor to a patient to the effect that he may be suffering from an *undefined* disease, and that he should therefore take any steps *he* thinks fit to cure it *rapidly*; but that, above all, he should not fail to announce publicly what he is doing about it.[239]

The crux of the matter, however, lay not in ambiguities, generalities and insinuations, but in the vision of development itself, the primary purpose and main criterion of which were postulated to be a rise in income. We know, Frankel wrote, that a significant portion of economic activity in different societies takes place without money; it therefore cannot be seen in statistics on national income. Thus, we cannot say for certain if a worker living in the slums of a big city "is better off" than when he lived in solidarity with his relatives and family in the countryside "with a different pattern of beliefs, hopes and ideals." Moreover, Frankel saw the concept of "income" as an accounting term. It did not include the goals it is intended to serve – it is merely an abstract category. "Planned development" could easily mean planning citizens' consumption ("authoritarian" decision-making), as well. From an economic point of view, the production of unnecessary objects, for example, too many locomotives or too many tonnes of steel, could increase national income, but would not increase prosperity. This risk was all the greater, since according to the recommendations of the UN report, planners were supposed to deliberately *ignore* market signals.

Written into the very idea of planning is, according to Frankel, "extreme oversimplification of the problem of structural change." He reminds us that this is not a game of chess, but the shifting of whole societies onto a new track: people

---

238 Ibid., p. 308.

239 Ibid.

adjust to new situations slowly and with difficulty, and their reactions and needs are difficult to predict in advance.

> What is significant in this view is the extreme oversimplification of the problem of structural change. For structural change is a vast process of slowly evolving social and economic reorientations. It is not at all like the switching of factors of production to making one product instead of another; and it cannot be adequately discussed in terms of mere "planning" decisions. To postulate major structural readjustment is to imply that the goal of change is known; whereas this is precisely what is not known – unless we are to trust to the intuition of the artist-planner. It is, indeed, unfortunate that the authors speak of the process [...] almost as a sculptor might speak of the inanimate materials which he uses as the medium of expression for his art. But human beings are not a medium of artistic expression; except for tyrants.[240]

From the perspective of hindsight, we have to acknowledge that these warnings proved all too justified. However, they went against the spirit of the times. They were also completely ignored. Frankel's article met with an angry response; the most violent response was written by Arthur W. Lewis, one of the authors of the report being criticized.[241] In response to Frankel, he wrote:

> It does not emerge from his review whether he favors the economic development of underdeveloped countries; development has some painful results, of which he is fully aware, and to which he makes extended reference. It is certain that he dislikes the idea of *speeding* up development. For him, development is a slow process of re-orientation of attitudes and institutions, and attempts to speed it up are certain to be disastrous, if not also unsuccessful.
>
> Every economist is familiar with the concept that every good has its cost, or price, and that it is not for economists to say whether the price is worth paying. We were asked, as technical economists, what measures were required, if development was to be speeded up, and we gave answers, to the best of our ability. I think Professor Frankel's review may be interpreted as arguing that we should have refused to answer any such question. We should have said "Speeding up economic development is bad; its costs in human happiness exceed any material benefit that it may confer. You ought not to want it, and we refuse to have anything to do with the matter." This is a rather unusual view of the role which the economist should play. Professor Frankel does not want to speed up the economic development of underdeveloped countries, but most member countries of the United Nations do. They asked us what measures would be required, if this end was given, and we did not think it improper to try to answer their question.[242]

---

240 Ibid., p. 312.

241 W. A. Lewis, "United Nations Primer for Development: Comment", *Quarterly Journal of Economics*, 1953, no. 2.

242 Ibid., p. 268.

Lewis's response is quoted here primarily because the same rhetorical techniques he used to crush his enemy here have been used successfully by followers of radical market reforms since the 1970s. Lewis distances himself from ideology; he believes that he is an impartial expert, a technocrat who is merely providing politicians with answers to their questions, and not affecting their decisions. His opponents in the discussion are pictured as pessimistic reactionaries attached to the anachronistic status quo, who in their practice show disregard for the needs of the impoverished citizens of underdeveloped countries. He also makes it clear to his opponents (and, more importantly, to his readers) who has political backing. Which side would prevail in a dispute between an aging university professor and the majority of members of the United Nations?

Thirty years after this debate, those defending the role of the state in the economy were treated in the same way – not only in relation to planning, but even regarding food subsidies, whether these were in the poorest of countries or in those with highly-developed social systems. They were strongly reproached by liberals – who, like Lewis, thought of themselves as neutral technocrats – for being enemies of development, who while posing as the ostensible friends of the poor (whom they in fact disregarded), were defenders of anachronistic and unjust institutions which bred corruption, inefficiency and wealth-destroying inflation.[243] They just as easily deflected the charges of the "reactionaries".

On a side note, the polemic between Frankel and Lewis also prompts some rather discouraging reflections on the mechanisms guiding intellectual life. Frankel has been forgotten; Lewis was awarded the Nobel Prize in 1979. From the standpoint of a public career, it is therefore safer to err in line with conventional thinking – to go along with the rest – than to be right and on your own. We cannot even rely on posthumous rehabilitation.[244] Milton Friedman was luckier; his memorandum to the Government of India warning against placing too much emphasis on capital investments and relying on a naïve faith in their automatically generating an increase in wealth, is at least still remembered today.[245]

In the 1950s, programmes and reports dedicated to the acceleration of development in underdeveloped countries proliferated like mushrooms after a rain. In 1948, at a UN conference in Havana, countries rich and poor formally set for themselves the goal of maintaining full employment and rapid economic growth.

---

243 Cf. Chapter 8.

244 In the chapter on the PRL, we will return to another famous debate (in which Lange, Hayek and Mises took part) over whether effective use of resources is possible in a planned economy without market pricing system.

245 M. Friedman, "A Memorandum to the Government of India", 1955.

In 1949 the first mission of the World Bank (then called the International Bank for Reconstruction and Development) to a third world country was sent to Colombia; Experts from various fields, from education to health, were to write a national development plan for Colombia, covering all fields of social life. After returning, they wrote in the report:

> Only through a generalized attack throughout the whole economy on education, health, housing, food and productivity can the vicious circle of poverty, ignorance, ill health and low productivity be decisively broken. [...] One cannot escape the conclusion that reliance on natural forces has not produced the most happy results.[246]

In 1951 the UN released the report, which aroused a strong protest from Frankel. A decade later, UN Secretary-General U Thant designated the 1960s as the first "Development Decade". He set a goal for national income in developing countries to increase by at least 5 percent annually until 1970 and "continue to expand at this annual rate thereafter." In his report on the plan, he noted:

> The concept of national planning—for social as well as for economic development. This is central to all the proposals for intensified action by the United Nations system during the development decade [...] Former objections to planning, based largely on a misunderstanding of the role envisaged for the private sector in most development plans, have died away. It is now generally appreciated that the purpose of a development plan is to provide a programme of action for the achievement of targets based on realistic studies of the resources available. Planning is proving to be a potent tool for the mobilization of existing and latent resources—human and material, public and private, domestic and external available to countries for the achievement of their development aims.[247]

Ignacy Sachs, the Polish delegate to the United Nations conference at which these ambitious plans were announced, noted then with evident satisfaction:

> Symptomatic of the prevailing sentiment today is the fact that at this great gathering of scholars meeting in Geneva under the aegis of the United Nations in February 1963 to discuss the salvation of the developing world, no one tried to defend *expressis verbis* the concept of free competition or an unplanned economy. Delegates from socialist countries listened with some satisfaction to how American professors urged the delegations from the developing world to adopt planning.[248]

---

246 Quoted in W. Sachs, *The Development Dictionary: A Guide to Knowledge as Power*, London 1992, p. 135.

247 U Thant, "Foreword to the United Nations Development Decade: Proposals for Action, June 1962", [in:] A. W. Cordier, M. Harrelson, *Public Papers of the Secretaries-General of the United Nations*, vol. 6, New York–London 1976, p. 142.

248 I. Sachs, *Drogi i manowce świata „B"*, Warszawa 1964, p. 37.

Sachs was writing the truth; his description had nothing to do with communist propaganda. He did note with concern, however, that the various "socialisms" put into practice in the developing countries differed from the Soviet pattern – sometimes so much so that they hardly deserve the name:

> It is not enough to just talk about freedom, reforms, plans and socialism. The reforms must be put into practice, plans implemented; socialist slogans in the mouth of a leader, and even his sincere, emotional engagement in the struggle against capitalism, do not stake out a non-capitalist path for development. [...] They do however always express a desire to gain the support of the masses through a programme which is juxtaposed against capitalism and its discredited colonial stigma. Hardly anyone today believes in the possibility of repeating the "classical" path of capitalist development in the developing world.[249]

Indeed, the planning projects in the vast majority of countries of the developing world did not assume total nationalization of the economy in accordance with the Soviet model. On the table were investments by the state in industry and nationalization of key sectors of the economy, especially the mining industry, but also banks and large factories. Native-born capitalists – always few in number – were often allowed to keep their property; in return, they had higher taxes imposed on them and were forced to help fulfil state plans.[250] (A good example of this was the lot of the Tata family's wide range of businesses in India. While after independence their airlines were indeed nationalized, they maintained control of the rest of their empire, which has been successfully expanding ever since.) Nationalization always remained, however, "within reach". The government could resort to this option if it considered it appropriate and politically viable.

The delicate issue of "political profitability" frustrated planners from the outset. Economists moved in a world of ideas, models and statistics. They often did not understand that politicians had to take into account in their calculations dozens of variables that did not fit into the planners' theories: they had to seek support from both within the country and outside of it; they faced constant competition from rivals seeking power, and finally, they had to feed their ego. Politicians also tended to handle matters in a manner dictated by (at least in part) by their country's political culture and the existing power relations; from the point of view of the planners, these actions often seemed irrational, as they were circuitous and costly. Most likely nobody has expressed this better than Albert O. Hirschman in his writings about his experiences in Colombia (1948–1952):

---

249 Ibid., p. 35.

250 S. Yusuf, *Development Economic through the Decades*, Washington 2009, p. 6.

> The task was supposedly crucial for Colombia's development, yet no Colombian was to be found who had any inkling of how to go about it. That knowledge was held only by a few foreign experts who had had the new growth economics revealed to them. It all seemed to be an affront to the Colombians who were, after all, struggling or tinkering with their problems in many fields through a great variety of private decisions and public policies. My instinct was to try to understand better their patterns of action, rather than assume from the outset that they could only be "developed" by importing a set of techniques they knew nothing about. True, this paternalistic mode of operation was given much encouragement by the Colombians themselves who were, initially at least, treating the foreign advisers as a new brand of magicians, and who loved to pour scorn on themselves by exclaiming at every opportunity "Aqui en el tropico hacemos todo al reves" (Here in the tropics we do everything the wrong way around). But the foreign advisers and experts took such statements far too literally. Many Colombians did not really feel all that inept. For at least some of them the phrase implied that, in the particular environment in which they operated, they might well have worked out by trial and error some cunning principles of action, of which they were themselves hardly conscious, that might seem perverse to outsiders, but have actually proven quite effective.[251]

Hirschman's reflections were indeed exceptional; however, they came too late (his most important book was published in 1958, these recollections are from 1984). More typical was the reaction of another expert, a farmer from Oregon, agronomist, and later head of the FAO, who gave some common-sense advice to the inhabitants of a small village in the north of Thailand. Seeing their astonished faces, he told a reporter accompanying him: "If I had been able to stay in that village another few hours, we might have changed the fundamental agricultural methods for hundreds of miles."[252]

While dealing with villagers was easy – or so the thinking went – politicians posed problems from the outset. Arthur W. Lewis quickly grew uncomfortable in the role of advisor to the Prime Minister of Ghana, Kwame Nkrumah. When he asked for the removal from the first Five Year Plan of several large construction projects in the capital, Nkrumah refused, reminding him that he must take into account the political consequences of the investments undertaken.[253] After just two years, Lewis resigned and left Ghana embittered.

Politicians also had their biases – not always in line with economic doctrine – which planners had no choice but to take into account. Another expert, Colin

---

251 A. O. Hirschman, "A Dissenter's Confession", [in:] *Pioneers…*, op. cit. p. 91.

252 Quoted in R. E. Mulcahy, *Readings in Economics from Fortune*, New York 1954, p. 137.

253 R. L. Tignor, *W. Arthur Lewis and the Birth of Development Economics*, Princeton 2006, p. 276.

Clark, in recalling years later a meeting with Gandhi, whom he was to advise on how to pull India out of poverty, wrote:

> Gandhi (nobody will believe this) proved to be a convinced free-market economist, strongly critical of the price controls, rationing, and compulsory purchase of farm crops which the Nehru government was then introducing. The right solution, he said, was to raise the price of food, then everyone would have to work harder. The source of India's troubles was that the people were thoroughly idle.[254]

A few weeks after this conversation, Gandhi was assassinated, leaving Nehru free to realise his vision unimpeded. The Indian Prime Minister believed in progress and technology. "I'm all for tractors and big machinery", he said, summing up his vision.[255] Politicians were familiar with the subtleties of power, but less so with the mysteries of economics; this had its consequences. In recalling Nehru, Colin Clark complained about how some development planners had concluded that industry – any industry – automatically enriches a country.

> What a disastrous error. India, under the guidance of a leading scientist, followed a most peculiar line of reasoning. Population, he pointed out, was increasing, therefore we need more food. To produce more food we need fertilizer. So far, correct. Then we must produce the fertilizer – the possibility of importing was apparently not considered. And to construct fertilizer plants we need steel. Therefore as much as possible of our available resources should go into building large steel works. Perhaps because of the extraordinary conditions under which it is produced, steel attracts emotional attributes which prevent rational discussion. Once when I was asked in India whether further investment in steel works should be undertaken, I replied that this was a problem in comparative religion.[256]

The "liberal" point of view then was likewise completely caught up in the politics of the time. (The word "liberal" has been placed in quotes for a reason; in fact, the advocates of laissez-faire economics who come along in the 1970s –convinced that free trade was the only recipe for growth – were not then present among the specialists on underdeveloped countries.) *A Non-Communist Manifesto* –this was subtitle of a book published in 1960 by Walt Whitman Rostow, a historian and economist who, from among all the authors of theories on "catching up" earned the greatest sympathy from the market. He was also a politician and a high official

254 C. Clark, "Development economics…", op. cit., p. 63.
255 Quoted in D. Yergin, J. Stanislaw, *The Commanding Heights*…, op. cit., p. 53.
256 C. Clark, "Development Economics…", op. cit., p. 64.

in the Kennedy administration; he said openly that he had formulated his doctrine on growth in order to counter the global threat of communism.[257]

In June 1961, Rostow, then Deputy National Security Advisor, delivered a commencement address to a very special group of graduates – officers who had just completed the U.S. Army Special Warfare Center's course in counter-intelligence strategy. The graduates included eighty officers from twenty different countries, the majority of which were poor American client states in Asia and Latin America facing a military threat from leftist guerrillas. The world, he warned, had become a dangerous place. In Cuba, the Congo, Laos and Vietnam – all poor, backward countries – the U.S. administration was facing a crisis that seemed impossible to solve. Each of them, Rostow said, "represented a successful Communist breaching-over previous years—of the Cold War truce lines which had emerged from the Second World War and its aftermath. In different ways each had arisen from the efforts of the international Communist movement to exploit the inherent instabilities of the underdeveloped areas."[258]

It was obvious to him that the cold war could not be won without giving the people of the underdeveloped countries the promise of a better life.[259] Rostow did not deny that the communist experiment ushered in modernity, but at the price of freedom.[260] He thought this was a poor trade-off, because if things were left to their natural course, you could have both one and the other. The officers being trained to fight the guerrillas in Vietnam were to become actively involved "in the whole creative process of modernization." This was the field where the battle would be decided. Rostow's theory would be an ideological response to the promise of a way out of backwardness that communism had brought to the

---

257 Rostow first published an oultine of his theory in a series of articles he began writing in the early 1950s (e.g. W. W. Rostow, "The Take-off Into Self-sustained Growth", *The Economic Journal*, 1961, no. 261); it was later rewritten for a general readership in the *The Economist* ("Rostow on Growth. A Non-Communist Manifesto", *The Economist*, 15 August 1959 and 22 August 1959), and finally in book form (W.W. Rostow, *The Stages of Economic Growth*, Cambridge 1960).

258 M. E. Latham, *Modernization as Ideology. American Social Science and "Nation Building" in the Kennedy Era*, Chapel Hill 2000, p. 3.

259 J. M. Hagen, V. W. Ruttan, "Development Policy Under Eisenhower and Kennedy", *Economic Development Center Bulletin* 87–10, University of Minnesota, November 1987, p. 35 ff.

260 "The tragedy of Communism is not so much its initial dictatorial character as its capacity to deny future choices to those who fall under it." W.W. Rostow, *Politics and the Stages of Growth*, Cambridge 1971, p. 289.

world's poorest countries.[261] Rostow himself was not among America's "doves"; in fact, he was said to be the one who convinced Nixon in 1972 to carry out the last wave of bombing raids on Hanoi – a needless action, since the political decision to withdraw from Vietnam had already been taken. What was at stake, he had explained to the president, was the prestige of the United States.

Rostow had written his doctorate in the 1930s on the history of the British industrial revolution. He was convinced that history repeats itself, obviously not in its details, but in the general course taken by all societies as they moved toward modernity. He thought the stages in this course were universal, as he believed, like Marx earlier, that he had discovered the universal laws of history, which he described in his book. This watershed moment Rostow called the "take-off". Afterward, national income increases dramatically – from a few percent to a double-digit increase – and the country is on the road to modern growth. Rostow thought that the "take off" had begun earliest in England, in the second half of the nineteenth century; other countries – he named, among others, Chile and Venezuela – were now on the threshold. He described this change in words worthy of a visionary, not a scientist:

> Usually from outside the society, but sometimes out of its own dynamics, comes the idea that economic progress is possible; and this idea spreads within the established *élite* or, more usually, in some disadvantaged group whose lack of status does not prevent the exercise of some economic initiative. More often than not the economic motives for seeking economic progress converge with some non-economic motive, such as the desire for increased social power and prestige, national pride, political ambition and so on. Education, for some at least, broadens and changes to suit the needs of modern economic activity. New enterprising men come forward willing to mobilise savings and to take risks in pursuit of profit, notably in commerce. The commercial markets for agricultural products, domestic handicrafts and consumption-goods imports widen. Institutions for mobilising capital appear; or they expand from primitive levels in the scale, surety and time horizon for loans. Basic capital is expanded, notably in transport and communications, often to bring to market raw materials in which other nations have an economic interest, often financed by foreign capital. And, here and there, modern manufacturing enterprise appears, usually in substitution for imports.[262]

The "take off" itself, a period of high investment and intensive development of the industry lasting several decades, could be triggered by an impulse from outside (for example, the sudden increase in demand for wood and coal in Sweden in

261 K. G. Nustad, "The Development Discourse in the Multilateral System", [in:] *Global Institutions and Development. Framing the World?*, London–New York 2004, p. 16.

262 W.W. Rostow, *The Take-off…*, op. cit., pp. 27–28.

the late nineteenth century); it could also, as in nineteenth-century Japan, be the result of the internal logic of the historical process. Rostow drew clear political conclusions from this – the West should stimulate development in underdeveloped countries by providing loans, technical support, and buying their goods. All this would sooner or later result in a "take off" to modernity. Communism, with its labour camps, expropriation, dictatorship and impoverished masses, was therefore, Rostow concluded, no longer needed: "the tricks of growth are not all that difficult", he wrote.[263] Rostow thought that for a "dedicated" country, the road from a traditional society to the stage of high mass consumption would take from 54 to 80 years.[264]

Rostow's theory was criticized by those economists – i.e., the majority – who did not believe in the spontaneous capitalist development of underdeveloped countries. They did not perceive the fact that although Rostow differed from his more radical colleagues in terms of his political prescriptions, he in fact had a great deal in common with them: like Nurkse, Lewis, Rosenstein-Rodan (and the Poles Lange, Kalecki and Sachs) he was convinced that there could be no development without industrialization, and, following from this, that the rate of investment needed to be rapidly increased, and that all societies moved toward modernity essentially along the same path – the road staked out by the history of the West. Whether a country was a bourgeois democracy or a dictatorship of the proletariat, the essential structure of economic and social modernity was the same – because it is shaped by the division of labour in industry, and this is a function of technology, which is the same in both America and the Soviet Union. All of these economists (Marxists and non-Marxists alike) could say following Marx that developed countries merely showed what the future looked like for underdeveloped countries. They differed, of course, on many issues, especially in such nontrivial matters as the methods by which you can accelerate progress; as to the point they sought to reach, however, their thinking was the same. They shared in common a belief in progress, the fact that people were guided primarily by economic motivations, the primacy of the "base" over the "superstructure", technophilia, a belief that there were no limits to growth, and that they represented a "scientific" doctrine. I need to make a digression here that is important for the rest of this narrative: in the 1980s, this same creed and these same structural similarities were shared by both Marxists and the ultra-liberal "Chicago school",

---

263 Quoted in J. M. Cypher, J. L. Dietz, *The Process…*, op. cit., p. 141.

264 G. Deng, *The Premodern Chinese Economy*, New York 1999, p. 6. For more on the disputes among U.S. politicians over development strategy, see W. W. Rostow, *Concept and Controversy. Sixty Years of Taking Ideas to Market*, Austin 2003, p. 197 ff.

followers of the next big economic narrative. Dudley Seers, one of the most renowned specialists in development, wrote in 1979:

> Though it seems provocative to say so, and always annoys both parties considerably, Marxism can be described as a neoclassical doctrine with precise accuracy. There is no dispute that, like the Chicago School, its origins can be found in the work of Adam Smith and Ricardo, early in the industrial revolution. [...] "The invisible hand" in Adam Smith's graphic metaphor is, on the whole and in the long run, benevolent. Somewhere in the future, justifying sacrifices by the present generation (and many political crimes), lies a utopia, an integrated world of prosperity and peace (capitalist or socialist as the case may be) to be achieved if not in the next generation, then two or three later. They differ profoundly about the mechanisms by which it will be achieved but not about its likelihood [...][265]

In the 1950s, the vitality and unprecedented prosperity of the affluent societies of the West – especially the United States – drove the imagination in a way that in postmodern times may seem incomprehensible. The transformation of a rural, traditional agricultural society into a modern, urban and industrial society (this was a sharp dichotomy in the theory of modernization) was not solely economic in nature: it was part of a wider process of modernization that included the most intimate spheres of an individual's life – from religion and family life, to politics and *the production of culture.*

Sociologists and modernization theorists presented the vicissitudes and goals of this process with a certainty equal to that of economists in relation to the vicissitudes and goals of industrialization.[266] Economists, moreover, read the work of modernization theorists; W.A. Lewis, for example, cited them often.[267] Modernization, wrote historian Cyril E. Black, was the "process by which historically evolved institutions are adapted to the rapidly changing functions that reflect the unprecedented increase in man's knowledge, permitting control over his environment."[268]

Perhaps the most succinct definition of modernization, as it was imagined at the time, was proposed in 1959 by sociologist Edward Shills at a conference

265 D. Seers, "The Congruence of Marxism and Other Neoclassical Doctrines", [in:] *Toward a New Strategy for Development. A Rothko Chapel Colloquium*, New York–Oxford 1979, pp. 3–4.

266 For a classic overview of this works, see *Modernization. The Dynamics of Growth*, ed. M. Weiner, New York–London 1966.

267 R. L. Tignor, *W. Arthur Lewis*..., op. cit., p. 96.

268 M. E. Latham, *Modernization*..., op. cit., p. 4.

devoted to the "new states" in the Middle East, Asia and Africa. Shills said that one word – *modernity* – summed up the ambitions of underdeveloped regions:

> In the new states "modern" means democratic and equalitarian, scientific, economically advanced and sovereign. "Modern" states are "welfare states," proclaiming the welfare of all the people and especially the lower classes as their primary concern. "Modern" states are meant necessarily to be democratic states in which not merely are the people cared for and looked after by their rulers, but they are, as well, the source of inspiration and guidance of those rulers. Modernity entails democracy, and democracy in the new states is, above all, equalitarian. Modernity therefore entails the dethronement of the rich and the traditionally privileged from their positions of pre-eminent influence. It involves land reform. It involves steeply progressive income taxation. It involves universal suffrage. Modernity involves universal public education. Modernity is scientific. It believes the progress of the country rests on rational technology, and ultimately on scientific knowledge. No country could be modern without being economically advanced or progressive. To be advanced economically means to have an economy based on modern technology, to be industrialized and to have a high standard of living. All this requires planning and the employment of economists and statisticians, conducting surveys to control the rates of savings and investments, the construction of new factories, the building of roads and harbors, the development of railways, irrigation schemes, fertilizer production, agricultural research, forestry research, ceramics research, and research of fuel utilization. "Modern" means being western without the onus of following the West. It is the model of the West detached in some way from its geographical origins and locus.[269]

To this long quotation we need to add an important footnote. "Democracy", as referred to here should not be understood in a narrow, formal manner – on the Western model, with a multi-party political system, a tripartite separation of powers, and civil rights guaranteed by the constitution and upheld by the authorities. While American writers on modernization theory generally held up the American system as a model ("The United States is Presiding at a general reorganization of the ways of living throughout the world" was an epigraph to Daniel Lerner's *The Passing of Traditional Society: Modernizing the Middle East* in 1958), the specifics of local traditions and the historical moment left open a wide range of options.[270] The will of the people could express itself in non-liberal forms of government, such as a one-party system. There was nothing extraordinary about this, especially at a time when making the leap into modernity required the breaking up of feudal social structures – and these old structures, even if doomed to oblivion, would not give in without a fight.

---

269 Quoted in N. Gilman, *Mandarins of the Future. Modernization Theory in Cold War America*, Baltimore 2003, pp. 1–2.

270 Quoted in N. Gilman, *Mandarins…*, op. cit., p. 1.

In the same year (1959), one of the most prominent modernization theorists, David Apter, analyzed the dynamics of the process by which the pursuit of modernity was pushing countries in the developing word to embrace authoritarian politics.[271] He wrote about this not only without hand-wringing, but with no particular regrets. The leaders of the "new" countries, wrote Apter, face a dilemma. They must reconcile the need for universal participation in public life, necessary to maintain public support, with the need to create an integrated, disciplined apparatus of power. Only an "oligarchy" can manage such a transformation of society. "We are familiar with the radical totalitarian solution to this problem. Can we find an optimal solution which falls short a totalitarianism?", he asked.[272]

Apter assumed that rapid industrialization required "tight organizational control" and therefore the need for a certain degree of authoritarian rule.

> Because a government needs a great deal of trial and error in order to chart its course, its strength and structure must be relatively secure. Such strength is a function of political party support, which in turn depends upon recruitment. There is a tendency for parties to become the private patrimony of the leader. The party leader tries to alter the social stratification system by making its curve less sharp and reducing the upper strata. He needs to create a new managerial and bureaucratic elite. [...] The modern nationalist movements of today attack traditional oligarchies and replace them with their own. The main difference between these oligarchies is that in the new ones recruitment is on the basis of political power, party loyalty, or expertise. Each of these categories of entry are relatively democratic.[273]

Authoritarianism works: Apter did not recommend it – his article is strictly descriptive in style – but he left room for no doubt:

> The combination of an elite core with a mass following is the most effective for development purposes. It provides the bureaucratic cadres to run the party, the government, and act as the coordinating arm of the state, while the mass party organization provides the informational core. The differences and antagonisms between local party factions provide both competition in ideas and allow the membership to serve as a communications source.[274]

Apter was thus an optimist: even if democratic mechanisms in the Western sense did not work, the system was not only capable of carrying out modernization efficiently, but also of assuring certain features characteristic of democracy, including

---

271 D. E. Apter, "Nationalism, Government, and Economic Growth", *Economic Development and Cultural Change*, 1959, no. 2.

272 Ibid. p. 117.

273 Ibid., pp. 120–121.

274 Ibid., p. 122.

competition within the ruling elite and a flow of information "from below" to the government. The party, he recommended, should be decentralized in its organization, but hierarchical in terms of its communication structures. Distributing wealth to its members (and thereby maintaining their support) would ensure the government's stability and open up possibilities for social mobility (i.e., a career inside the party apparatus). "If too strictly organized, such a party can become a punitive arm of the state. If it does, then the costs of coercion go up, and a very nasty situation can arise."[275]

Such a despotic government could be effective and was better than totalitarianism because it placed fewer restrictions on political freedom. However, this price was not what was most important. Democracy was neither possible nor in fact desirable, because it was too weak, too "soft", and the leap into modernity required a level of heroism that representative governments were unable to demand from their people. The collective aim – accelerated development – demanded precisely such a political structure; one could not conclude otherwise, but it could not be denied. "Authoritarian governments mix the proportions of nationalism and ideology so that sacrifice and self-denial are regarded as social virtues," Apter wrote.[276] The government was responsible – but not to the voters, but to interest groups, such as the urban intelligentsia and the heads of industry:

> Government may become impatient with accountability, which limits the freedom and autonomy of decision-makers and tempers their decisions and their plans by potential opposition. [...] Leaders search for certainty; social life becomes organized; those who go along with the regime receive benefits and rewards; purpose and direction is provided; development of the state becomes the new religion in which the dominant political party is the home of the faithful, and the messiah is the party leader who controls the government. Within this general framework there can be considerable freedom, often even political freedom [...][277]

Apter wrote this in 1959, so even before most former colonies had gained independence (although this was generally already at hand). He showed notable foresight: in the developing countries, alongside planning committees and government investments, single-party systems began to quickly multiply. Apter knew there was a natural tendency for non-democratic government to increase their control over the lives of citizens: "the more government controls, the more its costs rise. [...] Since increasing costs must be borne by the public, there is normally a

275 Ibid.

276 Ibid., p. 124.

277 Ibid., pp. 126, 132.

rise of dissatisfaction". According to Apter, once could hope that economic development would eventually push the political system towards democracy – in some distant and undefined time in the future.[278]

Life would quickly verify these theories. Western economists and sociologists and politicians from the Third World entered the 1960s, the first "Development Decade", with optimism. Success was possible. It was within arm's reach. It could be achieved with the help of the West – but also in spite of it, if the West did not abandon its colonial habits. "What excites the imagination most and evokes the most enthusiasm in our countries, especially among the younger generations, are the lessons learned from the Soviet methods of development", Raúl Prébisch wrote.[279]

This successful country was eager to share its experiences.

278 Ibid., pp. 134–136.

279 Quoted in I. Sachs, *Drogi i manowce…*, op. cit., p. 90.

Chapter 3. Internal colony

1. Land of the big bluff

In 1931, a twenty year-old New Yorker named John set out for Magnitogorsk via Berlin and Moscow. He had finished three semesters at an experimental college and worked for a few months at a General Electric factory, where he had trained as a welder. America was approaching the lowest depths of the Great Depression. It appeared that capitalism was collapsing under the weight of that crisis. In New York, long lines formed in front of the charity kitchens offering soup for the unemployed.

Scott was not a stereotypical Western *fellow traveller* of the Communists. He was not an intellectual who supported revolution for ideological or aesthetic reasons. The son of a radical university professor and member of the Communist Party until he was kicked out in 1928 for views that deviated from the party line, he was an idealist, but not a blind one: he was well aware of the terror and misery that reigned in the Soviet Union. He never in fact became a Communist, though neither was he an ideological opponent of communism.[280] He was fascinated by the scale of the Stalinist enterprise and its Utopian ambitions – wrenching an enormous, poor country out of centuries of backwardness.

In the Soviet Union there was no unemployment. There was, however, a war – for industry. Years later, Scott would recall:

> In 1940, Winston Churchill told the British people that they could expect nothing but blood, sweat, and tears. The country was at war. The British people did not like it, but most of them accepted it. Ever since 1931 or thereabouts the Soviet Union has been at war, and the people have been sweating, shedding blood and tears. People were wounded and killed, women and children froze to death, millions starved, thousands were court-martialed and shot in the campaigns of collectivization and industrialization. I would wager that Russia's battle of ferrous metallurgy alone involved more casualties than the battle of the Marne. All during the thirties the Russian people were at war. […] In Magnitogorsk I was precipitated into a battle. I was deployed on the iron and steel front. Tens of thousands of people were enduring the most intense hardships in order to build blast furnaces, and many of them did it willingly, with boundless enthusiasm, which infected me from the day of my arrival.[281]

---

280 He did not become a Communist, but it has not been ruled out that he may have been an agent for Soviet intelligence after his return to the United States in 1942; his name appeared on lists of "Communist sympathizers" and agents of the USSR.

281 J. Scott, *Behind the Urals…*, op. cit., p. 5.

The Magnitogorsk that Scott found (he arrived in 1933) looked different from the city that citizens of the Soviet Union could see in propaganda films and posters. Above all, it was not a city, but a gigantic, chaotic and dirty construction site, without roads or plumbing, and full of garbage and waste. Workers lived in long rows of hastily assembled barracks, huts and dug-outs. Only a colony of foreign specialists, mainly Americans and Germans, whom the Soviet Union was generously paying in hard currency, had better conditions. An American engineer in Magnitogorsk received as much as a hundred dollars a day, that is, more than a worker in America could earn for a month of hard work.[282] A foreign specialist did not go hungry, unlike a great many citizens of the USSR.

In 1933 agriculture was in a state of utter collapse following the collectivization campaign. Food was also lacking in Magnitogorsk. The Party's response was to introduce a brutal hierarchy in terms of access to food. Foreign specialists and local dignitaries ate best. Soviet specialists ate slightly better than most. In shops for workers even bread was often lacking. (Scott had access to a shop for foreigners; in his account, he obtained it only at the insistence of Russian friends, with whom he shared his food.) Sanitary conditions in Magnitogorsk were awful. People were dying on a daily basis in the process of building it.

There was nothing exceptional about this. A Soviet citizen in the time of Stalin's Great Turn lived in crowded, cold, and dirty conditions – and often went hungry. After the great famine in the Ukraine and in southern Russia in 1932–1933, there was also a less well-known, but very severe famine in the postwar years (1946–1947), which also encompassed areas not devastated by the war.[283] Between 10 and 20 million people had poured into the cities in the 1930s. Factories were built, but not housing. In 1930, for each Muscovite there were 5.5 square meters of living space; in 1940, there were less than 4 square meters. In provincial industrial cities, the situation was even worse. In newly founded Magnitogorsk and quickly growing Irkutsk, there was less than 4 square meters of living space per person, while in Krasnoyarsk in 1933 the per capita norm was 3.4 square meters.[284] In practice, many people had to fit into an even smaller space, since Stalin's Soviet Union did not implement the egalitarian slogans that it proclaimed (though it proclaimed them with decreasing conviction over time, as Stalin was opposed to *uravnilovki* and believed in the power of material incentives).

---

282 Ibid., p. 71.

283 J. Fürst, *Stalin's Last Generation. Soviet Post-War Youth and the Emergence of Mature Socialism*, Oxford 2010, p. 43 ff.

284 S. Fitzpatrick, *Everyday Stalinism. Ordinary Life in Extraordinary Times. Soviet Russia in the 1930s*, Oxford 2000, p. 46.

Power relations were transparent: they were visible even in the spatial organization of Soviet cities. In Magnitogorsk the local soviet was housed in a small building next to the main square. In the middle of the square stood a statue of Stalin. The council was overwhelmed by the enormous edifice of the factory administration and the NKVD building, located on the hill above the city. The factory chief lived in a fourteen-room villa.[285] Half of the workers lived in barracks, and every fifth worker lived in a dug-out.[286] While an expensive metro was built deep under the ground in Moscow, with stations decorated as Socialist Realist palaces, basic infrastructure was often lacking in the provinces. As late as 1933, Dniepropietrovsk, a city of 400,000 people, still had no sewage system. The Russian archives contain many letters from desperate citizens begging Stalin, Molotov or Kaganovich for help; one came from a six-person family in Moscow, residing in an alcove under the stairs of an old tenement house. The windowless room of about six square meters had one meter per person.[287]

A Polish reporter several years older than John Scott, Aleksander Janta-Połczyński – decidedly less enchanted with Magnitogorsk than the American–wrote in a book on the USSR published in 1933:

> You have not seen the dug-outs here yet. You should take a look at them," one of the Germans told me yesterday. [...] Beyond the hill one of these colonies spread across a meadow. Huts thrown together from a few boards or dug out of the earth stretched out in a long row over the swampy area of the meadows. They were densely packed: smoke was rising from the tin pipes stuck into the makeshift roofs. More often, fires were burning in front of the dug-outs, with some dubious food being prepared over them in a jagged pot. Dirty, half-naked children were running around. At the entrance to one of the huts sat an old woman, a second, younger woman rested her head on her lap. The old woman, sifting through the girl's hairs one by one, searched through her black hair for bedbugs or lice with a monkey-like, precise movement, murmuring each time she caught a specimen. [...] A half hour before, the police had passed through with an order for everyone to get out within three days, since after that the area would be cleared out, the huts "mechanically smashed," and whoever did not leave voluntarily would be removed by force. Nothing was given in compensation, no other place or barracks were proposed; they were left to fend for themselves.[288]

---

285 S. Kotkin, *Magnetic Mountain. Stalinism as a Civilization*, Berkeley–Los Angeles 1997, p. 289.

286 S. Fitzpatrick, *Everyday Stalinism...*, op. cit., p. 49. Data from 1938.

287 Ibid., p. 47.

288 A. Janta-Połczyński, *W głąb Z.S.R.R.*, Warszawa 1933, quoted in *Spojrzenie na Rosję*, ed. J. Kochanowski, Warszawa 1994, p. 73.

Differences in the standard of living among the citizens of the USSR were enormous. Equality existed only in slogans. The Party-state elite (including the security apparatus) not only had access to better shops and bigger apartments, but also earned considerably more. In 1946 the head of a department in the Ministry of the Interior, the recently renamed NKVD, earned 4200 rubles a month: this was many times greater than the average monthly earnings of a worker (475 rubles at the time, but many earned much less). Officers of the Cheka not only earned more and had better rations, they also had additional opportunities for improving their standard of living. Local NKVD offices were full of eatables and furniture given as "presents" by frightened factory and kolkhoz bosses. Seizing and appropriating goods, particularly apartments, from "enemies of the state" was also a daily occurrence. During the hunt for Polish Communists in 1938, an NKVD officer acquired an apartment by writing "Pole" instead of "Jew" in the nationality rubric for a Party member he was interrogating; he thus unmasked a dangerous counterrevolutionary, whose apartment he then received.[289]

Soviet industry not only produced goods of low quality, since it did not have to take into account consumer tastes. More importantly, it produced very few of them. In 1946 – a year, it is true, of rebuilding what had been destroyed by the war – the average Soviet citizen bought half a pair of leather boots, a third of a pair of galoshes and 1.5 kilos of soap; industry produced one fourth of an undergarment per citizen and less than one pair of socks.[290] Not until the early 1950s did the level of consumption of a Soviet citizen significantly rise above what it had been in 1928, the last year of the quasi-capitalist New Economic Policy (NEP), and the last year before the great campaign of agricultural collectivization and the great Stalinist Five-Year Plans. A year before Stalin's death, the average level of consumption reached three pairs of domestically produced socks and one pair of boots: more than during the difficult postwar period, but not much higher. Durable goods such as refrigerators and televisions were in practice unattainable.[291] Even if someone managed to avoid dying of hunger (that is, he was not one of the millions of peasants who perished during collectivization) and did not get shot, imprisoned, or exiled during one of the waves of terror that shook Russia in the 1930s, his life was one of grim poverty.

---

289 P. R. Gregory, *Terror By Quota. State Security from Lenin to Stalin (An Archival Study)*, New Haven–London 2009, pp. 72–74.

290 D. Filtzer, *Soviet Workers and Late Stalinism. Labour and the Restoration of the Stalinist System after World War II*, Cambridge 2004, p. 43.

291 D. Filtzer, *Soviet Workers and De-Stalinization. The Consolidation of the Modern System of Soviet Production Relations, 1953–1964*, New York 1992, p. 1.

What was built at the price of famine, terror and poverty? The scale of Stalinist undertakings acted on the imagination even of observers who were unfavourably disposed toward them. Non-Communist and sceptic Janta-Połczyński wrote of the "record-breaking, in spite of everything, achievement of the construction of Magnitogorsk":

> On 25 June 1930, came the first strike of the shovel that began the building of the factories. On 1 February 1931, the construction of the first tall furnace began. And here, a small "but". [...] But the blueprints for Magnitogorsk – the basic blueprints – were only ready in May of 1931. So until then the work was done without any "general plan"!? Now, in mid-July 1932, Magnitogorsk has 230,000 inhabitants (divided as follows: 80,000 construction workers, 10,000 in the working parts of factories [...] two great working furnaces, two active batteries of coking ovens, half of a power station in service. It produces fire bricks, and has its own repair workshops. Daily production comes to 2000 tonnes of brick. Not to mention the great number of works begun and finished. [...] The hour was getting late when we finally went out to look at Magnitogorsk by night. The deep darkness in the valley is punctured by a thousand points of light. The air is transparent, and glimmers and specks of electric lights can be seen only through the hazy range of the trail of smoke rising from the factories. The bloody gleam of the cokery, the faraway clamour of the high furnaces mix with the sounds of a storm heading toward us from somewhere in the Urals. The whole span of the sky is lit up by piercing flashes of lightning. This view contains un-European dimensions, riveting with its expanse, enfolding with its perspectives, hypnotizing with its depth.[292]

2. We would be sitting at a broken trough

"Was Stalin really necessary?" Historians who work on the USSR are still to this day attempting to answer this question, posed in the early 1960s by the eminent Sovietologist Alec Nove.[293]

At the time, it referred to the contemporary situation and had a clear political dimension. The motives behind Sovietologists' research were to a large extent practical. They were trying to describe how the Soviet system functioned in order to assess how big of a threat it posed to the West and how it could be restrained at minimal cost. They relied on thin and obscure sources, and thus needed to expend considerable effort on establishing basic facts. Debates over the nature of the system took place against the backdrop of ideology and politics, to which the facts were subordinate. They debates were always accompanied, as

292 A. Janta-Połczyński, *W głąb Z.S.R.R...*, op. cit., pp. 69–70.

293 A. Nove, *Was Stalin Really Necessary? Some Problems of Soviet Economic Policy*, New York 1964, p. 33 ff.

another outstanding historian, Aleksander Gerschenkron, wrote in his review of Nove's book, by a practical question: do changes in the USSR's internal policies indicate that the regime is strengthening or weakening?[294]

Ideological disputes had some bearing on these discussions – for example on assessments of the Soviet dictatorship's ability to act effectively. There was no shortage of Sovietologists inclined to judge that in the Soviet Union, the inherent evil of totalitarianism triumphed over the rational exercise of power (ruthless and genocidal perhaps, but still a form of rationality).[295] From this point of view, the evil empire was founded on evil, and was a land of ideological insanity. That insanity, however, in fact hurt the system itself, which as a result could only be grasped in the categories of rational description with difficulty and only to a limited extent.

Today the subject of research for historians working on the USSR – a much smaller group than Sovietologists in days gone by – is the increasingly distant past. They undoubtedly have better sources than Alec Nove or Adam Ulam had. Though contemporary Russia guards the secrets of the Brezhnev and later eras closely, files from the Stalinist era are more easily accessible. Stalin's correspondence with members of the Politburo; NKVD reports on the mood in Soviet society; real data on the results of the five-year plans (more precisely, data which the Party possessed and did not release) – all have become the subjects of detailed studies.[296] We know more about the costs and achievements of Stalin's Great Turn; we also know more about the lives of ordinary citizens of the USSR during Stalin's time – not only in the cities, but in the provinces as well. The question posed by Nove remains current, but historians increasingly tend to look for answers in the sociology of Soviet institutions, the mechanisms by which information flowed within the structures of power, or in the channels for advancement.[297] These authors do not deny that the pathological personality of Stalin left a mark on the system, like the tradition of Russian despotism and an ideology that proclaimed the need to radically rebuild the world at any cost. All of these combined to form a system that another excellent specialist, Stephen Kotkin, has called – notwithstanding the apparent contradiction in his formulation – an Enlightenment "theocracy."[298] In analyses made in the last two decades,

---

294 A. Gerschenkron, review (untitled), *The Economic History Review*, 1965, no. 3.

295 Cf. e.g. D. W. Lovell, *From Marx to Lenin. An Evaluation of Marx's Responsibility for Soviet Authoritarianism*, Cambridge 1984

296 It is worth mentioning here the works of S. Fitzpatrick, L. Siegelbaum, S. Kotkin, D. Filtzer, O. Klhevniuk and P. R. Gregory.

297 Cf. e.g. P. R. Gregory, *The Political Economy of Stalinism*, Cambridge 2003.

298 S. Kotkin, *Magnetic Mountain…*, op. cit., p. 286 ff.

the mechanics of the system have, through this description, assumed a more rational form. It has not become less inhuman or more economically efficient in the process; its internal functioning has simply become easier to explain.

Here it is worthwhile to pause for a moment and consider two questions posed in the past by Sovietologists, and now by historians. The first is: could Russia perhaps have developed more rapidly and at a lesser cost without the revolution? The second question relates to the nature of communism: perhaps the Jacobin (ascetic, ideological, and bloody) dictatorship of Stalin was not an inevitable development after the system was founded (contrary to what many of its critics have sought to assert, including, for example, Leszek Kołakowski[299]), but resulted from a historical coincidence? It would thus be possible to imagine a revolutionary Russia governed by a more liberal dictator – a different comrade of Lenin. It would no doubt have been an undemocratic Russia, but without mass terror, possibly more socially just and with an economy joining together elements of capitalism and socialism, without the catastrophe of collectivization and accelerated industrialization. From this perspective – usually favoured by authors with views more to the left of the spectrum – the reign of Stalin is seen as a betrayal of the ideals of the revolution, rather than a consequence of them.[300]

This is not the place for summary answers to these questions, especially since they are only indirectly linked with the subject of this book. It is worth noting, however, the most recent important voice in this discussion about Russia's potential for capitalist development. The American economic historian Robert C. Allen, author of an influential book on the roots of the British industrial revolution and a comprehensive history of Soviet industrialization, in which he enumerates the arguments of historians who pronounce Stalinist industrialization to have been a failure.[301]

First, Soviet economic growth was not at all impressive; many capitalist countries developed just as quickly (for example, Japan). Stalin's crimes, therefore, brought no economic benefits.

Second, before 1917 the Russian economy had already entered onto a path of rapid growth (the "take-off" in Rostow's categories). If not for the revolution, it would have caught up with the West after a few decades.

---

299 Cf. L. Kołakowski, *Main Currents of Marxism*, London, 197.

300 S. F. Cohen, *Bukharin and the Bolshevik Revolution. A Political Biography*, Oxford–New York 1980, p. 186 ff.

301 R. C. Allen, *Farm to Factory. A Reinterpretation of the Soviet Industrial Revolution*, Princeton 2003.

Third, the growth of production under Communist governments was limited to steel, machines and arms. Until the collapse of the USSR, its citizens' standard of living grew very slowly because the country was ruled by a dictatorship focused on the preservation of its own power and international expansion. In practical terms, Capitalist governments would therefore have better served the interests of the Russian working class than the ostensible "dictatorship of the proletariat." The collectivization of agriculture is an example that springs to mind here: several million deaths and gigantic material losses brought about, above all, by the will to consolidate power and achieve total control over society.

Fourth, Soviet socialism was economically irrational. It generated and then tolerated enormous surpluses of employment and waste. It created an economy unnaturally geared toward maintaining ineffective institutions (for example, the kolkhoz) and military production, rather than consumption. It was also incapable of innovation, except in military technology. It succeeded in building gigantic steelworks and tank factories, but could not compete with the West in the sphere of advanced technology; this led to economic stagnation throughout the entire Soviet bloc beginning in the mid-1970s.

All of these arguments, Allen notes, are disputable, except perhaps the last.[302] It is by no means certain that Russia would have caught up with the West if it had become a capitalist country. The experience of other countries at the same level of development at that time show it to be anything but a foregone conclusion. The countries that were developed in 1989 were already distinctly richer than the "rest of the world" in 1820; since then, the distance between the two groups has only increased, and transitioning from one to the other become increasingly difficult. On the other hand, even the poor areas on the periphery of Europe – for example, the countries in the Mediterranean basin – had a much more modern social structure in 1917 than did Russia, where peasants constituted 80 percent of the population. Likewise, the institutions of the modern state, such as the banking system, governmental structures, and judicial system, were either in their infancy in Russia, or were developing in a form distinct than their western counterparts.

Probably the most interesting argument Allen makes, however, concerns fundamental elements of the social structure: models of the family and the division of land in the countryside. By the twentieth century, rich and poor countries had already had different models of the family for centuries. In Western Europe (and in countries colonized by Europeans) women married late – sometimes

---

302 For an extensive summary of this discussion, see R. C. Allen, *Farm to Factory…*, op. cit., Chapter 1.

well above the age of twenty – and many of them never found a life partner. In non-European countries, women entered into permanent unions considerably earlier. A higher birth-rate had not only cultural, but also economic significance, since faster population growth made it harder for non-European countries to extract themselves from the Malthusian trap. On the eastern outskirts of Europe, the line of division between European and non-European family structures ran from Petersburg to Trieste; Russia – with the exception of the Kingdom of Poland and the Baltic countries – found itself on the Asiatic side.

According to Allen, one factor in the tendency of Russian peasants to have many children was their particular method of farming land. In Russian rural areas, the land was not the private property of those who tilled it; every so often the community would divide the land anew among its members. This institution not only made peasants reluctant to invest personally in raising the standard of efficiency, it also inclined them to produce the largest possible number of children, since larger families could count on a larger apportionment of land at the next "distribution." As Allen writes:

> Russia's large families were the result of the same traditional, patriarchal values that have led to large families in many poor, non-European countries.
>
> In the twentieth century, countries where the non-European pattern predominated had population explosions that have frustrated development efforts and contributed to the divergence in per capita income. The demographic patterns c. 1900 suggest that Russia's destiny was closer to India's than to Germany's.[303]

This digression has not answered the question of whether Stalin was *really* necessary. It does show, however, that answering this question is not so simple: left to its own devices, tsarist Russia was by no means fated to become another Japan.[304]

Historians agree, however, in their assessments that for the Bolshevik dictatorship, the modernization of Russia – understood by them to mean the rapid development of industry and urbanization – was, from the very beginning of their rule, the key political task from several perspectives: ideological, strategic and economic. It is also a known fact that simply nationalizing the whole economic life of a country – perhaps combined with currency devaluation – leads to catastrophic results. The policy of "war communism" in the years 1918–1921, during which time even one-person workshops were nationalized, led to a breakdown of production and made reconstruction after the war's destruction more

---

303 R. C. Allen, *Farm to Factory…*, op. cit., p. 13.

304 G. Tanquary Robinson, *Rural Russia under the Old Regime*, Berkeley–Los Angeles 1969, p. 116.

difficult. In 1921 industrial production in Russia still reached barely one quarter of prewar levels.

The Bolsheviks had no illusions: the road to the bright future could not be easy for anybody. In his book *The Politics and Economics of the Transition Period*, published in 1920, Bukharin – at that time one of Lenin's closest colleagues and the leading Party ideologue – explained (polemicizing with Kautsky, who recommended a gradual transition to socialism):

> The proletarian revolution is, however, a breach of the civil peace – it is civil war. And civil war reveals the true physiognomy of a society split into classes. The national fetish is destroyed in the fire of civil war and the classes take their places, weapons in hand, on either side of the revolutionary barricades. It is not surprising, therefore, that in the process of the proletariat's revolutionary struggle, all these forms, establishments and institutions which bore the semblance of being "national" inevitably collapse. Once again this is an unavoidable and historically absolutely inevitable process, whether individuals, groups or even certain intermediate classes want it or not.[305]

Bukharin recalled Marx's admonition that the workers would have to go through "15, 20, 50 years of civil wars and national struggles not only to bring about a change in society but also to change yourselves." In the party program that he wrote together with Preobrazhensky in 1919, he imagined society as one great production organization, from which the anarchy of capitalist production would be eliminated.[306] These lofty words were but words, however, and the task of rebuilding the country and putting it on the path of rapid development set challenges of a very practical nature. War Communism was revealed to have been a mistake; the pragmatic Lenin did not hesitate to admit as much. In October 1921, *Izvestia* printed his speech delivered at the 10th Party Congress in which he criticized himself and the Party for their premature frontal attack on capitalism in Russia. War Communism was a "mistake" and a "jump," which arose "in complete contradiction to all we wrote" concerning "the transition from capitalism to socialism."[307]

Economic planning offered an obvious solution to the problem of the "transition to socialism," about which Marx himself, unfortunately, wrote very little.

---

305 N. Bukharin, *Politics and Economics of the Transition Period*, London–Boston 1979, p. 42.

306 P. J. Boettke, *The Political Economy of Soviet Socialism*, vol. 8, London–New York 2001, p. 86. Marx quote from *Revelations Concerning the Communist Trial in Cologne*, Part I, "Preliminaries." Marxists Internet Archive. https://www.marxists.org/archive/marx/works/1853/revelations/ch01.htm.

307 Quoted in A. Kaufman, "The Origin of 'The Political Economy of Socialism'", *Soviet Studies*, 1953, no. 3.

The Bolsheviks observed with admiration how the Germans were able to mobilize their resources during the First World War. One of them wrote in 1915:

> Contemporary Germany has given the world a pattern of the centralized direction of the national economy as a single machine working according to plan. In contemporary Germany the keys of the machine are held by Siemens, Borsig, Gwinner, Bleichroder representatives of the biggest banks and the biggest accumulations of industrial capital in the country. He who holds the keys of the machine runs it according to his own conception; but the experience in the practical life of a vast country of the possibility of constructing such a unified machine within the complicated framework of modern civilization retains its theoretical interest and all its social scientific significance.[308]

The Germans submitted their economy to planning and control by degrees.[309] The first laws limiting economic freedom went into force on 3 August 1914. The state gradually took control over citizens' savings, foreign trade, production and the sale of food products, and set price limits on various goods, as well as introducing "raw-materials unions", supervising the distribution of scarce raw materials according to the needs of the war economy.[310] In November 1916, a ministry of planning was created and total mobilization of resources and manpower was implemented.[311] Industry was organized into 170 "war companies", based on the old trade unions. This program halted the decline in military-related production, though agriculture and the production of consumer goods continued to shrink. The prices of basic foodstuffs rose during the war eight-fold, and millions of Germans were forced to live on starvation-level rations, amounting to 700–900 kcal a day.[312] Widespread hunger brought down morale.[313] Nonetheless, contemporaries had no doubts regarding what a great achievement the Germans' war mobilization was.[314] Walther Rathenau, an industrialist and politician, wrote in

---

308 Quoted in E. H. Carr, *The Bolshevik Revolution 1917–1923*, Harmondsworth 1972, p. 359.

309 A. Ritschl, "The Pity of Peace. Germany's Economy at War, 1914–1918 and Beyond", [in:] *The Economics of World War I*, ed. S. Broadberry, M. Harrison, Cambridge 2005.

310 H. Strachan, *The First World War*, vol. 1, Oxford 2001, p. 1039 ff.

311 T. Hunt Tooley, "The Hindenburg Program of 1916. A Central Experiment in Wartime Planning", *The Quarterly Journal of Austrian Economics*, 1999, vol. 2, no. 2.

312 B. J. Davis, *Home Fires Burning. Food, Politics and Everyday Life in World War I Berlin*, Chapel Hill–London 2000, p. 180.

313 D. Welch, *Germany, Propaganda and Total War, 1914–1918*, New Brunswick 2000, p. 124.

314 R. Bessel, "Mobilization and demobilization in Germany, 1916–1919", [in:] *State, Society and Mobilization in Europe During the First World War*, ed. J. Horne, Cambridge 2002, p. 212 ff.

1918, that it was "an economic development closely connected with the methods of socialism and communism," and that "what came to fruition in the war years should have taken decades or centuries to come to fruition […] The economy went from being a private matter to a social matter."[315] Socialists considered the state's control of the economy to be a solution based on principles that drew on their ideology.

From the perspective of these experiences, the "new economic policy" (NEP), declared by Lenin was a step backward – a tactical and temporary concession granted by the New to the Old, as Lenin himself admitted in his last public speech.[316] In a socialist country, the private sector still existed – mainly in agriculture, crafts, trade and services. It was governed by the laws of the market. Alongside this there existed the state sector – industry, transport, banks, wholesale and foreign trade. In the era of the NEP, the private sector constituted only 9 percent of the Soviet GDP, but a disproportionately larger proportion of consumer goods.[317] Currency regained its value; goods returned to the shops.[318] The new Soviet rubles were backed by gold, and maintaining their value was a permanent concern of the Party comrades seated in the Politburo.[319] Deliverance from the tyranny of market chaos and its replacement by rational (planned) management remained ever in the economy's future. Bukharin formulated the problem as follows:

> Only in a society where production is anarchic, and likewise the distribution of goods, do the economic factors governing the life of the community manifest themselves in the form of "natural" and "spontaneous" laws independent of the will of individuals and collective bodies, laws which function with the same blind necessity as the force of gravity […] Indeed, as soon as we take an organized social economy, all the basic 'problems' of political economy disappear: problems of value, price, profit and so on. […] The social economy is regulated not by the blind forces of the market and competition, but by a

---

315 Quoted in E. Nabiel, *Gospodarka wojenna Niemiec, 1914–1918*, Warszawa 1959, pp. 27–29, 324–325. See also W. O. Henderson, "Walther Rathenau. A Pioneer of the Planned Economy", *The Economic History Review*, New Series, 1951, vol. 4, no. 1.

316 M. Lewin, *Lenin's Last Struggle*, Ann Arbor 2005, p. 66.

317 V. Shlapentokh, *A Normal Totalitarian Society. How the Soviet Union Functioned and How it Collapsed*, Armonk–London 2001, p. 103.

318 A. B. Ulam, *The Bolsheviks. The Intellectual and Political History of the Triumph of Communism in Russia*, Cambridge – London 1998, p. 449 ff.

319 D. M. Woodruff, "The Politburo on Gold, Industrialization, and the International Economy, 1925–1926", [in:] *The Lost Politburo Transcripts. From Collective Rule to Stalin's Dictatorship*, eds. P. R. Gregory, N. Nalmark, New Haven–London 2008, pp. 199–200.

consciously followed plan. In this case [...] there will be no room for a science which studies the blind laws of the market, since there will be no market[320].

After a few years of the NEP, the Soviet economy was ripe for a change of course. The country was rebuilding itself from the devastations of the recent past: around the turn of 1925–1926, industrial production had returned to prewar levels, and agricultural production was almost caught up. Nonetheless, the Party continued to have serious trouble managing the economy; this presented a constant political threat to the Party's power.

The first and most fundamental problem was food.[321] Before the war, peasants had sold grain, tobacco, wool or leather in cities in order to buy industrial products: salt, sugar, matches, fabrics, tools. In the second half of 1922, that natural order of things began to be threatened by emerging "price scissors": industrial goods were growing more expensive and peasants were able to buy ever fewer (or, more often, could not afford to buy any). They thus had no motivation to bring their foodstuffs to the cities to sell. In the autumn of 1923, the relative prices of industrial products compared to the prices for foodstuffs were three times higher than before the war and revolution.[322] This was the subject of extremely anxious discussions in the Politburo (during which the word "scissors" was declined in every grammatical case; it was taken from the shape of a graph showing the diverging levels of prices for farm and industrial goods). Cities were threatened with famine, but the Party managed to lower prices on industrial goods through administrative means (orders and threats), and peasants began to sell their foodstuffs again. Towards the end of 1926, however, the prices of industrial goods began to rise again, and this time they could not easily be stabilized. In 1927, unlike four years earlier, Soviet industry did not have unused powers of production left from the war that were relatively easy to mobilize. The state was already then beginning to invest in heavy industry, rather than produce for the market; there was simply a lack of goods that might interest peasants.

In response, the Party abolished the market once again, this time for good. A stenograph of a Politburo meeting in January 1927 throws some light on the direct political and economic motivations for this decision. The discussion involved Nikolai Rykov, formal head of the Soviet state (removed a few years later

---

320 N. Bukharin, *The Politics...*, op. cit., p. 57.

321 S. Pirani, *The Russian Revolution in Retreat, 1920–24. Soviet Workers and the New Communist Elite,* London–New York 2008, p. 139.

322 M. Harrison, "Prices in the Politburo, 1927: Market Equilibrium Versus the Use of Force", [in:] *The Lost Politburo Transcripts...*, op. cit., pp. 225–226.

and then condemned to death in a show trial) and Kosior, head of the Party in the Ukraine (likewise murdered during the Great Terror).

> Rykov complained: "Does industrialization offer anything for price cuts this year? It doesn't. Not even in the branches of industry, such as glass, that we have mechanized more than others. The STO [Council of Labor and Defense] was told recently that mechanization has been carried out in such a way that glass prices will rise this year."
>
> Voice: "Why?"
>
> Rykov: I asked the same question myself, but I got no clear answer. Sergo [Ordzhonikidze, Politburo member, at the time head of the party control commission] is currently in correspondence with the glass factories on this issue. We've built factories that are better than "in Europe" but glass prices have become even more expensive. [...]
>
> Kosior reported that "the workers asked me: 'Why are prices for baked bread not coming down, when we can buy grain more cheaply?' I myself don't know why bread prices are unchanged."
>
> Rykov: "It's the 'mechanization' of baking."
>
> Kosior: "We see this sort of thing everywhere" [...].[323]

Stalin then suggested an answer: the mechanization of industry combined with inadequate work norms were lifting wages faster than the workers' productivity was increasing. In other words, as historian Mark Harrison remarks, according to Stalin, workers were seizing the benefits from industrialization at the state's expense.[324] This was at best an incomplete diagnosis, since the low output of Soviet industry resulted from many reasons, but Stalin undoubtedly believed it to be true. Soon he would take care to keep workers' pay from rising too quickly.

However paradoxical it may seem today, it was easier for the Soviet leaders to control millions of small peasant producers – or at least they thought it was – than for the Party to manage the apparatus of industrial production from above. At a meeting in January 1927, Anastas Mikoyan, a faithful colleague of Stalin who was at that time responsible for trade, said as much.

> We have reached a point such that peasant muddle and the peasant grain market are wholly and completely in our hands, we can raise or lower grain prices at any time, and we have all the levers of influence in our hands. But in relation to state trade and the co-operatives, we don't have these levers for industrial commodities, or, more accurately, we utilize them badly. At present it is easier to raise or lower grain prices in a short period of time across the entire Union territory; and more difficult, and it demands unbelievably

323 Quoted in M. Harrison, "Prices in the Politburo...", op. cit., p. 231.
324 Quoted in M. Harrison, "Prices in the Politburo...", op. cit., p. 231.

> more effort, to cut prices for industrial commodities in the state-trading or cooperative sphere, because no one stands up for the peasant [muzhik] and gets in our way, whereas various organizations stand up for cooperation and state trade and defend them. Some comrade or other turns up from cooperation and state trade and says we can't cut prices just like that, there has to be a profit, all are good guys—and the result is none of the necessary pressure and none of the necessary results[325].

Mikoyan was being brutally frank: the peasants would have to pay, since they were politically weakest. The Party apparatus had to be reckoned with, while the peasants did not. For the time being, however, an effort was made to encourage them to sell foodstuffs.

After an intensive campaign conducted over ten months, the government was able to force producers to lower prices on industrial products by an average of 7 percent. (This was more than they had expected: Mikoyan had observed in January that it would only be possible to reduce them by 2–3 percent.) The result was empty shops, queues, and high prices on the black market, since goods were simply not available elsewhere. The peasants still did not want to sell grain to the state, since there was not much they could buy with the money they were able to earn. From the point of view of the members of the Politburo, this situation was creating a political threat. The Soviet authorities thus became hostage to the 25 million peasant families, small property owners who could starve the Soviet Union by stopping food deliveries to the cities.

That was unacceptable to the Party. The response to the poor results of the purchasing effort was a massive action carried out by the GPU in rural areas in autumn 1927 that forced peasants to cooperate. A campaign urging the collectivization of agriculture (beginning with propaganda) was close to follow.

The ruling elite in the USSR also had less extemporaneous reasons for confiscating the peasants' land from them. At issue was not only the regime's security, but also ideology. When the Bolsheviks sanctioned the division of large land holdings, they did so for tactical purposes in order to obtain peasant support for the revolution. The return of the land to the peasants created a caste of small landowners. As Rosa Luxemburg observed at the time (from distant Berlin), the Soviet authorities created "a new powerful layer of popular enemies of socialism in the countryside, enemies whose resistance will be much more dangerous and stubborn than that of noble large landowners."[326] Lenin would perhaps have been inclined to admit that she was correct, but he yielded to the demands of the

---

325 Ibid., p. 238.

326 Quoted in L. Siegelbaum, *Soviet State and Society Between Revolutions, 1918–1929*, Cambridge 1994, p. 40.

moment. "Liquidation of the kulaks as a class" could be postponed, but it did not cease to be a long-term goal.

At the same time, Soviet industry was desperately in need of investment. Red Russia was cut off from Western sources of capital (in part by choice, as it had discontinued payment of the tsar's debts) and the foreign investment that had to a large degree financed economic growth in the last decades of tsarist rule. In truth, production had returned to its prewar level, but machinery was aging. In the state coffers there was a constant lack of funds for investment. In 1925–1926, the first heated argument over the course of investment policy broke out in the Politburo: Felix Dzerzhinsky (at that time supervising state industry) and his deputy Grigorii Piatakov clashed with People's Finance Commissar Grigorii Sokolnikov, who advised a reduction in imports (and thus limiting investment) and a restrictive financial policy, leading to a stabilization of the economy and development surpluses in foreign trade. "The lack of hard currency is the fundamental noose that is strangling the development of industry," Piatakov shouted during a Politburo meeting.[327] To obtain hard currency, it was necessary to export; the USSR exported, among other things, gold and wood, but above all, grain. The peasants nonetheless did not want to sell it to the state.

Debates over how to get out of this pitfall went on in an atmosphere of constant menace. By 1921, hopes for revolution in the West had been decisively dashed and the Soviet Union was forced to build "socialism in one country"; it was an enormous and potentially rich country, to be sure, but at the moment a poor one surrounded by enemies. Stalin, who towards the end of the 1920s had attained all but absolute power, in particular, had an obsession with external threats (we should note that the German invasion in 1941 showed this obsession to be not entirely irrational). In the 1920s, it was estimated in the Politburo that an invasion would occur within five or, at most, ten years.[328] In 1928, in a speech in which he settled accounts with so-called "right-wing deviationism" in the Party – meaning Bukharin and his allies – Stalin laid out this strategic thinking very clearly:

> We have assumed power in a country whose technical equipment is terribly backward. Along with a few big industrial units more or less based upon modern technology, we have hundreds and thousands of mills and factories the technical equipment of which is beneath all criticism from the point of view of modern achievements. At the same time we have around us a number of capitalist countries whose industrial technique is far more developed and up-to-date than that of our country. Look at the capitalist countries

327 D. M. Woodruff, "The Politburo on Gold…", op. cit., p. 200.

328 A. Erlich, *The Soviet Industrialization Debate, 1924–1928*, Cambridge 1960, p. 28.

> and you will see that their technology is not only advancing, but advancing by leaps and bounds, outstripping the old forms of industrial technique. And so we find that, on the one hand, we in our country have the most advanced system, the Soviet system, and the most advanced type of state power in the world, Soviet power, while, on the other hand, our industry, which should be the basis of socialism and of Soviet power, is extremely backward technically. Do you think that we can achieve the final victory of socialism in our country so long as this contradiction exists?
>
> What has to be done to end this contradiction? To end it, we must overtake and outstrip the advanced technology of the developed capitalist countries. We have overtaken and outstripped the advanced capitalist countries in the sense of establishing a new political system, the Soviet system. That is good. But it is not enough. In order to secure the final victory of socialism in our country, we must also overtake and outstrip these countries technically and economically. Either we do this, or we shall be forced to the wall[329].

Stalin also reminded his listeners about Peter the Great, who had "feverishly built mills and factories," and underscored that it was "in its way an attempt to break out of the grip of this backwardness." It was a failed attempt, of course. Even Peter the Great could not accomplish this – only socialism could accomplish it, under his, Stalin's, leadership.[330] (This reference to Russian tradition, in which technical and economic modernization had for centuries served mainly military goals, was not accidental.[331])

The technical debate over how to "catch up" continued in Russia throughout the 1920s and provided theoretical arguments to the proponents of rapid industrialization. From the start, however, it was entangled in Stalin's adroit and cynical manoeuvring in his struggle for power within the Politburo. As would soon be revealed, what was at stake in these debates was not only economic policy, but also the health and life of its participants. The two most important authors of the theory behind Stalin's economic policies, Grigorii A. Feldman and Yevgenii A. Preobrazhensky, would never receive any awards or honours for their accomplishments. Instead, Feldman spent many years in the Gulag, from which he emerged an ailing and broken man only in the year of Stalin's death (he died five years later, in 1958). Preobrazhensky was arrested at the beginning of the 1930s, then released and sentenced to exile, only to be arrested again a few years later

---

329 J. Stalin, *Industrialisation of the Country and the Right Deviation in the C.P.S.U.(B.). Speech Delivered at the Plenum of the C.P.S.U.(B.), November 19, 1928*, https://www.marxists.org/reference/archive/stalin/works/1928/11/19.htm

330 Ibid., p. 257.

331 W. J. Blackwell, *The Beginnings of Russian Industrialization 1800–1860*, Princeton 1968, p. 169 ff.

and finally sentenced to death as a Trotskyite during the Great Terror. (He had in fact worked with Trotsky in the early 1920s as a member of the Central Committee, and, briefly, the Politburo; however, suspicions of any kind of oppositional activity were almost certainly fabricated by the Cheka).[332]

In the 1920s, Soviet economists could not find many suggestions in the classic works of Marxism about what should be done. Marx had anticipated that revolution would break out in the countries where capitalism was most advanced. He had little to say about *how* a backward socialist country could catch up with the leading capitalist countries. Preobrazhensky therefore referred to the Marxian concept of primitive accumulation (which Marx, in turn, had taken from Adam Smith). Marx wrote that in capitalism the bourgeoisie reproduces its capital and takes possession of the surplus from the workers' labour. The point of departure for this process is the accumulation of capital; however; this had to start somewhere.[333] In this process, primitive accumulation plays "about the same part as original sin in theology," Marx wrote.

---

332 Another victim of the purge was the Soviet economist most widely known in the West, Nikolai D. Kondratiev, one of the authors of the theory of long-term conjuncture cycles (lasting 50–60 years) in capitalist economies. The Institute of Conjuncture founded by Kondratiev in Moscow – maintaining contacts with many Western scholarly centres– was dissolved in 1928, though its head had not participated directly in the debate on Soviet industrialization. The actual reason for the liquidation of the institute, according to historian of Soviet economic theory Vincent Barnett, was its market approach to problems of investment and development. As early as January 1928 there was a discussion of the national economy's interest at an institute meeting that treated it as the sum of interests (that is, profits) of individual actors on the economic stage. Kondratiev's institute, devoted to rigorous and methodical study of the market economy, Barnett writes, "existed in a context where the stated political objective was the complete elimination of markets and hence cycles from all aspects of economic life, whether this be in the short or medium term. Members of the Conjuncture Institute must have realised that their personal positions within the Soviet economic bureaucracy were inextricably connected to the fate of the actual markets which they studied and analysed in such an enthusiastic and original manner." V. Barnett, "A Long Wave Goodbye. Kondrat'ev and the Conjuncture Institute, 1920–28", *Europe-Asia Studies*, 1995, no. 3, p. 417. Kondratiev himself was arrested in 1930 and sentenced to 8 years in prison in a show trial of one of the opposition groups invented by the NKVD. Though he served out the sentence, he was then shot in 1938.

333 A. Erlich, "Preobrazhenski and the Economics of Soviet Industrialization", *The Quarterly Journal of Economics*, 1950, vol. 64, no. 1.

> The legend of theological original sin tells us certainly how man came to be condemned to eat his bread in the sweat of his brow; but the history of economic original sin reveals to us that there are people to whom this is by no means essential. Never mind! Thus it came to pass that the former sort accumulated wealth, and the latter sort had at last nothing to sell except their own skins. And from this original sin dates the poverty of the great majority that, despite all its labour, has up to now nothing to sell but itself, and the wealth of the few that increases constantly although they have long ceased to work. [...] In the history of primitive accumulation, all revolutions are epoch-making that act as levers for the capital class in course of formation; but, above all, those moments when great masses of men are suddenly and forcibly torn from their means of subsistence, and hurled as free and "unattached" proletarians on the labour-market. The expropriation of the agricultural producer, of the peasant, from the soil, is the basis of the whole process.[334]

Marx did not mince words: "conquest, enslavement, robbery, murder, briefly force" – these were the methods by which primitive accumulation was achieved. What form might it take in a socialist nation?

Preobrazhensky answered: the capital needed for major investments in industry must be "pumped" from the capitalist sector of the economy to the state's coffers.[335] In his most important work, *The New Economics*, he wrote:[336]

> In the period of primitive socialist accumulation the state cannot do without the alienation of a part of the surplus product of the countryside and of artisan labour [...] The idea that a socialist economy can develop by itself without touching the resources of the petty bourgeois, including the peasant, economy is beyond doubt a reactionary, petty bourgeois utopia.[337]

This process could not take place spontaneously. Nor would it be possible to wait until socialist industry developed a sufficiently high surplus, because that, in Preobrazhensky's view, would mean extending the period of introductory accumulation indefinitely. It is worth underscoring here that Preobrazhensky rejected violence: the methods described by Marx, such as colonialism, plunder, and piracy, were unacceptable to him. He did, however, use a similarly sinister phrase

---

334 K. Marx, *Capital. A Critique of Political Economy,* https://www.marxists.org/archive/marx/works/1867-c1/ch26.htm

335 The best analysis of Soviet debates of that time, still widely cited to this day, is found in A. Erlich's *The Soviet Industrialization Debate, 1924–1928*, Cambridge 1960.

336 Originally published in Moscow in 1926 as *Novaya Ekonomika*, the book came out in the West many years later; see E. A. Preobrazhensky, *The New Economics*, Oxford 1965.

337 Quoted in E. H. Carr, *A History Of Soviet Russia Socialism In One Country: 1924 1926*, New York 1958, pp. 203–204.

in referring to the Russian countryside as an "internal colony."[338] Preobrazhensky was positively disposed towards foreign loans: he believed that even though they had to be paid back with high interest, ultimately, they were beneficial, since they made the import of technology and Western *know-how* possible.

The state would take possession of part of the "surplus value" produced by peasants using mainly indirect methods that did not call for the use of an expensive police apparatus. Preobrazhensky promoted controlled inflation (he knew that it would impoverish the petty bourgeoisie, operating as an additional tax) in addition to direct taxation of trade and crafts. All of this was secondary relative to the principal mechanism, however: the state was to buy grain from peasants cheaply and export it; the hard currency earned would be used to import machines needed for new state factories (under no circumstances for consumer goods). To that end, the state would need to establish a monopoly on the purchase of grain and a monopoly on foreign trade, allowing it to set prices.

This technique of "taking over the private sector surplus" would, naturally, have its limits. Preobrazhensky knew that purchasing prices could not be set too low, since farmers would then stop selling their grain. As an economist, he was nevertheless pleased with the elegance and low cost of this solution: the establishment of additional, high taxes would demand building an expensive treasury apparatus, whereas his idea, as he wrote, "does not require even a kopek to be spent." Of course the peasants' standard of living could be temporarily lowered, but the benefits of accelerated development would quickly compensate for that. Technologically advanced production would soon allow for the cheap production of industrial goods: their low prices would signify a *de facto* universal wage increase, for peasants as well. Taking a longer-term perspective, Preobrazhensky envisioned the moment when the socialist sector of the economy would be strong enough to function independently and cover the costs of investment with its own moneys. It could then stop siphoning off capital from peasant labour, as this would no longer be necessary.

Preobrazhensky thought that his method indicated a way out of backwardness, not only for the NEP-era USSR, but every backward country that wanted to tear itself out of that state in attempting to build socialism, and in which there existed a capitalist economy alongside the socialist sector. He wrote that the more "economically backward, petit-bourgeois and peasant" a country transitioning to a socialist organization of production was, the greater the degree to which

338 R. Conquest, *The Harvest of Sorrow. Soviet Collectivization and the Terror Famine*, New York 1986, p. 65.

socialist accumulation would have to be based on appropriating part of the surplus production of pre-socialist forms of economy, and the less accumulation would be based on its own production base. This meant it would rely less on surplus production created by workers in socialist industry, and more on the seizure of the surplus from the traditional production sector.

Though Preobrazhensky's works did not enter into scholarly circulation in the West until after the Second World War, an interesting connection can be traced between Preobrazhensky and Rosenstein-Rodan, a pioneer of Western theory on the development of backward countries. There is no proof that Rosenstein-Rodan read the works of Preobrazhensky, but he was certainly familiar with developments in the Soviet Union. Paul A. Baran, a student of Preobrazhensky in Russia in the 1920s, later studied with Paul Rosenstein-Rodan at Harvard (Baran himself was also an important forerunner of dependency theory and was the author of the book *The Political Economy of Growth*, which created a stir in the late 1950s and early 1960s).[339]

Primitive socialist accumulation would not have been a painless process even if the state were not to use direct coercion. It should be remembered, however, that from the perspective of a Marxist and a careful reader of *Das Kapital*, who really believed that at the roots of primitive capitalist accumulation lay violence and force, the socialist state would still behave in a more humanitarian way than the protocapitalists.

Perhaps it would not be necessary to lower the general standard of living even temporarily. This was the view of growth taken by the second economist who had a major role in this debate, Grigorii A. Feldman. An electrical engineer by education, he worked for Gosplan (the central planning office) in the 1920s, and published an extensive, two-part article in its magazine in 1928 in which he proved the economic rationality of investing in heavy industry. Feldman was not interested in a situation where the state would buy machines from abroad in exchange for exported grain. He focused on domestic sources of accumulation – and tried to construct a mathematical model that would correspond to the question of whether accelerated investment necessarily demanded a lowered standard of living.[340]

Feldman came to the conclusion that in fact the two were by no means inextricably linked. (As a contemporary historian put it, that "one could have one's

339 M. Hatziprokopiou, K. Velentzas, *Preobrazhensky and the Theory…*, op. cit., p. 191.

340 Feldman's two-part 1928 article appeared in English as "On the Theory of Growth Rates of National Income", I & II, [in:] *Foundations of Soviet Strategy for Economic Growth*, ed. N. Spulber, Bloomington: Ind. 1964, pp. 174–199, 304–331.

cake and eat it too."[341]) Paradoxically, investments in heavy industry, meaning the production of steel, factory machinery or locomotives, rather than clothing or furniture, would lead to a rapid rise in consumption (Feldman took this division of the economy into the manufacture of consumer goods and the means of production from Marx). The economist thought that the rate of production of consumer goods – furniture, clothes, or houses – was dependent on previous investments in the development of the means of production (and thus industrial and construction machinery, railway tracks and locomotives). The greater the investment in heavy industry in the first period of industrialization, the faster the growth of consumption later: Feldman constructed a mathematical model of this process.

But what did the word "later" mean for him? Feldman assumed a perspective of several, at most a dozen or so years. His model allowed for a certain decrease in consumption in the first period of industrialization, but by no means considered this inevitable: everything depended on the political decisions of planners, the amount of resources they initially earmarked for investment. A politician or planner in charge of making economic decisions would thus have a choice between two extreme scenarios resulting from his path (both of which assumed investment in heavy industry): in the first, consumption continued to rise steadily, very slowly early one, and later very quickly; in the second, it fell somewhat initially (during the jump in investment), then bounced back even faster than in the first scenario. In this way, the economist proposed to politicians a transparent trade off: the more we tighten our belt at the beginning, the better we will live later on.

In any case, Feldman considered huge investments in heavy industry to be necessary. Without them, the economy, left to run its natural course, would attain a low rate of investment, and thus the level of consumption would rise very slowly – more slowly over a period of a few years than in either of the "great leap" scenarios proposed by Feldman. A *piatiletka* (five-year plan) was crucial. The only alternative, he argued, was stagnation.

The ideas of Preobrazhensky and Feldman formed the basis of the Stalinist industrial revolution, although Stalin never acknowledged the debt of gratitude that he owed these two Soviet economists. Economic policies in many Third World countries after 1945 were also based on these ideas. Nehru's chief planner, Prasanta Mahlanobis (whose ideas, as we saw, were bitterly mocked years later by

341 R. C. Allen, *Farm to Factory…*, op. cit., p. 54.

one outstanding British expert on development), created Indian five-year plans according to Feldman's model.[342]

The brutal and ruthless struggle for power in the Soviet Union after the death of Lenin was superimposed onto these theoretical conceptions. How it played out has been described in detail elsewhere, so there is no need to give an extensive account of it here. The main actor was Stalin, who masterfully played the members of Lenin's Politburo against one another, simultaneously taking advantage of his power as head of the Party apparatus to build a base of faithful political supporters. In the course of these political battles, Stalin did not take a clear and unambiguous position on matters concerning economic policy: he usually expressed support for those members with whom he had entered into a political alliance.

From the early 1920s on, Trotsky and his adherents had pursued the aims of rapid industrialization and large investments in heavy industry at the expense of agriculture: Preobrazhensky expressed their thinking well. Bukharin, at that time the editor-in-chief of *Pravda* and the Party's main ideologue, was propounding a more market-based and generally "softer" economic policy (Stalin appeared to support him at that time). Bukharin argued that the idea of sudden industrialization carried out at the peasantry's expense would bring about serious political and economic difficulties in its wake. According to Bukharin, the peasants were not so stupid as to fail to grasp that the state was manipulating prices to its disadvantage. As a result, he claimed, they would not only be unfavourably disposed toward the Soviet authorities, but would stop selling their grain – without which it would be impossible to build up industry in starving cities.

Bukharin proposed a different solution – uniform development of industry and agriculture, that is, a reversal of the pricing system proposed by Preobrazhensky. Lower prices on industrial products would stimulate consumption, and therefore production as well, and greater profits from industry would permit financing of investment. Bukharin wanted, for example, to lift the ban on the hiring of agricultural workers by rich peasants. In the spring of 1925, he declared in a famous speech: "To the peasants, to all the peasantry, we must say: Enrich yourselves, develop your farms, and do not fear that constraints will be

342 Colin Clark's views on Mahlanobis's economic planning were quoted in Chapter 2. This model of growth is sometimes called the Feldman-Mahlanobis model in the literature. It should be noted that Mahlanobis, like Feldman, had not been educated as an economist: he was a physicist (he studied at Calcutta and Cambridge), and later worked as a statistician. See also Chapter 6.

put on you."[343] He did not believe in the threat of a renascent capitalism in the countryside. He thought that trade cooperatives and state farms would be more productive than private farms: socialism would defeat capitalism in a fair fight. Moreover, Bukharin thought that major growth in production would require only small investments. According to his ally, Rykov, "the possibilities of increase in yields even by such relatively elementary devices as replacing the wooden hoe by plow, improvements in seeds, introduction of the simplest agricultural machinery and of fertilizers are tremendous at the present level in our villages."[344] Bukharin warned against forcing peasants to join kolkhozes (cooperative farms): he believed that this would merely lead to the rise of "parasitic Communist institutions" living on state subsidies, which would only strengthen the peasants' conviction "that the private economy is a very good thing." The road to the kolkhoz was supposed to lead through classical trade cooperatives that dispensed credit and bought grain, and whose efficiency would convince the peasants of the superiority of collective farming. They would come to believe in collective farming if they saw with their own eyes that it could make life more comfortable.[345]

The old Communists were taken aback by Bukharin's views: his attempt to rehabilitate capitalism was too overt. The slogan "enrich yourselves", with which the conservative Guizot had exhorted the French bourgeoisie in the nineteenth century, elicited a resounding protest. Stalin at that point defended Bukharin, but he would remember these accusations well and would himself use them against Bukharin a few years later.

At the Sixteenth Party Congress in July 1930, Stalin finally settled accounts with his last remaining political opponents. He now cited their economic prescriptions. In the political report of the Central Committee at the Congress, Stalin pronounced the NEP to be a "regrouping of forces." Condemning "Right deviators" for its concessions to alleged "village capitalists," he appeared to rehabilitate the ideas of the "left opportunists" against whom he had earlier fought. Their mistake was to have sought to implement the program of industrialization prematurely – when the dictator was not yet ready for it.

---

343 Quoted in R. W. Davies, "Grain, Class, and Politics During NEP. The Politburo Meeting of December 10, 1925", [in:] *The Lost Politburo Transcripts…*, p. 183. The speech was printed in *Pravda* on 14 April 1925.

344 Quoted in R. C. Allen, *Farm to Factory…*, op. cit., p. 59.

345 S. Cohen, *Bukharin and the Bolshevik Revolution. A Political Biography, 1888–1938*, Oxford–New York 1980, p. 195.

3. Mechanics of the Great Leap

When Stalin publicly condemned Bukharin for "right deviationism," the campaign of industrialization and collectivization had been ongoing for over a year. The Soviet Union was preparing for the leap into modernity that would follow almost to the letter the prescriptions outlined by Preobrazhensky and Feldman. Stalin added one important new element to the program: violence. The peasants, as Bukharin had anticipated (but Preobrazhensky had not foreseen), in fact did not want to sell their grain. The Soviet authorities thus resolved to take it from them – forcing a mosaic of millions of small peasant farms into the framework of the kolkhozes which were fully under its control.

The direct impulse for starting collectivization was provided by the miserable results of efforts to purchase grain in 1928. According to official statistics, the amount purchased fell from 10.6 million tonnes in 1926 to 10.1 million tonnes in 1927 and 9.35 million tonnes in 1928. In that year, for the first time in history, Russia had to import grain.

In May 1928, Stalin presented to the comrades in the Politburo a report demonstrating that although grain harvests were at their prewar level, the amount of that yield that made it to market was barely half of the prewar level. He accused "kulaks" and owners of middle-sized farms of deliberately concealing grain in order to weaken the Soviet authorities. In reality, the state's purchasing prices were so low that they did not cover the costs of production; in autumn of 1927 many peasants preferred to symbolically burn their grain rather than sell it to the state.[346] This was now more than an economic problem: it was a political crime. The peasants had declared war on the Soviet state. The army and the Cheka were now enlisted into the buying campaign. Party dignitaries were informed that they were personally responsible for the results of the purchasing effort in their regions. Grain was confiscated at local markets, and checkpoints were set up on the roads to inspect peasants' carts. The punishment for private trade in grain was a stiff prison sentence.

Stalin – in the assessment of a noted expert on Soviet archives, including the dictator's correspondence – was far from economically illiterate, and often based his decisions not on Party reports or intelligence, but on his own intuitions. He was keenly aware of how markets work, and thus knew that raising the purchasing price would incline the peasants toward selling their grain.[347] In August 1930, in a letter to Molotov – at that time premier of the USSR and one of Stalin's chief

346 P. R. Gregory, *The Political Economy…*, p. 32.
347 Ibid., p. 36.

colleagues – he wrote: "We have one and a half months to export grain: starting in late October (perhaps even earlier), American grain will come on the market in massive quantities, and we won't be able to withstand that. If we don't export 130–150 million puds of grain in these six weeks, our hard currency situation could become really desperate." In another letter to Molotov, he wrote: "If we can beat this grain thing, then we'll prevail in everything, both in domestic and foreign policies."[348] In all of Stalin's preserved correspondence from that time – including, for example, telegrams to Kaganovich – agricultural matters play a leading role.[349]

The dictator prevailed, though the price of his victory was high. Beginning in 1929, an increasing amount of grain was flowing into the state reserves, though the harvests remained at a more or less fixed level. "The eyes of our rightists are popping out of their heads in amazement," he commented with satisfaction in a letter written in the winter of 1929–1930. Up until the mid-1930s, Stalin took an interest in every detail of successive grain campaigns: he knew which region was not fulfilling its plans, and personally decided whether to raise or lower delivery quotas to the authorities. He knew that these plans could not be executed without the use of ruthless coercion. His correspondence with the Politburo members closest to him at that time, Kaganovich and Molotov, is full of wrathful recommendations to hunt down the "vermin," "criminals and bandits," and "enemies of the state" (he had in mind peasants who were allegedly concealing grain and those trading privately in foodstuffs).

Preobrazhensky, now under arrest, submitted a statement of self-criticism. In an attempt to save his own life, he beat his breast and paid tribute to the genius of Stalin: "Collectivization – this is the crux of the matter. Did I have this prognosis of collectivization? No, I did not."[350] In fact, he had simply lacked the imagination to foresee that the state could declare war on its own citizens, condemning them to hunger and almost unimaginable suffering. In 1929, according to secret statistics gathered for the supreme authorities of the USSR, over 1300 rebellions broke out in rural areas. In February 1930 alone, a quarter of a million peasants took part in 736 demonstrations. Twenty thousand were shot.

Nevertheless, the worst was still to come. In July 1929, only 4 percent of peasant farms had joined a kolkhoz. In November, the figure was 7.6 percent.[351]

---

348 Quoted in P. R. Gregory, *The Political Economy*..., p. 37.

349 R.W. Davies, "Stalin as Economic Policy-maker. Soviet Agriculture, 1931–1936", [in:] *Stalin. A New History*, ed. S. Davies, J. Harris, Cambridge 2005, p. 124.

350 Quoted in P. R. Gregory, *The Political Economy*..., p. 40.

351 R. Conquest, *The Harvest of Sorrow*..., op. cit., p. 112.

Though Stalin publicly praised the pace of collectivization, in reality he was not satisfied and obliged his subordinates to accelerate it. In December 1929, he declared the official policy of "liquidation of the kulaks as a class"; in January 1930, the Politburo approved the relevant resolution. At that point there began the massive exile of alleged "kulaks" to the far north or the Asiatic steppes. There was not even a shadow of economic rationality in this: this pure orgy of terror had the result of shattering peasant support for the regime. Practically speaking, there were no kulaks left, since they had long since been driven to ruin; fewer than one in 100 farms hired even one worker. The average value of the confiscated property from a "kulak" family amounted to between 170 and 400 rubles (roughly equal to the monthly wages of a worker); the income of such a "kulak" was lower than the income of the government clerk sentencing him to deportation. As Robert Conquest, a historian of the Great Famine, observes, the costs of deportation itself were probably higher than 400 rubles.[352]

It is now difficult to harbour any doubts about the famine having been the deliberate result of Stalin's policies, implemented with the consistency and ruthlessness fitting an oriental despot.[353] The state confiscated grain, even the portion designated for sowing; it introduced internal passports and attempted to eliminate starving peasants from the streets of the cities where they sought help. The peasants, forced into a corner, had stopped sowing and were slaughtering their cattle en masse. Soviet archives contain reports by survivors who speak of slow death in the agonies of hunger, suicides, and even cases of cannibalism. In 1933, the OGPU intercepted a letter written by a boy deported from the Ukraine to Siberia:

> What a wicked fate has befallen me, I still can't believe that they did this to me, and why they are tormenting me this way, as if I were a rich man or hurt somebody, they are bunglers and bloodsuckers and nothing more. We are starving here, and there's nothing to buy, nothing to eat. It's incredible how they abuse us, prisoners have it much better, they get special work clothes, three pounds of bread, but we get nothing, that's the kind of criminals we are, they'll probably torture us to death, the snakes. A lot of people are already starving to death. The damned scoundrels, I feel sorry for the people, and myself as well. What are they tormenting us for, for our property? Is it really possible the scoundrels won't come to their senses and let us live freely?[354]

---

352 Ibid., p. 117.

353 *Memoirs of Nikita Khrushchev, Commissar 1918–1945*, ed. S. Khrushchev, University Park 2005, pp. 63–64.

354 Cf. *The War Against the Peasantry 1927–1930. The Tragedy of the Soviet Countryside*, ed. L. Viola, V. P. Danilov, N. A. Ivnitskii, D. Kozlov, New Haven–London 2005, 319 ff.

The greatest number of victims of famine died in the Ukraine and southern Russia. Reports from the small number of foreigners who witnessed the events are full of information about depopulated villages in which out of a few hundred inhabitants there remained at most a few dozen, wandering through the empty fields like shadows.[355]

In July 1934, Władysław Gomułka, at that time a low-level Communist Party activist, travelled by train to a sanatorium in Crimea. He was warned of possible attacks or robberies on the train. Years later, Gomułka would write:

> In reality, these were serious and widespread occurrences. They grew in number and spread over the territory of the Soviet Union during the period of intensive collectivization of agriculture. The bands of marauders consisted mostly of peasants who had been kicked off their farms and dispossessed of their lands. As I later learned from certain workers at the Party school, the collectivization of agriculture, conducted using brutal administrative methods, had aroused resistance and opposition from the peasants everywhere, which was manifested in many different forms. In the period immediately preceding collectivization that had been previously announced by the authorities, one widely used form of opposition was the peasants' restricting their cultivation of the land to an area whose harvesting would be sufficient to provide only for the needs of their own family. The peasants left the rest of the land fallow. If collectivization was being applied to areas already sown and cultivated, the peasants' protest manifested itself in the form of limiting the harvest of crops to an amount that met their own food needs. The part of the crops in the peasants' fields not taken would be destroyed.[356]

The future leader of Communist Poland was startled by what he saw and heard. For Gomułka, collectivization was "the original sin underlying all the evil that manifested itself on such a massive scale in the Soviet Union under Stalin." He wrote: "Nobody can state the extent of the harmful consequences, particularly of a moral nature, that it had on Soviet society, and which weighed on its traditions."[357].

According to recent estimates by historians, using previously classified data from Soviet statistical bureaus, between 5.5 and 6.5 million people died of hunger in the Soviet Union in the years 1928–1934.[358] Historian Timothy Snyder estimates the number of famine victims in the years 1932–1933 at 3.3 million.[359] Overall, in the 1930s, according to the estimates of historian Robert Conquest,

---

355 R. Conquest, *The Harvest of Sorrow…*, p. 244.

356 W. Gomułka, *Pamiętniki*, vol. 1, ed. A. Werblan, Warszawa 1994, p. 341

357 Ibid.

358 R. W. Davies, S. G. Wheatcroft, *The Years of Hunger. Soviet Agriculture, 1931–1933*, New York 2002, p. 401.

359 T. Snyder, *Bloodlands. Europe Between Hitler and Stalin*, New York 2010, pp. 44–46.

14.5 million citizens of the USSR died as a result of repression relating to collectivization.[360]

Stalin bought the Five-Year Plan – the Soviet ticket to modernity – at the price of widespread famine and millions of human beings. This assessment does not suggest that the transaction was praiseworthy, moral or even economically advantageous. On the contrary, there are many arguments in favour of the view that the Five-Year Plan was accompanied by colossal waste – not only of energy, health and human life, but also of the capital extracted from millions of peasants by the Soviet authorities at such an expenditure of sweat and blood.[361] The collective farms turned out to be a great disappointment: in 1938 almost half of farm production came from private peasant farmsteads (one half hectare per family), which constituted only 3.9 percent of cultivated acreage.[362] The Cheka and the GPU reported on the terrible state of state-run farms even before the beginning of collectivization, but Party discipline and ideology demanded that Communists believe such problems to be temporary.[363]

From the beginning, historians and Sovietologists have differed in their assessment of the results of Soviet industrialization: estimates of the rate of economic growth in the USSR during the period under discussion are highly divergent. No one doubts, however, that such growth was a fact.[364] The goal that had been set was achieved. In the 1930s the USSR became an industrial power.

The transformation of Soviet society from an agrarian to an industrial society also looked quite different from the way the Soviet Utopians of the 1920s had imagined it. As late as 1929, on the threshold of the first Five-Year Plan, the economist and high-ranking Gosplan clerk L. M. Sabshovich published a booklet entitled *The USSR in Ten Years*: it was published in a mass edition and translated into a

---

360 R. Conquest, *The Harvest of Sorrow…*, op. cit., p. 306.

361 The scope of this transfer is disputed. According to some studies, the value of the farming machines sent to the countryside, necessary for the replacement of the draught-animals slaughtered by the peasants, was equal to or greater than the value of the agricultural products "extracted" from the villages. The Great Leap would thus have been achieved by a lowering of living standards everywhere (not only in the countryside). See P. R. Gregory, J. Sailors, "The Soviet Union during the Great Depression. The Autarky Model", [in:] *The World Economy and National Economies in the Interwar Slump*, ed. T. Balderston, New York 2003, p. 206.

362 M. Lewin, *The Making of the Soviet System*, New York 1994, p. 180.

363 V. Brovkin, *Russia After Lenin. Politics, Culture and Society 1921–1929*, London–New York 2005, pp. 168–169.

364 Cf. e.g. A. Bergson, *The Real National Income of Soviet Russia Since 1929*, Cambridge 1961.

number of foreign languages. The Soviet Union in 1939 was to be a country where the "material and social base of socialism" had already been built: free of private ownership, free of classes, free of big cities, and even free of natural disasters. Industry and the populace were to be equally distributed throughout the enormous country in agglomerations of 50,000–75,000 inhabitants; the author believed these to be the optimal social and public health conditions for life. In here vision of the future, there were no longer any rural areas, and the "peasant mentality" had been utterly eliminated. Kolkhoz and sovkhoz farms would surround farming towns, and shared life in communes would replace private domestic farms, that "plague that deforms the life of adults and children." Thanks to the commune, women would be liberated from family duties and the slavery of domestic life. Everyone would live in enormous hotel-houses, automated dormitories housing 1400–2000 persons each (children would be separated from their parents and raised collectively). The work week would be shortened to three days.[365]

By 1939 these visions had been entirely forgotten. The country was poor, hungry and cold. People often worked seven days a week, without a single day off. In place of Utopia, Dnieprostroi and Magnitogorsk had been built.

While the numbers do not fully convey the scale of these changes, it is useful to adduce them here. Between 1928 and 1937, industrial production rose annually by 11 percent. The share of agriculture in the GDP fell from 49 percent to 29 percent. Every fifth resident of the USSR had moved from working on a farm to working in industry, one of the largest migrations to cities in the history of the world. The share of consumption in the GDP fell from 80 percent to 53 percent; the share of investment doubled from 13 percent to 26 percent. During that decade, the prices of consumer goods rose by a figure of seven: the retail price of agricultural products rose by 539 percent.[366] According to contemporary estimates (as opposed to overstated Soviet data) GDP growth in the years 1928–1955 amounted to an average of 5.2 percent annually; if we take into account the collapse in production brought about by the war, from which the economy of the USSR only recovered in the late 1940s, estimates would run still higher. During the first two Five-Year Plans (1928–1937), the Soviet GDP doubled.

There is no doubt that in the early years of the first Five-Year Plan – at least until 1932 – the standard of living dropped substantially. There is no shortage of experts, however, who state that consumption grew minimally throughout the

365 R. Stites, *Revolutionary Dreams. Utopian Vision and Experimental Life in the Russian Revolution*, New York – Oxford 1989, p. 199.

366 P. R. Gregory, J. Sailors, *The Soviet Union during the Great Depression…*, p. 200.

first two Five-Year Plans.[367] If true, that would mean that Feldman was right – a simultaneous jump in investment could coincide with a rise in consumption, though the abrupt growth in prosperity he predicted in the later phases of the Great Leap materialized late and at best incompletely in the era of Khrushchev, the golden age of the Soviet economy. Specialists continue to engage in a long and very technical debate on the level of official and black-market prices and wages, and the caloric value of food per Soviet citizen.[368] The question thus remains open. Regardless of statistical discussions, however, both Russians and foreigners remember the 1930s in the USSR as a time of universal misery.

New industrial projects provided reasons to be proud, but their work on them too was not proceeding entirely according to plan. The technology was usually imported from the West, together with the specialists needed to start up operations. The USSR provided raw materials, capital, and manpower. Magnitogorsk was just such an industrial enterprise. It was designed in 1928 by the Leningrad construction company Gipromez, but the McKee Company from Cleveland, Ohio, which received a contract for 2.5 million dollars in gold, was responsible for the greater part of its construction. The model for the works and the city was supposed to be Gary, Indiana, in which a gigantic metallurgical works had been built by U.S. Steel. Magnitogorsk appeared to be an ideal location to the planners: placed almost exactly on the border between Europe and Asia, it was secure from foreign invasion. The factory was erected right near the "magnetic mountain," a gigantic deposit of high-grade iron ore estimated to hold 228 million tonnes.

The plan placed unrealistic obligations on the shoulders of the builders, which proved impossible to meet, thus providing the authorities with a pretext for the use of repression and constant replacement of personnel. In 1932, the first operating furnaces in Magnitogorsk fulfilled only 44.9 percent of the plan: the plant's

---

367 This is the opinion of R. C. Allen, among others; Allen writes that consumption in the late 1930s was considerably higher than in the late 1920s, judging from, among other sources, tables of the caloric value of the food eaten by a citizen of the USSR (*Farm to Factory…*, p. 132 ff.); P. R. Gregory and J. Sailors (who estimate annual growth in consumption at a level of 0.8 percent; see *The Soviet Union During the Great Depression…*, p. 201) concur.

368 S. G. Wheatcroft, *The first 35 Years of Soviet Living Standards…*; the author, analyzing discussions of wages and prices in the USSR conducted since the 1950s by western scholars and the findings of his own archival research, reaches the conclusion that the standard of living in the USSR in the late 1920s was not reached again until a few years after the Second World War.

managers were replaced three times.[369] Similar problems plagued all of the great construction Five-Year Plans. The building of Dnieprostroi, a gigantic dam on the Dnieper, had begun in 1927 even before the announcement of the first Plan. Lenin thought that electrification would change and modernize Soviet Union; the plan for electrification in the early 1920s was the Soviet state's first large, co-ordinated economic enterprise. Dnieprostroi was to provide energy for industry as well as hasten the implementation of Lenin's vision.

From the outset, its construction was plagued by problems. Assessments by foreign engineers and Party overseers found the efficiency of the work to be low, largely as a result of the workers' wretched living and housing conditions and poor diet. Thousands of people came to build the dam and thousands quickly left. Work was often halted due to a lack of raw materials and crucial construction elements: for example, in 1931 electric turbines that had been ordered for the dam were lent to another factory. although thousands had been hired (17,000 in 1929, 30,000 in 1930) local Party members complained of a lack of hands for work. In 1930 the plan was nearly completely executed, but only because its targets had been lowered.[370]

The plans were highly flexible. What would have most shocked proponents of rational, planned industrialization in the poorest countries in the 1950s and 1960s would have been to learn that Soviet planning in the Stalinist period was primarily a ritualistic and propagandistic enterprise. Firstly, its degree of precision left much to be desired. In 1951, more than 20 years after the start of the first Five-Year Plan, a detailed version of the plan was broken down into no more than 127 products. Secondly, the numerical values inscribed in the plan were based – as one historian specializing in this area writes – "on experience, intuition, and bargaining," and sometimes simply the arbitrary decisions of a dictator.[371] In the 1930s, Stalin often dispatched decisions about investment costs and production goals from Crimea, where he was vacationing, without consulting anybody. Sometimes he guessed right – he was usually well-informed – but sometimes he made faulty decisions.

Thirdly, the Five-Year Plans did not translate directly into short-term planning: they merely designated the general direction of economic development. As a rule they also were not executed in full. The goals of the first Five-Year Plan (1928–1933) were met, on average, at a level of 60 percent; those of the

369 J. Scott, *Behind the Urals…*, op. cit., p. 71.

370 A. Rassweiler, *The Generation of Power. The History of Dneprostroi*, New York – Oxford 1988, pp. 3, 132–134, 173.

371 P. R. Gregory, *Political Economy…*, p. 114.

second – rather lower – at a level of 70 percent. Almost all of the plans were approved many months after their formal initiation: the first (1928–1933) was approved in the spring of 1929, and the fifth (1950–1955) in August 1952.

Every Five-Year Plan carried a propaganda message.[372] In November 1929, Stalin wrote about the first:

> We are advancing full steam ahead along the path of industrialization—to socialism, leaving behind the age-old "Russian" backwardness. We are becoming a country of metal, a country of automobiles, a country of tractors. And when we have put the U.S.S.R. on an automobile, and the *muzhik* on a tractor, let the worthy capitalists, who boast so much of their "civilisation," try to overtake us! We shall yet see which countries may then be "classified" as backward and which as advanced[373].

It was announced at that time that industrial production – then equal to 5 percent of the USA's industrial production – would catch up in the early 1940s. Planned production results were arbitrarily changed (usually from above): from April to December 1929 the planned amount of iron to be smelted was increased fivefold, from 1.3 million to 6.1 million tonnes.[374] The cult of steel production surpassed even the cult of Stalin: there was not a great deal of "rationality" in this.[375] In 1937, during work on a subsequent Five-Year Plan, a wave of purges swept through the Gospłan: among those shot were two successive heads and many workers (they shared the fate of statisticians and demographers). There could be no talk of "rational, scientific" planning in such conditions.

In practice, the Soviet economy was managed by means of short-term operational plans that were not published and could be changed at any moment (and very often were). This involved a great deal of steering by hand. The Politburo could at any given moment change allocations of materials and production goals. It could also give orders for a change in the production profile. It did both of these things constantly. It was, at least in theory, all-powerful.

Every authority has its limits, however. The men governing the USSR were permanently overworked. Their lives consisted of endless meetings, at which hundreds of decisions were taken on various matters, often very insignificant ones. The drive toward total control over the life of society remained in irremediable

---

372 M. Lenoe, *Closer to the Masses. Stalinist Culture, Social Revolution, and Soviet Newspapers,* Cambridge–London 2004, p. 66.

373 J. Stalin, "A Year of Great Change. On the Occasion of the Twelfth Anniversary of the October Revolution", *Pravda*, November 7, 1929, https://www.marxists.org/reference/archive/stalin/works/1929/11/03.htm

374 Examples taken from P. R. Gregory, *Political Economy…*, pp. 118–120.

375 S. Fitzpatrick, *Stalin's Revolution*, Oxford 2008, p. 131.

contradiction with the need to delegate tasks to lower levels of the hierarchy. When attempts were made to do so – inconsistently and timidly – the clerks at the lower level were afraid to make decisions, and therefore sent them back to their superiors. In January 1930, the whole Central Committee apparatus amounted to barely 375 people, Gosplan – only 900, counting clerks and cleaning women. The Energetics Department at Gosplan, one of the most important departments, then had 30 essential workers. In the 1930s the Politburo was making from 2300 to 3500 decisions a year, but this was turning out to be too few to run a huge country. Stalin – aside form his obsession with controlling everyone and everything and his tendency to micromanage policy – realized that such a system could not be maintained for long. In 1932 he proposed limiting the list of matters dealt with by the Politburo to 15 per meeting. This rule was quickly broken: in the mid-1930s the agenda for some meetings encompassed over 100 points.[376]

The dictator's letters to his closest colleagues allow us a glimpse of his daily work style. He took most of his decisions during meetings with a small group of associates; these were not recorded in shorthand. There were no drastic differences between what he said publicly and privately. Stalin appears truly to have believed that he was surrounded by enemies, saboteurs and troublemakers, and that the system's (and its rulers') survival depended on the development of industry at any cost. He had a good memory for crucial economic data – the size of the investment budget, the current state of the largest projects, production figures for grain and steel, transport capacity. Stalin often evaluated the effectiveness of economic plans based on intuition, and when he took a decision, it was difficult afterwards to dissuade him from it (and few had the courage to attempt to do so).[377] Regional Party leaders had some influence over decisions about where to build a factory or power station, but not as much as under Stalin's successors, whose position was weaker and who had to exert more effort to gain support for the Party apparatus.

In economic affairs – according to economic historian Paul R. Gregory – Stalin was "well informed and consistent. He had well-defined goals, he gathered his facts carefully, and he listened to advice and sometimes changed his mind as a consequence of such advice."[378] Rationality went hand-in-hand with an obsession with threats that bordered on paranoia. These two dimensions of his personality are illustrated nicely in a letter to Molotov (written on or around 6 August 1929):

---

376 P. R. Gregory, *Political Economy…*, pp. 127–129.

377 E. Belova, P. R., Gregory, "Dictator, Loyal, and Opportunistic Agents. The Soviet Archives on Creating the Soviet Economic System", *Public Choice*, 2002, p. 113.

378 P. R. Gregory, *Political Economy…*, p. 14.

> 1. Transfer Comrade Mirzoian to the Trade Union International. 2. Purge the finance ministry and state bank of wreckers despite the wails of dubious communists and definitely shoot two or three dozen wreckers from these *apparaty*, including several dozen common cashiers. 3. Kondratieff, Groman and a few other scoundrels must definitely be shot. 4. A whole group of wreckers in the meat industry must definitely be shot. 5. It is a mistake to issue nickel coins now. 6. It is a mistake to import shoes from England. 7. It is good that the United States has allowed the importation of our timber. 8. How are things with German credits? 9. Force grain exports; credits will come. 10. Pay attention to the Stalingrad and Leningrad tractor factories. Things are bad there.[379]

Stalin's obsessions frequently conflicted with rational economic calculation – and they usually won. Coercion and control, ubiquitous in the system the dictator built around himself, were unbelievably costly, in part because they affected educated specialists whom the economy needed.[380] Millions of people whose qualifications would have been useful to the Soviet economy were murdered in the purges and exiled to work camps (between August 1937 and November 1938 alone, at the height of the Great Terror, 700,000 people were shot).[381] The response to the crisis in the Soviet economy and decrease in the rate of growth was more repressions.[382] The number of security guards and Chekists, who were very costly to employ, continued to grow in number. In 1939, among the masses of citizens working in the USSR, officially estimated at 78.8 million people, there were as many as 2.1 million security guards keeping watch over factories, offices, railway stations and bridges: this was four times the number of miners, and more than twice the number of railwaymen (and these figures do not include those working in the ranks of the NKVD).[383] The response to accidents at work or failure to adhere to a plan typically consisted of accusations of espionage and sabotage. When in the late 1930s, the Soviet railways, due to underinvestment and overuse, were besieged with accidents and breakdowns, which occurred on average every five minutes, Lazar Kaganovich, Stalin's faithful subordinate and

---

379 Ibid.

380 R. T. Manning, "The Soviet Economic Crisis of 1936–1940 and the Great Purges", [in:] *Stalinist Terror. New Perspectives*, eds. J. A. Getty, R. T. Manning, Cambridge 1993, p. 116 ff.

381 O. Khlevniuk, "The Economy of the OGPU, NKVD, and MVD of the USSR, 1930–1953", [in:] *The Economics of Forced Labor. The Soviet Gulag*, eds. P. R. Gregory, V. Lazarev, Stanford 2003, p. 49.

382 M. Harrison, *Soviet Planning in Peace and War, 1938–1945*, Cambridge 2002, pp. 5–34.

383 R. Conquest, *The Great Terror. A Reassessment*, Edmonton 1990, 275; see also J. Arch Getty, *Origins of the Great Purges. The Soviet Communist Party Reconsidered, 1933–1938*, Cambridge 1985.

colleague, announced that he had uncovered a "Trotskyite-Japanese" diversionary network in the transport industry. He thus gave the signal for a purge of the railways to begin. It began at the top, with the People's Transport Commissariat: in August 1937, ten high-ranking officials were arrested, accused of sabotage, and shot. Next, regional railway chiefs were advised to track down saboteurs: on a single line in southern Russia, 1700 out of 45,000 railwaymen were arrested – so many that temporary prisons were organized at railway stations.[384] If a director failed to unmask sabotage, it usually meant that he himself would be found guilty of sabotage and end up in a camp, if not shot, and his family would also likely meet with repressions.

In such an atmosphere of espionage mania and an obsession with "wreckers" and sabotage, Communist managers protected themselves the only way they knew how. The numbers imposed on them by planners were usually unrealistic, but admitting failure meant immediate arrest. By necessity, they played a kind of game with the planners: they would lower production capacity, conceal reserves, and falsify statistics in order to fulfil the plan. When the chasm between the official figures and reality became too great, the factory leadership would end up in work camps. But their successors had to do the exact same thing. The system allowed them no choice.

The placement of millions of people in work camps also did not make economic sense, and not only because their skills would have been more beneficial elsewhere. In 1940 there were two million prisoners in the Gulag system. In 1950, despite the very high death rate during the war (when food rations were cut drastically) there were 2.5 million. That meant that every twentieth Soviet worker was a prisoner.[385] Towards the end of the 1930s, the Gulag was the largest construction enterprise in the USSR; the prisoners also cut down trees for export and excavated gold, which provided an important source of hard currency for Soviet industry. Stalin judged that unpaid prisoner labour, and the apparent ease with which they could be moved from place to place, made it possible to cheaply carry out large-scale construction projects – gigantic canals and railway lines built in the heart of the Russian wilderness. In practice, the situation was different, a fact of which the NKVD was particularly well aware: prisoners worked considerably less efficiently than free labourers, the camps regularly failed to fulfil production norms, and maintaining them cost a fortune (only the terrifying gold mines in

384 R. Conquest, *The Great Terror…*, pp. 276–277.

385 P. R. Gregory, "An Introduction to the Economics of the Gulag", [in:] *The Economics of Forced Labor…*, p. 19.

Magdan turned a profit).[386] Stalin clearly overestimated the economic efficiency of forced labour. Starting from the end of the Great Terror, the administrative leadership experimented with a system of material incentives, including, among other things, paying prisoners, which was supposed to motivate them to work harder. From 1949 onward, the deputy to Beria, head of the Ministry of Internal Affairs – the newly-renamed postwar incarnation of the NKVD – three times proposed a radical revision of the system in extensive reports: freeing 75 percent of the prisoners and replacing work camps with a system of forced deportation. He received a hearing a few weeks after Stalin's death.[387] (In an ironic twist of fate, the author of this proposal did not benefit from its mercies: as a collaborator of Beria's, he was sentenced to 15 years in a camp after his boss's downfall and execution. He served out his entire sentence.) Contrary to what seems intuitively obvious, the security apparatus did not have an interest in building up a system of work camps; on the contrary, it was particularly conscious of the system's inefficiency and strove for its liquidation, primarily out of economic motives, as documents reveal.

The problem of motivation beleaguered the economy beyond the Gulag as well. Towards the end of the first Five-Year Plan, employment in industry was rising, but work efficiency was falling – poor living conditions, hunger, queues and a high turn-over among workers had their price. If wages were not sufficient to ensure survival, people would sooner or later rebel; Stalin was aware of this fact. Documents from the 1930s show that he devoted a significant amount of time to providing workers with necessities, sometimes publishing precise directives as to what quantity of goods to send to a particular city or region. In the first quarter of 1930 alone, 92 strikes were recorded, and the efficiency of industrial work fell by 10 percent compared to the previous year.[388] In reality, the Politburo was trying to carry out a very meticulous and difficult operation in the realm of social engineering – establishing a level of wages high enough for workers to survive on, so the state would not be threatened with widespread revolt, but that would simultaneously force them to their work more efficiently.

Stalin also involved himself with the system for motivating people to work. In 1931, in a speech to "economic activists," widely publicized by the propaganda service, he severely condemned the idea of an *uravnilovka* or levelling of wages, deeming it a harmful leftist fantasy. Instability in the work force, negligence, the

---

386 M. Parrish, *The Lesser Terror. Soviet State Security, 1939–1953,* Westport–London 1996, p. 46.

387 A. Tikhonov, "The End of the Gulag", [in:] *The Economics of Forced Labor…*, p. 73.

388 P. R. Gregory, *Political Economy…*, pp. 94–95.

low quality of products – the reason for all of these things, he claimed, lay in the need "to organise wages properly":

> The cause is the wrong structure of wages, the wrong wage scales, the "Leftist" practice of wage equalisation. In a number of factories wage scales are drawn up in such a way as to practically wipe out the difference between skilled and unskilled labour, between heavy and light work. The consequence of wage equalisation is that the unskilled worker lacks the incentive to become a skilled worker and is thus deprived of the prospect of advancement; as a result he feels himself a "visitor" in the factory, working only temporarily so as to "earn a little money" and then go off to "try his luck" in some other place.[389]

Equality of wages, Stalin taught, had nothing to do with Marxism-Leninism: "whoever draws up wage scales on the 'principle' of wage equalisation [...] breaks with Marxism, breaks with Leninism."[390] Wages would become equalized when communism arrived, in the distant future. A demanding system of norms and piece work pay rates quickly began to be introduced that provided incentive for competition between workers and overfulfilment of plans.

Psychological incentives were soon added to material ones. From the early 1930s "shock brigades" were organized and workers exhorted to intensify their efforts, but the real propaganda campaign was yet to come. Its kicked off by the achievement of miner Aleksei Stakhanov, who during his night shift from 30–31 August 1935 managed to excavate 102 tonnes of coal, amounting to 1400 percent of his norm.

There is no doubt today that Stakhanov had been chosen by Party bosses and his record achievement preceded by careful preparations, assuring him assistance and comfortable work conditions on which he could not have counted under normal circumstances. His success was publicized by *Pravda*, which had been entrusted a few weeks earlier with discovering "New Soviet Men" by the commissar for heavy industry himself, Sergo Ordzhonikidze ("In capitalist countries, nothing can compare with the popularity of gangsters like Al Capone," he was quoted as having told journalists. "In our country, under socialism, heroes of work [...] must become the most famous.")[391] Ordzhonikidze probably saw some small piece on Stakhanov's success in a trade paper and called the offices

389 J. Stalin, *New Conditions–New Tasks in Economic Construction. Speech Delivered at a Conference of Business Executives. June 23, 1931.* https://www.marxists.org/reference/archive/stalin/works/1931/06/23.htm

390 Ibid.

391 L. Siegelbaum, *Stakhanovism and the Politics of Productivity in the USSR, 1935–1941*, Cambridge 1990, p. 73.; see also D. Filtzer, *Soviet Workers and Stalinist Industrialization. The Formation of Modern Soviet Production Relations, 1928–1941*, London 1986.

of *Pravda* to point them toward this potential hero. On 8 September 1935, *Pravda* began issuing calls for a massive work competition under the slogan "From Competition of Individuals to Mass Competition". Two days later it used the expression "Stakhanovite movement" for the first time.[392]

It is difficult to find persuasive proof that the Stakhanovite movement actually raised the level of labour efficiency or work discipline. It certainly aroused opposition from among workers, which was carefully kept secret.[393] It was useful to the authorities for many reasons, among others because it allowed them to exert additional pressure on the middle management (to which Stakhanovites were often promoted) and induced workers to learn new production techniques (which brought measurable improvements). It also motivated people financially: on his record-setting night, Stakhanov earned 200 rubles instead of the 23–30 he received on an average shift. He was then awarded an apartment and a prize.[394] On the other hand, it stood in contradiction to the ideals of collective effort (and collectively accomplished innovation) proclaimed by the system. Stakhanovites often caused disruption in the work of their colleagues, as the work of an entire department would be reorganized in such a way as to assure the best possible conditions for beating successive records. These leading workers were also unpopular because their successes made the authorities raise the norms for everyone. Since the late 1930s, the authorities had begun to use more traditional methods for increasing efficiency and maintaining work discipline; for example, miners were offered a five-year contract with high premiums for uninterrupted work to keep them from switching to neighbouring mines.[395] At the same time, the state's drastic punishments were aggravated – one could be sent to a work camp for a quarter of an hour's tardiness. The difficulty of motivating workers towards more efficient work represented one of many defects in the system that time would reveal to be ineradicable.

4. Stalin, rational modernizer?

The answer to the question of how rational the system built by Stalin was is both commonplace and far from obvious. It is a commonplace to speak of how criminal and inefficient it was, how badly it wasted the time and effort of Soviet

---

392 Ibid.

393 S. Davies, *Popular Opinion in Stalin's Russia*, Cambridge 1997, p. 32.

394 L. Siegelbaum, *Stakhanovism…*, p. 70; see also L. Siegelbaum, A. Sokolov, *Stalinism as a Way of Life*, New Haven–London 2000, 161 ff.

395 L. Siegelbaum, *Stakhanovism…*, pp. 292, 302.

citizens, and how gray and miserable it made their everyday lives. To the extent that we accept the criteria for rationality, based on its classical dictionary definition, to include the expediency of the means adapted toward a desired end, the answer becomes more complicated. Stalin wanted to make the Soviet Union an industrial and military power in the lifetime of one generation and to protect its system from external intervention. There is no doubt that he achieved both of these aims.[396] It would be naive to think that this dictator, who personally approved long lists of persons condemned to death during the Great Terror, was not aware of the price demanded by that success. In this sense, his choices can be considered rational – although, obviously, marked by the stain of his pathological personality, which allowed him to overlook the cost in human life while making his calculations.

In the 1990s, two contemporary adherents of the classical school of political economy, Mancur Olson and Ronald Wintrobe, described the system of the dictatorship within the categories of rational choices made by individual actors in public life. Each makes a rational decision in the sense that he looks after his own security and strives to gain maximal advantage (power, prestige, material goods), simultaneously lowering costs (for example, taking care to reduce the scope of external control, to keep down the payments made to bosses in the hierarchy, and so on). From this perspective, immoral behaviour (that is, publicly condemned behaviour, often in conflict with the interest of the political community as a whole) can be – and often is – very rational from the point of view of individual or group interests. For example, a director of a Soviet factory in the 1980s behaved rationally by lobbying for a reduction in the plan in the capital city, concealing his production capabilities and reserves from inspection (in order to receive an award every year for exceeding the plan), and buying the good favour of his colleagues in the power apparatus with a variety of goods (to which he, as a director, had access). At the same time – and using precisely these same incentives – he could alternately bribe and intimidate workers in his factory who rebelled against their low wages and long work hours and his authoritarian management style.

A tyrant who feels insecure in power only looks after his short-term gain, since his long-term perspective for wielding power is doubtful. From his perspective, therefore, confiscations, very high taxes or ordinary plunder begin to pay off even if they hurt the long-term interest of the community; he thus behaves like a "roving bandit" who robs the people over whom he temporarily holds power

396 A. Nove, *Stalinism and After. The Road to Gorbachev*, London–New York 1992, p. 67.

by every possible means at his disposal, as he is indifferent to their fate. The "stationary bandit" – a hereditary monarch or a dictator firmly in control of the reins of government – has an interest in the largest possible gains from a long-term perspective: he therefore restrains his tendencies toward quick plunder.[397]

Olson postulated that a dictator's interest demands he "extract" the largest possible amount of resources from his subjects. He wrote that Stalin was no different in this sense from the rulers who built the Egyptian pyramids or Versailles.[398] Though a comparison (even an implicit one) with cattle is of course insulting to the citizens of the USSR, there is no lack of historians who find Olson's metaphor to make sense.[399] Those were precisely the intensions of "Team Stalin" – to extract the largest possible surplus from the Soviet economy and to concentrate it in their own hands, allocating it on military expansion and spectacular construction projects. Stalin differed from Rameses XIV in that he had more effective tools at his disposal: Communist ideology and the new totalitarian technique for managing the economy. The selective modernization of the country coincided with his own interests, but only in part: Stalin's interests included Magnitogorsk and the atom bomb, but not refrigerators or plumbing in every citizen's flat (those would only weigh down the budget).[400]

From the perspective of the criteria he adapted, he was successful; it also seems fairly plausible – although this remains open to question – that Stalinism may have brought social advancement to millions of people who had no such chance before the revolution. He moved them to the cities and gave them an education, though they were forced to live in poverty and cramped quarters, and their schools were of low quality.[401] The flaws in the system of the Soviet economy – permanent trouble with quality standards, a low level of innovation, waste, the planners' disconnect from reality – were already clearly visible during Stalin's rule. Repression and terror allowed for short-term mobilization: this potential had to be exploited. When Stalin died, the USSR found itself plunged

---

397 M. Olson, "Dictatorship, Democracy and Development", *American Political Science Review*, 1994, 3. I use Olson's terms "stationary bandit" and "roving bandit".

398 Ibid.

399 See, e.g. E. Belova, P. R. Gregory, "Dictator, Loyal, and Opportunistic Agents. The Soviet Archives on Creating the Soviet Economic System", *Public Choice*, 2002, p. 113.

400 M. Harrison, *Communism and Economic Modernization,* Centre for Competitive Advantage in the Global Economy, University of Warwick, working paper no. 92, 2012.

401 S. Fitzpatrick, *Education and Social Mobility in the Soviet Union*, Cambridge 2002, p. 239 ff.

into a profound crisis.[402] The Party leadership realized that a change of course was necessary.

The death of Stalin brought a paradigm shift in the exercise of power. When his colleagues took power, they became both representatives and hostages of the bureaucracy Stalin had created. The "new class" (to use Milovan Djilas' term) was above all interested in the security and financial benefits associated with power. The system lost its dynamism – irreversibly, as it turned out.[403]

Soviet leaders were perfectly aware of this fact; as a contemporary specialist in Soviet history writes, nobody was more critical of the bureaucracy than they were.[404]

In spite of everything, average Russians lived better than they had in Stalin's time. The second half of the 1950s was the golden age of the Soviet economy: it grew considerably faster than the American economy and at a pace comparable to those of Japan and Germany, while a somewhat stabilized investment policy brought goods back into stores. Every Soviet citizen was employed – the Party knew that this provided the foundation for internal stability. It also promised a rising standard of living: radios, televisions, washing machines and refrigerators began appearing in homes. In the late 1950s Khrushchev could truly believe that the Soviet Union, developing at its current pace, would surpass not only the GDP but also the consumption level of the United States (in a few decades, admittedly, but then permanently). Many Western analysts believed so, as well. According to CIA estimates from 1999, the Soviet Union came closest to achieving this aim in the year 1970: its GDP at that time amounted to 57 percent of America's.[405]

American intelligence was shocked by the pronounced decrease in the pace of economic growth in the USSR after 1975: in the later years of Brezhnev's rule the Soviet GDP practically stood in place.[406] Although the plan for the years 1976–1980 assumed the lowest rate of growth of any Five-Year Plan (4.1–5.1 percent

402 See especially *Late Stalinist Russia. Society Between Reconstruction and Reinvention*, ed. J. Fürst, London–New York 2006.

403 A. Ogushi, *The Demise of the Soviet Communist Party*, London–New York 2005, p. 10.

404 S. Fitzpatrick, *Everyday Stalinism. Ordinary Life in Extraordinary Times. Soviet Russia in the 1930s*, Oxford 2000, p. 28.

405 S. Morewood, "The Demise of the Command Economies in the Soviet Union and Its Outer Empire", [in:] *Economic Disasters of the Twentieth Century*, eds. M. J. Olivier, D. H. Aldcroft, Cheltenham–Northampton 2007, p. 275.

406 M. Harrison, "Economic Growth and Slowdown", [in:] *Brezhnev Reconsidered*, ed. E. Bacon, M. Sandle, Houndmills–New York 2002, 38 ff.

annually), even that was just wishful thinking.[407] From the mid-1970s onward, the USSR's imperial ambitions were financed through profits from oil, whose prices on world markets rose fourfold after the energy crisis of 1973. American intelligence only took official note of the economic stagnation in the USSR in the year 1977.[408]

In a speech given on 11 June 1971, Brezhnev admitted publicly that "without major defense expenditure we should have moved our economy forward faster": in real terms arms spending was growing more rapidly than the GDP. A CIA report in May 1976 estimated that Soviet defence spending had risen from 40–50 billion rubles in 1970 to 55–60 billion in 1975 (at 1970 prices).[409] This meant it had expanded from 8 percent to 11–13 percent of the GDP. When Gorbachev took power, defense spending was probably more than 15 percent of the GDP.

Every year the USSR spent about 2 percent of its GDP on aid to Soviet bloc countries, including Cuba. Since the first loan extended by Khrushchev to the Hungarians after the 1956 uprising and designated for the stabilization of the economy, the USSR's client states had become an ever greater burden on its budget (2 percent of GDP was a more than twice the level of development aid provided by the most generous capitalist countries to the poorest ones).[410] These expenses had a negative effect on the level of investment, and thus on economic growth.

The system's biggest Achilles' heel, however, remained the way sectors of the economy were structured within the Soviet bureaucracy inherited from Stalin's times.[411] In 1989 there were 36.4 million people working in Soviet industry, and their number grew each year. At the same time, the United States had been reducing the number of industrial workers since the 1970s (to 18.4 million in 1989), while production continued to rise. Although the world had changed, the power relations within the Politburo promoted the preservation of the Stalinist investment structure; the method that had assured Stalin's strategic success had become a burden on his successors. The USSR imported a significant part of its modern technology, purchasing it or stealing it from the West: economic success began increasingly to depend on the country's ability to compete in a race for

407 V. Mau, I. Starodubovskaya, *The Challenge of Revolution. Contemporary Russia in Historical Perspective,* Oxford 2003, p. 230.

408 *CIA's Analysis of the Soviet Union, 1947–1991,* ed. G. K. Haines, R. E. Leggett, Washington 2001, p. 173.

409 S. Morewood, "The Demise of the Command Economies..., op. cit., p. 277.

410 Ibid., p. 278.

411 P. Gregory, *Restructuring the Soviet Economic Bureaucracy*, New York 1990, p. 123.

advanced technology, for which – despite having educated the masses – it was ill-prepared to win.[412]

A second fundamental and irremovable weakness in the system was the poor flow of information. In a dictatorship everyone lies, and the greater the dictator's power, the more he is surrounded by lying. In his classic book on dictatorships, Ronald Wintrobe describes the problem thus:

> The more threatened they are by the ruler, the more the subjects will be afraid to speak ill of or to do anything which might conceivably displease him or her. Therefore, it would seem, the less the dictator knows what they are really thinking, and the more reason for him or her to be insecure! Hence the paradox: The greater the dictator's power, the more reason he or she has to be afraid. Finally, and most important, the problem is two-sided. The dictator's dilemma could equally be called the subject's dilemma: As much as dictators want to be loved, the subjects want them to believe that they are loved, for only then are the people safe from them. If they can make their dictator believe that they truly worship (or even that they support) him or her, then he or she need not fear them; and if in turn the ruler does not fear them, they need not fear him or her.[413]

Low-level officials protected themselves against pressure from the "centre" by creating what Winrobe calls "horizontal trust networks" (what were called "cliques" in the language of Communist Party members). They cooperated with one another not only in order to safely take advantage of the privileges associated with power – homes and apartments, cars, and other goods provided to public servants – but also in order to protect themselves from the centre's planning control. In short, they made a pact to deceive the dictator together (if we treat the post-Stalinist Politburo as a collective dictator). That weakened the system and reduced its effectiveness.

---

412 During the times of the USSR, economists and Sovietologists offered extremely diverse interpretations of the slowing of economic growth that began in the second half of the 1960s. Among the reasons proposed were capital-absorptiveness and the low efficiency of work in the Soviet economy (see e.g. M. L. Weitzman, "Soviet Postwar Growth and Capital-labor Substitution", *American Economic Review* 1970, no. 4); difficulties in managing an increasingly complicated economy (see G. Schroeder, "The Slowdown in Soviet Industry, 1976–1982", *Soviet Economy* 1985, no. 1); lifelong guarantees of employment, which lowered the motivation to work (D. Granick, *Job Rights in the Soviet Union. Their consequences*, Cambridge 1987); lack of rewards for innovation (J. S. Berliner, *The Innovation Decision in Soviet Industry*, Cambridge 1976). The role of problems with the flow and coordination of information is underscored by P. Rutland, *The Politics of Economic Stagnation in the Soviet Union*, Cambridge 1993.

413 R. Wintrobe, *The Political Economy of Dictatorship*, Cambridge 2000, p. 22.

These inner systems often originated, paradoxically, in plans imposed from above that could not be carried out by legal means. During the first Five-Year Plans (and later on) there was an enormous black market in the USSR, not only for consumer goods but also for unofficial trade (mainly in the form of exchange) between enterprises. In 1933, in Stalingrad as many as 40 percent of registered cars disappeared – according to official data, they "were not repairable." In practice, as a commission appointed by the Party discovered, organizations that did not officially have the right to be issued a car would buy it on the black market or build one from replaceable parts they were able to somehow "organize" by unscrupulous means.[414] In diaries from the 1930s, there are many descriptions of unofficial "trade representatives" from Soviet enterprises – people whose (state) companies sent them out with suitcases full of rubles to obtain parts or raw materials essential to production that were not available through official channels. The connections thus formed turned into close and permanent collaborative relationships, which weakened the authority of the Politburo and pushed an ever greater portion of the USSR's economy into the gray market. One diarist, head of the planning department at a large Russian sawmill in the 1930s, described how this system arose:

> Once I dropped in on Neposedov and found an unfamiliar, impressive looking man in a leather coat in his office. Neposedov was enjoying himself: "Well, what do you propose? A tank? Or machine guns? Those we do not need; we are peaceful people. Cannons we don't need either. Or maybe we could organize an army in the factory?" Laughing, Neposedov turned to me. The man in the leather coat was the representative of a large munitions plant near Moscow. They had a shortfall in lumber and needed several train-car loads in order to complete an important construction job. They had sent dozens of couriers to various factories. Perhaps one of them would get lucky. "Why a tank or bullets?" retorted leather-coat. "We can give you makhorka [cheap tobacco], manufactured items. We have them." This representative concluded an agreement to the effect that we would give them two or three carloads of lumber in return for several crates of makhorka, a cask of vegetable oil for the dining room, and other products. Our deal with the munitions plant was quite providential. Another factory, which made parachutes, balloons, and dirigibles for the military, gave us several hundred yards of percale – a silky, thin, and surprisingly durable fabric used in balloon making – in exchange for lumber. The bolt was so wide that you could get a whole man's shirt out of little more than a yard of fabric. Everyone in the factory was supplied with percale shirts and blouses.[415]

One could be sent to the camps for such transactions, but circumstances made them an unavoidable necessity. After Stalin's death, however, they could be

---

414 P. R. Gregory, *Political Economy...*, p. 147.

415 G. Khomiakov-Andreev, *Bitter Waters. Life and Work in Stalin's Russia*, Boulder 1997, pp. 74–75.

conducted for profit (no longer by necessity), and relatively safely.[416] Stalin maintained competition within the bureaucracy by means of purges that shook the system and broke up informal communication networks within elite circles. He smashed their mutual solidarity in an unspeakably brutal fashion – with shots in the back of the head. When that method ceased to be applied, the system began to ossify, until it became the fossil of the final Brezhnev years.

Historians of Stalinism often write that Stalin destroyed the Party, that it ceased to exist as an independent ideological movement, becoming not only the Party of Stalin, but his podium and footstool, as well.[417] If Wintrobe is correct, that means that the Party's failure – the destruction of true, disinterested Communism and its replacement with Stalinist doctrine – was a condition for the USSR's successful leap to modernity: if Stalin had not destroyed the Party, the system would have changed sooner into a lethargic oligarchy.

In an essay written in 1997, economist Paul Krugman put forward a somewhat less cynical explanation for the collapse of the Soviet system:

> Were the supposed productive triumphs of the Soviet Union under Stalin merely a hoax? Tell that to the soldiers of Germany's Army Group Center – the few who survived. The fact is that Stalin did transform Russia into a massive industrial power – a power tested in the most unambiguous way imaginable. And his successors did achieve real technological triumphs – not just showy triumphs like sending cosmonauts into orbit, but the creation of a highly sophisticated scientific and engineering establishment. True, Russia was never any good at producing high-quality consumer goods. But it was not always the bumbling, incompetent system we now imagine.[418]

Krugman (like many historians) finds that the decline and collapse of the system resulted primarily from the fact that the ideology at the source of its dynamism had withered. Like any great enterprise, the Soviet state was organized, according to Krugman, on the model of a great industrial syndicate; what the USSR needed to continue its existence was a purpose. That purpose was provided by its ideology. When people stopped believing in its ideology, the system fell apart. He argues that "the basic problem was not technical, but moral," continuing:

---

416 S. Alasheev, "Informal Relations in the Soviet System of Production", [in:] *Management and Industry in Russia, Formal and Informal Relations in the Period of Transition*, eds. S. Clarke, Edward Elgar, Aldershot–Brookfield 1995, p. 28 ff.

417 See, e.g. J. Arch Getty, O. V. Naumov, *The Road to Terror. Stalin and the Self-Destruction of the Bolsheviks, 1932–1939,* New Haven–London 1999.

418 P. Krugman, "Capitalism's Mysterious Triumph" (1997); http://web.mit.edu/krugman/www/.

> A market system, of course, works whether people believe in it or not. You may dislike capitalism, even feel that as a system it will eventually fail, yet do your job well because your family needs the money you earn. Capitalism can run, even flourish, in a society of selfish cynics. But a non-market economy cannot. The personal incentives for workers to do their jobs well, for managers to make good decisions, are simply too weak. In the later years of the Soviet Union, workers knew that they would be paid regardless of how hard they tried; managers knew that promotions would depend more on political connections than on performance; and nobody was offered rewards large enough to justify taking unpopular positions or any sort of serious risk.[419]

Capitalism, Krugman concludes, won because egoism and cynicism are written into its system.

In the 1950s and 1960s, that victory nonetheless looked very distant. Third World countries were creating planning commissions and dreamed of building up heavy industry, since it was widely thought that the USSR had triumphed. From the perspective of the 1990s, it is very easy to forget that Western experts long believed in the Soviet system's competence and its economic results. People knew, of course, that the standard of living in the USSR and Eastern bloc countries was lower than in the West, that goods were often lacking in shops (or, if available, were poorly designed and produced). That, however, did not overcome their belief in the basic effectiveness of the system. In the fifth edition of a popular American university economics textbook from 1961, Nobel laureate Paul Samuelson published a chart demonstrating that GDP in the USSR was significantly higher than in the USA (the same author suggested that the gap between the two countries would remain permanently).[420] As late as 1989, just before the collapse of the system, Samuelson wrote that "the Soviet economy is proof that, contrary to what many sceptics had earlier believed, a socialist economy can function and even thrive."[421] In 1987 another respected and at that time widely quoted specialist, Gur Ofer, estimated the average rate of growth in the Soviet economy in the years 1928–1985 at 4.2 percent annually – "among the best for such an extended period."[422]

---

419 Ibid.

420 D. M. Levy, S. J. Peart, "Soviet Growth & American Textbooks", SSRN research paper, 3 December 2009, http://ssrn.com/abstract=1517983

421 Quoted in M. Skousen, *The Making of Modern Economics. the Lives and Ideas of the Great Thinkers,* Armonk 2015, p. 424.

422 R. Wintrobe, *The Political Economy of Dictatorship*…, p. 199.

We could easily find dozens more such quotations. In the USSR itself, opposing economic views were practically non-existent until the very end.[423]

Given that celebrated experts shared these views, it is easy to understand how they were embraced by the political leaders of poor, newly-independent countries, who dreamed of creating modern, powerful states, of catching up with and surpassing the West. The Soviet Union showed them a path they could take, even if they were not Communists and rejected elements of the system.

423 P. Sutela, "Soviet Economics after Stalin. Between Orthodoxy and Reform", [in:] *Economics in Russia. Studies in Intellectual History*, eds. V. Barnett, J. Zweynert, Aldershot–Burlington 2008, p. 162.

So many deeds cry out to be done,
And always urgently;
The world rolls on,
Time presses.
Ten thousand years are too long,
Seize the day, seize the hour!
The Four Seas are rising, clouds and waters raging,
The Five Continents are rocking, wind and thunder roaring.
Our force is irresistible,
Away with all pests!
Mao, 1950[424]

"Greater, Faster, Better, More Economical."
One of the most popular slogans from the time of the Great Leap Forward[425]

Chapter 4. The Four Seas are rising

1. Somebody told Mao

In the 1980s, economist Colin Clark, a pioneer in the theory of development in underdeveloped countries, recalled that:

> Somebody had told Mao [...] that about one-third of China's agricultural labor force was redundant and should be transferred to other employment. This was in fact attempted in the Year of the Great Leap Forward, 1958, when Mao apparently believed (at any rate for a time) what had been told him about the harvest having been doubled in a single year. The result was what now has been admitted to have been a disastrous famine.[426]

Clark added that one needed only to make "reference to the already abundant information" on the Chinese economy in order to learn the truth: there was simply a shortage of hands available for work. "After all, to put it simply, if you are going to cultivate a country the size of China with hand hoes – very few draft

424 Mao Tse-Tung, *Reply to Comrade Kuo Mo-Jo,* in *Poems,* Open Source Socialist Publishing 2008, p. 41

425 Quoted in J. Shapiro, *Mao's War Against Nature. Politics and the Environment in Revolutionary China*, Cambridge-New York 2001, p. 66.

426 C. Clark, "Development Economics. The Early Years", [in:] *The Pioneers of Development*, op. cit., pp. 64–65.

animals and still fewer tractors were available – you are going to need the labor of something like 600 million people."[427]

Mao's recipe for backwardness had, generally speaking, much in common with the idea for how to make the leap into modernization, a prevalent concept at the time. The nationalization of industry and government planning were to allow consumption to be kept under control and the "extraction" from the economy of reserves for investment – ostensibly squandered earlier by rich, parasitical elites. These investments were of course to be made by the state, mainly in heavy and machine industry, and ideally on projects that were grand in scale – in keeping with the conviction that scale guarantees more effective results. Only at some vaguely defined but not too distant point in the future, after the country's productive energies had been more fully developed, would the moment come to invest in raising the standard of living, that is, in residential construction and light industry.

As in the case of the USSR, Mao's primary strategy was based to a considerable extent on the export of agricultural products, and later basic industrial products at low prices (the state needed hard currency for the import of machines and unavailable raw materials). The plan promised success – socialism and comfortable living – at the price of one or two generations' blood, sweat and tears. In the 1950s, this sounded more realistic than today: at the time, it was possible to think that a similar strategy was working wonderfully in the USSR, which was then enjoying the best period, economically speaking, in its short history (in the late 1950s various consumer goods began to appear in the homes of ordinary citizens; Stalinist asceticism quickly faded into the past). From the point of view of the Communist Party's collective interest, this economic ideology also had the important benefit of providing added justification (in addition to a purely doctrinal rationale) for the concentration of all mechanisms of power in its hands.

From the perspective of Western economic theory in that era, as well, the ideas being proposed in China did not seem blatantly absurd. After all, the development models that were popular then – those of Nurkse and Lewis – proposed that underdeveloped countries replace capital with labour and control over consumption, as well as with foreign trade. China, a poor country, did not possess capital, and the West would not have lent it – at any rate, not on terms that would have been politically acceptable to both sides at the time. There appeared to be an abundance of free hands available for work. Therefore, China was to reach modernity by the work of its own hands – the way Baron Münchhausen in the famous tale pulled himself out of the swamp by the pigtail of his wig.

---

427 Ibid., p. 65.

Mao's economic thinking thus fits into the broader current of statist thought of his epoch. As an economic ideologue he was nevertheless exceptional, and not only due to his historically rare level of unscrupulousness and nonchalant disregard for the life of his subjects. He even made his own particular ideological contribution to economic theory: the conviction, carried to its extreme consequences, that every aspect of social life is political, and that politics is a force that can bring about a radical transformation of society – even in the most unfavourable material conditions. When material incentives to work were liquidated during the Cultural Revolution, this was an expression of precisely this conviction: that, in fact, ideology determines everything, the superstructure determines the base. Classical Marxist relations between political and economic structures were reversed in his thought.

In 1949 Mao became absolute ruler of an enormous and ancient country, but one that was incredibly poor and weak economically and militarily. In 1937, before the war with Japan, the railways in China covered a length of some 20,000 kilometres, approximately the same distance as in the Second Polish Republic, which was 1/30 its size (furthermore, Poland was then by European standards a poor country with an underdeveloped infrastructure). China also had 30,000 km of paved roads – less than half of that in Poland.[428]

Mao ruled a country that was almost certainly poorer than Russia before Lenin's revolution – the GDP per capita was 2/3 lower in China even in 1949 compared to Russia in 1913. The economic structure of both giants was nonetheless similar: in both countries about 80 percent of the population worked in farming, producing slightly more than half of the GDP. The average life expectancy for a Chinese citizen born in 1930 was under 35 years. Historian and economist Charles Bramall claims that China in the 1950s was not only lagging behind Europe by at least two centuries, but more underdeveloped than Great Britain before the industrial revolution.[429]

2. Five meals a day

On 4 August 1958, Mao visited the region of Xushui in the province of Hebei not far from Beijing. He was in a rapturous mood: reports were coming in from throughout the country about records harvests of cotton, rice and wheat. He

428 Mao Tse-Tung, *Wojna Chin przeciwko Japonii*, Warszawa 1949, p. 105.

429 C. Bramall, *Chinese Economic Development*, London 2008, p. 55.

walked through fields surrounded by journalists and local dignitaries, wondering out loud what to do with the food surplus:[430]

> "How are you going to eat so much grain? What are you going to do with the surplus?"
>
> "We can exchange it for machinery," Zhang responded after a pause for thought.
>
> "But you are not the only one to have a surplus, others too have too much grain! Nobody will want your grain!" Mao shot back with a benevolent smile.
>
> "We can make spirits out of taro," suggested another cadre.
>
> "But every county will make spirits! How many tonnes of spirits do we need?" Mao mused. "With so much grain, in future you should plant less, work half time and spend the rest of your time on culture and leisurely pursuits, open schools and a university, don't you think? … You should eat more. Even five meals a day is fine!"[431]

Soon after the Chairman made these prescriptions, people were not only not eating five meals a day, but were beginning to die of hunger on a massive scale.

The road to this catastrophe was long and complex. The Communists carried out agrarian reform (by today's estimates 5 percent of the rural population classified as "landlords" owned between 37 percent and 44 percent of all arable land).[432] The process was bloody – Mao himself admitted that around 700,000 "counterrevolutionaries" were shot or beaten to death in the years 1950–1952. It also had far-reaching consequences, because families classified as having "'bad class' backrounds" were discriminated against on the basis of their status as late as the 1970s. In spite or perhaps because of that, the reform turned out to be popular. It was also radicalized and accelerated after the outbreak of war in Korea: by other estimates, between 2 and 5 million "landlords" lost their lives during the reform.[433]

In cities – after an initial purge carried out against "spies and counterrevolutionaries," during which a few hundred thousand people were killed – Mao early on demonstrated astonishing restraint (he advised executing only "10 to 20 percent"

430 This chapter was informed by a number of biographies on Chairman Mao, in particular P. Short, *Mao: A Life*, New York 2000; M. Meisner, *Mao Zedong. A Political and Intellectual Portrait*, London 2007.

431 F. Dikötter, *Mao's Great Famine: The History of China's Most Devastating Catastrophe, 1958–62*, London 2010, p. 41.

432 C. Bramall, op. cit., p. 68.

433 L. Feigon, *Mao: A Reinterpretation*, Chicago 2002, p. 96.

of those "deserving capital punishment," and granting the rest a reprieve).[434] The regime also had spectacular successes: in a short and brutal campaign, the Communists eliminated a number of social plagues, including prostitution, gambling and drugs. Poppy cultivation was wiped out, dealers were shot, and drugs publicly burned during great mass propaganda rallies (according to meticulously gathered government statistics, exactly 764,423 such events were organized, with 74,595,181 people attending). By the end of 1952, all addicts, according to official data, had been cured and drug addiction had ceased to exist as a problem.[435]

Hyperinflation, which had plagued the final years of the Kuomintang governments, had disappeared, and the property of foreigners nationalized. The new regime appeared to be resistant to corruption, which positively distinguished it from the previous one. Even beggars had been eliminated from the streets and sent to re-education collectives, and those working in now-closed brothels – to factories, where they would be trained to perform socially useful work. A "patriotic health campaign" was also carried out, in which people were mobilized to clean up cities and dig new latrines.

The 505 km-long railway line from Chongqing to Chengdu, stuck in the planning stages for over 40 years, was finished in two years.[436] What earlier had been unfeasible suddenly turned out to be possible.

Mao's policy toward Chinese business was also relatively liberal at first: today's historians often compare it with Lenin's NEP. The government spoke of a "united national front" in which the working class would lead the bourgeoisie and petty bourgeoisie toward a strong, modern China.

The time for revolutionary acceleration was fast approaching, however. In December 1949, shortly after coming to power, Mao took a Chinese delegation to Moscow. In addition to a not very favourable friendship agreement (with no formal terms concluded for technical assistance and in which the USSR lent China only $300 million – less than was lent to Poland's Bierut), he brought back a

---

434 Mao, "Comment on Suppressing and Liquidating Contrrevolutionaries, 8 May 1951", [in:] *The Writings of Mao Zedong 1949–1976*, eds. M. Kau, J. Leung, M. Sharpe, Armonk-London 1986, p. 190.

435 Z. Yongming, "Nationalism, Identity and State-Building. The Antidrug Crusade in the People's Republic, 1949–1952", [in:] *Opium Regimes. China, Britain and Japan 1839–1952*, eds. T. Brook and B. Tadashi Wakabayashi, Berkeley-Los Angeles-London 2000, p. 392.

436 J. Gittings, *The Changing Face of China. From Mao to Market*, Oxford 2006, p. 23.

model of socialist industrialization.[437] It was more an idea than a precise prescription. Among the several hundred books hastily translated at that time from Russian, few were devoted to technology and economics: most were works of Marx, Engels and Lenin, and textbooks on dialectical materialism.

Beginning in 1950, Mao created an apparatus for planning and managing industry based on the Soviet model, which the Chinese imitated without being aware of its weaknesses. In the first phase of investment, 700 factories were to be built, 156 of which were to be supplied by the USSR, including 24 power stations, as well as steelworks, refineries and chemical plants. Shortly before the initiation of the first Five-Year Plan in 1953 (in keeping with good socialist tradition, its ultimate shape was finalized two years later, after it had already begun) Mao also began the Five-anti Campaign, intended to purge "bourgeois experts" from industry. Nationalization accelerated and single-person management was introduced in state enterprises together with systems of norms and payment contracts based on Soviet models. This plan envisaged that industrial production would double over five years, and that agricultural production would rise by a quarter. Twenty percent of the GDP was allocated toward investment, while over half of the investment budget was to be earmarked for heavy industry – more than in the first Soviet Five-Year Plan!

The first plan proved to be an impressive success – not only on paper, but in all likelihood, in reality as well.[438] Production was supposed to grow by 14.7 percent yearly; it was almost certainly 3 percent higher than that.[439] As in the case of Stalin, the investment was financed at the expense of rural areas – buying peasants' goods at artificially low prices set by the state. And, like Stalin, Mao had problems with agriculture, to which he sought solutions in collectivization.

After these first experiences, in March 1955, Mao shared with his fellow Chinese the thought that building socialism was going to take some time:

> It is no easy job to build a socialist society in a large country like ours with its complicated conditions and its formerly very backward economy. We may be able to build a socialist society over three five-year plans, but to build a strong, highly industrialized socialist country will require several decades of hard work, say, fifty years, or the entire second half of the present century.[440]

---

437 D. A. Kaple, *Dream of a Red Factory. Legacy of High Stalinism in China*, New York-Oxford 1994, p. 12.

438 GDP rose 8.9 percent annually, industrial production - 18 percent. R. Guo, *How the Chinese Economy Works*, Houndmills-London 2009, p. 213.

439 L. Feigon, I. R. Dee, op. cit., p. 100.

440 Mao Tse-Tung, *Selected Works, vol. 5*, Beijing 1977, p. 155.

Paradoxically, the Chairman was right – 50 years later, China was in fact one of the world's great economic powers. Credit for this achievement, however, was not due to Chairman Mao.

In texts written in late 1955, as noted by historian of Maoism and critical editor of Mao's letters Stuart Schram, foreshadowings of the coming Great Leap Forward and Cultural Revolution are already beginning to appear: among these were "Mao's belief in the omnipotence of the subjective efforts of the mobilized masses to transform themselves and their environment."[441] This was a reversal of classical Marxist thought, which placed emphasis on the material base of production and property relations, while tending to perceive social phenomena as secondary and derivative. For Mao, China's peasant class, not the great industrial proletariat, was to carry out the great transformation. Writing on the successes of farming cooperatives, which through their own efforts in three years had accumulated "a large quantity of the means of production", Mao commented: "In a few decades, why can't 600 million paupers, by their own efforts, create a socialist country, rich and strong?" Elsewhere, in December 1955, he added that "Chinese peasants are even better than English and American workers."[442]

Collectivization accelerated dramatically, and although it took with it – according to very approximate estimates – as many as two million victims, Mao considered it a success. In spite of the high number of deaths, the operation was carried out more efficiently and humanely than its Soviet counterpart: the kulaks were usually not liquidated or resettled, only dispossessed,[443] and farm production did not collapse as it did in the USSR.

This success led Mao to publish his first critical consideration of the Soviet model of socialism. In April 1956 he had this to say on collectivization:

> We have done better than the Soviet Union and a number of Eastern European countries. The prolonged failure of the Soviet Union to reach the highest pre- October Revolution level in grain output, the grave problems arising from the glaring disequilibrium between the development of heavy industry and that of light industry in some Eastern European countries – such problems do not exist in our country [...] The Soviet Union has taken measures which squeeze the peasants very hard [...] The method of capital accumulation has seriously dampened the peasants' enthusiasm for production. You want

441 S. Schram, *The Thought of Mao Tse-Tung*, London 1989, p. 113.

442 Ibid., pp. 112–113.

443 F. C. Teiwes, "The Estabilishment and Consolidation of the New Regime: 1949–1957", [in:] *The Politics of China. The Eras of Mao and Deng*, ed. R. MacFarquhar, Cambridge 1997, p. 59.

the hen to lay more eggs and yet you do not feed it, you want the horse to run fast and yet you don't let it graze. What kind of logic is this?[444]

After the short and abandoned experiment with open public debate during the "Let a hundred flowers bloom" campaign in 1956 – this debate had quickly begun to evolve in a direction that was uncomfortable for Mao and the party, and was therefore shut down – the Chairman, at the Third Plenum of the Chinese Communist Party in 1957, announced the Great Leap Forward.

Putting aside poetic metaphors, the Great Leap Forward consisted of a few simple but radical economic policy prescriptions. The most important of these was an increase in investment to record levels, unseen anywhere else in the world at the time (or afterward in Mao's China). According to later estimates, in 1960 China invested over 31 percent of its GDP.[445] That meant a radical reduction in consumption levels, and thus – in such a poverty-stricken country – the risk of famine.

The second element in the plan was an enormous transfer of the workforce from the production of consumer goods – particularly food – to the production of such goods as steel and iron.

The third element in the Great Leap Forward was a radical restructuring of the institutions where production took place. That meant chiefly the establishment of a new type of trade cooperative – the "people's communes" – in autumn 1958. Collectivization, which had not yet been completed, was to be accelerated. The new communes were considerably larger than the village production cooperatives created earlier: the aim was to take advantage of the positive (it was felt) effect of this larger scale. In the communes, production and consumption were to take place in conjunction. People ate in great cafeterias, and 70 percent of food was allocated at no cost, with 30 percent awarded as a bonus for good work results. This cut the link between the quality of work and subsistence – a member of the collective, at least in theory, could get enough to eat regardless of whether he worked productively or not (motivation was supposed to be other than material). Another aim was to liberate women from domestic duties. Cooking separately for each family appeared to be a manifest waste of time and effort that could be put to more socially beneficial uses. This gigantic social and economic restructuring project included ambitious production goals, which, in addition, were systematically raised.

Enthusiasm for the Great Leap Forward was, if one believes contemporary reports, to a great degree authentically felt. Novelist Zhou Libo described the

444 Quoted in S. Schram, *The Thought…*, op. cit., pp. 149–150.
445 C. Bramall, op. cit., p. 125.

future plans of a communist youth group leader in a village in southern China, who was fascinated by the "Iron Buffalo" – that is, the village's first tractor:

> After the co-operative is established, I'm going to propose that we do away with all the ridges between the fields, and make small plots into large ones. With large fields, the Iron Buffalo [tractor] can go into the water. [...] When we've built a reservoir, all the dry fields in the village will be irrigated, and even after paying tax we shan't be able to eat all the grain we grow. We'll send the surplus grain to help feed the workers in industry. Won't that be wonderful! Then they, all smiles, will come in their jeeps to the countryside, and say to us, "Hello, peasant-brothers, would you like to have electric light here?" "Yes, paraffin lamps are really too inconvenient and wasteful." "Very well, we'll install it. Do you want the telephone?" "Yes, we want that as well"[...] With electric light, telephone, lorries, and tractors, we shall live more comfortably than they do in the city, because we have the beautiful landscape and the fresh air. There'll be flowers all the year round and wild fruit, more than we can eat [...].[446]

Mao's radicalism arose from his belief – apparent in all of his later writings – that any pause on the road to socialism, in the process of reshaping social and economic relations, threatened to move things backward. Agrarian reform had been correct at the previous stage; now there was a threat of capitalist relations returning to the countryside, "as the better-off peasants strove to get richer while the poorer fell into debt." The communes were a revolutionary improvisation: at the beginning of the collectivization campaign in 1955, Mao was not yet thinking in this direction. He also had an economic argument – production results indicated convincingly that small farms were less productive – and an increase in farming productivity was absolutely necessary, due both to the quickly growing population and to the needs of industrialization.

The beginning of the Great Leap was signalled by a water-conservancy and irrigation campaign carried out in the winter of 1957–1958, when people were free from farming work. Cooperatives and neighbouring (still) private landholders carried out work that was impressive in its scale. According to estimates made by the Chinese press, every sixth Chinese citizen – 100 million people – went into the fields with shovels. As a result of this "crash campaign", construction work was shoddy and badly planned, and there were "disastrous" changes in the ground-water table and soil quality that only came to light later.[447]

The notion of using the surplus manpower in the countryside to upgrade/modernize the backward infrastructure was not new – it was being popularized in the

---

446 Quoted in J. Gittings, *The Changing Face of China. From Mao to Market*, Oxford 2006, p. 31.

447 J. Gittings, *The Changing Face...*, op. cit., p. 32.

West at that time by the economist Ragnar Nurkse. Mao, however, took it to an absurd extreme. The 1958 harvests were good, but the yield was mostly taken from farmers for export abroad: the Russians were demanding remuneration for their technical support, and hard currency was needed for the importation of machines. In addition, relations with the USSR (which had given China 7.4 billion rubles in the years 1952–1957, at that time equivalent to almost 2 billion dollars) were beginning to worsen, and whether further aid could be counted on was unclear.[448] Between 30 percent and 44 percent of the harvest was taken from the peasants.[449] Farming was also being deprived of manpower, with communes ordered to build industry and villagers being sent to work in factories.

In 1957, it was already clear that collectivization had negatively impacted farm production, which had grown by 1 percent that year, less than the population. Worse yet, at the very beginning of the great industrialization program, Chinese farming was already 50 percent less productive than Soviet farming in 1929. The attempt to "squeeze" the peasantry for resources – both labour and capital – to build heavy industry therefore brought with it the threat of an even greater societal catastrophe than in the USSR.

All of this, however, remained outside the reach of Mao's interests; sooner or later, Mao would silence anyone who might have directed his attention to these growing problems. In 1956 a purge took place among "bourgeois rightist economists", including those like Lin Lifu of the Chinese Academy of Sciences, who claimed that excessive acceleration of the collectivization of farming could lead to unfavourable results, or those like Chen Chenchan of the University of Beijing, who claimed that China might have something to learn from Western, bourgeois economics. Both were publicly condemned and never heard from again.[450] In 1957 the office of statistics was reformed; now nobody would dare to question the reports sent in by provincial Party leaders to the Chairman, which were notoriously tampered with at the higher echelons of the bureaucracy, becoming sheer ministerial fiction by the time they reached the Politburo.

Mao was well aware, of course, that his subordinates often lied. For this reason, he spent time travelling around the country and personally inspecting the progress of the "Great Leap." He eagerly talked with ordinary people, as well. From the technicians in the Ministry of Metallurgy he learned that China could

---

448 Y. Chen, *Transition and Development in China. Towards Shared Growth*, Farnham-Burlington 2009, p. 15.

449 J. Fenby, *Modern China…*, op. cit., p. 403.

450 C. Chichren Lin, "The Reinstatement of Economics in China Today", *The China Quarterly*, 1981, no. 85.

overtake Great Britain in the production of iron not in fifteen years – as he had postulated as one of the campaign's main goals – but in ten. In Sichuan, he saw how workers in a steelworks increased production by retooling aging machinery according to their own designs. Elsewhere he heard that thanks to the expansion of the irrigation system, yields had risen by a factor of 70. These absurdly high results were confirmed by Chinese scientists and trumpeted in propaganda.

Still, Party secretaries sometimes managed to outsmart the Chairman. Village furnaces were built specially close to the tracks so that Mao could see them from the train. Women were told to wear colourful, festive clothing. In the province of Hubei, the Party secretary ordered rice to be moved from distant fields and planted along the route of Mao's journey, so that he could not miss how plentiful the harvest was. The rice was planted so densely that it had to be surrounded with electric fans – otherwise, the too-densely packed crop would have rotted.

The Chairman was carried away by this atmosphere of success – as did his inner circle. "My enthusiasm," he said, may seem "madly arrogant", but he believed that it was simply "revolutionaries who seek the truth from facts … uniting the Russian revolutionary zeal with the American spirit of realism!"[451]

By the end of 1958, the whole country had been collectivized into 26,000 communes. Outwardly, everything was going wonderfully. The harvests were splendid – as it would soon turn out, this was due to unusually favourable weather, not Party policy. There was also a jump in industrial production, but mainly because of the recent activation of the first factories built through a Chinese-Soviet partnership (with black clouds already gathering overhead, since Russia was in the midst of de-Stalinization, which was viewed with suspicion by Mao, who saw a threat in this to himself).

The Chairman singled out for praise two solutions introduced in the communes which would prove to be catastrophic. The first was the cafeterias, where eating together was mandatory for everyone. Because there was no direct connection between what a peasant gathered in the field and what he ate, this greatly weakened people's motivation to work (only 30 percent of the food allowance was dependent on work productivity).[452] Later it emerged that in the regions where the cafeterias were most popular, famine was fiercest.[453] The second, equally catastrophic idea was the introduction of the *Dazhai* reward system of "points" awarded for work. In practice, however, the points were awarded not

451 L. Feigon, *Mao. A Reinterpretation*, Ivan R. Dee, Chicago 2002, p. 121.

452 C. Bramall, *Chinese Economic Development…*, op. cit., p. 125.

453 L. Feigon, *Mao…*, op. cit., p. 132.

so much for work as for revolutionary fervour and political engagement. This was another break with the Stalinist system, which had not given up on money as an incentive to work harder, and which always, by rewarding high-profiled "shock workers"[Rus. udarnik], had placed heavy emphasis on material incentives (which posed no obstacle to talking at length about the struggle for socialism). The contract system of payment introduced in the USSR in the 1930s brutally enforced productivity. Mao believed that faith and fervour would provide stronger motivation.

The first unsettling signs of impending economic collapse reached members of the Politburo toward the end of winter in 1959, when they were visiting the communes. What they saw gave them an unpleasant shock. The old marshal Peng Dehuai – who was soon to turn against Mao publicly – visited several provinces and saw everywhere starving peasants, while from party activists he heard complaints (in private) about the excesses of the Great Leap.[454]

The Chairman began to retreat, though not very deftly, from certain ideas. In February 1959 he tried halting the transfer of peasants' private property to the communes without recompensation and criticized the policy of equal remuneration for all work brigades without regard to their productivity. In the months that followed, he encouraged the provincial secretaries to exercise moderation and reprimanded those who claimed that peasants were hiding rice. In early spring, while meeting with state planner Chen Yunem, an economist with moderate views, Mao agreed to dissolve the communes and return to the brigade system (meaning in practice the older, smaller form of cooperative), dissolve the cafeterias, return private peasant land, and reduce steel production goals.

It is very possible that if there had not been an attempt to remove Mao from power, the Great Leap might have ended there – and we would not today be counting the victims in the tens of millions. According to Chinese estimates, by the middle of 1959 120,000 people had died of hunger.[455]

3. The Great Famine

The attempt to oust Mao from power took place during a Party conference in the beautiful mountain district of Lushan in July 1959. How real the threat was in reality remains a matter of dispute among historians.

---

454 D. Goodman, *Deng Xiaoping and the Chinese Revolution. A Political Bbiography*, London-New York 1994, p. 60.

455 F. Dikötter, *Mao's Great Famine…*, op. cit., p. 89.

Mao's challenger, if he really had one, acted alone. Peng Duhai, Defence Minister and an old comrade of the Chairman's from their days fighting as partisans, wrote a letter to Mao that was essentially a protest against the abuses of "the Great Leap. "I am a simple man and indeed I am crude and lack tact," the letter began. "For this reason, whether this letter is of value or not to you is for you to decide. Please correct me wherever I am wrong." Peng praised the achievements of Chinese industry, including the farmstead furnaces, and foresaw that China would overtake Great Britain not in ten years, but in four. At the same time, he wrote about problems: the waste of natural and human resources and the overstatement of production figures. Although the letter was on the whole measured and cautious, some passages were insulting to the Chairman, including mentions of "petty-bourgeois fanaticism leading to leftist errors" and the statement that "dealing with economic construction does not come quite as easily as bombing Quemoy or dealing with Tibet" (Mao's most recent foreign policy successes).[456]

The Chairman reportedly was unable to sleep that night. Two days later he called a meeting of the whole Politburo in his villa, where he greeted his comrades in a bathrobe and slippers. He condemned Peng Dehuai bitterly: the old marshal, he said, was part of a rightist attack on the "Great Leap". He declared Peng a "right opportunist" with aspirations to power, and refused to allow him to respond or defend himself, skilfully dodging his accusations. He remarked to the remaining comrades that they were all jointly responsible for the Great Leap Forward and demanded that they declare their loyalty. "If the Chinese People's Liberation Army should follow Peng Dehaui, I will go to fight guerilla war," he threatened theatrically.[457] In August the Central Committee officially pronounced Peng Huhai to be the leader of an "anti-Party clique": this marked his end.

If this was what an attempt to seize power from Mao looked like, it had been executed with exceptional ineptitude. Nobody stood in Peng Duchai's defence. Perhaps their fear resulted from the fact that purges had been carried out among Party elites during the "anti-right" campaign in 1957, and this was still fresh in everyone's memory. Perhaps Peng acted alone, or, as some historians speculate, without informing his followers, if he had any, that he was writing a letter to Mao.[458]

In practical terms, the condemnation and downfall of the marshal also meant that any criticism of the Great Leap whatsoever had now become unthinkable – since Mao had placed his critic among the ranks of "right opportunists." He,

456 Quoted in F. Dikötter, *Mao's Great Famine…*, op. cit., p. 93.

457 D. Goodman, *Deng Xiaoping…*, op. cit., p. 62.

458 This is the view of D. Goodman, the author of the previously cited political biography of Deng Xiaoping.

too, was now unable to turn back, though it is not clear that he desired to do so. Although the Chairman admitted that the plans for an increase in steel production were unrealistic, he quickly went back to this idea and declared: "We'll do 100 million tons in ten years, and then we'll be in heaven."[459] Paradise seemed within reach. In 1958, 10.7 million tonnes of iron were produced in backyard furnaces – the target set by the Chairman – but it was low in quality and essentially useless, and a great many tools and machines had been melted down in the process.[460] Any doubts voiced were drowned out by propaganda. A professor of agricultural sciences, who was a student at the time, recalled many years later in a conversation with an American historian:

> There was a saying about Daqing, the model oilfield, "When the oil workers shout with all their might, the great earth will shake and tremble." This slogan says the earth must listen to the orders of humans. It is wrong. It violates the laws of nature. That's what they tried to do during the Leap. There was a photograph of some children standing on top of a field of rice. It was impossible, but that's how dense our rice was supposed to be. Our university also falsified figures. By the university gate there is a field about a mu large. [...] The leaders decided that this one little piece of land should produce 10,000 jin of rice. We students had to take the rice shoots from several mu of fields, and, all day and all night, even by lamplight, bind them together and squeeze them into the field, although they were already rotting. The peasants came from the surrounding farmland to see what on earth we could be doing – after all we were an agricultural college! But even the professors had no way of resisting, because everyone was competing with each other to produce higher figures. It was not a normal time. There was pressure everywhere.[461]

The enormous country was plunged into chaos and destruction. It is unclear to what extent Mao was aware of what was going on. At the Party's instructions, people killed flies, mosquitoes and rats. Sparrows were killed as well, since Mao was convinced they were eating the harvest; when he finally understood that they eat insects, he redirected the campaign toward the fight against bed-bugs.[462] This resulted in a catastrophic famine. In terms of the number of victims, it was the greatest such disaster in history.

The famine was not only the result of the Party's economic policies. The scale of the tragedy was further heightened – as in Ukraine in the 1930s – by requisitions carried out to feed the cities. The portion of grain harvested allocated for

---

459 L. Feigon, *Mao...*, op. cit., p. 134.

460 J. Shapiro, *Mao's War...*, op. cit., p. 75.

461 Quoted in J. Shapiro, *Mao's War...*, op. cit., p. 77. A *jin* is equal to approx. 0.6 kg; one *mu* is approx. 0.66 hectare.

462 L. Feigon, *Mao...*, op. cit., p. 123.

each city dweller rose by 70 percent in the years 1958–1960, but due to poor harvests, food was lacking in the cities, as well. In Beijing, as Mao's doctor remembered, "there were almost no people on the streets, and those who were, were thin and listless."[463] Like the USSR during its famine, Mao's China continued to export food abroad even as its people starved.[464] China also instituted a costly policy of buying favour with newly independent African countries by giving them loans in hard currency that could have been used to import food; for example, in 1960, at the height of the famine, Mao lent Guinea 25 million dollars.[465]

There is no way to estimate the full extent of the damage caused by the Great Leap Forward. Beginning in 1958, old mud buildings were systematically demolished in order to use them as fertilizer; wooden constructions were burned in backyard furnaces to smelt iron. Forests and parks were cut down. Militias seized whatever they deemed suitable for use by the communes – sometimes killing the owners in the process. In 1960 the situation in the countryside was so dire that families were eating cotton. Animals were slaughtered *en masse*; according to official statistics, in the province of Hunan the number of pigs decreased by ¾ in the years 1958–1961.

The country was ceasing to function. Transport came to a halt; factories lacked parts for their machinery. To make matters worse, the weather, which had been favourable for the Party in 1958, took a turn for the worse. The Yellow River flooded, killing – directly and through hunger brought on by the destruction of the harvest – almost 2 million people. Industrial production collapsed: in 1961 it fell from the previous year by nearly half.[466]

People ate the bark off trees – those that were still standing. Cases of cannibalism were reported. Husbands sold their wives – for food, because money had lost its value. Bands of starving peasants attacked trains and warehouses containing food. "'Nobody cried when a family member died. You just carried on as usual,' she said. 'No fear of death, no emotion for the living,'" a female survivor of the famine later recalled in an interview.[467]

In 1960, the first, fragmentary information about the famine reached the West, but the Chinese government pronounced it to be merely propaganda and

---

463 J. Fenby, *Modern China...*, op. cit., p. 416.

464 C. J. Mitcham, *China's Economic Relations with the West and Japan, 1949–79. Grain, Tade and Dplomacy*, London-New York 2005, p. 40.

465 D. Brautigam, *The Dragon's Gift. The Real Story of China in Africa*, Oxford-New York 2009, p. 32.

466 D. Goodman, *Deng Xiaoping...*, op. cit., p. 65.

467 J. Fenby, *Modern China... op.cit.*, p. 416.

rejected offers of aid. The true scale of the catastrophe remained unknown for a long time, though many refugees from China – a great many people crossed into Hong Kong, for example – brought with them horrifying news.[468]

Throughout the summer of 1960, a group of Politburo members who understood what was happening tried to convince Mao of the need for "consolidation" after the recent series of natural disasters, and that China should begin importing grain. In October the Chairman's office received its first report from the region of Xinyang in the province of Henan, which Mao had earlier deemed a model. The report spoke of a massive famine, which had killed not 18,000 people, as earlier estimates asserted, but 80,000. Mao was shocked, but immediately perceived in the situation the hostile actions of class enemies. He agreed to send a mission composed of members of the Politburo to study the matter on the ground.

In Xinyang they found an empty, devastated land. The few peasants who survived were sheltering themselves from the winter cold in the ruins of demolished buildings, which had no windows, doors, or roofs – they could be burned for fuel. In the barren fields there were only graves. In total, over a million people died or disappeared in Xinyang in 1960, and of these, 67,000 were clubbed to death by militia squads composed of Party activists assigned to requisition the last grains of rice.

> Bad people have seized power, causing beatings, deaths, grain shortages and hunger. The democratic revolution has not been completed, as feudal forces, full of hatred towards socialism, are stirring up trouble, sabotaging socialist productive forces.[469]

This was Mao's diagnosis. He put the burden of blame on "rich landowners" and "counter-revolutionary elements". He never admitted making a mistake. A radical purge of local Party dignitaries, however, was immediately carried out – thousands of people were arrested for merely having zealously done what a few months earlier had been expected of them. After having caused 45 million deaths, the Great Leap Forward was officially ended.

American intelligence reports on China give us an idea of what the Western world was able to find out about the situation. In 1961–1966, analysts wrote mainly about China's economic problems, which were thought to make it impossible for it to achieve an international position on a par with that of the US or the USSR. First of all, they considered China to be overpopulated, and its low level of technological development and enormous birth rate meant that China

---

468 C. Yik-yi Chu, *Chinese Communists and Hong Kong Capitalists: 1937–1997*, New York 2010, p. 46.

469 F. Dikötter, *Mao's Great Famine…*, op. cit., p. 117.

was condemned to face constant problems feeding its citizens. China's fate was, in the words of one such report, a constant "race between food production and population growth." In addition, China was investing badly, according to American analysts, both from an ideological perspective, but also because its elites were driven by "extreme nationalism." That was why the bitter lesson of the Great Leap Forward would, in their view, be quickly forgotten.

Beginning in 1964, the Americans predicted that China would return to a path of accelerated investment in heavy industry and armaments, even if doing so threatened a return of hunger. "China [could] not become a modern industrial state for many years", they concluded. The Special National Intelligence Estimate (SNIE) of 1961 predicted that China would become one of the three most important producers of coal, steel and electricity over the next ten years, but that "its people will continue to subsist on a barely adequate diet in good [harvest] years, and suffer shortages in bad years."[470] This was not far from the truth: China would not return to the per capita food production levels achieved during the good harvests in 1956–1958 until twenty years later.[471]

4. Politics above everything

Just when the economy was beginning to recover from the losses caused by the Great Leap Forward, the Chairman applied another shock to it.

The purpose of the Cultural Revolution, which lasted (with interruptions and crises) nearly ten years (1966–1976), was much broader than that of the Great Leap Forward. Economic matters were only one part of it, one element in a great project to rebuild society.

It is not known how many people died during this last experiment of Mao's. Official figures remain secret (and are not necessarily complete), and estimates by specialists vary widely, with numbers ranging from 750,000 to nearly 8 million.[472] Some of these people were shot to death in battles, as the process

---

470 E. Goh, *Constructing the U.S. Rapprochement with China, 1961–1974. From "Red Menace" to "Tacit Ally"*, Cambridge 2005, pp. 50–51.

471 C. Riskin, "Feeding China: The Experience since 1949", [in:] *The Political Economy of Hunger*, vol. 3, eds. J. Drèze and A. Sen, Oxford-New York 2007, p. 33.

472 On the basis of analysis of available data from 1520 county-level rural districts, A. G. Walder and Y. Su estimate the number of victims at between 750,000 and 1.5 million ("The Cultural Revolution in the Countryside: Scope, Timing and Human Impact", *The China Quarterly*, 2003, no. 173). In contrast, R. J. Rummel puts the number at 7,731,000 victims (*China's Bloody Century: Genocide and Mass Murder*

culminated in outright combat between various parties within the Hong Weibing (Red Guard), as well as between the Red Guard and the army, but most were murdered: starved to death, buried alive, beaten to death or forced to commit suicide. A wave of killings of "class enemies" also swept across the country; for example, in just five days, from 27 August to 1 September 1966, in Daxing – a suburb of Beijing – 325 people were killed in such actions. In other mass killings, the death toll reached the thousands.[473]

There are also major divergencies in estimates of the number of people repressed – beaten, imprisoned, starved, publically humiliated and exiled from cities to work camps and manufacturing cooperatives, where they would undergo "re-education" – with numbers ranging from 35 to 125 million. The revolution rolled across China in stages: it first encompassed the country's main academic centres, where it reached its height in 1967–1968; around 1968, it began to spread to industry and transport; in the years 1969–1971 it moved to the countryside (which was also impacted by the cultural revolution, despite the fact that until very recently it was generally believed to have been mainly an urban movement).

Historians often look for the driving force behind the Cultural Revolution in the struggle for power at the top levels of the Party leadership. In the mid-1960s, after the failure of the Great Leap Forward, the Chairman is thought to have lost *de facto* influence in favour of a group of fellow Politburo members, among whom the most important figure was Liu Shaoqi. Mao initiated the Cultural Revolution and stood at its forefront in order to regain power; just as Stalin's power was consolidated by purges among the Party apparatus, the mainstay of Mao's rule was the Red Guard, comprised of students and young workers. This comparison overlooks one important difference, however: where Stalin's purges were carried out from above by the specialized machinery of Party-state violence, the massacres of the Cultural Revolution were carried out by a social movement that, although inspired by Mao, came "from below." Thus, visible in the background is a rebellion against Party elites, the "new class", who had obtained privileges at the expense of "the people."

Mao still regretted the failure of the Utopian and egalitarian ideals of the revolution. After the failure of the Great Leap Forward, he handed over management of most state matters to his comrades in the Politburo; there remains some

since 1900, New Brunswick 1991). Other estimates tend to put the number in the range of 1.5–2.5 million victims.

473 Y. Su, "Mass Killings in the Cultural Revolution: A Study of Three Provinces", [in:] *The Chinese Cultural Revolution as History*, eds. J. Esherick, P. Pickowicz, A. Walter, Stanford 2006, p. 96.

disagreement as to what extent he did so voluntarily. In the autumn of 1962, when the country was slowly getting back on its feet, he announced the slogan "Never forget the class struggle!" and began to prepare the ground for continuing the revolution.[474] The idea that the revolution is a never-ending process can already be found in texts Mao wrote as a student, but its full expression appeared in his works written on the eve of the Great Leap Forward, in early 1958:

> Our revolution is like fighting a war. After winning one battle, we must immediately put forward new tasks. In this way, we can maintain the revolutionary enthusiasm of the cadres and the masses, and diminish their self-satisfaction, since they have no time to be satisfied with themselves even if they wanted to; new tasks keep pressing in, and everyone devotes his mind to the question of how to fulfil the new tasks.[475]

Aside from the struggle for dominance and the ideological conviction of the need for permanent revolution, conflict among the party elite was also fuelled by fundamental disagreements concerning economic policy. During the Cultural Revolution, Mao had criticized Liu, accusing him of attempting to "rebuild capitalism." His words should not be taken literally – at the time, Mao was accusing the Brezhnev regime of doing the same thing in the USSR. Liu was also a proponent of forced socialist industrialization, to be conducted along the lines of the Soviet model, based on central planning combined with price and wage controls in order to maximize workers' productivity.[476] He believed in the power of material motivation. In many ways, he was like those reformers in the socialist bloc who wanted to increase the role of "incentives" at different levels of the production process – from the enterprise level down to the worker.[477] Behind this lay the belief – expressed around the same time in a more elegant form in Western theory – that lowering wages to the level of biological subsistence was harmful to the pace of growth because it reduced workers' motivation; the planner should therefore establish wages not at the lowest possible level, but at the optimal level for growth (which does not preclude being economical or a high rate of investment).[478]

---

474 S. Schram, *The Thought of Mao*, op. cit., p. 164.

475 S. Schram, "Mao Tse-tung and the Theory of Permanent Revolution 1958–69", *China Quarterly*, 1971, no. 46, p. 227.

476 Y. L. Wu, "Economics, Ideology and the Cultural Revolution", *Asian Survey*, 1968, vol. 8, no. 3.

477 Y. Y. Kueh, *China's New Industrialization Strategy. Was Chairman Mao Really Necessary?*, Edward Elgar, Cheltenham-Northampton 2008, p. 3 ff.

478 J. C. H. Fei, A. C. Chiang, "Maximum-speed Development Through Austerity" [in:] *The Theory and Design of Economic Development*, eds. I. Adelman and E. Thorbecke, Baltimore 1969, p. 67 ff.

Mao took a completely different view: he thought that material motivation to work should be replaced by political control and revolutionary fervour – which not only would bring obvious political benefits, but also make it possible to reach a considerably higher rate of investment and capital accumulation. This difference of opinion translated into Liu and his circle's preference for industry that produced consumer goods. Mao, who himself led a lifestyle that was far from ascetic, saw sacrifice as necessary, as well as being useful to the revolution. He must at the same time have known that, for example, in 1956, workers' bonuses alone amounted to 10 percent of the country's entire wage-fund. By bringing everyone, beginning with the peasants, to the brink of starvation, Mao was able to extract more resources from the economy for what he saw as the accelerated investment in heavy industry (and such costly endeavours as, to name one, China's atomic program).[479] The asceticism imposed by the Chairman on 600 million Chinese was, in effect, a confiscatory tax designated for investment.

In economic terms, the Cultural Revolution was thus a reprise of the Great Leap Forward, except on a smaller scale and carried out in a more anarchic fashion. Beginning in the spring of 1968, the press continued to report successive magical over-fulfilments of production plans (the original plans were never revealed). Only the fact that the revolution was late in reaching the countryside and not as far-reaching there explains why the catastrophic famine caused by the earlier campaign did not repeat itself.

The Cultural Revolution began in schools and universities, and shortly thereafter, moved to factories. During many months of confusion– at least up to autumn 1967 – official articles in the press urged people to "remain at their production posts, and not leave their factories to engage in exchange of revolutionary experiences."[480]

However, the wave could not be held back. In early November 1967, workers at 17 factories in Shanghai– influenced by news delivered from the capital by Red Guards – organized the Workers' Revolutionary General Headquarters in Shanghai and sent 2,500 of their members, led by 32 year-old "commandant" Wang Hongwen, who had earlier worked as a factory security guard, to Beijing. Premier Zhou Enlai ordered the train stopped, in order to deal with the problem on the spot. In protest, the workers sat on the tracks and for 31 hours blocked an important railway connection to Nanjing, paralyzing the transportation system.

---

479 Y. Y. Kueh, *China's New Industrialization…*, op. cit., p. 4.

480 R. MacFarquhar, M. Schoenhals, *Mao's Last Revolution*, Cambridge–London 2006, p. 141.

The high official sent from Beijing to negotiate with the workers agreed to all of their demands and blamed the earlier standstill on the local Party organization.

At a conference of economics ministers not long afterward, a quarrel broke out: if workers "are permitted to set up all kinds of organizations, there will be even more problems [...] Either they will begin fighting, or they will stop production," complained one of the participants.[481] He was right.

The centre nonetheless decided that the revolution should continue. A decree issued by Mao on 9 December 1966 entitled "Ten Points On Industry" permitted workers to form "revolutionary organizations," though it also placed upon them the duty to maintain production. At the turn of 1966–67, armed workers' militias had gained *de facto* control over the city of Shanghai. In the summer of 1967, regular battles broke out, including in some factories, among various factions of the revolutionary Red Guard: these battles centred on the question of who better represented Mao's thought – and in the course of them, all manner of local conflicts were brought out into the open.

The scale of these clashes resembled a creeping civil war. In one such battle, at Chongqing in August 1967, over 10,000 heavy artillery shells were fired, and a 1000 people were killed. In another place in the province of Hunan, the work of a giant steelworks was held up for six weeks due to fighting in which six workers were killed. In Shanghai, Wang Hongwen ordered his fighters to attack a diesel motor factory; in the fighting that ensued, 18 people lost their lives, and another 983 were wounded. Production was halted for two months. Throughout China, in the third quarter of 1967 only half of planned production was achieved.[482] To this day it is difficult to estimate the losses caused by the removal of qualified engineers and supervisors from factories and other plants, after they fell victim to the "class struggle" conducted in Mao's name and directed against what had hitherto been the nation's elite. On 18 August 1967, dressed in military fatigues for the first time in years, Mao greeted a procession of several hundred thousand Red Guards on Tiananmen Square: he was once again back in his element.[483]

Factory life had been turned upside down. For most revolutionaries bookkeeping, profitability, and earnings were bourgeois ideas, while control and oversight limited the free expression of workers' creative power (hence the slogan "Better Red than Expert"). Planning was also rejected because it merely stood in the way of unlimited growth in production. The entire previously existing system

481 Ibid., p. 142.

482 Ibid., pp. 217–220.

483 J. Chang, J. Halliday, *Mao. The Unknown Story*, New York 2005, p. 517.

of management was discarded as being worthless and hindering the initiative of the working class. Workers were discovering that they were better educated and prepared than the engineers and supervisors who were "contaminated with bourgeois habits," and who often not only had university degrees, but had obtained them abroad.[484]

Likewise, in keeping with the postulate that all creative work is class-oriented and the source of creativity is the working class, innovation was to be generated by the workers themselves. (In accordance with Mao's thought in the *Little Red Book*: "The masses have boundless creative power. They can organize themselves and concentrate on places and branches of work where they can give full play to their energy; they can concentrate on production in breadth and depth and create more and more undertakings for their own well-being."[485]) This fit perfectly with the spirit, dominant in Maoism, but with deeper, older roots stretching back to imperial times, of autarchy. In the 1970s, a Western Maoist described it thus:

> The notion of "relying on one's own strength" has a profound effect on the attitude toward the requirements of accumulation. "In keeping with Chairman Mao's teachings," a member of the revolutionary committee explained, "a three-in-one team has been organized in our factory for the purpose of achieving a technical revolution. This is a specialized team, but a campaign is under way to enlist mass participation in this effort. We must not rely exclusively on this specialized team which, at any rate, consists of few people.

Innovation in the economy was an element of the revolution, and an ongoing process, not simply a series of steps. The Western sympathizer was shown a machine that had been improved by the workers:

> The experts and specialists had always claimed that this type of machine could not possibly dye and print jersey in two colors. The workers said: "Why can't it be done? Let's try it!" After the Cultural Revolution, they proposed the attempt be made, and after a few trials it turned out to be quite practical to print in two colors. Nevertheless, we still have problems.[486]

Propaganda again became deafening and offered clear, unambiguous models. For example, on 15 March 1969, Beijing Radio transmitted a broadcast about the

---

484 S. Andors, *China's Industrial Revolution. Politics, Planning and Management 1949 to the Present*, New York 1977, p. 200.

485 *Quotations from Chairman Mao Tse Tung*. Marxists Internet Archive, https://www.marxists.org/reference/archive/mao/works/red-book/ch11.htm.

486 C. Bettelheim, *Cultural Revolution and Industrial Organization in China. Changes in Management and the Division of Labor*, New York-London 1974, pp. 27–28.

discovery of a new insecticide, the text of which illustrates both revolutionary management methods and the thriving cult of Chairman Mao:

> Trial manufacture began in the factory in October 1966. Harbouring inveterate hatred for this new born thing, the handful of capitalist roaders in the Party and the class enemies in the factory did everything they could to obstruct and sabotage the undertaking. They slandered the revolutionary workers, saying, "scientific experiments are the affair of technicians and university graduates. How can you workers expect to produce any bacteria? You don't know how high the sky is and how big the earth is!"
>
> The revolutionary workers replied firmly in words like these: "Chairman Mao says: 'The humble are the most intelligent; the lofty are the most ignorant'. Armed with Mao Tse-tung's thought, the working class is capable of performing wonders which you cannot even imagine!" They chose four comrades with only primary school education to study for one month at a unit which was then carrying out experiments in making the new insecticide. After the four comrades, returned the workers borrowed a microscope, bought several flasks, made some wooden cases and immediately started their experiments [...] Devoted to serving the people "wholly" and "entirely", they went to the villages to make investigations and canvass the poor and lower-middle peasants for their views. In doing this, they made more and more progress in their experiments. Over 900 experiments in all were conducted and they finally succeeded in trial producing the new type of insecticide.[487]

In this atmosphere, decisions concerning production were to be made collectively by workers, though it is hard to say from a distance how much say they actually had. The result, beyond any doubt, was total chaos in production.[488] Additional losses to the economy caused by repressions against educated people and the closing of universities (some for several years) are difficult even to estimate.[489] Many schools never opened again. The number of institutions of higher education in China fell during the Cultural Revolution by more than half – from 1300 to slightly more than 400 – and began to rise again only after the Chairman's death.[490]

Although the army's intervention in the second half of 1968 put an end to the worst excesses of the Cultural Revolution, fighting in the provinces continued as late as 1976, a year before Mao's death.

---

487 Quoted in *The Miracles of Chairman Mao. A Compendium of Devotional Literature: 1966–1970*, ed. G. Urban, London 1971, p. 122.

488 A. Eckstein, *China's Economic Revolution*, London-New York 1978, p. 91.

489 R. Dernberger, "Radical Ideology and Economic Development in China: The Cultural Revolution and Its Impact on the Economy", *Asian Survey*, 1972, vol. 12, no. 12, p. 1062.

490 D. Guthrie, *China and Globalization. The Social, Economic and Political Transformation of Chinese Society*, New York-London 2009, p. 177.

5. Society is certainly a bit coarse

It is easy nowadays to look at the Maoist experiments as aberrations and condemn the regime's crimes. For contemporaries, and not only Chairman Mao's admirers, this was not so obvious. In 1975, in one of the most prestigious economic development journals, it was possible to read the following assessment:

Standards for evaluating China's performance are open to dispute, but certain features of the economy are generally ranked among the regime's outstanding accomplishments. These features include, above all, the near equality of income (at least compared to most developing countries) and the fact that in areas visited by foreign travelers, everyone seems to enjoy a standard of living above bare subsistence, despite the pressure of people against scarce resources.[491]

The author praises the contrast between clean and tidy Chinese cities and the dirty and chaotic metropolitan areas of Asia's capitalist countries – at that time full of unemployed and hungry people, which China did not have. The same author cited several foreign observers, including Joan Robinson, an economist fascinated by Mao at the time:

> [T]he flood of observers' reports concerning everyday life in China are almost uniformly positive. They describe Chinese citizens under communist rule as disciplined, well-fed and clothed, forward looking and proudly nationalistic, healthy [...]. The society is, to be sure, somewhat drab [...] rather dull at times, and lacking in many of the amenities and freedoms of Western life. But observers are impressed with the contrast they perceive with other developing societies.[492]

Numerous Western observers were inclined to make light of the nearly total elimination of private property and personal autonomy in Maoist China. In practical terms, for example, Chinese people had no free time. In Mao's time this was not in fact studied because the very idea smacked of a bourgeois lifestyle. In 1980, when reforms were just beginning, collectives allowed the average citizen barely 2 hours and 21 minutes a day for rest and recreation (in 1991, the figure was already more than twice that).[493]

The average rate of growth for the Chinese economy from 1952 up until the 1970s was estimated after Mao's death at 4–6 percent annually, which indicates that it considerably outstripped the pace of population growth (2 percent

---

491 D. B. Keesing, "Economic Lessons from China", *Journal of Development Economics*, 1975, no. 2.

492 J. Robinson, *Economic Management – China 1972*, London 1973, quoted in D. B. Keesing, "Economic lessons..." op. cit.

493 J. Friedmann, *China's Urban Transition*, Minneapolis-London 2005, p. 79.

annually). China also unquestionably outpaced the other Asian giant, India, leaving it far behind. According to estimates made in 1980, China's GDP rose seven-fold in the period 1950–1980; India's grew by less than three-fold. Taking population growth into account, the average Chinese person was almost four times richer in 1980 than in 1950. In presenting this comparison, Economist Wilfred Malenbaum pronounced the Chinese achievement to be "spectacular", attributing it to, among other things, centralized investment on a grand scale.[494] He also observed that even if other Asian countries achieved an even higher rate of growth due to exports, such a strategy would not have been possible for China, as it was too big, in his view, for such a solution to be effective there.[495]

By today's estimates, as well, Mao's China comes out looking good compared to the rest of what we used to call the "Third World", and now call the developing countries – with assessments of China's average rate of growth in GDP ranging as high as 6.7 percent annually, though it was subject to extreme oscillations during Chairman Mao's periods of experimentation.[496] China's profile looks even better if we take into account not only the pace of the rise in GDP, but other development indicators, such as average life expectancy, which was unmistakably higher than in other countries with a comparative level of income.[497] The Chinese were also relatively better-educated than the country's level of wealth would indicate.[498] Another achievement of modernization consisted of far-reaching gains in gender equality, an effort consistently imposed by the regime from the beginning of its rule. It has also been observed that if one overlooks subtle questions of "superstructure" – the omnipresence of ideology, the level of the regime's control over society and the number of victims – the economic policy of the final period of Mao's rule was in fact quite similar to what was being attempted at the time in other poor countries, i.e., raising the level of investment, particularly in industry.

---

494 W. Malenbaum, "Modern Economic Growth in India and China. The Comparison Revisited, 1950–1980", *Economic Development and Cultural Change*, 1982, vol. 31, no. 1.

495 C. Bramall, *Chinese Economic…*, op. cit., p. 155.

496 R. F. Dernberger, "The People's Republic of China at 50: The Economy" [in:] *The People's Republic of China After 50 Years*, ed. R. L. Edmonds, Oxford-New York 2000, p. 45. A. Maddison estimates economic growth in China in the years 1952–1978 to have been 4.4 percent annually (A. Maddison, *Chinese Economic Performance in the Long Run, 960–2030 AD,* OECD, Paris 2007, p. 60).

497 C. Bramall, *Chinese Economic…*, op. cit., p. 3.

498 K.-Y. Tsui, "Forces Shaping China's Interprovincial Inequality" [in:] *Inequality and Growth in Modern China*, ed. G. Wan, Oxford-New York 2008, p. 81.

In the final years of Mao's life, the socialist engine of growth was already showing signs of fading. Toward the end of the 1970s, the GDP growth rate fell to 1.5 percent annually, lower than the rate of population growth. The economy was also becoming increasingly capital intensive, like the USSR and communist Eastern Europe at that time. Whereas in the 1950s it was necessary to invest 2.51 yuan in industry to achieve a rise in growth of 1 yuan, in the first half of the 1970s it required 5.49 yuan (in 1993 in post-reform China, a mere 1.35 yuan was sufficient). Furthermore, private consumption grew at a rate three times slower than GDP, a problem typical of socialist countries.

As Mao was dying, a number of problems that were endemic to planned economies were reaching a critical stage: production was weighed down by logistical problems and underinvestment in transport, obsolete light industry, bottlenecks in the supply of raw materials and energy. At the same time, the Politburo continued to insist on setting daily production targets for most sectors of the economy.[499]

For a short period after Mao's death, the Politburo was engulfed in a power struggle. By the end of the 1970s, however, it was clear to the new team in power that the time had come to find a different path forward. The party leadership, now comprised of new faces, quickly moved onto the path Mao had feared most: a road one of his Western admirers called "the Great Leap Backward".[500]

---

499 F. C. Teiwes, W. Sun, *The End of the Maoist Era. Chinese Politics During the Twilight of the Cultural Revolution: 1972–1976*, Armonk-London 2007, p. 199.

500 C. Bettelheim, "Great Leap Backward" [in:] *China since Mao,* eds. N. Burton, C. Bettelheim, New York-London 1978, p. 37.

A number, when it grows hot with fervour,
Enters boldly into worlds of prophetic dreams
And produces epics about factories
Or poems about elaborate dreams.
From a publication issued on the 75th anniversary of the founding of the H. Cegielski Stock Company, 1930s.[501]

We are witnessing the collapse of the last bastions of global capitalism, which as a political system is reaching the end of its era. We bid it farewell, noting that it leaves behind the tainted seeds of hatred among nations, classes and sectors of society, savage rivalries between states, criminal theories about one man's rule over another, enslavement of the spirit and enslavement to work.
Declaration of the Coordinating Body of Democratic, Socialist and Syndicalist Parties, containing basic guidelines for the political system in postwar Poland, Warsaw, 4 March 1944.[502]

Chapter 5. Polish planism[503]

1. Polish poverty

In the summer of 1938, Polish journalist Melchior Wańkowicz made his third trip to observe progress on the construction of the Central Industrial District (Pol. Centralny Okręg Przemysłowy, abbrev. COP). One of the most highly acclaimed journalists of the Second Republic, he was gathering material for a book solicited by the government about the success of its program to build Polish industry. In the book, *Relay Race* (Pol. *Sztafeta*, 1938), Wańkowicz wrote:

> Ten million people living from farming lack food and jobs. Ten million unemployed people living in the countryside (in addition to those registered in the cities) are a dead weight we cannot shoulder, who are as yet unworthy to be called citizens because they first need to be nourished, given some kind of surplus social income to allow them to think about more than just their most primitive animal needs.

---

501 Quoted in M. Wańkowicz, *Sztafeta. Książka o polskim pochodzie gospodarczym*, Warszawa 2012, p. 113.

502 Quoted in *Programy polskich partii politycznych i ugrupowań partyzanckich lat wojny i okupacji hitlerowskiej*, ed. K. Przybysz, Warszawa 1987, p. 148.

503 The apt term "planism" comes from an article by Fr. A. Wóycickiego: "Ku ustrojowi korporacyjnemu", *Przegląd Ekonomiczny*, 1938, no. 2, p. 16.

> And then – the COP appeared. Five-sixths of Poles live outside its borders, but they still dream about it, holding their heads high, awaiting a better future, and reassessing how they view Poland.[504]

Wańkowicz's prewar reporting is full of harrowing descriptions of misery: dirty, ragged children with eyes damaged by trachoma, the poor clustered in dark, damp cellars, peasants slowly dying from untreated tuberculosis and syphilis, vegetating in misery and squalor in towns and villages in Poland's poorer eastern "B-Side". The literary concept behind *Relay Race* was to contrast descriptions of such poverty with visions of the prosperity and growth promised by the government's investments. The author notes in the book's Preface:

> Poland is a very poor country. Each page of the Statistical Yearbook tells us so. [*Relay Race*] does not dispute this state of affairs. The book merely wants to demonstrate that our lives today are not so terribly wretched, that we can remain hopeful, and that if we do so, we will improve our situation. This will require generations of hard work, just as it took the "work" of generations to squander away a once rich and prosperous Poland.[505]

Development is not something that will occur at some undefined time in the future: it is happening here and now, right before the reporter's eyes, thanks to the far-sighted and ambitious policies of the government. The spiritual kinship between this writing and socialist realism is striking. The cult of production and industry is the same in both. Even the graphical elements of the book - pictures of welders on scaffolding, miners at work digging, power lines, jackhammers, red-brick factory buildings standing in an open field - bring to mind, as one historian noted years later in his introduction to a new edition of Wańkowicz's book, the iconography of the Stalinist era, which would arrive in Poland only after the cataclysm of the Second World War.[506]

In Wańkowicz's reporting, industry - the aesthetics of which seem to fascinate him - is to bring civilization to a place it has never previously been. This is to be more than a purely technological revolution. After the factory come doctors, schools, social insurance and new, improved rules of life:

> I walk to the house where the welders live. The welder is the highest category of worker; you have to be good with your hands to be a welder; but you also earn six hundred zlotys per month; it's no surprise that they get paid so well; imagine if the pipes carrying natural gas under pressure had cracks in the seams [...] the Jewish innkeeper, who runs the place where we go to drink beer, praises these welders as easygoing people who save

504 M. Wańkowicz, *Sztafeta...*, op. cit., p. 314.

505 Ibid., p. 268.

506 Cf. B. Brzostka's Introduction to *Sztafeta...*, p. 9.

their money to send back to their families. One old man, fumbling with his tobacco pouch, sees fit to add his own two cents: "This Johnny-come-lately [...] may be a worker, but he wears fancy clothes and lives like a city boy. He eats meat every day, and not just cooked up plain, but minced with onion, and pan-fried on both sides, and he washes it down with vodka. He's a clever bastard, not like our peasant-folk. He doesn't deny himself a thing, he knows you only live once in this world. He doesn't watch what he spends because he's never short of cash. He's the kind of person who knows which end is up.[507]

This miracle could only have been decreed from above. In *Relay Race*, it is the government – far-sighted ministers, directors and military officers, who have assumed the burden of responsibility for Poland - who took up the task of building the Central Industrial Region. In doing so, they simultaneously realised two collective aims, tying progress to building the nation's military strength.

The structural parallels between ideas from the 1930s and 1950s – and even later – about how to promote Poland's economic development are much more pronounced than they appear at first glance. It was commonly and sincerely believed that the free market did not work (or worked only in relation to consumer goods), and that the only chance for achieving significant growth and catching up to the West after centuries of backwardness was planning and centralised state investments, directed by an elite - before the war, the government, and after the war, the communists. The belief was common that only by such means could Poles be made "full-fledged citizens", although this "citizenship" did not necessarily mean that Poles would have the freedom to choose between different political parties. The social objective of industrialization was freedom from poverty and meeting people's basic needs, such as participation in the national culture – of course in a form defined by the ruling elite. Both before and after the war, the government faced similar pressures, those posed by a growing population and a large military budget - though the international contexts were, of course, quite different. The two periods also shared a common sense of optimism. As Wańkowicz wrote:

The day they get their first day's pay – from a lifeless block of ten million have-nots, one tiny piece breaks away once again. On the other side, 400,000 new citizens are born here every year. The race to a Poland inhabited by full-fledged citizens is a hard one.[508]

507 M. Wańkowicz, *Sztafeta...*, op. cit., pp. 319–320.

508 Ibid., p. 319.

Prewar Poland was indeed a very poor country.[509] Polish historians write about this in a less harsh manner than Westerners, who systematically group the Second Republic with countries such as Romania, Portugal and Greece. Before 1939, more than half the population in Poland worked in agriculture, compared with slightly less than half in the countries of southern Europe and more than 70 percent in the Balkans. Peasant life was short – life expectancy was 47 years in 1938. This was more than ten years shorter than in the West, and living conditions in general were often very primitive in comparison with Germany or France. Poland had modern industry, but these factories were islands in the sea of a primitive, semi-feudal economy. Even here, however, performance levels remained much lower than in the West.[510]

Nevertheless, the Second Republic was not in last place in Europe's second division. In contrast to the Balkan countries, for example, it had its own industrial sector, somewhat fewer people worked in agriculture, and a larger proportion of citizens could read. The nineteenth century, when the Polish lands were divided between three foreign powers, had not been good to Poles, but the industrial revolution had not passed them by entirely.

Economic historians have argued for decades about the pace of economic development in Central Europe during the era of industrialization. Opinions and estimates differ, but the general conclusion is that despite the changes in borders, political systems and economic theories, the gap between the West and Central Europe has remained relatively constant.[511] Poland's per capita GDP before 1939

---

509 Cf. J. Kochanowicz, "Polska w epoce nowoczesnego wzrostu gospodarczego", [in:] *Modernizacja Polski. Struktury. Agencje. Instytucje*, ed. W. Morawski, Warszawa 2010, pp. 153–180.

510 D. H. Aldcroft, *Europe's Third World. The European Periphery in the Interwar Years*, Aldershot–Burlington 2006, p. 4.

511 E.g. David F. Good in summing up this debate says that growth in Central Europe in the years 1870–1989 was somewhat higher than in Western Europe (1.40 percent annually versus 1.19 percent). See D. F. Good, "The State and Economic Development in Central and Eastern Europe", [in:] *Nation, State and the Economy in History*, eds. A. Teichova, H. Matis, Cambridge–New York 2003, p. 139. Various estimates of the growth rate in Central Europe show it was either somewhat higher or lower than in Western Europe: it was lower before 1939, markedly higher in the years 1950–1973, and comparable (given a lower starting point) later on. Ivan Berend writes that although Central Europe was mired in stagnation up until 1939, the period of real socialism up to 1973 allowed Poland to close a large part of the gap separating it from the West, which again began to grow in the 1980s. (Ivan T. Berend, *Central and Eastern Europe 1944–1993. Detour from the Periphery to the Periphery*, Cambridge–New

never exceeded half the average in Western Europe. The disparity was even more clearly visible in the level of consumption, which in Poland in the 1920s was less than one-fourth the level in the West; consumption levels fell further during the Great Depression, returning to pre-crisis levels only just before the war. In 1937, the number of cars per capita in Eastern Europe was 25 times lower than in the West (not to mention the United States).[512] In spheres that determine the comfort and quality of life - such as income, education, road infrastructure, home size and furnishings, doctors per capita - interwar Poland lagged far behind the West.[513] Poorer citizens, particularly those living in rural areas, were chronically undernourished.[514] The economist Ludwik Landau wrote at the time:

> At their height in 1929, white-collar workers' wages in Poland, like those of physical labourers, were among the lowest in Europe, and remained both in nominal terms and – despite the low food prices in Poland – in real terms far from the level of wages in Western countries.[515]

Landau added that Polish wages were also characterized by a greater discrepancy between the intelligentsia and the workers and farmers than in the West – a situation typical of underdeveloped countries. While a Polish government official had an income comparable to his colleagues in Austria or the Czech Republic (although lower by half to that in Germany or France), Western workers already earned much more than Poles. According to Landau, this distance stemmed primarily from the difference between the production generated in Poland (estimated by him to be 610 zlotys per year per capita, compared with e.g. 600 zlotys in Romania) and in the countries of the industrialized West (1800 zlotys per capita), not to mention the U.S. (4500 zlotys).[516]

York 1996, p. 187 ff.). Cf. also P. Bairoch, *The Economic Development of the Third World since 1900*, London 1975. Cf. also A. Maddison, *The World Economy…*, op. cit.

512 D. H. Aldcroft, *Europe's Third World…*, op. cit., p. 175.

513 J. Żarnowski, *Społeczeństwo Drugiej Rzeczypospolitej, 1918–1939*, Warszawa 1973, p. 82.

514 J. Żarnowski, *Polska 1918–1939: praca, technika, społeczeństwo*, Warszawa 1992, p. 230.

515 L. Landau, "Płace w Polsce w związku z rozwojem gospodarczym" [in:] *Wybór pism*, Warszawa 1957, p. 253.

516 L. Landau, "Gospodarka światowa. Produkcja i dochód społeczny w liczbach" [in:] *Wybór pism*, Warszawa 1957, p. 418.

2. Life during the Depression

The Great Depression hit Poland particularly hard: industrial production declined by as much as 40 percent, and the deflationary policies of successive governments (including tax increases, spending cuts, maintaining the gold standard) only deepened the economic collapse.

From the outset, the interwar period had been difficult for newly-independent Poland. Derek H. Aldcroft estimates that industrial production fell by up to 15 percent in 1920 during the Polish-Bolshevik War, and by 1929, on the eve of the Great Depression, had not yet returned to prewar levels – meaning that Poland's economic performance was the worst in Central Europe and only slightly better than the Soviet Union's.[517] According to other estimates, in particular, those of Stephen Broadberry and Alexander Klein, Polish GDP per capita reached prewar levels only in 1937, a result on par with those of other countries in central and southern Europe.[518]

These problems were rooted not only in the economic policies of successive governments, but also in radical changes in the country's post-independence geopolitical situation.[519] To the east, Russia, the primary market for the former Polish Kingdom's industrial output, was now closed to Poland. To the west, Germany had been engaged in a customs war with Poland since the mid-1920s. At home, merging the various partitions into one entity and rebuilding after the devastation of the First World War were extremely costly, as was the hyperinflation that plagued the country for several years.

The Great Depression was quick to reach Poland. A fall in food prices led to weakness in its banks, which had issued loans for agricultural production. The government's response to this crisis was the nationalization of factories and

517 D. H. Aldcroft, *Europe's Third World…*, op. cit., p. 111.

518 S. Broadberry, A. Klein, "Aggregate and Per Capita GDP in Europe, 1870–2000: Continental, Regional and National Data with Changing Boundaries", *Scandinavian Economic History Review*, 2012, vol. 60, no. 1.

519 Cf. Z. Landau, "National Income in Historical Research (On Material from the Period of Interwar Poland)", *Acta Poloniae Historica*, 1976, no. 33; The article also contains a discussion of the methodological difficulties in calculating national income and its relation to the actual level of agricultural and industrial production.

banks at risk of collapse.[520] Private banks held 40 percent of deposits in 1926, but only 20 percent in 1934.[521]

In the early 1930s, journalist Konrad Heather wrote in a report on Zawiercie, "the city of the unemployed":

> I walked through the factory halls. Just a year earlier, they had been filled with the roar of machines; today they stand mute. What do we see now in these deserted halls, whose maze of looms has been left silent? Today, rather than thousands of workers bustling about these factory halls, we have a handful of caretakers, recruited from among the former work crews. They wear scarves and caps as they make their rounds in the empty factory's unheated halls. These cold rooms instil a feeling of dread. Pieces of silk or plush cloth hang here and there from the looms, as if someone had left suddenly in the middle of work. Will the workers return to finish the job, will they return to the print shop, to the laundry and the finishing line, to the bleachery, to the spindles and looms? Will they ever return to work? There are currently 7,854 people on the unemployed rolls in Zawiercie. If we consider that they are mostly the heads of families, and the average family consists of three to four people, then we can estimate that as many as 25,000 people are receiving support from the social welfare services. According to the last census, Zawiercie had 32,000 residents. It is thus no exaggeration to say that three-quarters of the Zawiercie population live on public assistance.[522]

The government had no idea how to remedy the situation. Polish politicians' actions were focused, above all, on efforts to maintain financial stability by preventing both a financial crisis and a return of hyperinflation, which was still fresh in Poles' memories. They also sought to maintain Poland's credibility as a solvent, reliable and stable member of the international community. Another reason for inaction was, says Nikolaus Wolf, the desire to defend Poland's economic independence and maintain access to French capital (France was then the pillar of the "gold bloc").[523] This issue was finally decided by Marshal Pilsudski, who objected to any form of monetary "experimentation", when he assumed dictatorial powers in 1926.[524]

---

520 Cf. W. Roszkowski, "Etatyzm przemysłowy w Polsce w latach kryzysu", *Przegląd historyczny*, 1972, vol 63, no. 1, p. 67.

521 C. H. Feinstein, P. Temin, G. Toniolo, "International Economic Organization: Banking, Finance, and Trade in Europe between the Wars", [in:] *Banking, Currency, and Finance in Europe Between the Wars*, ed. C. H. Feinstein, Oxford 1995, p. 45.

522 K. Wrzos, *Oko w oko z kryzysem: reportaż z podróży po Polsce*, Warszawa 1985, p. 152.

523 N. Wolf, "Should I Stay or Should I Go? Understanding Poland's Adherence to Gold, 1928–1936", *Historical Social Research – Historische Sozialforschung*, 2007, no. 4.

524 J. Kaliński, Z. Landau, *Gospodarka Polski XX wieku*, Warszawa 2003, p. 125.

All these arguments seemed reasonable, but the price citizens paid for these policies ended up being extremely high.[525] Budget expenditures fell by a third in 1930–1934. There was also a comparably drop in real value of loans granted by banks, which essentially put a stranglehold on the economy.

The crisis brought about a breakthrough in thinking: it became widely read as a great moral defeat for capitalism. In the 1930s and 1940s, the vast majority of reporting on the economy – from both right and the left – associated liberalism and the free market with poverty, irrationality, chaos and waste on a massive scale. Perhaps not without reason: at its low point in the winter of 1933, the Great Depression was, as the American economic historian Bradford DeLong writes, "a form of collective insanity":

> Workers were idle because firms would not hire them; firms would not hire them because they saw no market for their outputs; there was not market for output because workers had not incomes to spend.[526]

There was a general feeling that the world had been turned on its head, and was full of meaningless suffering. The economist Włodzimierz Brus, who had grown up in the 1930s, and would later spend decades trying to reform the economy of real socialism, recalled that decade:

> In the less developed countries of Eastern and Central Europe, the Great Depression brought more misery and hopelessness than elsewhere else. Having been born in Poland in 1921, I was quite aware in the mid-1930s of the suffering being caused by mass unemployment, the wide-spread homelessness in the cities, the catastrophically low incomes of the rural population, especially in Central and Eastern Poland, where the "surplus" rural population was estimated to be in the millions. Although the situation of my own family was relatively good (my father, a white-collar worker in a Jewish volunteer organization, kept his job throughout the interwar period), the juxtaposition of idle factories and unwanted production against an army of people desperately seeking work and fighting for survival led to questions that could not be ignored.[527]

In Poland, approximately 40 percent of workers in the cities were out of work. The absurdity of factories sitting empty while millions were unemployed and starving, made a particularly striking impression and is mentioned often in memoirs.

---

525 Z. Landau, W. Roszkowski, *Polityka gospodarcza II RP i PRL*, Warszawa 1995, p. 66.

526 J. B. DeLong, *Hopeless Unemployment*, Project Syndicate, 1 August 2012, http://www.project-syndicate.org/commentary/hopeless-unemployment.

527 W. Brus, "Zmora reformowania socjalistycznego systemu ekonomicznego", *Teoria Ekonomii. Prace i materiały*, 1997, no. 4. My thanks to prof. Tadeusz Kowalikow for suggesting the article.

In his search for a better economic order, Brus turned first to a classical economics textbook, which left him disappointed, and then to the texts of Soviet Marxists. He found them convincing.

The formative experience of the Great Depression as a discrediting of capitalism and the free market left an impression on an entire generation. Here is another recollection of that era by the poet and prominent intellectual Czesław Miłosz:

> I condemned the capitalistic system, but was suspicious of becoming enmeshed in philosophical intricacies. [...] The dates are important. The years 1930–1935. Mass unemployment. The destruction of wheat and coffee. Hitler's seizure of power. All those aroused a violent protest from everyone who was not ready to accept the absurd. The poems I wrote then did not call for revolutionary action, but there was terror in them and a foreboding of what was to come. [...] Our university politics underwent the same polarization as the politics of all countries: the Right became more and more Fascist, and the Left more and more Stalinist.[528]

Brus's conviction of the absurdity and irrationality of capitalism was not shaken even by the experience of a stay in the Soviet Union, during which he saw up close – first working as a piece worker producing metal parts for parachutes, and then as the head of the planning office in a factory producing two-finger gloves for the military – how a centrally planned economy operated in practice/reality:

> I learned a lot in the factories, not in a positive sense, but in a negative one: how distant the realities of central planning were, viewed from the level of the factory floor, from the schemes taught in the classroom: poor organization, the harmful role of plan fulfilment as the primary indicator of success, a system of incentives which encouraged waste instead of the conservation of resources - matters of the utmost importance in wartime; quality control was only effective if it was carried out from outside by a military delegation. Thus, the microeconomics of Soviet industry were frightful.[529]

At the same time, and this was a paradox characteristic of many observers, seeing this mismanagement and disorder with his own eyes, Brus remained impressed by the scale of investment that Stalinism made possible, especially given the very difficult wartime conditions.

> The industrialization programme created a number of new factories in Saratov, including large plants producing combine harvesters and ball bearings, large oil refineries, etc. They were quickly converted to military production (the combine factory began production of fighter aircraft) and formed a base for industrial plants that had been evacuated from the western part of the country. The possibility of mobilizing resources in conditions of necessity were also obvious: one example from my personal experience

---

528 C. Miłosz, *Native Realm. A Search for Self-definition*, Berkeley 1981, pp. 115–116.
529 W. Brus, "Zmora reformowania...", op. cit.

was the building of a gas pipeline to Saratov from newly discovered fields in the seemingly impossible conditions of the winter of 1942–1943.[530]

The Great Depression marginalized in Poland the political influence of liberal economists from the Kraków school, supporters of laissez-faire who had been influential in the 1920s. The suddenly found themselves in the same situation as the advocates of "market socialism" after 1989 – no one would listen to them. Moreover, they themselves sometimes experienced moments of doubt. In a book published during the Second World War in London, one of the most important representatives of this group, Ferdinand Zweig, wrote that now he could see the positive effects of central planning efforts undertaken even before the war:

> The experiment of planning the Central Industrial District is one of those experiments that merits attention when considering the specific issues involved in rebuilding Poland's economy after the war.[531]

The prewar journalism of Polish liberals – Adam Krzyżanowski, Adam Heydel and Ferdynand Zweig – was full of familiar-sounding warnings against the expansion of the state, the danger collectivism poses to freedom, the inefficiency of statism. If not for its archaic language, it would have not been out of place in the 1990s. It was written, however, at a very bad time for the free market. In practice, the voices of the "Kraków school" were almost completely forgotten for several decades, and were reintroduced into the public debate only after 1989.[532]

3. The antiliberal 1930s

The debate about statism in the interwar period was won decisively by its supporters, certainly in terms of political practice, and, according to the prevailing view, in terms of theory, as well.[533] "Life itself" put an end to the debate: capitalism had collapsed under its own weight, and now – as they wrote at the time – you would have to be naive to believe in "economic automatism".[534] Moreover, even avowed liberals "contrary to the beliefs they professed, were forced to pursue a policy of state intervention, often one bearing the hallmarks of statist politics."[535]

---

530 Ibid.

531 F. Zweig, *Poland Between Two Wars*, London 1944

532 K. Rogaczewska, *Ekonomiczny wymiar polskiego liberalizmu…*, op. cit., p. 224.

533 Cf. S. Duda, "Liberalizm a etatyzm: dyskusja o gospodarczej roli państwa w drugiej Rzeczypospolitej", *Rzeszowskie Zeszyty Naukowe: Prawo-Ekonomia,* 1997, vol. 22; J. Gołębiowski, *Sektor państwowy w gospodarce Polski międzywojennej,* Warszawa 1985.

534 K. Dziewulski, *Spór o etatyzm. 1919–1939*, Warszawa 1981, p. 11.

535 R. Wapiński, *Historia polskiej myśli politycznej XIX i XX wieku,* Gdańsk 1997, p. 220.

This is visible in the political programmes written of the period. The historian Andrzej Friszke divides Polish political life in the 1930s into three main (and internally diverse) camps: democratic, nationalist and "sanation", i.e., supporters of the Pilsudski dictatorship.[536] Without questioning the differences between them, it is worth noting here one common element in their views on the economy: they all shared an aversion to the free market as the sole (or even primary) regulator of economic processes. State intervention was widely recognized as the solution to the Depression, although the Soviet model was widely rejected as too radical and incompatible with Polish realities.[537]

On the left, the Polish Socialist Party called for the expropriation of large estates and large factories and the "collectivization of production"; there were differences of opinion within the party as to whether statism was an unsuccessful attempt to save capitalism (as assumed by the authors of the more radical "Project Programme" of 1937), or a path to greater social control over the economy, as can be inferred from the programme ultimately adopted.[538] Ultimately, however, the Socialists' plans called for, among other things, the collectivization of large estates, the introduction of a monopoly on foreign trade, the confiscation of land without compensation, and the introduction of a planned economy, i.e., the protection of "worker-peasant" interests.[539] The socialist left was going to leave in private hands only small-scale production: industry was to be managed by mixed teams of workers, buyers and state commissioners.[540] The agrarianist ideologues of the Peasant Party also proposed the expropriation of large estates, as well as reliance on family peasant farms and the transfer of industry to small towns.[541]

The right also abandoned liberal economic ideas, and it is worth devoting more attention here to them than to the ideas of the Left, which was by nature supportive of public or social ownership. Roman Rybarski, an economic theorist affiliated with the nationalist National Democrats and closest to the liberal Kraków School was politically marginalized in the 1930s.[542] In 1936, he warned against a "state monopoly", which admittedly could achieve economic successes,

536 A. Friszke, *O kształt niepodległej,* Warszawa 1989, p. 325.
537 Ibid., p. 330.
538 K. Dziewulski, *Spór o etatyzm…*, op. cit., p. 122.
539 J. Tomicki, *Polska Partia Socjalistyczna 1892–1948,* Warszawa 1983, p. 366.
540 A. Friszke, *O kształt…*, op. cit., p. 342.
541 Ibid., p. 340.
542 K. Rogaczewska, "Myśl ekonomiczna Narodowej Demokracji w kontekście konfliktu liberalizmu i socjalizmu", [in:] *Narodowa Demokracja XIX–XXI wiek. Dzieje ruchu politycznego,* vol. 1, *Koncepcje – ludzie,* Toruń 2012.

but "this very modernized, rationalized state factory would produce a standardized man, a human-robot, rather than a living man."[543] In its programme from 1928, the National Party condemned "statism", but wanted the state to play a very active role in an economy subordinated to "national" aims – including the promotion of small industry and handicrafts.[544]

In the 1930s, right-wing ideologues writing about the economy could write about the sanctity of private property and criticize sanation statism because it did not meet their expectations, but the ideas they put forward on the "national economy" were far removed from free-market principles and rested upon far-reaching state intervention.[545] Stanisław Grabski wrote in 1938:

> With the current state of our cash reserves, we cannot expect an increase in private capitalization of more than 100 million annually. And if the state takes none of this – then a private enterprise, based on private capitalization, could create new jobs for at most 150,000 people annually. […] With its current resources, private capitalization is able to provide jobs for barely half of the growth of our working-age population. […] But then for the other half of this increase, and for one and a half million of the most long-term unemployed, the state must create sufficient earning opportunities.[546]

These types of proposals could be combined with criticism of the government's policy of statism (Grabski called it "bureaucratism"), which had not lived up to the high expectations set for it.[547] This did not prevent Grabski – who still had an affinity for the free market – from writing about the "tasks of our planned economy", i.e., establishing a state lending programme and directing the development of industry.[548] His conclusion, which he reiterated repeatedly, was clear: "The liberal economy is no longer sufficient for us (it may still function quite adequately in England and France) as a means for staking a course out of the poverty that has been growing deeper for years".[549] "The essence of a planned national economy is directing the nation's economic development toward a predetermined goal."[550]

---

543 A. Friszke, *O kształt…*, op. cit., p. 334.

544 R. Wapiński, *Historia polskiej myśli…*, op. cit., p. 226.

545 S. Żurawicki, *Myśl ekonomiczno-polityczna w Polsce okresu międzywojennego*, Warszawa 1970, p. 106 ff.

546 S. Grabski, *Ku lepszej Polsce*, Warszawa 1938, p. 85.

547 Cf. W. Wojdyło, *Koncepcje społeczno-polityczne Stanisława Grabskiego,* Toruń 1993; S. Wójcik, *Ekonomia społeczna według koncepcji Stanisława Grabskiego,* Lublin 1995.

548 S. Grabski, *Ku lepszej…*, op. cit., pp. 99–100.

549 Ibid., p. 111.

550 Ibid., p. 207.

This "goal" of state control over the economy was to strengthen the armed forces and the nation's collective strength and "creative potential", which was described by means of a biological and naturalistic rhetoric. In *Wyście z kryzysu*, another popular book on the radical right, Jędrzej Giertych wrote:

> In some areas of Poland there is widespread hunger. The urban intelligentsia sometimes fail to realize the appalling living conditions of the Polish people in some densely populated, but less developed parts of the country. There are areas of Poland where the average peasant family usually eats nothing but potatoes boiled in salted water, and serving them with anything, not to mention wholemeal bread, is considered a rare delicacy seen only on special occasions; that in such areas, even older peasant children do not know what sugar tastes like because they have never had it in their mouths (they are more likely to know the taste of black-market saccharin); that the prayer for "our daily bread" is for many Poles a prayer unfulfilled. In these areas, Polish people's physical strength quickly wanes: the young generation, as a result of malnutrition (and even – in families which have now cows, or which sell all the milk they produce – of not drinking milk during childhood), do not properly develop physically. We may even be threatened in the future with the degeneration of our race.[551]

A radical reorganization of the economy was therefore needed immediately. Giertych was aware that Poland would not quickly become wealthy, but he also did not think this was essential. For him, improving living conditions did not mean luxuries, which only demoralized people. Like many other critics of capitalism – on both the right and the left – he thought that capitalism created "artificial needs": the state was to ensure its citizens a life that was dignified, but also free of the demoralization caused by consumer excesses. In its "Principles of the National-Radical Programme" published in 1937, the far-right ONR "Falanga" wrote:

> Any industry where the main source of profit is not the owner's own work will be expropriated [...]. All credit institutions will be in the hands of the state or public organizations, appointed by the various professional divisions of the Political Organization of the Nation.[552]

In most writings about the "national economy", as in the programmes of the socialists, there were very few specifics. Jędrzej Giertych, however, began to stand out among Poland's right-wing publicists in this regard:

> If it is to base its economy on strong foundations, Poland must return to traditional, age-old economic principles. The principles of thrift, work, foresight, individual initiative

551 J. Giertych, *O wyjście z kryzysu*, Warszawa 1938, p. 303.
552 Quoted in R. Wapiński, *Historia polskiej myśli...*, op. cit., p. 230.

and energy, the avoidance of unnecessary debt and needless extravagance, and finally, conscientiousness and integrity. We are not and we will not be a rich nation. But we can be [...] a well-managed country of average means. What do we need to do in order to reach this objective? Here is a list of measures leading to this objective that will be adopted by the national government.

Point A, the best described, called for the "removal of the Jews", who the author – and the movement in general – believed were parasites preying on the weak Polish body, and one of the main causes of the nation's calamities (Giertych even meticulously calculated that there was one Jewish "parasite" for every 17 Poles).[553] The rest of the plans for a national industrial and credit policy were, as in all such programmes, very vague. The state was to supply funds for a major investment effort, but it was not explicitly stated what exactly was to be built or how. Giertych condemned the government, complaining it "produces raspberry juice, slaughters calves, builds coffins, catches fish, sows grain, manufactures nails, weaves cloth and canvas, grinds flour, mines coal, salt and kerosene, processes sugar, provides the public with bus transport, builds homes, lets apartments, takes tourists by cable car up to mountain peaks, buys, sells [...]".[554] According to his vision, all this would be handled by private companies – but under the strict supervision and direction of the "national government". He firmly rejected "statism" as practiced by the Doboszyński government.[555]

In perhaps the most quoted right-wing vision of the Polish economy, that of Adam Doboszyński in *The National Economy*, these contradictions were even more pronounced. Doboszyński called for the breaking up of large estates as compensation – mainly for political reasons – because he envisioned a nation of small-scale, but secure private ownership. He also sought to "enfranchise the masses" and the "collectivization of big industry" (as distinguished from nationalization, although it is not clear exactly upon what this distinction, besides the subtle issue of a formal title deed, would be based).[556] He wanted to ban the construction of new factories in industrial areas, and called for "uniform distribution of factories throughout the country; a worker would continue to live in his home village and commute to work (by bicycle, train, bus) [...] This postulate was in no way utopian," he asserted, as if he realized how outlandish it sounded.[557]

---

553 J. Giertych, *O wyjście...*, op. cit., p. 313.

554 Ibid., p. 320.

555 T. Włudyka, *"Trzecia droga" w myśli gospodarczej II Rzeczypospolitej: koncepcje Adama Doboszyńskiego*, Kraków 1994, p. 25 ff.

556 A. Doboszyński, *Gospodarka narodowa*, Wrocław 2004, p. 116.

557 Ibid., p. 110.

At the heart of Doboszyński's book – besides a vaguely outlined utopia supervised by the state in union with small producers and owners and worker affiliated in corporations – was the issue of the Jews.[558] Liberalism had to be abandoned because, among other things, it was a Jewish invention (even if it brought an increase in wealth, which the author – unlike most of his contemporaries – did not rule out on principle):

> We are aware that any restriction on economic freedom comes at the price of an overall lowering of the standard of living (a relative slowing of the rate at which prosperity increases), but we believe that acquiring wealth as quickly as possible is not a proper goal for the life of the nation, if as a result, its spiritual and structural development suffers. [...] [E]xcessive economic freedom degenerates into the economic and political supremacy of an organized minority in the nation, or even, as in today's Poland, of a payot-wearing "national minority."[559]

The book is mainly an angry diatribe against the Jews, and in its most emotionally-charged chapter, it claims that the Jews are responsible for both communism and capitalism ("the product of the slow transformation of the Aryan economic system under the influence of Jewish customs").[560] According to Doboszyński, Jews' materialism manifests itself when they are oppressed as a people; when they gain power, as in Russia after the revolution, a collectivist voice and the messianic aspect of their dual nature come to the fore.

Similar statements appear repeatedly. What is essential here is the general anti-market trend. Economic nationalism and planning dominated economy thought – even in concepts that originated outside the left, where the market and private property still had a place. During the interwar period, the most well-known advocate of these views was the Romanian Mihail Manoilescu, an engineer by training, an economist by predilection, and a politician by ambition. Manoilescu propounded a theory of "Unequal Exchange" (one of the forerunners of dependence theory) between the countries of a rich centre and poor periphery nations. He believed the exchange of agricultural products for industrial goods was dictated by the rich countries, who determined the terms of trade. Manoilescu saw the only way out of this trap in a state focused on accumulation and industrialization, the purpose of which was to eliminate any dependency on imports. This process, of course, was to be planned and controlled by the state.

558 Cf. also S. Żurawicki, *Myśl ekonomiczno-polityczna w Polsce okresu międzywojennego*, Warszawa 1970, p. 117.

559 A. Doboszyński, *Gospodarka...*, op. cit., p. 108.

560 Ibid., p. 81.

"An agricultural country", he wrote: "cannot raise slowly and uniformly the income of all producers.... The real work of progress begins in the centers, or nuclei ... and such nuclei can only be provided by industries, which require superior productivity."[561] Such an undertaking requires centralization and coordination: in a typically modernist manner, Manoilescu believed a modern society resulted from the careful planning work of an engineer, and he considered liberal democracy, with its quarrels and divisions, to be a pernicious anachronism. His most important book, *The Theory of Protectionism and International Exchanges*, the best known of the era's many manifestos on economic nationalism, was published in 1929, at the outset of the Great Depression, which in the eyes of many Europeans had utterly compromised the ideals of liberalism. The book was translated into English, French, Italian, Portuguese and German, and very read widely in Latin America, especially in Brazil; in Poland it was invoked by the publicists associated with Leviathan, a lobby group which represented the interests of big industry.[562] The rest of his prescription – prohibitive tariffs to promote the development of Romanian industry and its "Romanization", the use of the "surplus population" from the overpopulated countryside in the construction of industry, an obsession with "scientific" planning – was very typical of the era, and reappeared in different forms, as we have seen, in various parts of the world.[563]

A key feature of the book was the belief, shared by those on both the left and the right, and in the pro-government camp, that only the state could solve the Second Republic's economic problems – both those resulting from the Great Depression, as well as those resulting from centuries of backwardness. Laissez-faire

---

561 Quoted in Andrew C. Janos, *East Central Europe in the Modern World. The Politics of the Borderlands from Pre- to Postcommunism*, Stanford 2000, p. 179.

562 J. Kofman, *Nacjonalizm gospodarczy – szansa czy bariera rozwoju. Przypadek Europy Środkowo-Wschodniej w okresie międzywojennym*, Warszawa 1992, pp. 20–21;
As a politician, Manoilescu was less fortunate: in the early 1930s, he was named Minister of Public Works, then Minister of Industry and Commerce, and finally, Governor of the National Bank, but his career was suddenly interrupted when he refused to grant a loan to a company belonging to a close friend of the King (the king became furious when the company failed). He returned to government in 1940, when, under heavy presssure from the Germans, he signed an agreement ceding much of Transylvania to Hungary. This was a grim task, especially for a nationalist, and he reportedly fainted during the ceremony. Within a week the signing, his career was over. After the war, he was publically condemned and imprisoned for collaborating with the Nazis, and died in prison of diseases he acquired while incarcerated.

563 J. L. Love, *Crafting the Third World. Theorizing Underdevelopment in Rumania and Brazil*, Stanford 1996, p. 60.

had not worked, and belonged to the past: the future was in coordination and planning.

What was important in all of these programmes was not only how much they shared in common (which was more important than their differences on particulars), but also what they left unsaid. In all of them, we hear a clear echo of the modernist fascination with scale and methods for organizing industrial production. This echo was universal, heard equally on the left and right, and gave rise to remarkably similar (if vague) practical prescriptions. At the end of the 1930s, this primarily meant abandoning deflationary policies, extending lines of credit and initiating a large-scale investment programme – by necessity to be carried out by the state, because no one else could do it.

These ideas were not unknown to the ruling camp in Poland, but it was faced with a much more challenging task than just writing a programme – it also had to implement its ideas. These, in turn, had originated within Stefan Starzyński's "First Economic Brigade" before the Great Depression (this informal group began operating in 1928, when its most important programmatic work, *On the Economic Front*, was published. The ideas contained in the book, however, had originated earlier). For Starzyński, the economy it was one front in the "struggle to empower the State", with "State" obviously being written with a capital letter. In another place, he adds: "Even the most rational economic policy by the government will not achieve much if economic life itself does not keep up with the times and is not guided by planning and rationalization in its functioning."[564]

From Starzynski's calls for "rationalization" and making economic policy "more scientific" – there was still no talk of a major investment programme in his plan – the road to statism was a short one. In 1928, he proposed protectionist duties as a means of supporting industry, active tax and credit policies to support selected branches of the economy, and the building of new infrastructure, especially a seaport.[565]

Throughout the 1930s, the Polish State systematically expanded its role in the economy, first by taking control of companies threatened with collapse, and later by establishing it own, as well. By the end of the interwar period, state-owned

---

564 Quoted in P. Janus, *W nurcie polskiego etatyzmu. Stefan Starzyński i Pierwsza Brygada Gospodarcza 1926–1932*, Kraków 2009, p. 235.

565 P. Janus, *W nurcie polskiego etatyzmu…*, op. cit., pp. 237–239. Cf. also M. Łapa, *Modernizacja państwa. Polska polityka gospodarcza 1926–1929*, Ibid., Łódź 2002.

enterprises generated more than 25 percent of industrial production, and a number of key sectors of the economy were completely under government control.[566]

The paradox of this situation lies in the fact that the State was not an effective manager, knowledge of which may have been the source of ritualistic condemnations of "statism" (though these did little to dissuade anyone from thinking that the state should solve Poland's economic problems). Critics of "statism" remained on the sidelines: they were active and visible, but they were ignored. In 1935, Tadeusz Bernadzikiewicz, an economist and journalist associated with the Leviathan lobby group, carried out a devastating critique of the management style of state-owned enterprises, which he estimated comprised as much as 1/4 of the nation's social wealth. As a manager, the state was incompetent, inefficient and prone to handing out political sinecures. No one knew the exact number of enterprises that were state owned or in which the state had a stake: they formed an inscrutable tangle of interrelated, often semi-private companies which the state guaranteed a profit, very often at the expense of its citizens, and which the bureaucratic and political elite used to enrich themselves. "We often learned of the existence of such companies by chance", wrote Bernadzikiewicz, recalling how it once came to light, quite by chance, that the state owned 31 printing houses. The State Armaments Works produced bicycles, padlocks, typewriters, office furniture, and machines for making cigarettes; the State Aviation Works – bicycle rims and fenders.[567] All of this production was subsidized by the state (i.e., the citizens) in one way or another. Officials were ordered to buy only telephones produced by state-owned enterprises. Taxes were lowered for state-owned mines (they paid 45 cents per tonne of coal, while private mines paid 1 zloty). In 1931, the National Engineering Works were given a waiver on customs duties on Fiat automobile parts to help them build a car assembly plant, and later a production plant. The factory was never built, but the company profited on the import of parts to Poland duty-free (which was facilitated by the introduction in 1932 of prohibitive tariffs on the import of auto parts, which made the lives of other importers more difficult).[568] As a result of this policy, the automotive industry in Poland not only came to a standstill, but even declined: from 1931 to 1934, the number of automobiles registered in Poland fell by 29 percent, and only one person in 1,245 owned a car, while in much poorer Albania the figure was 1 in 1,200.

---

566 J. Beksiak, T. Gruszecki, U. Grzelońska, J. Papuzińska, D. Żochowski, *Polska gospodarka w XX wieku. Eseje historyczno-ekonomiczne*, Łódź 2003, p. 22.

567 T. Bernadzikiewicz, *Przerosty etatyzmu. Uwagi o gospodarce państwowej w Polsce,* Warszawa 1935, p. 23.

568 Ibid., p. 40.

At the same time, in Germany, which was also in the midst of a deep economic crisis, the number of registered vehicles tripled during this period.[569]

Following the death of Pilsudski, the government responded to Starzyński's proposals with the implementation of a state investment programme. To legitimize its rule the Pilsudski camp chose to demonstrate its efficiency and experience in ensuring national security and economic strength – understood primarily in military terms.[570] They rejected democracy as ineffective and weak, and incapable of modernizing the country.[571] Pilsudski supported the economy's autonomy and independence from ideological interference; however, he also believed that objective economic mechanisms operated within a particular historical, geographical, natural and social context, and that the economy should serve non-economic objectives – of which the most important was ensuring the security and stability of the state.[572]

The heart of this grand planned investment programme was to be the Central Industrial District (Pol. Centralny Okręg Przemysłowy, abbrev. COP), which would be focused on military projects. According to the assumptions presented by Deputy Prime Minister Eugeniusz Kwiatkowski in June 1936, over the course of a four-year plan – running from July 1936 to June 1940 – the state planned to spend the astronomical sum (given Poland's capabilities) of 1.65–1.80 billion zlotys, most of which would be spent on infrastructure, though funds would also targeted to industrial investment.[573]

There was a burning necessity for action. In 1935, Kwiatkowski had presented the Sejm with a bleak picture of the Polish economy in crisis:

> The structure of our economy is extremely unfavourable and resistant to stimulus. Poland's countryside in the twentieth century has largely returned to a natural economy. Rather than develop its capacity as a natural and seemingly inexhaustible market, rural

569 Ibid., p. 97.

570 Cf. W. Paruch, "Autorytarna formuła legitymizacji władzy w piłsudczykowskiej myśli politycznej – warianty, kontrowersje, poszukiwania", [in:] *Kryzysy i sposoby ich przezwyciężania w myśli politycznej XX wieku,* ed. W. Wojdyło, Toruń 2004.

571 W. Paruch, "Założenia systemowe antydemokratycznej modernizacji Rzeczypospolitej – rozważania o piłsudczykowskiej myśli politycznej (1926–1939)", [in:] *Demokracja. Centrum i peryferie. Procesy modernizacyjne państwa w polskiej myśli politycznej XX–XXI wieku,* eds. A. Bałaban, J. Faryś, T. Sikorski, P. Słowiński, Szczecin 2008.

572 W. Paruch, "Przejawy i ograniczenia liberalizmu w piłsudczykowskiej myśli politycznej (1926–1939)", [in:] *Polskie zbliżenia z liberalizmem,* eds. T. Godlewski, D. Karnowska, Toruń 2006.

573 "Plan budowy COP", *Polska Gospodarcza*, 1938, no. 40.

> areas have become in every respect merely a modest and crowded addition to the urban market [...]. Many of the needs of those living in the countryside are being met in a peculiar and extremely primitive manner: matches are being split into parts, and candlewood used for light; foot and wagon transport, even over significant distances, have once again – after a break since the late nineteenth century regained – regained their importance.[574]

It quickly became clear that private capital, which the government had initially counted on (state investments were focused primarily on infrastructure), was not being invested in the building of factories – and that the state would have to get involved here as well.[575] Salvation would not come from outside in the form of loans and capital: Poland had to cope with the crisis alone, and do so quickly.[576]

The effectiveness of these investments will never be assessed because the construction of the Central Industrial Region was interrupted by the war. Recent research indicates, however, that we have good reason to believe their effect would have been modest. For one, the programme created a mere 110,000 new jobs.[577] Moreover, while GDP per capita in the late 1930s averaged an impressive annual growth rate of 11 percent, the profitability of public investments remained low, and were being pursued at the cost of an already rising debt and increasing economic instability. A modern historian can see striking similarities between state capitalism at the end of the Second Polish Republic and the economic policies of the Polish People's Republic.[578] On the other hand, between 1935 and 1938, industrial production in Poland increased by 30 percent, which was one of the best results in the world.[579] Even the propaganda of the interwar period sounded familiar to that after the war: for example, it was announced that the first four-year

574 Quoted in Z. Landau, "Kwiatkowskiego wizja gospodarki polskiej", *Zeszyty naukowe Uczelni Warszawskiej im. Marii Skłodowskiej-Curie* 2011, no. 33.

575 Z. Landau, W. Roszkowski, *Polityka gospodarcza...*, op. cit., p. 70.

576 M. Drozdowski, *Polityka gospodarcza rządu* polskiego 1936–*1939*, Warszawa 1963 p. 68.

577 C. Bobrowski, *Wspomnienia ze stulecia*, Lublin 1985, p. 80.

578 Cf. P. Koryś, *The State as an Entrepreneur: Reorientation of the Economic Policy of the Republic of Poland in Late 1930s and the Developing of State Capitalism*, upublished manuscript. My thanks to the author for providing me with access to this work.

579 J. Kaliński, "Przyspieszenia wzrostu w dziejach gospodrczych Polski", [in:] *Między zacofaniem i modernizacją. Społeczno-gospodarcze problemy ziem polskich na przestrzeni wieków*, eds. E. Kościk, T. Głowiński, Wrocław 2009, p. 34; Cf. also Z. Landau, J. Tomaszewski, *Gospodarka Polski międzywojennej 1918–1939*, vol. IV, *Lata interwencjonizmu państwowego 1936–1939*, Warszawa 1989

plan had been realized ahead of schedule in 1939; the next plan was designed to cover 15 years.

Kwiatkowski's economic ideas typified those of the pro-modernization elite in peripheral countries. He believed that in the modern world – of which, in his opinion, Poland should be a part – the only countries that truly mattered were those with a modern industrial sector (projects like the construction of the port in Gdynia were matters of "national ambition").[580] Industry was also extremely important in that it determined a state's military potential. A second problem was the need to provide jobs for the country's growing population: hidden unemployment in the countryside was accompanied by visible unemployment in cities. The expansion of industry would create jobs for the unemployed, and was therefore as much an aspect of social policy as an economic venture.[581]

The common threads linking prewar and postwar ideas on how to move out of backwardness are more visible when we matter through the lens of the military programmes adopted by Poland's political parties, and how they foresaw the nation's future. The young economists associated with the journal *National Economy* (Pol. *Gospodarka Narodowa*), headed by Czesław Bobrowski, were already heralding the coming of a new era:

> We unanimously rejected the basic assumptions of the pre-May and post-May economic policies, which are based on the illusion that Poland's development can be grounded in the inflow of foreign capital, for which we should provide greenhouse conditions by tolerating cartel pricing policies, erecting customs barriers, etc., etc. Against this background, three basic thematic trends arose in the club's writings and discussions: the need to fight against deflationary policies; recommendations for bolder actions to stimulate economic activity; and a call for changes in industrial policy […].[582]

4. Wartime programmes

The war, everyone realized, both in Poland and abroad, marked a radical break with the past. It was clear that after this calamity there could be no return to the poverty and injustice of prewar Poland. Virtually all political programmes that were being put together at that time, called for radical social and economic reforms. The programme of the Polish Socialist Party – Freedom, Equality, Independence

580 E. Kwiatkowski, *Dysproporcje. Rzecz o Polsce przeszłej i obecnej*, Warszawa 1989, p. 235. The book was first published in 1932.

581 Z. Landau, "Kwiatkowskiego wizja…", op. cit.

582 C. Bobrowski, *Wspomnienia…*, op. cit., p. 83.

(Pol. Polska Partia Socjalistyczna – Wolność, Równość, Niepodległość, abbrev. PPS-WRN), written in 1941, stated:

> The First Government of Independent Poland, backed by the decisive will of the people, upon its formation will issue a decree establishing the framework of both the political and socio-economic structure of the new Republic. In particular, these decrees call for:
>
> a) agrarian reform through the expropriation of large estates and the creation from them of a land reserve to be parcelled out [...];
>
> b) expropriation of industrial enterprises and their transfer to the state, local governments and established cooperatives for collectivization, as well as the creation of a collectivized management structure for them;
>
> c) reform of the tax system, aimed at the just allocation of the tax burden on all levels of society.

It also called for a "special tribunal" to put on trial sanation officials, who were said to share responsibility for the government's oppression and impoverishment of the "masses".[583] Socialists associated with the Polish Socialist Party – Freedom, Equality, Independence (PPS-WRN) predicted the postwar triumph of the socialist system, and its ideals of humanism, freedom and equality. A world full of "boors and criminals" was to be replaced by a world of freedom, peace and prosperity.[584] The idealism of this vision is striking in retrospect.[585] PPS-WRN put forward the idea of a postwar federation of Central European states, based on socialist principles, and eventually creating from them a federal state modelled on the U.S.[586]

The political programmes of various parties grew more radical as the war progressed, the occupation grew more brutal and destructive, and Soviet troops drew nearer to Poland. Nearly all the parties' plans called for "collectivization of the economy", land reform, planning, and the elimination of unemployment. Differences between the programmes of parties on the left and right remained significant (e.g., on the issue of compensation for nationalization, the fate of foreign-owned property, the minimum size of the companies that would be nationalized and of the farms that would be subject to land reform, and the form

583 Quoted in *Programy polskich partii*..., op. cit., p. 18.

584 E. Ponczek, Aksjologiczny wymiar lewicowości w polskiej myśli politycznej w latach II wojny światowej, [in:] *Polska Lewica w XX wieku. Historia – ludzie – idee,* eds. T. Ślęzak, M. Śliwa, Kraków 2004, p. 168.

585 Cf. K. Dunin-Wąsowicz, *Polski ruch socjalistyczny 1939–1945,* Warszawa 1993.

586 S. Stępień, "Polska – Europa – świat w myśli politycznej PPS-WRN", [in:] *Świat wokół Rzeczypospolitej*..., op. cit., p. 451.

of the institutions that would manage the economy) but nobody even considered a return to laissez-faire. This idea seemed as absurd to the authors of these programmes as the idea of a return to central planning would have seemed in 1990. Far-reaching agreement among the political parties can be seen, for example, in the programmes for land reform. According to the Council of National Unity – the quasi-parliamentary political body representing the underground state – postwar Poland would parcel out agricultural property and increase the size of small family farms. All private property in excess of 50 hectares would be subject to immediate parcelling-out; plans called for the creation from them of farms 8–15 ha in size depending on the quality of the soil, the farm's location and the type of crop grown. The construction of rural roads, electrification and the expansion of cooperatives and education were announced.[587] This programme was accepted by the Peasant Party "Ruch", PPS-WRN, and the Labour Party. It was rejected only by the National Party, which was not opposed to the idea of reform, but had concerns about its planned pace and the lack of compensation for the owners of expropriated property.[588]

Private property was to be limited in nature, both in its scale and scope. For example, the Democratic Party – the party of the intelligentsia – called in its programme from 1943 for leaving small-scale production in private hands, but also wrote:

> Maintaining the principle of private property as a stimulus for initiative and a factor contributing to the welfare of the people and the country, it should be abandoned when it conflicts with the sense of social justice. [...] Land reform must be carried out in such a manner that the broad masses of peasants are granted a path to ownership without compensation [...] Privately owned farmland will be allowed only in the form of independent family farms. [...] The exchange of goods in the countryside in the future system will be based primarily on cooperatives. [...] Remaining private enterprises will be subject to social and state control, representing producers and employees, who will have a voice in production decisions and receive a share of profits.
>
> Income revenues should be reinvested and used to create new sources of production and employment, or otherwise be used for the public good.[589]

---

587 K. Przybysz, "Program przeobrażeń politycznych w myśli politycznej Rady Jedności Narodowej oraz opozycji demokratycznej w latach 1945–1947", [in:] *Elity władzy w Polsce a struktura społeczna w latach 1944–1956*, ed. P. Wójcik, Warszawa 1992.

588 K. Przybysz, *Polska myśl...*, op. cit., p. 190.

589 Quoted in *Wizje Polski. Programy polityczne lat wojny i okupacji*, ed. Kazimierz Przybysz, Warszawa 1992, p. 200. I would like to thank dr hab. Andrzej Krzysztof Kunert for help in locating these materials.

Disputes of course, existed – over the forms of state control over the economy, the terms of agricultural reform and the forms of planning to be used. There were no doubts, however, in terms of the direction of change, even in the London government. In 1942, Stanisław Grabski, head of the National Council of Poland in London, noted:

> Various parties among us have put forward a programme for the nationalization of heavy or key industries. This demand is being made not only by the Socialists. It has been incorporated into the ideological declaration of the National Radical Camp immediately after its split from the National Party and Camp for a Great Poland.[590]

Even the rightist National Party, which strongly defended private property, and warned that the state, by imposing various levies and restrictions on property, could easily lead it – without formally abandoning it – to become a "fiction", wrote in the 1944:

> The meaning of the concept of private property is undergoing a fundamental change. An individualistic concept of the inalienable rights of the individual in relation to ownership is giving way to a new formulation, accenting first and foremost the social function of private property. Private property will find here its justification and far-reaching legal protection if ownership rights are established in accordance with the needs of the national economy. [...] Faith in the economic automatism that underlies economic liberalism now belongs to the past. Experience has taught us that, beyond a doubt, the free play of economic forces does not lead automatically to harmonization of the economy, neither in terms of its particular parts or as a whole, nor to the proper coordination of economic goals with the overall objectives of national life.[591]

The National Party did not unequivocally reject "socialism".[592] What it wanted was "national democracy", understood by its activists as "calling on the broad masses of the nation to work for the good of the whole [...] not through the governments of small cliques or irresponsible Fuehrers, but through the collective efforts of society as a whole, the adoption of a great, common national idea, a joint sense of unity and an awareness of hierarchy, and finally, by defining

---

590 J. W. Gołębiowski, "Sprawa nacjonalizacji przemysłu i odbudowy gospodarki narodowej w programach ważniejszych stronnictw politycznych podczas II Wojny Światowej", [in:] *Wojna i okupacja na ziemiach polskich*, ed. Władysław Góra, Warszawa 1984, p. 530.

591 Quoted in *Programy polskich partii...*, op. cit., p. 144.

592 S. Rudnicki, "Koncepcje niepodległego państwa w myśli politycznej obozu narodowego", [in:] *Wizje Polski w myśli politycznej lat I i II wojny światowej*, ed. M. Tanty, Warszawa 1990.

personalism in a Catholic spirit."[593] In addition, the party wanted a "universalization of property", but also a "just division of national income" and strict state control over the economy under a national plan. The "universalization of property" was thus in practice to accompany restrictions on owners' rights.[594]

Both the left and right drew up plans for far-reaching state control of the economy, planning, and subordinating private property to collective – social or national – interests (or in some cases simply abolishing it). Historian Marci Shore writes:

> Against this gradualist ethos and patience with human imperfection, liberalism's offspring rebelled; both nationalism and communism were utopian variations on liberalism. What made them utopian was not only a more fervent optimism, but also an aspiration toward totalism.[595]

Anti-liberal programmes on the left and right had more in common than the supporters of either side were willing to admit. But the differences between them should not be glossed over – the socialists spoke about emancipation, freedom and humanism; the right, about the national interest – but their visions of the future economic system combined anti-liberalism and collectivism (to which the Socialists added the demand for full political and cultural freedom, which prewar capitalism had not provided to the masses).[596] It was possible – like the socialists or Peasant Party – to assign a major role to local governments in Poland's future political system, but that did not necessarily indicate support for a free market.[597] "Both the Socialists and National Democrats", wrote Krystyna Rogaczewska, "believed it was possible to create the economic sphere without regard for the laws of

---

593 W. Woydyło, "Wizja ustroju politycznego państwa w myśli politycznej Stronnictwa Narodowego w drugiej wojnie światowej", [in:] *Między otwartą a domkniętą myślą polityczną. Szkice o najnowszej refleksji politycznej,* eds. R. Bäcker, J. Marszałek–Kawa, Toruń 2006, p. 66.

594 K. Przybysz, *Polska myśl polityczna…*, op. cit. p. 165.

595 M. Shore, "Cosmopolitanism, the Avant-Garde, and a Lost Innocence of Central Europe", [in:] eds. M. Gordon, H. Tilley, G. Prakash, *Utopia/Dystopia: Conditions of Historical Possibility,* Princeton 2010, p. 176.

596 K. Przybysz, *Polska myśl polityczna…*, op. cit., p. 167.

597 B. Poboży, "W walce o Polskę Ludową. Wizje przyszłej Polski w myśli politycznej ruchu ludowego w latach 1939–1945", [in:] *Dylematy historii i polityki. Księga dedykowana profesor Annie Magierskiej,* eds. R. Chwedoruk, D. Przastek, Warszawa 2008 p. 187.

economics."[598] Marxists could talk about the objective laws of history, and nationalists about the cyclical nature of history – but this nevertheless united them.[599]

Against the background of the wartime programmes of other political parties, the declarations of the Communists in no way stood out for their radicalism. Nationalization of large parts of the economy was written into the Manifesto of the Polish Committee of National Liberation (Pol. Polskiego Komitetu Wyzwolenia Narodowego, abbrev. PKWN) and other political declarations by the communists who were preparing to assume power in accordance with Stalin's will, could be seen as almost moderate: their project included "big industry", i.e., steel mills, mines, the armaments and machinery industries, banks and transport.[600] There was to be planning, but also worker control of enterprises.[601] The programme's moderation was a conscious political choice, and shows the hand of Stalin, who at this stage believed that radicalism was harmful to his political plans.[602]

On the evening of 17 May 1944, two months before the announcement of the manifesto, Oskar Lange, then already well-known as an economist with leftist but non-Communist views, met in Moscow with Stalin and Molotov. Lange later described the course of their conversation:

> I noted that the views of soldiers and officers [of the Polish Army in the Soviet Union] were more radical than the views of members of the Union of Polish Patriots. While the vast majority of soldiers expressed support for the nationalization of big industry and banks, the Union of Polish Patriots was reluctant to take a position. Most of all, the Polish Communists were now in the right wing of the Union of Polish Patriots (compared with the socialists and Peasant Party), because they opposed the nationalization of big industry in the belief that it would undermine national unity. Stalin smiled and said: "That's because I told them off". He added that he was very glad to hear that there were clear demands for the nationalization of big industry, which was, in his opinion, very beneficial.

Lange noted that Stalin underestimated the radicalism of Poles – because the Polish Army in the USSR consisted "mainly of military settlers and wealthier peasants" and were thus not representative. The poor and "landless proletariat" would be given a voice after the liberation. Stalin replied that in his opinion the

---

598 K. Rogaczewska, *Myśl ekonomiczna Narodowej Demokracji…*, op. cit., p. 95.

599 Ibid., p. 95.

600 M. Nadolski, "Programy przeobrażeń ustrojowych w Polsce komunistów i ugrupowań prokomunistycznych w latach 1941–1948", [in:] *Elity władzy w Polsce a struktura społeczna w latach 1944–1956*, ed. P. Wójcik, Warszawa 1992.

601 K. Przybysz, *Polska myśl polityczna…*, op. cit., p. 184.

602 Ibid., p. 185.

German occupation had ended class divisions and that reactions from various social strata would be rather uniform.[603]

Stalin was largely correct: the war had indeed radically flattened Poland's social structure, pauperizing or eliminating a large part of the prewar elite. In the east, they were destroyed by the Soviet Union; in the West, by Germany, which had also assumed control of a large part of industry. The shift in society to the left was confirmed by reports being sent from Poland to London.[604] This made carrying out a radical programme of social reform much easier.

Such changes were also anticipated in the documents and studies being produced by those associated with the Polish government in London. At the end of 1939, the government-in-exile announced that the new Poland would embody the principle of "social justice", giving peasants the right to land, and workers – to the means to work.[605] Work by the Committee on Constitutional Affairs on a vision for Poland's future political system had been gaining momentum since the autumn of 1941, and Gen. Sikorski took a personal interest in its progress. Ready in its final form in 1942, the document assumed the necessity of introducing economic planning, wide-ranging state intervention, and nationalization of key and leading industrial enterprises. Private property was to be preserved in the form of small businesses and family farms created as a result of wide-scale reforms.[606] The Council of National Unity issued a key statement in March 1944 – "What the Polish Nation is Fighting For"; in addition to calling for democracy, decentralization and the "rule of law", it heralded major changes in the economy: "the universalisation of ownership", "raising national income" (which was to be the task of the state), full employment, a planned economy and the "Poland's rising to the level of the countries of Western Europe in economic terms through targeted public and private investment."[607]

---

603 Quoted in W. Skrabalak, *Polscy socjaliści w XX wieku. Ich rodowody oraz uwarunkowania ich działalności*, Warszawa 2010, pp. 133–134.

604 K. Przybysz, "U źródeł Trzeciej Rzeczypospolitej. O przyszłości społeczeństwa i państwa w latach 1939–1945", [in:] *Dylematy historii i polityki. Księga dedykowana profesor Annie Magierskiej*, eds. R. Chwedoruk, D. Przastek, Warszawa 2008.

605 K. Przybysz, *Polska myśl polityczna 1939–1945. Zarys problematyki*, Warszawa 2000, p. 163.

606 W. Wojdyło, "Wizja ustroju polityczno-gospodarczego powojennej Polski w projekcjach Komisji Spraw Ustrojowych Rządu Rzeczypospolitej Polskiej na uchodźstwie 1939–1945", *Athenaeum*, 2005, no. 13.

607 A. Friszke, *O kształt niepodległej*…, op. cit., p. 502.

The radicalism of these proposals was in part dictated by the state of affairs (i.e., "depriving the Soviets of initiative in terms of social reform in Poland and immediately proposing legal initiatives that would inspire confidence among the rural and urban masses in [the Council's] leadership abilities", cabled Gen. Bór-Komorowski to Kazimierz Sosnkowski in July 1944).[608] An extensive memorandum several dozen pages in length, written in London in 1944, outlined plans for the government's first decisions after returning to Poland. It provided for nationalization of the main instruments of industry and explicitly rejected prewar corporatist ideas, calling instead for direct state intervention:

> Any attempt to establish economic organizations designed to work on behalf of the state or simply assume its role in terms of economic policy, has been politically and socially discredited, having failed to demonstrate the organizational values their creators expected from them.[609]

The document warned of the threat of "centralization" and "the formation of a manager caste", and anticipated a mixed form for management of the economy, involving private entities, the state and local government – "big industry" and heavy industry would remain the direct responsibility of the state. Smaller enterprises would be controlled through resource and credit policies that would be national in scope.

The whole of Europe was veering to the left, as well.[610] In France, in January 1946, a Plan Commission (Fr. Commissariat général du Plan) was established, and a national economic plan drawn up that envisioned major investments being made in heavy industry and infrastructure, which would be coordinated and in part carried out by the state.[611] France nationalized its mining, gas and power industries, along with some major banks, insurance companies, and Renault's commercial fleet and factories.[612] The plan was originally intended to guide the country's reconstruction.[613] It was later adapted to include the assistance provided by the United States under the Marshall Plan (announced in 1947), which the countries of Eastern Europe rejected under pressure from Moscow: In total, U.S.

---

608 J.W. Gołębiewski, *Sprawa nacjonalizacji…*, op. cit., p. 542.

609 My thanks to prof. Marcin Kul for providing me with this manuscript.

610 Cf. Chapter 2.

611 B. Eichengreen, *European Economy Since 1945. Coordinated Capitalism and Beyond*, Princeton–Oxford 2007, p. 105.

612 J. Holzer, *Europa zimnej wojny*, Kraków 2012, p. 98.

613 T. Judt, *Postwar: A History of Europe Since 1945*, New York 2005, pp. 70–71.

aid granted to Western Europe totalled 24.8 billion dollars, most of which was spent on the reconstruction of infrastructure and investment in key industries.[614]

Historians disagree on the extent to which postwar growth in Western Europe resulted from reconstruction, the flourishing international trade and the expansion of the labour force – and how much it resulted from structural modernization.[615] In the early 1950s, the western world began two decades of the fastest economic growth in its history, along with the expansion of the welfare state.

Poland's course was a foregone conclusion, although it had not been chosen through a democratic process. That does not mean, however, that many people longed for the unemployment and hunger of the prewar era. On 6 February 1946, the eminent economic historian Witold Kula, one of the most astute analysts of Polish backwardness, gave a habilitation lecture at the University of Łódź entitled "Social Privilege and Economic Progress" (Kula's economic views were rooted in the experience of the Great Depression). In it he said:

> History has never before witnessed a culture that deliberately choose to plan and finance investments to allow it to keep pace with or even surpass population growth, thereby raising the general standard of living, but which, at the same time, would not seek to justify any new form of social privilege.
>
> Today's world is the first to undertake such a task.
>
> The future will show how well this task was fulfilled.
>
> But unlike facing the worries of everyday life, in order to meet the challenges of a task that nobody has ever tried to accomplish – we need to remain aware that this is precisely where the ambitious, heroic beauty of our era lies.[616]

Such a task required a rational, comprehensive multi-year plan and the mobilization of society.

5. The road to Stalinism

By November 1945, the Central Planning Office had already been set up, staffed by a group of economists led by Czesław Bobrowski, who had been associated

---

614 J. Holzer, *Europa…*, op. cit., pp. 102–103; J. Kochanowicz, "Początki planowania w Polsce po II wojnie światowej w perspektywie porównawczej", [in:] *Ekonomia i ekonomiści w czasach przełomu*, eds. E. Mączyńska, J. Wilkin, Warszawa 2010.

615 For a survey of this literature, see T. Vonyó, "Post-war Reconstruction and the Golden Age of Economic Growth", *European Review of Economic History*, 2008, no. 2.

616 W. Kula, "Przywilej społeczny a postęp gospodarczy", *Przegląd Socjologiczny*, 1947, no. 1–4, p. 193.

with the prewar non-communist Left. At first, planned management covered coal mining, transportation and food supplies. The country lay in ruins, and masses of people had been transferred from one place to another. But already in 1946, the first National Investment Plan was launched; initially it was very simple, assuming only financial limits on investment.[617]

Bobrowski was a staunch opponent of the Stalinist economic model: he believed that three sectors – private, cooperative and state – should co-exist in Poland, with the latter including major enterprises and banks, and acting as the engine of the economy. The Central Planning Office prepared an edition of Oskar Lange's classic work on market socialism, *On the Economic Theory of Socialism* (1936). *Socialist Review* also printed his wartime essay, in which he warned against "a concentration of economic power, dangerous for democracy, in the hands of the state bureaucracy."[618] He also wrote about the need to maintain multiple forms of economic and social control over the government.

The rebuilding plan was a success, and was probably the only one in the history of communist Poland which was not only met, but exceeded. Gross national income per capita rose from 506 zlotys in 1938 to 860 zlotys in 1949, mainly due to the annexation of the more industrialized western lands and the decline in population (from 36 to 26 million). Real wages, especially white-collar workers, however, remained significantly lower than before the war.

The Central Planning Office soon – in February 1948 – fell victim to purges. This was an element of the communists' plans for switching the country's economy onto Stalinist tracks. The authorities quickly began systematically discriminating against private businesses – those which had survived the postwar wave of nationalization, which were often carried out in an arbitrary and chaotic manner, and in violation of relevant legal provisions.[619] In the archives of the Economic Department of the Polish Workers' Party (Polska Partia Robotnicza, abbrev. PPR), a few reports written "in the field" in 1945–1946 have survived: envoys from provincial towns reported to headquarters on the number, condition and equipment of industrial plants, indicating which should be nationalized and which could be left in the hands of their owners.

617 *Ustawa o planie 3-letnim*, ed. J. Kaliński, Lublin 1981, p. 8.

618 T. Kowalik, *Spory o ustrój społeczno-gospodarczy w Polsce, lata 1944–1948*, Warszawa 2006, p. 61.

619 Cf. M. Zaremba, *Wielka trwoga. Polska 1944–1947. Ludowa reakcja na kryzys*, Kraków 2012.

1 May 1947, Hilary Minc, speaking in Katowice, said: "We have won the battle over production, we will now try to win the battle over trade."[620] He had mentioned this latter battle earlier in 1945, when he accused "speculators" and trade cooperatives of creating market troubles.[621] His aim, at least officially, was to put a halt to rising prices and fill stores with goods. It was easier for the government to blame the "excessive purchasing power" of some groups of the population, in particular, peasants and urban dwellers who had enriched themselves on the wartime chaos and postwar looting, than blame its own economic policies. In June of 1947, a law was passed "On combating high prices and excessive profits", and an extensive inspection apparatus quickly set up: these included various pricing commissions and "social commissions for inspecting prices". Most of those who sat on these bodies were representatives of the authorities, including local delegations of the Special Commission to Combat Fraud and Economic Sabotage. Established in 1945, this institution was free of judicial review, and could sentence those accused of misconduct to as much as two years in a forced-labour camp (in 1945–1954 more than 90,000 people were thus sentenced).[622] The price control commissions possessed a rich arsenal of repressive measures – they could seize a business' assets or shut it down when they believed the law was being broken. Overall, the Commission carried out 359,000 inspections, wrote up 69,000 protocols and imposed 800 million zlotys in criminal fines – sending 788 people to forced-labour camps.[623]

In July 1947, the first lists of maximum prices were announced; these imposed such low profit margins on private trade that they often did not even cover transport costs. This was a deliberate effort to ruin private enterprises. This culminated in the closure of companies without a business license. Applying for a license and paying the relevant fee – from 2 to 24 percent of trading volume! – was payable by November 1947: of the 20,000 companies that did not submit applications by this deadline, 15,000 simply closed down voluntarily. The local governmental and tax authorities were actively involved in this campaign, raising rental fees for premises and imposing arbitrary surtaxes.

All this destruction and the accompanying draining of money from the market –plans called for raising 4 billion zlotys from merchants alone – led to a drop

620 J. Kaliński, *Bitwa o handel 1947–1948*, Warszawa 1970, p. 80.

621 T. Kowalik, *Spory o ustrój…*, op. cit., p. 65.

622 D. Jarosz, T. Wolsza, *Komisja Specjalna do Walki z Nadużyciami i Szkodnictwem Gospodarczym 1945–1954*, Warszawa 1995, p. 8.

623 J. Kaliński, *Bitwa…*, op. cit., pp. 97–101.

in inflation from 28 percent in 1947 to 3.2 percent in 1948.[624] The costs of this policy were passed onto citizens, who afterward were left with no choice but purchase goods from state-run enterprises.

By destroying the remnants of private enterprise, the government simultaneously achieved several objectives: it increased its control over the economy, preparing it for rapid industrialization on the Soviet model (which required curbing consumption); it increased its political power, weakening those groups that were not dependent on the state's material base; finally, it eliminated the remnants of the capitalist class system. Its economic, political and ideological goals were fully synchronized. The evident inefficiency of the state economy – visible on a microscale to the naked eye – did not interfere with the plans for massive structural and social transformation envisaged by the authorities. The new, six-year plan assumed growth in national income of 70–80 percent, and a rise in industrial production of 85–90 percent. These indicators were then arbitrarily raised, and in the final version, national income was to increase by 112 percent, and industrial production by 158 percent.[625]

Minc's plan differed from Bobrowski's plan significantly, not only in terms of its focus on investment, but also in how the economy was to be managed. The first investment plan already called for a command economy – the tasks written into the plan read like a set of instructions.[626] A typical centralized economy was thus in the making from the outset.[627] Only after 1949 was a rigid, centralized system for managing the economy introduced: according to its provisions, "enterprises were created to perform tasks arising from national economic plans" and "economic calculations" were just one of many (and not the most important) criteria for assessing their usefulness.[628] There was full overlap in terms of personnel between the state apparatus, political parties and the economy: corporate executives and the managers of various bodies sat in different party bodies, and key decisions on the economy were taken at the political level.[629] This was fundamentally different from how planning was implemented in the West, where

---

624 Ibid., p. 161.

625 M. Bałtowski, *Gospodarka socjalistyczna w Polsce*, Warszawa 2009, p. 170.

626 T. Stankiewicz, *Działalność inwestytycjna państwa w Polsce w latach 1945–1947*, Warszawa 1993, p. 35.

627 T. Stankiewicz, *Działalność…*, op. cit., p. 177.

628 M. Tymiński, *PZPR i przedsiębiorstwo. Nadzór partyjny nad zakładami przemysłowymi 1956–1970*, Warszawa 2001p. 31 ff.

629 J. Kaliński, "Zarządzanie gospodarką", [in:] *PZPR jako machina władzy*, eds. D. Stola, K. Persak, Warszawa 2012, p. 201.

objectives were stipulated rather than production volume; moreover, targets were arbitrarily adopted by planners, with rigid divisions into different areas of the economy and types of goods.[630]

This departure from the market had far-reaching consequences. Costs, quality and the level of technological advancement in products ceased to be relevant to companies. Fulfilment of the plan was not motivated by profit (or fear of bankrupcty), but a system of premiums, commands and penalties. As a result, fully rational enterprises focused on meeting those targets in the plan that brought them the greatest benefits, that is, on quantitative production results over quality and innovation. This was not accidental, as the main aim of planners for a long time was to increase production in key industries.

In response, planners tried to incorporate as many details as possible into their plans: e.g., in companies supervised by the Ministry of Light Industry, even 100 percent of production was precisely written into the plan, while in others the share exceeded 90 percent. Centralized control and harsh penalties for failure to comply with the plan led to growth in the bureaucracy. Since enterprises themselves tinkered with the plans, evermore rigorous regulations were introduced, and more details demanded. Enterprises were organized in a hierarchical pyramid. While in the 1940s investments were defined by value, rather than production volume, and banks had a say in the investment process, by the 1950s everything had become rigid and formalized.[631]

This process occurred in all countries in Central Europe under Soviet domination. In just the first half of 1951, each coal mine in Hungary received 1025 government regulations and circulars. Gathering such a volume of data exceeded the capabilities of most enterprises – and only a fifth of the data collected was actually used in the planning process.[632]

In the Archives of New Records in Warsaw, hundreds of folders filled with giant sheets full of numbers, intended to regulate production in the socialist economy, have survived, although usually lack descriptions and are now completely incomprehensible.

At the same time, however, the authorities retained the right to manual control: Hilary Minc reportedly never parted with a notebook in which he maintained

630 Cf. T. Judt, *Postwar…*, op. cit., pp. 69–72.

631 T. Stankiewicz, *Działalność…*, op. cit., p. 178.

632 I. T. Berend, *Central and Eastern…*, op. cit., p. 77; Cf. also T. Vonyó, "Socialist Industrialisation or Post-War Reconstruction: Understanding Hungarian Economic Growth, 1949–1967", *Journal of European Economic History*, 2010, no. 2.

a running list of changes in production targets.[633] He was meticulous, organized and had an excellent memory: he was perfectly suited to run a Stalinist economy.[634] His announcement of a transition towards the Soviet model in a speech delivered at the meeting of the Central Committee of the Polish Workers' Party in April 1947 is a classic call for state control: the word "State" occurs five times just in the definition of socialist industry, and is mentioned 30 times throughout the speech. "Marxism has always understood collectivization of the means of production as their transfer to public ownership," he said.[635]

Making the economy similar to that of the Soviet Union was also the result of pressures coming from Moscow. A document from April 1948 has been preserved, in which Russian envoys wrote to Stalin reprovingly about his incorrect – in their opinion – economic policy, accusing the leaders of the PPR of "nationalist deviation" and "lagging behind in both theory and practice on the peasant question." "Comrade Stalin in 1929 warned that the theory of the spontaneous development of socialist construction is an anti-Marxist theory," Minc reminded, mentioning the name of Gomułka.[636]

While the exact mechanisms of dependence are not yet known, it is clear that the Soviet Union benefitted economically from its satellites – which it began subsidizing on a large scale only during the times of Khrushchev and Brezhnev. In 1945 alone, Soviet troops transported out of Poland machinery and rolling stock worth at that time 500 million dollars (for comparison, the USSR loaned Poland that year 28.8 million dollars for food purchases.). In the Stalinist period, the main mechanism for extracting money from the Polish People's Republic was an agreement concluded with the USSR in August 1945. In it, Poland committed itself to selling coal at special, low prices, far below world prices (1.22 dollars per

633 I would like to thank prof. T. Kowalik for this anegdote about Minc.

634 H. Różański, *Śladem wspomnień i dokumentów, 1943–1948*, Warszawa 1988, pp. 166–167.

635 T. Kowalik, *Spory o ustrój…*, op. cit., pp. 66–67.

636 "Memoriał kierownika Biura Informacji KC WKP(b) Leonida Baranowa oraz instruktorów KC WKP(b) Nikołaja Puchłowa i Władimira Owczarowa 'O antymarksistowskiej orientacji w kierownictwie PPR'" [in:] *Polska-ZSRR. Struktury podległości. Dokumenty WKP(b) 1944–1949*, eds. G. A. Bordiugow, et al., Warszawa 1995, pp. 212–214; Cf. also A. Skrzypek, *Mechanizmy klientelizmu. Stosunki polsko-radzieckie 1965–1989,* Warszawa 2008.

tonne). Prior to 1956, Poland sold more than 54 million tons of coal under this agreement, losing a whopping sum of 630 million dollars.[637]

Two sectors of the economy did not surrender easily to central planning – foreign trade (because the products of a socialist economy had to compete on unpredictable capitalist markets) and agriculture, because the peasants were stubborn, conservative and self-seeking, and it was therefore difficult to persuade them to participate voluntarily in the great work of building socialist industry. In foreign trade, the state tried to cope by assuming a monopoly on trade. Moreover, at the height of Stalinism, Poland was, in practice, a closed country; almost nobody could leave the country for private purposes.[638]

Like in the USSR, control over food production was both a political and economic challenge: without it there was no possibility of either full control, nor of rapid industrialization. In the Communist Party itself, there were disagreements on the appropriate pace and methods for "liquidating the remains of capitalism" in agriculture, though these were quickly resolved. Władysław Gomułka, Deputy Prime Minister and Minister of the Recovered Territories, was an opponent of collectivization, as he had seen it carried out in the Soviet Union in the 1930s and considered it a moral and economic failure. Indeed, this was one of the reasons for his removal from power in 1948. During the meeting of the Politburo when he was denounced for having deviated from the party line, he defended himself saying:

> I believed that the transition from a system of small peasant farms to a socialist economic system should be voluntary in nature and based on the free choice of working peasants. It is therefore to be a long-term process. The forward pace of this process is dependent on proving to the peasant masses the superiority and greater profitability of collective over individual farming. I believe a major role can be played by state-owned farms, provided they are well organized and raised to a satisfactory level.[639]

Gomułka in his stubbornness would not budge, but he was doomed to fail because Stalin insisted on haste (The Cominform had recommended collectivization to communist parties in June 1948). In Poland, shortly after the removal of Gomułka, Minc provided a motto for action in a speech delivered on 3 September 1948 at the plenum of the Central Committee of the Polish Workers' Party. The peasant-capitalist, the *kulak* employing and exploiting the poor, was

---

637 J. Kaliński, "Pomoc czy wyzysk? Stosunki gospodarcze między Polską i ZSRR", [in:] *Białe plamy – Czarne plamy. Sprawy trudne w relacjach polsko-rosyjskich (1918–2008)*, eds. A. D. Rotfeld, A. W. Torkunow, Warszawa 2010, p. 631 ff.

638 D. Stola, *Kraj bez wyjścia. Migracje z Polski 1949–1989*, Warszawa 2012, p. 27 ff.

639 Quoted in D. Jarosz, *Polityka władz komunistycznych w Polsce w latach 1948–1956 a chłopi*, Warszawa 1998, p. 19.

the obvious enemy: he could be overcome only by a radical change in the structure of agriculture. Minc estimated that by 1949 cooperatives made up 1 percent of the total value of farms. He distinguished three types of cooperatives; in the most collective of these, revenue was to be divided according to the amount of work performed, and not the amount of land or means of production supplied. Collectivization was to bring, he optimistically assumed, an increase in food production of 35–45 percent during the six-year plan (1950–1955).[640]

The unspoken goal of collectivization was the same as in Stalin's Soviet Union. Establishing food prices too low for it be profitable for peasants to increase production. Farmers defended themselves against the unprofitability of production and forced deliveries. They also fought against what they perceived as expropriation, an invasion from the cities and a threat to their traditional existence.[641] Here is an account of one such action:

> The tractors started into the field, and the people started in pursuit of the tractors. Women began to a cry out and make a commotion. They began holding up holy paintings and singing devotional songs. One of the women lay down in front of the tractor and hugged the earth, because this had all begun on her field. All the people, the whole village, everyone who could breathe, left their cottages – women, men, children, old men – and went into the field. They had with them the images of saints and sticks and shovels and pitchforks and other items. One woman struck a tractor, damaging it. That's how it all started. Men stood on the sides, while the women pushed forward. Nobody left the fields, everyone guarded his field. This continued throughout the night; in the morning, a group of young party activists arrived from Rzeszów, followed by a cordon of troops and police. The party activists were supposed to reassure the people and explain things to them. The army and police were supposed to protect the activists and the equipment, because one tractor had already been damaged. At the sight of so many visitors, the people put out the alarm. The bell from the church tower began to ring vigorously. From all sides, people began to appear on the horizon. They were people from all the nearby villages coming to their aid. They walked in a phalanx through the fields towards the machines, holding holy paintings, reciting prayers and singing songs.[642]

The government sought to take control of the entire food production process, and this would only be possible through collectivization. In theory – and perhaps even believed at the highest levels of government – the peasants were supposed to agree to this voluntarily, and therefore, a system of incentives that was gradually expanded was developed. Cooperatives were given tax breaks, and priority in

640 D. Jarosz, *Polityka władz...*, op. cit., pp. 19–20.

641 S. Skieterski, "Świadomość chłopów okresu kolektywizacji w świetle pamiętników", *Przegląd Humanistyczny*, 1990, no. 4.

642 Quoted in Ibid.

obtaining assistance with rebuilding and expansion, land reclamation and electrification, the setting up of youth clubs, and the delivery of supplies. In addition, they were offered special loans, exempted from mandatory quotas for supplying milk during their initial period of activity, their quotas for compulsory deliveries of grain were lowered, and children from cooperatives were guaranteed easier access to studies.[643]

Yet all of this did little to help, and at the "lower levels" of the bureaucracy many abuses occurred. Local officials exerted strong pressures on peasants, often simply forcing them to join cooperatives. For example, in the Żagań district in 1951 the local Party secretary issued a command to the district secretary in Witoszyn that "by this and that day a cooperative must be established". A low-level apparatchik complained that "if it isn't established, I'll be the one who gets a sound thrashing. I'll be the deviationist."[644] When the authorities condemned such abuses – first publicizing in 1951 some particularly extreme cases that had occurred in Gryfice, and then again in 1953 when a similar situation took place in the Lublin region – the local power apparatus felt wronged and confused: in the end, they were just doing what was expected of them.

Collectivization in Poland did not prove to be as much of a disaster as in the USSR, perhaps only because it was carried out using less brutal methods, and as a result, was never fully completed. The peasants were unshaken in their convictions. "Collective farms make a beggar out of a man", heard one party activist who had been instructed to go into the fields and convince the people from his native village to join the cooperative. Propaganda also did not work: the films peasants most enjoyed watching were fairy tales and war stories, and on the radio, they only listened to music, news and the weather report.[645] Any visible hesitation by the authorities on the issue of collectivizing was read by the peasants as a call to retreat: after the fraud in Gryfice was disclosed, 200 cooperatives in Poland were immediately dissolved.[646]

The communist authorities had reasons not to use a Stalinist model of coercion. The country had a significant excess of labour, and it was thus more convenient – for the moment – for peasants to remain in the countryside than to have masses of unemployed workers in the cities that industry was not yet able to absorb. Besides, the ruling elite, quite reasonably, did not trust the efficiency of its

643 D. Jarosz, *Polityka władz…*, op. cit., pp. 35, 48–49.
644 Ibid., pp. 60–61.
645 Ibid., p. 62, 65.
646 Ibid., p. 20.

own administration – which discouraged them from making sudden moves.[647] In 1956, when Gomułka's return to power gave the signal to retreat, cooperatives quickly disappeared. Of the total number of 10,203 cooperatives registered at the end of September 1956, by the end of the year only 1528 remained.[648]

At the price of a loss of private property, low wages, market deficiencies and widespread impoverishment, the Polish People's Republic's ruling elite had obtained an impressive investment success. As Oskar Lange wrote in 1958 during a post-thaw debate on the reform of socialism, the Stalinist mobilization resembled a war economy. It assured a very high rate of accumulation with complete control of official wages, prices and production. While the traditional rate of accumulation in Central European countries – including Poland – did not exceed 6 percent, GDP in the first half of the 1950s reached 22–30 percent. Moreover, these investments could be focused on selected sectors of the economy.

Historians today are inclined to doubt that the rate of growth in GDP (according to official figures – 7 percent annually) was actually so high during the Stalinist period.[649] Certainly, the armaments industry helped Poland both increase production and achieve the structural transformations they desired. Moreover, masses of people moved from villages to cities, thereby breaking free – at least in theory – from a timeless existence, which Marx had called "the idiocy of rural life". During the six-year plan, employment in industry increased by 2.2 million people, most of whom had moved from the countryside to urban areas.[650]

6. Brus, Lange, Kalecki. "The bane of reform"

In 1955, reporters from the weekly *Po Prostu* [Eng. *Frankly Speaking*] travelled to Zambrów, a small town in which the state had built a large textile plant. What they saw there terrified them – and the story they wrote became one of the most well-known Polish texts of the thaw.

---

647 R. A. Francisco, B. A. Laird, R. D. Laird, *The Political Economy of Collectivized Agriculture: A Comparative Study of Communist and Non-communist Systems*, New York 1979, p. 99.

648 D. Jarosz, *Polityka władz…*, op. cit., p. 150.

649 Cf. e.g. A. Maddison (*The World Economy, vol. 2*, op. cit.) estimates the rate of growth in GDP in the Polish People's Republic was significantly lower, somewhere in the range of 2–2.5 percent annually during the Stalinist era. W. Orłowski (*Gospodarka polska w ostatnim tysiącleciu*, http://www.nobe.pl/gospodarka-pol-1000.htm) believes that real growth during this period may have been closer to zero.

650 M. Bałtowski, *Gospodarka socjalistyczna…*, op. cit., p. 171.

We stand facing a red barracks building. Above the door is a sign reading "Home for Young Workers". In spite of the warm weather, we feel a chill. A dirty set of wide stone stairs leads upward. [...] The beds are covered with gray blankets, the floors are unwashed, and in the large undraped windows are dust-covered cotton child-sized aprons. They live here 10 or more to a room, without any chairs or tables. They aren't needed here. Besides, they would only get in the way. The girls sit idly huddled on their beds or on the window sills. There is a puddle in the hallway. Someone spilled water from a bowl. She was afraid to wash herself in the bathroom. It is a military-style bathroom, with a dozen or so faucets lined up in a row, beneath them runs a trough. [...] It is cold and dark. [...] Cold water won't wash away the dirt, it won't keep you clean.[651]

In Zambrów success was achieved: the plant realized its plan, but at the cost of enormous sacrifice and suffering – which to the reporters often seemed unjustified, irrational and unnecessary.

The year 1956 brought the collapse of the Stalinist model of accelerated industrialization. The workers' revolt in Poznań, and then the revolt in Hungary showed the limits of people's endurance. There are good reasons to believe that the growth rate imposed by the six-year plan was unsustainable – e.g., in Hungary the level of waste (failed investments, unsold inventory, idle machinery) reached as high as 20 percent of GDP.[652] There is no reason to assume that the economy of the Polish People's Republic was managed any more efficiently.

During the October plenum, Hilary Minc was forced to admit his errors. His downfall was sealed. He confessed that the six-year plan had assumed an "unrealistic rate of growth in agriculture" and an "unsatisfactory rate of technical progress", and in addition, had been burdened with massive defence spending during the Korean War (1950–1953), when a "semi-war economy" had been introduced. Minc also admitted that Poles were living in poverty:

It seems to me that the fundamental mistake of the six-year plan, both in its design and its execution, was the lack of harmonization between the targets for improving the material and cultural conditions of the population and the targets for the long-term development of productive forces and the reduction of disparities in relation to the most advanced countries.[653]

All the defects listed by Minc – difficulties in completing investments, the heavy burden of military expenditures, the primacy of heavy industry over

651 J. Ambroziewicz, R. Wiśniowski, "Tam zapomniano o socjalizmie", *Po Prostu*, 1955, no. 39, quoted in A. Zawistowski, *Kombinat,* Warszawa–Białystok 2009, pp. 350–351.

652 I. T. Berend, *Central and Eastern...*, op. cit., p. 79.

653 "Wystąpienie Hilarego Minca na VIII Plenum KC PZPR, 19–21 października 1956 r.", *Nowe drogi*, October 1956, no. 10, pp. 123–125.

consumption – would prove to be structural defects in the system, and not just ailments affecting his version of a Stalinist economy.

In the face of social protests and economic collapse, in 1956 the ruling elite had to listen to the economists – or at least pretend to do so. Thus far, their impact on policy had been limited: a huge gap divided them and the party technocrats. "Those who are called upon as experts on economic matters were never informed about what was really as stake, and no one asked them to express their views on this issue," Wlodzimierz Brus said years later, recalling the Stalinist era. However, as one of the party's leading economists at that time, he may have somewhat underplayed his own role, which was something he was not proud of.

Brus gave the government what it needed from him at the time, but he did not forget about the need to treat matters objectively. After 1956, he became increasingly critical of the government's economic policies, evolving towards opposition to the system (after having been one of Poland's leading Stalinists, in 1948 he helped break up the Central Planning Office, criticising it harshly for publishing a book on planning that strayed too far from Stalinist economics, and which he said was an example of "the fruitless nature of a subjectivist theory of economics" and "an expression of bourgeois ideas").[654]

Established during the leadership crisis in 1956, the Economic Council – whose chair was Lange, and vice-chair, Czesław Bobrowski, had been sidelined during the Stalinist era – proved to be powerless body. A report published in June 1957 recommended, among other things, balancing supply and demand through price increases and a slowdown in wage increases, reducing the influx of people from rural to urban areas, reducing the amount of capital and energy consumed by new investments, "shortening the investment front", and using part of the defence industry to produce market goods.[655] It aimed to reduce the "command-nature" of the economy and democratize the governance of business enterprises. Workers' councils were to be a counterweight to the power of the bureaucracy; these were to be, in conjunction with the central plan – at least in the opinion of one of the important members of the Economic Council, Michał Kalecki – a key element of socialism with a human face.[656] All of these reforms, however, threatened the power of the power apparatus and undermined the government's control over the economy.

---

654 T. Kowalik, *Spory o ustrój…*, op. cit., p. 96.

655 Rada Ekonomiczna przy Radzie Ministrów, *Przegląd bieżącej sytuacji gospodarczej kraju i zadania stojące przed polityką gospodarczą*, Warszawa 1957.

656 T. Kowalik, "Michał Kalecki a pierwsze reformy gospodarcze w Polsce", *Nauka Polska* 1989, no. 2.

In practice, therefore, the communist authorities adopted only a portion of these recommendations – cancelling a number of new investments and raising wages (which increased in real terms by more than ten percent in 1956 and by almost as much the following year). Part of the government's investment funds were shifted to industries producing consumer goods.

This calmed the public's mood, but the issue of structural reform of the economy remained an open question. A key point in the discussion among economists was the role of market mechanisms in a socialist economy – and what could possibly replace them in setting prices and production levels. This discussion took place in two parts. The first of these was a dispute about the role of the "law of value" under socialism. The issue had a long history, dating back to Marx and his reflections on the economic theory of value based on work (which, in turn, drew on the work of Adam Smith and David Ricardo), and later, a long and ideological debate (in which Stalin himself spoke out) about whether the law of value works in socialism. In practice, however, it was really just an ideological front, with the "law of value" usually being invoked merely to justify price increases (both in the Soviet Union in 1947, and in Poland in 1953; Gomułka would later prove to be an enthusiast of the "law of value"). After Stalin's death, it was used by dissidents and reformers who sought to discredit the planned economic system and introduce more market elements into it.[657]

After 1956, a discussion returned in a new guise, that had been ongoing for two decades, and before the war had sparked a hot dispute between two liberal economists from the Austrian school, Ludwig von Mises and Friedrich von Hayek, and the socialist economist Oskar Lange. The dispute's history reached back to the 1920s, and to even earlier theoretical considerations from before the First World War. At stake was an essential question: was rational economic planning possible? This debate has been well described, so there is no need to summarize the whole of it here; however, the outlines of the two main positions are worth mentioning.[658]

In an article written back in 1920,[659] Mises claimed that the socialist system was unable to solve the problem of rational pricing (he also rejected the Marxist

---

657 G. Temkin, *Dyskusje o gospodarce socjalistycznej: Marks-Lange-Mises-Hayek,* Warszawa 2011.

658 E. Łukawer, *Spór o racjonalność gospodarki socjalistycznej. Z historii problemu,* Kraków 2005.

659 Cf. also L. von Mises, "Economic Calculation in the Socialist Commonwealth" trans. S. Adler, [in:] *Collectivist Economic Planning*, ed. F.A. Hayek, London 1935, pp. 87–130, available at https://mises.org/library/economic-calculation-socialist-commonwealth; von Mises expands his argument in *Socialism: An Economic and Sociological*

view that economic calculations can be made by measuring the amount of socially necessary labour – and converting complex labour into simpler tasks; he saw this as a dangerous utopia).[660] Rational prices were shaped by the market – through millions of individual decisions by producers and consumers, which together comprised knowledge that no central planner could possibly possess. His access to knowledge is always limited, and he must process information sent up "from below", and resend it "back down"; All of this would take time, if it were even technically and mathematically possible (even if Hayek was willing to admit that it was theoretically possible, he was convinced it remained impossible in practice).

This structural defect meant that socialism was doomed, according to Mises and Hayek, to market imbalances and inefficiencies, because prices, the main regulator of the economy, are by necessity determined arbitrarily. Lange's response to this objection was a model of "market socialism" (as described in 1936–1937).[661] In his model, the Central Planning Office would substitute for the market – and through a process reminiscent of an auction, would locate equilibrium prices through a process of trial and error (with the exception of work whose value is determined by/within a social contract). Lange wrote:

> If the quantity demanded of a commodity is not equal to the quantity supplied the price of that commodity has to be changed. It has to be raised if demand exceeds supply and lowered if the reverse is the case. Thus the Central Planning Board fixes a new set of prices which serves as a basis for new decisions, and which results in a new set of quantities demanded and supplied. Through this process of trial and error equilibrium prices are finally determined.[662]

Lange's model had numerous advantages. Not only did it theoretically achieve the same thing as the free market, but it also dealt effectively with some persistent and ineradicable maladies that afflicted capitalism: these included the existence of monopolies and oligopolies, and the external costs (e.g. social costs – at the time there was no thought about environmental costs) of economic decisions, which could be taken into account by planners, but which did not fit into the narrowly defined calculations of a capitalist. It was also assumed that market

Analysis, New Have 1951, available at https://mises.org/library/socialism-economic-and-sociological-analysis.

660 E. Łukawer, *Spór o racjonalnosć…*, op. cit., p. 42.

661 O. Lange, "On the Economic Theory of Socialism", *The Review of Economic Studies*, 1936, no. 1 (Part One); 1937, no. 2 (Part Two); O. Lange, *On the Economic Theory of Socialism*, Minneapolis 1938.

662 O. Lange, "On the Economic Theory of Socialism: Part One", *The Review of Economic Studies*, 1936, no. 1, p. 66.

socialism would eliminate cyclical crises and allow for a reduction in social inequalities. Income from work would consist of two parts: one for the services rendered, and the other being the individual's share of income derived from collectivized means of production. The level of the first would be decided by the "negative marginal utility of work"; the second, a kind of social dividend, would be fixed in such a way that it would not influence the choice of activity (e.g. per head of population, or according to age or number of family members).[663]

From Lange's point of view, market socialism had one cardinal advantage, of special importance in a backward country: it provided the option of considering social (which really meant "political") needs when making decisions about the level of investment. Under capitalism, these were the result of individual choices of individual companies, and as a result, it was difficult for the government to directly affect them. It could only do so indirectly, through a complicated system of institutions and incentives, such as interest rates, and loans from specialized investment banks. Meanwhile, escaping backwardness required a leap in investment. Capitalism, according to Lange, made this impossible.

Although the rate of saving imposed by the state would be arbitrary and compulsory, Lange wrote:

> A rate of accumulation which does not reflect the preferences of consumers as to the time-shape of the flow of income may be regarded as a diminution of social welfare. But is seems that this deficiency may be regarded as overbalanced by the advantages [...].[664]

This view was a widely held one. In often reprinted essays on capitalism, the influential British Marxist economist Maurice Dobb, repeatedly expressed his own formulation of this idea: capitalist societies are structurally incapable of making an informed choice between the present and the future, i.e., to sacrifice consumption "now" in order to ensure a better future.[665] It was long believed that Lange had won this argument. In 1942, Economist Joseph Schumpeter predicted that "a socialist form of society will inevitably emerge from an equally inevitable decomposition of capitalist society."[666] Schumpeter believed that capitalism would dig its own grave: its success would undermine the institutions upon which it rested because wealthier and better educated people would not put up with the imperfections of capitalist institutions. A year later, he added: "Many readers will

663 E. Łukawer, *Spór o racjonalność...*, op. cit., pp. 194–195.

664 O. Lange, "On the Economic Theory of Socialism: Part Two", *The Review of Economic Studies*, 1937, no. 2, p. 127.

665 M. Dobb, *Political Economy and Capitalism*, London 1950, pp. 244–245.

666 J. Schumpeter, *Capitalism, Socialism and Democracy*, New York 2003, p. 410.

wonder why I thought so laboriously and complex an analysis in order to establish what is rapidly becoming the general opinion, even among conservatives."[667]

It is not clear whether Lange believed his model could be realized in practice. In 1940, he wrote in a letter to Hayek that he considered his "central planner" to be merely a "methodological tool".

In response to Lange's model – published in a two-part article in the late 1930s – Hayek wrote his famous 1945 essay "The Use of Knowledge in Society", in which he wrote:

> The peculiar character of the problem of a rational economic order is determined precisely by the fact that the knowledge of the circumstances of which we must make use never exists in concentrated or integrated form, but solely as the dispersed bits of incomplete and frequently contradictory knowledge which all the separate individuals possess. The economic problem of society is thus not merely a problem of how to allocate "given" resource ... it is a problem of the utilization of knowledge not given to anyone in its totality.[668]

Every planned economy is thus inherently inefficient because no central brain is able to gather and process the required amount of information. It is theoretically and technically infeasible, and therefore Lange's central planner is an unachievable and dangerous utopia, because it would limit human freedom and wealth. Lange never accepted (or – as writes Gabriel Temkin, a historian involved in the dispute – may have never understood) this argument.[669]

Another liberal economist, Lionel Robbins, thought Lange's model was theoretically possible, but unachievable in practice. This, according to the Pole, would be resolved by means of technology. In the 1960s, he became fascinated with computers, which – he thought – could cope with the problems that prevented the creation of a perfect central planner. In his last article, "The Computer and the Market," he wrote:

> Were I to rewrite my essay today my task would be much simpler. My answer to Hayek and Robbins would be: so what's the trouble? Let us put the simultaneous equations on an electronic computer and we shall obtain the solution in less than a second. The market process with its cumbersome *tâtonnements* appears old-fashioned. Indeed, it may be considered as a computing device of the pre-electronic age.[670]

---

667 Ibid.

668 F. A. Hayek, "The Use of Knowledge in Society", *The American Economic Review*, September 1945, vol. 25, no. 4, pp. 519–520.

669 G. Temkin, *Dyskusje o gospodarce socjalistycznej*..., op. cit., p. 68.

670 Originally published as "Maszyna licząca i rynek" in 1966, Lange's article appeared in English under this title in *Capitalism, Socialism and Economic Growth: Essays Presented to Maurice Dobb*, ed. C. Feinstein, Cambridge 1967, pp. 158–161.

In the debate during the 1950s and 1960s over how to reform the Polish economy, market mechanisms remained a taboo – a postulate that was not only censored, but even unthinkable. The ideas that arose after 1956 on how to reform the socialist economy leaned in the direction of loosening the political straitjacket of central planning and introducing more democracy into the management of enterprises. A return to capitalism was not only impossible for political reasons, the postulate itself could not be raised no only due to censorship: it was also unthinkable. Just as the "oppositionist/revisionists" wanted to improve the system, not to abolish it, the "economist/revisionists" sought a better form of socialism. Their influence on economic policy, however, remained negligible.

Planning would, of course, remain in place: the state was to be involved in such things as determining the size of the wage fund and carrying out the largest long-term investment projects. But, at the same time, however, it was to be less pedantic and leave more freedom to enterprises. Michal Kalecki, a prominent economist and an important figure among Poland's would-be reformers believed that workers' councils would help increase efficiency, but his evolution towards market mechanisms – from 1956 up to his death in 1970 – was gradual and never fully realized. In 1956, after just three weeks, the committee he headed produced a proposal for reform: it included a new plan providing state-owned enterprises with greater autonomy (the number of indicators for which they were to be held accountable was reduced from a few dozen to eight in the version ultimately adopted by the government); and a law establishing an "Enterprise Fund", which set out rules for employee participation in profits.[671] Legislation was also drafted creating workers' councils, and giving them powers similar to that of a supervisory board in western companies (e.g., a vote in annual plans, strategy development, and the distribution of profits).

At the same time, a fascination arose in Poland with the Yugoslavian economic model, about which people had begun to write more willingly and extensively during the "thaw", and which was considered to be not only more efficient, but also more democratic (both of these aspects were clearly idealized). Brus himself travelled to Yugoslavia at the end of 1956, and his experiences there were printed in *Economic Life* (Pol. *Życie Gospodarcze*) – the country's main economic weekly – on the first page of the 1957 New Year issue. Today, his dreams of smoothly operating trade and services sectors are moving – and say more about the Poland that Brus left, than about Yugoslavia:

---

671 W. Brus, *Zmora ref ormowania…*, op. cit., p. 30.

Customers display extreme confidence in their actions, compared to relations here: namely, they do not show the seller any fear, they are just plain fussy as they pick and choose, sift through the goods, make up their minds, check sizes. […] How long I sat in a Yugoslav restaurant was entirely up to me. Because you hardly ever had to wait for a waiter – neither when ordering, nor when waiting for the main course or the check. There was no set formula to prevent people from satisfying their individual tastes, and the assortment of dishes coming out of the kitchen always matched those on the menu […] The response of the store manager to a question about how they proceed in cases of doubt was characteristic: "we prefer not to argue with the customer."[672]

In articles written about underdeveloped countries, Polish economists at the time wrote – in line with global trends – that the key to escaping backwardness was to increase accumulation and that only the state could achieve this.[673] There could be no such thing as "automatism in development," Bobrowski wrote in 1965, "If there could, we simply wouldn't have the problem of underdeveloped countries on the scale and with such tensions, as exists today."[674]

Kalecki, in turn, was convinced that unemployment in capitalist countries was the result of class politics pursued in the interest of "so-called economic experts closely connected with banking and industry".[675] During the Great Depression in the 1930s, Kalecki had arrived at ideas for stimulating economic activity – very similar to Keynes' ideas but preceding them – through public spending and working toward full employment. He believed that if capitalist states did not adopt these recommendations, it was only to protect the interests of the ruling classes – about whom Kalecki had no illusions. Capitalism, not socialism, was the political system he considered incapable of reform – precisely because of the structure of political interests. Democratic economic planning required a revolution.[676]

In *Introduction to the Theory of Growth in a Socialist Economy*, published in 1963,[677] Kalecki refuted the dogma of that day on the socialist economy, including the belief that increasing the share of accumulation in the national income would lead in the long term to an increase in consumption; Kalecki's theory

---

672 W. Brus, "System jugosłowiański z bliska", *Życie Gospodarcze*, 7 January 1957, no. 1.

673 B. Popławski, *Polska szkoła rozwoju…*, op. cit.

674 C. Bobrowski, *Planowanie gospodarcze. Problemy podstawowe*, Warszawa 1965, p. 45.

675 J. López, M. Assous, *Michal Kalecki*, Houndmills–New York 2010, p. 198.

676 J. Osiatyński, *Michał Kalecki o gospodarce socjalistycznej*, Warszawa 1983, p. 13.

677 Originally published in Warsaw in 1963 as *Zarys teorii wzrostu gospodarki socjalistycznej*, Kalecki's book appeared in English in volume four of a seven-volume collection of his works: J. Kalecki, *Collected Works of Michal Kalecki*, ed. Jerzy Osiatyński, Oxford–New York 1991–1997.

showed that this is not always the case – and that when mismanaged, investments can lead to even lower consumption rates in the long term. These views, however, were not well received. "Polish economists were not yet ready to discuss the problems of socialist reproduction in such a language and style," noted Jerzy Osiatyński, a researcher of Kalecki's thought.[678] Soviet economist T. S. Khachaturov, author of the preface to the Russian edition of Kalecki's book offered a principled criticism, writing that it did not clearly explain the superiority of a socialist economy over a capitalist one.[679]

In the late 1950s and 1960s, Kalecki, who was now politically sidelined in Poland, remaining convinced that capitalism merely perpetuated underdevelopment. He devoted this time to advising governments of Third World countries and constructing multi-decade plans for communist Poland. In the spirit of the era, he wrote that the key challenge for poor countries was to significantly increase investment. If private investment was not forthcoming – which was likely – then the state should intervene, surmounting the institutional barriers that stood in the way of the rapid development of agriculture and adequately taxing the rich and more affluent. This, he wrote, would require social change more sweeping "than the upheaval created in eighteenth century by the French Revolution."[680]

7. Gomułka and Gierek

Gomułka had his own ideas on the economy but, more importantly, he was unwilling to loosen his grip on power; his memory for numbers and interest in economics were conducive to the pursuit of control.[681] The problem of a socialist economy was – as revisionists like Brus in Poland or Kornai in Hungary were soon to discover – its institutional character and the fact that it was essentially political. Stalinism had created an apparatus of power whose interests in practice always towered above the need for economic reform. Gomułka's attitude towards economists was described by historian Wojciech Morawski:

> Gomułka's pragmatism resulted in, among other things, a distance between himself and professional economists (all of whom were Marxist, since there was no other kind).

678 Quoted in J. Kalecki, *Collected Works of Michal Kalecki. Volume 4, Socialism: Economic Growth and Efficiency of Investment*, ed. Jerzy Osiatyński, trans. B. Jung, Oxford–New York 1993, p. 241.

679 Ibid., pp. 242–258.

680 J. López, M. Assous, *Michal Kalecki…*, op. cit., pp. 174–175.

681 J. Ptasiński, "Gomułka – jakiego znałem", [in:] *Władysław Gomułka we wspomnieniach*, ed. B. Szyzdek, Lublin 1989, p. 293.

Gomułka felt a certain insecurity towards them related to gaps in his own education. At the same time, however, he also regarded them as irresponsibly doctrinaire, ready to bring political misfortune down on the country just to have an opportunity to test out their theories. He believed that whatever the economists proposed, he had to filter through the sieve of his own common sense. I do not want to offend anyone with this comparison, but Gomułka's attitude towards economists was like to Hitler's to his generals. Hence the career of Bolesław Jaszczuk – who was not an economist, but an engineer and ideological technocrat who impressed Gomułka with his adroit use of a slide rule.[682]

Gomułka quickly put a stop to experiments with local workers' councils. In the latter half of the 1960s, it was already clear, however, that the economy required new, more fundamental reforms. Real wages were stagnant, and economic growth had remained at a low level of 2–3 percent per year, despite numerous new investments, especially in the chemical industry, one favoured by Gomułka and which he regarded as a "driver of modernity". The first two years of the plan for 1966–1970 brought increasing tensions on the domestic market and a poor performance in terms of foreign trade. The effectiveness of investments also declined. Those managing the economy would not listen to the economists, especially those whom they considered suspicious revisionists, but they also realized that the impressive growth of the Stalinist era could not be repeated and had resulted from the transfer of millions of people from the countryside – where labour productivity was low – to industry, which even in the messy conditions of socialism automatically brought about a jump in productivity. This mechanism for growth, despite continued population pressures, had clearly been exhausted. Thus, in journalists' reporting in the 1960s there were constant exhortations to move away from "extensive" growth and transition to a more "selective", "intensive" model.

A reform package was announced in the atmosphere of political repression that followed the events of March 1968. It assumed, among other things, increasing the importance of financial results as a criterion for assessing an enterprise, an emphasis on profits, and the need to motivate employees by means of wages "according to their contribution to achieving results". There was so much talk of "material incentives" in propaganda that it begged for sarcastic jokes. Stefan Kisielewski, an opposition but tolerated journalist, noted in his diary: "What does a cow have on its head? Not horns, but incentives."[683]

682 W. Morawski, "Poglądy gospodarcze Władysława Gomułki", [in:] *Gospodarka i społeczeństwo w czasach PRL-u (1944–1989)*, eds. E. Kościk, T. Głowiński, Wrocław 2007, p. 327.

683 S. Kisielewski, *Dzienniki*, Warszawa 2001, p. 419.

Naturally, no one was willing to entrust investment planning to the efficiency of the market: decisions about investments were to continue to be made by planners. In a speech at the XII Plenum in 1968, Jaszczuk said that the market "cannot dictate the direction of economic growth" because "the phenomena that take place within it do not provide a basis for assessing long-term social needs; this is necessary, for example, so that funds allocated for investment, which will bear fruit after several years, are spent as efficiently as possible."[684]

One could discuss the organization of state-owned enterprises, the scope of their freedom, and the necessity of holding them accountable for their results, as well as the need to increase the efficiency of investment, and motivate employees with better wages. But no one questioned the need for state investment on a large scale ("social control over the economy"), long-term planned development, and the need to maintain a tight rein on social inequality (i.e., wage controls). In a thousand-page official textbook entitled *The Political Economy of Socialism*, published in 1973, Bronisław Minc levelled a number of charges against markets: price signals were conveyed to markets with too much delay, they could not be used to determine the level of changes required in production, and they often expressed momentary fluctuations on the basis of which only uncoordinated, piecemeal decisions could be taken. Planning, he taught, was a "higher form of economic regulation".[685] Likewise, revisionists like Brus, Kalecki and Lange, who were always advocates of widening the scope of freedom and liberties in the Polish People's Republic, including economic freedoms, also believed that the social foundations of communist Poland's economy and the defects of capitalism could probably be reconciled.

In 1972, at the peak of the Gierek regime's success, publicist Aleksander Bocheński, who had been associated with the right before the war, but allied himself with the regime after the war, published a small book in which he explained how Gierek's ideas for Poland differed from Gomułka's asceticism. In an attempt to expose the roots of Poles' negligent (or so he thought) attitude to work, he wrote:

> In order to grasp the difficulty of activating psychological motors for high-quality work, you have to first realize the material fact that rapid industrialization of the country means building the largest possible number of new factories, mines and other plants […] this forced the Poland's socialist government to spend the greatest part of social income on this construction, and thus, to spend the least amount possible on consumption by the population beyond its basic needs. If a country has a hundred thousand

684 Ł. Dwilewicz, *Reformy…*, op. cit., p. 79.
685 B. Minc, *Ekonomia polityczna socjalizmu*, Warszawa 1973, pp. 134–135.

dollars at its disposal, it can use this money to import a hundred automobiles or ten machine tools. It cannot use the same money to buy both one and the other.[686]

Bocheński added that under conditions of hunger and exhaustion one can only build by using strong means of coercion. Gradually, however, human needs must come to the fore – and grow to include "automobiles, houses, and elegant apartments with bathrooms. Later, needs appear which are completely unnecessary."[687] In the 1950s, the Polish People's Republic attempted both to encourage people to make voluntary sacrifices, and to force them to work; in the 1970s, it was time for gentler methods.

The Gierek regime's promise, as Bocheński summed it up, however, sounded different: "I don't think that the ascetic model of socialism, at the stage of industrialization we have in 1970, has to be universally enforced."[688] The government carried out large investments and did not promise a standard of living equal to that in the West. This belonged to the future. But it did promise a steady improvement in living standards. It no longer expected sacrifices from citizens in the name of a beautiful future. This was also a necessity, because dissatisfaction was palpable, and had by no means died out after the regime change. In February 1971, textile workers in Łódź went on strike, protesting, among other things, atrocious, nineteenth-century working conditions (three shifts, no breaks for meals, widespread use of piece-work payment schemes).[689]

The Gierek regime's economic ideas for promoting growth were made possible by the détente in international relations and the resulting opening of international financial markets to communist Poland. These plans also assumed (and in this aspect alluded to the ideas of Jaszczuk and his team) an increase in exports, greater specialization in industry, and changes in the types of goods produced – exports were to consist for the most part of technologically advanced products. Poland would purchase new technologies from the West on credit and then repay these loans through the export of finished products. At the same time, consumption in the country would increase, thanks to which the regime – which felt insecure after the bloody riots on the Baltic coast in December 1970 – would assured itself support.

---

686 A. Bocheński, *Rzecz o psychice narodu polskiego*, Warszawa 1972, p. 53.

687 Ibid.

688 Ibid., p. 76.

689 M. Mazurek, *Społeczeństwo kolejki. O doświadczeniach niedoboru 1945–1989*, Warszawa 2010, pp. 154–155.

The influx of hard currency from abroad allowed Gierek to avoid facing temporarily the structural dilemma that had plagued the authorities of the Polish People's Republic since the outset. Poland's socialist economy had developed in cycles that started with a rise in investment (focused on heavy industry and production of the so-called "means of production"), then led to stagnation or a decline in living standards, and finally provoked a social explosion – after which a regime change followed.[690] The new ruling clique began by curbing investment, increasing consumption, placing more emphasis on light industry and increasing production for the domestic consumer market. But this was always temporary: after a few years, the pressure to invest in big industrial projects returned and the cycle was repeated. The injection of hard currency and licenses from the West in the early 1970s led to – for a few short years – an investment boom and simultaneous increase in consumption.[691] For a short time, you could believe that Poland was on the rise, and that people were truly living the good life. The Gierek regime succumbed to the optimism of its own propaganda. Zdzisław Rurarz, an economic adviser to Gierek, assumed an annual growth rate of 10 percent over two to three decades (!) and an accumulation rate of 40 percent of GDP – higher than called for in the six-year plan.[692] Amid cheers at a party conference in October 1973, the increase in national income planned over five years (1970–1975) was raised from an already impressive 39 percent to 55 percent.[693]

There was, of course, a rationale behind these investment pressures. Poland had one of the highest rates of population growth in Europe. The authorities had to find employment for all these young people – and the first signs of unemployment, which were already appearing after the dismissals of apparatchiks in 1956, was fuelling panic and fear among those who still remembered prewar times.[694] It was also believed, at least in party circles, that a higher level of investment meant higher growth – although in reality its effectiveness systematically declined.

However, these investment pressures, which people began to speak and write about in the 1960s, were largely a result of the institutional structure of the government apparatus, which resembled a giant pyramid, with the first secretary at

690 Z. Landau, "Etapy rozwoju Polski Ludowej", *Przegląd Historyczny* 1987, no. 2.

691 Cf. A. Müller, "Przyspieszony wzrost gospodarczy w Polsce w latach 1971–1975", *Zeszyty naukowe Uczelni Warszawskiej im. Marii Skłodowskiej-Curie*, 2011, no. 33.

692 J. Kaliński, *Gospodrka Polski w latach 1944–1989. Przemiany strukturalne*, Warszawa 1995, p. 153

693 M. Bałtowski, *Gospodarka socjalistyczna…*, op. cit., p. 224.

694 skarżyli się na nie np. autorzy listów do tygodnika *Po Prostu* – Cf. A. Leszczyński, *Sprawy do załatwienia. Listy do "Po Prostu" 1955–1957*, Warszawa 2000.

the top. The position of the first secretary depended on the support of the party apparatus, and the party apparatus was "fed" with investments.

The ambitions of all levels of the power structure were focused on carving out the largest possible piece of the investment pie for themselves. Local party secretaries competed to have a new factory built in their area. Managers thought about the promotion that the completion of a new project would bring them, and how their prestige would grow along with the growth of their enterprise, association or department. Local authorities sought to develop their cities and create jobs for the people in their region. Everyone lined up in front of the same cashier's window – which was in the hands of the planner – creating territorial and special-interest coalitions and pressure groups.[695] Of course, new investments built from scratch were more desirable than less expensive upgrades of existing plants.

The system did not have any means of preventing such bottom-up pressures for investment. Attempts were made to create a system of indicators that would set strict ceilings on expenditures for particular ministries and associations, but these did not work. Investors and contractors were always able to work around them, wresting for themselves as much as possible from the available investment pool, and often blackmailing planners with the threat of leaving uncompleted construction that had already begun.[696] During such "horse-trading" with planners, it was argued that a plant's production capacity was being underutilized, that the goods it produced were in demand, that it was in a priority industry, that it was growing, that it had export quotas to fulfil, and that any loss of employment had to be avoided because this could provoke social unrest. All of these arguments worked.[697]

Even in the best Gierek years (1972–1973), the overall fulfilment of reported investment needs did not reduce the pressures from enterprises on the central planner: "on the contrary, initially surprised by the attitude of the central planner, the following year, they made even greater investment demands."[698] Enterprises always played the system for their own benefit: they lowered cost projections (then asked for more money because the investment could not be left unfinished), failed to

---

695 Te zjawiska próbowali opisywać już w latach 70. socjologowie. Cf. np. A. Rychard, "Władza i gospodarka" [in:] *Zmierzch socjalizmu państwowego. Szkice z socjologii ekonomicznej*, ed. W. Morawski, Warszawa 1994, p. 48 ff.; also W. Narojek, *Społeczeństwo planujące, próba socjologii gospodarki socjalistycznej*, Warszawa 1973, p. 281 ff.

696 J. Kotowicz-Jawor, *Presja inwestycyjna…*, op. cit., p. 22.

697 E. Balcerowicz, *Przetarg planistyczny. Mechanizm i skutki społeczno-gospodarcze*, Warszawa 1990, p. 64.

698 J. Kotowicz-Jawor, *Presja inwestycyjna…*, op. cit., p. 76.

report problems with investments, and did not coordinate short-term plans with the long-term plan theoretically in force. It paid to produce goods as expensively as possible, because production value was calculated on the basis of gross indicators.[699] The regulations introduced in the 1970s making managers personally responsible for unsuccessful projects and requiring them to carry out economic analyses before applying for credit proved to be defunct.[700] Enterprises and industrial groups competed for resources using any means possible – which included falsifying statistics.[701] Ever-increasing sums of money were locked up in unfinished construction sites.[702]

The collapse of the Gierek miracle was accelerated buy a major shake-up in the global economy – the oil crisis of 1973 and the resulting drastic increase in energy prices that drove the developed countries of the West into recession. Due to the system used to settle crude oil purchases within the Comecon system, the impact on Poland of rising oil prices was delayed (the USSR changed rates every five years along with its new five-year plan, but it was unwilling to sell oil to its satellites for less than half the price it could get on world markets).[703] But there were many more problems facing the country. Foreign trade still remained the Achilles heel of the Polish economy. Manufacturing machines with the use of Western technologies often required components to be imported from abroad, and thus paid for with hard currency. The quality of Polish products was often poor, and were therefore difficult to sell on demanding international markets, so most made their way to other socialist countries. According to official data, in 1979 up to 28.7 percent of electronic equipment was produced at a loss; for Rubin televisions, the margin of loss reached 91.9 percent.[704] Coal exports remained one of the Polish Peoples' Republic's main sources of foreign exchange. However, by August 1974 revenues from exports were no longer sufficient to cover the costs of loans and imports.[705] In December 1975, Poland for the first

699 E. Balcerowicz, *Przetarg planistyczny…*, op. cit. p. 112.

700 J. Kotowicz-Jawor, *Presja inwestycyjna…*, op. cit., p. 113.

701 M. Bałtowski, *Gospodarka socjalistyczna…*, op. cit., p. 253.

702 Cf. W. Kuczyński, *Po Wielkim Skoku*, Warszawa 2012.

703 B. Eichengreen, *The European Economy since 1945. Coordinated capitalism and beyond*, Princeton 2007, p. 300.

704 M. Zaremba, Zimno, ciepło, gorąco. Nastroje Polaków od "zimy stulecia" do lata '80, in press. I would like to thank dr. Marcin Zaremba for making the article available to me.

705 P. Bożyk, *Marzenia i rzeczywistość, czyli anatomia polskiego kryzysu*, Warszawa 1983, p. 80.

time exhausted its foreign currency and had to be bailed out with a loan from the USSR.[706] Queues and power outages become commonplace: Poland had fallen into a crisis from which it could not lift itself.[707]

8. The system's problem

Since the 1960s, analyses of the weaknesses of the socialist economy have been shifting towards institutions – especially power structures. This can clearly be seen in the evolution of the writings of Janos Kornai, one of the leading economists of the region, and probably the most acute analyst of the weaknesses of planned economies. In a socialist economy, competition among various interests prevented any far-reaching change from occurring. Enterprises could be given a little less or a little more freedom; they could be held more or less accountable for their financial results; Big Economic Organizations could be created or broken up into smaller, decentralized entities. But the problems lay deeper. Kornai estimates, for example, that in Hungary in the years 1973–1983, despite two oil crises and a clear slowdown, the authorities were unable to alter the country's investment structure, giving preference to heavy industry and machine production (though differences existed between countries: while Hungary allocated 35 percent of investment to industry, in Bulgaria and Romania this percentage reached 45–49 percent).[708]

Kornai started out as a journalist writing articles about the Hungarian economy under Stalinism in the propaganda press (there was, of course, no other kind). Years later he recalled:

> Never for a moment did I think that the troubles were *systemic*, originating in the system itself. On the contrary, while perceiving many problems and faults in it, I was still convinced that socialism was superior to the capitalist system. Any difficulties would be transitory. I subscribed to Ernő Gerő's notion, taken from Stalin, that these were just growing pains. We would grow out of them! State ownership *had* to ensure higher productivity than private ownership. Central planning *must* be more efficient than market anarchy. There was utter confusion in my mind between the normative and the positive approach, the demands facing the socialist system and the realities of it.[709]

706 M. Bałtowski, *Gospodarka socjalistyczna…*, op. cit., p. 236.

707 M. Zaremba, "'Bigosowy socjalizm'. Dekada Gierka", [in:] *Polacy wobec PRL. Strategie przystosowawcze,* ed. G. Miernik, Kielce 2003.

708 I. T. Berend, *Central and Eastern Europe…*, op. cit., p. 184.

709 J. Kornai, *By Force of Thought: Irregular Memoirs of an Intellectual Journey,* Cambridge 2008, p. 51.

In the mid-1950s, Kornai began describing the institutional defects of socialism, which culminated in his acclaimed book *Economics of Shortage*, the inspiration for which, as he explained in his memoirs, was his attempt to purchase tiles for the house he had built outside of Budapest, through the socialist system of commerce. In the early 1990s, he came to the conclusion that even the concept of "market socialism" was misconceived: it did not provide a clear definition of ownership, it did not create incentives to respond to price changes, and it inclined managers not to engage in market competition, but rather, to fight for a share of the subsidies paid out of the "state pocket". It was indeed a better solution than a rigid socialist model, as it provided more room for market mechanisms, but it still remained ineffective.[710]

In his magnum opus, *The Socialist System. The Political Economy of Communism*, a penetrating and thorough analysis of the failure of the command economy – and thus of "the socialist system". Kornai also wrote about another of its fundamental traits: a lack of innovation. The colour television, photocopier, synthetic fibre were all invented in capitalist countries, because the market created incentives to compete through innovation.[711] Communist modernization was imitative, energy-intensive, duplicated a model that had been obsolete in the West since the 1970s, and the key to which lay in the political system that created it and from which it was inseparable.[712] The system's crash in Poland after just a few short years of prosperity under Gierek was only one of many proofs of this.

In practice, the system proved to be a brake on growth: real growth in the countries of Central Europe amounted to approximately 2.4 percent annually for the first postwar decade (compared with 3.2 percent annually in Western Europe). The gap in living standards separating the east and west grew steadily, and in 1989 was greater than it had been in 1939.[713] The system was capable of accumulation and growth despite massive waste, mainly due to the fact that it had carried out a major social transformation – moving tens of millions of people from the countryside, where they were languishing on the margins of the economy, to work in industry in cities, which automatically resulted in a jump in productivity, even

710 B. Eichengreen, *European economy…*, op. cit., p. 301.

711 J. Kornai, *The Socialist System. The Political Economy of Communism*, Oxford 1992, p. 296.

712 J. Chumiński, "Strukturalne uwarunkowania nieefektywności gospodarki socjalistycznej", [in:] *Modernizacja czy pozorna modernizacja. Społeczno-ekonomiczny bilans PRL 1944–1989*, ed. J. Chumiński, Wrocław 2010.

713 W. Orłowski, *W pogoni za straconym czasem. Wzrost gospodarczy w Europie Środkowo-Wschodniej 1950–2030*, Warszawa 2010, pp. 53–60.

under the messy conditions of socialist mismanagement. Later, however, the institutions hampering growth made their presence felt fully, and proved to be an insurmountable obstacle. If we look at this from a distance, as did economists Daron Acemoglu and James Robinson in their acclaimed book on the causes of poverty and wealth in nations, *Economic Origins of Dictatorship and Democracy* (2009), it is easy to say that the lack of democracy and free markets, and the authoritarian power of a ruling elite focused solely on its own narrow interests were the obvious reasons for the failure of this gigantic experiment.[714] The story however is more complex. What we consider to be obvious today is not necessarily quite so self-evident – and clearly was not so decades ago. Economic theory at that time clearly suggested that only a planned economy could pull backward countries out of the hopeless lethargy in which they been had stuck for centuries.[715]

The experience that shaped an entire generation of economists and politicians from the 1940s to the 1970s was the Great Depression, just as the experience that shaped the next generation was the inefficiency of the planned economy: without this in mind, we cannot understand either the former or the latter.

Winning Polish elites over to the free market took a long time – the whole of the 1980s. Even the economic programmes of Solidarity spoke about building a better socialism, and not a free market.[716]

714 D. Acemoglu, J. Robinson, *Why Nations Fail. The Origins of Power, Prosperity, and Poverty*, New York 2012, p. 126.

715 Cf. also J. Kochanowicz, "Początki planowania w Polsce po II wojnie światowej w perspektywie porównawczej", [in:] *Ekonomia i ekonomiści w czasach przełomu*, eds. E. Mączyńska, J. Wilkin, Warszawa 2010, pp. 203–205.

716 Cf. *Sprawy gospodarcze w dokumentach pierwszej "Solidarności", vol. 1, 16 sierpnia 1980–30 czerwca 1981*, eds. J. Luszniewicz, A. Zawistowski, Warszawa 2008.

Socialism is more than mere logic.[717]
Jawaharlal Nehru, 1957

The division of labor among nations is that some specialize in winning and others in losing.[718]
Eduardo Galeano, 1973

Chapter 6. Dilemmas of the periphery

The dialectic of development in the "Third World" 1945–1980

1. The black star of Africa

Ghana gained its independence on 6 March 1957. One minute after midnight, the British Union Jack was lowered from the flagpole, and the red-green-and-gold flag of a new country hoisted in its place. Over 2000 delegates from around the world took part in the new country's birthday celebration. There was no end to the banquets. People were dancing in the streets.

The next evening, after the ceremonial transfer of power, Prime Minister Kwame Nkrumah danced to the melody of the hit blues song "Gotta Be This or That" with the Duchess of Kent, who had been sent to represent Queen Elizabeth. The banquet took place in the marble-clad rooms of the newly built State House. The atmosphere was full of optimism: a new, post-colonial order was taking shape, better than the former colonial model. Ghana, the black star of Africa, was to represent the hopes of the entire continent for emancipation and modernity. A better tomorrow was within reach.

In his autobiography, published during that first year of independence, Nkrumah would write:

> As a ship that has been freshly launched, we face the hazards of the high seas alone. We must rely on our own men, on the captain and on his navigation. And, as I proudly stand on the bridge of that lone vessel as she confidently sets sail, I raise a hand to shade

717 Quoted in P. Chatterjee, *Nationalist Thought and the Colonial World*, London 1993, p. 157.

718 E. Galeano, *Open Veins of Latin America*, New York 1973, p. 1.

> my eyes from the glaring African sun and scan the horizon. There is so much more beyond.[719]

At the time, no one could imagine just how quickly this ship would hit the rocks. Nine years later, the catastrophe was complete. Nkrumah's government was hated and universally seen as corrupt and discredited. When a military coup d'état finally removed Nkrumah from power, Ghana was bankrupt, and its citizens were considerably worse off than on the day the country gained independence.[720]

The story of Ghana is instructive because it is nearly an archetype of the post-colonial fate of many other countries – including its hopes and ambitions, joy and disappointment. Nkrumah was more than just a leader: he was a prophet of Pan-Africanism, a star of world politics, and one of the creators of the Non-Aligned Movement, which sought to find its own way in a world divided between the Eastern and Western blocs, which were in the midst of a titanic struggle.

> Ghana's fight for freedom inspired and influenced us all, and the greatest contribution to our political awareness at that time came from the achievements of Ghana after its independence. It was from Ghana that we got the idea that we must do more than just the UN to bring about our own independence.

This was how Sam Nujoma, the first president of Namibia, remembered the period.[721]

Nkrumah loved media attention and was aware of his own charisma. It was thus not surprising that he agreed publically to a wager proposed by Félix Houphouët-Boigny, leader of the most important party in neighbouring Ivory Coast, during a visit to Ghana in April 1957 aimed at building Pan-African relations. The Ivory Coast was then still a colony, but independence was already within sight (it would be achieved in 1960). Houphouët-Boigny had a completely different vision for the future of his country: he wanted gradual development without radical experiments, based on agriculture and the know-how of French experts (tens of thousands of which were employed there in the 1970s). He believed in capitalism and the free market, which made him an exception at the time. He made a wager with Nkrumah on which country would develop faster over the next decade. Everyone expected that Houphouët-Boigny would lose.[722]

---

719 K. Nkrumah, *Autobiography*, New York 1957, p. 290.

720 R. Betts, *Decolonization*, New York–London 2004, p. 65.

721 Quoted in A. Biney, "The Legacy of Kwame Nkrumah in Retrospect", *The Journal of Pan African Studies*, March 2008, vol. 2, no. 3.

722 See J. Woronoff, *West African Wager: Houphouët versus Nkrumah*, Metuchen 1972.

The leader of Ghana had no idea that he would already be out of power by the time the bet was settled.

When Ghana obtained independence, it faced truly bright economic prospects. Its monetary reserves amounted to 269 million dollars, and the country had one of the highest levels of per capita income in sub-Saharan Africa, comparable with the level of income in South Korea or Taiwan. Ghana was the largest cocoa producer in the world, and had significant reserves of gold, bauxite and magnesium.

At the same time, however, as Nkrumah was well aware, Ghana remained economically dependent on Western demand for its products, mainly cocoa, whose price was determined by a world market in which American and European buyers dominated. Ghana sold cocoa and gold, and imported machines, automobiles and most other consumer goods. Thus, Nkrumah thought, it remained at the mercy of the former colonizers, and there could be no talk of real independence as long as that was true.

The leaders of newly established countries like Ghana had good reason not to trust their former colonial masters. The British had begun to think about the economic development of their colonies quite late, only towards the end of the 1930s, when cracks in their empire were already visible. It had earlier been believed that the presence itself of Europeans, in whose wake came trade and civilization, would bring progress to the people they subjugated.

Parliament approved the first programme for development of Britain's colonies during the war, in 1940, though immediately afterward even the modest funds allocated for this purpose were cut.[723] From the negligible five million pounds yearly that were finally approved, very little was ever spent: through 1948, real spending in whole amounted to 24 million pounds. This was supposed to dramatically improve the life of 68 million people in 47 dependent territories, which in practice meant spending seven shillings per person over the nine years the programme was in force.[724]

This charity was accompanied by bombastic rhetoric, and not just from the Tories. The Labour Party Programme in 1949 declared that "Great Britain and the colonies have gone into partnership to liquidate ignorance, poverty and disease," and the Labour Speaker's Handbook for 1948–9 added that "[i]mperialism

723 S. Constantine, *The Making of British Colonial Development Policy 1914*–1940, London 2005, p. 197 ff.

724 R. Palme Dutt, *Britain's Crisis of Empire*, London 1949, p. 80.

is dead, but the Empire has been given new life".[725] A British voter could further learn from the book that:

> In the colonies Labour Britain has given a tremendous impetus to social and economic progress. Under the Colonial Development and Welfare Scheme, £120 million is given, to colonial governments to assist local planning. The Colonial Development Corporation with a capital of £110 million has been established to finance special projects of large-scale economic developments. Further still the Overseas Food Corporation is empowered to spend £55 million on great plans for increasing food production in the colonies.[726]

In the postwar Britain of food rationings, these numbers might look impressive, but in practice they amounted to mere pennies. The richest colonies, such as Nigeria, allocated a shilling for education a year, but many had no access to schools of any kind. Even in Nigeria there was only one doctor for every 133,000 inhabitants (in postwar Britain the figure was one in 1200, and in pre-war Poland, one in 10,000). The colonial system of rule did not inspire hope for improvement of the situation.

Among the most spectacular colonial development projects were the gigantic peanut plantations in Tanzania mentioned earlier, on which 24 million pounds were spent in 1946; they cost an additional 7 million pounds a year to maintain, and were supposed to employ more than 30,000 Africans. The project was in fact intended to serve the British more than Africans. Its main purpose was to supply Britain's cities with half of their needs for fats by 1950. In practice, after four years of failures and delays, instead of the planned 228,000 tonnes of nuts, barely 2150 tonnes had been gathered, from an area covering 2% of the intended acreage. In practice nothing worked as planned. The land was not suitable for cultivation, machines broke down, and the colonial administrators complained that Africans did put enough effort into their work.[727]

Independence and industrialization seemed to Nkrumah to be the only way to break with colonial dependency and simultaneously pull the country out of poverty. In 1963, when his programme was crumbling, and Ghana stood on the verge of bankruptcy, he wrote: "the vicious circle of poverty which keeps us in our rut of impoverishment, can only be broken by a massively planned industrial

725 Ibid., p. 82.
726 Quoted in Ibid., p. 80.
727 Ibid.

undertaking."[728] Nkrumah's views did not set him apart – they were more or less universally shared.

While the first five-year development plan, begun in 1954 when Ghana was still an autonomous British colony, concentrated on education and the road-building, the next plan, officially labelled "Building a Welfare State", was focused primarily on the development of industry: its central point was the construction of dams on the river Volta and a formidable aluminium steelworks.[729] The next plan, announced in 1964 under the heading "Work and Happiness", was intended to cover seven years. It called for investment expenditures of the then-astronomical sum of a billion British pounds and for tightening control over businesses, which had hitherto operated under free market conditions. The newly appointed National Commission on Economic Planning was now to designate production goals for them.

Planned industrialization in Ghana left a lot to be desired, however: construction projects dragged out mercilessly, and costs were higher than planned, with disappointing results. For example, the government built a mango processing plant, though it admitted that there was no local market for its products, and that its production capacity was several times higher than world demand. That is, if the enterprise ever got off the ground.

The government's report on the factory is illuminating:

> Project: A factory is to be erected at Wenchi, Brong Ahafo, to produce 7,000 tons of mangoes and 5,300 tons of tomatoes per annum. If average yields of crops in that area will be 5 tons per acre per annum for mangoes and 5 tons per acre for tomatoes, there should be 1,400 acres of mangoes and 1,060 acres of tomatoes in the field to supply the factory.
>
> The Problem: The present supply of mangoes in the area is from a few trees scattered in the bush and tomatoes are not grown on commercial scale, and so the production of these crops will have to start from scratch. Mangoes take 5–7 years from planting to start fruiting. How to obtain sufficient planting materials and to organize production of raw materials quickly become the major problems of this project.[730]

---

728 K. Akonor, *Africa and IMF Conditionality. The Unevenness of Compliance*, New York–London 2006, p. 19.

729 K. Botwe-Asamoah, *Kwame Nkrumah's Politico-Cultural Thought and Policies. An African-Centered Paradigm For the Second Phase of the African Revolution*, New York–London 2005, p. 115.

730 Quoted in T. Killick, *Development Economics in Action*, New York 1978, 233. The book tells the entire story in great detail.

Another telling example was a coconut oil factory – the Esiama Oil Mill – built by the government of Ghana in 1961. On paper, this project seemed to make sense. It was true that no studies had ever been conducted that supported the planners' optimistic view that local forests could provide sufficient raw materials, but the managers did at least make surveys of the local forests before making the decision to build it. Plans for the factory were commissioned from foreign experts and technologically advanced (for the period) machines were purchased with foreign currency. Two years after completion of the factory's construction, its planned production capacity was additionally increased. Construction dragged on, the factory turned out to have been poorly designed, machines broke down due to poor operating conditions, and their operators lacked proper training. Due to rationing of foreign currency, the import of replacement parts took as long as three months, resulting in long pauses in production. In practice, this meant that the coconut oil produced by this modern factory cost considerably more than the oil local villagers had been producing by means of their own primitive methods. The oil from the Esiama Oil Mill cost almost a thousand cedis a tonne, whereas the world price was the equivalent of 600 cedis a tonne. The factory management wanted to lower costs, but when it turned out that this was beyond their means, a simpler solution presented itself: they simply demanded the government give them a monopoly on the purchase of raw materials – and, naturally, were given one. Poor farmers were thus made to pay for a large, inefficient factory.[731]

This was typical of many African industrial enterprises – from Ghana and Nigeria to Tanzania. Machines were ordered in offices very far from the places where they were to be used, and were thus often not suited to local conditions. Transport took a long time, and equipment often arrived damaged or in poor condition. When it did finally arrive, it was often installed improperly: a lack of educated cadres presented another enormous problem. All of these issues raised costs, as did the fact that imported equipment often could not be used to process local raw materials, which it proved incapable of handling. As a result, production was very expensive, and the survival of these companies ended up being financed by local consumers and contractors. The government subsidized production by means of a number of creative techniques: it limited the import of competing products or prohibited it entirely, lowered taxes, and provided local raw materials at a reduced price (which always meant that it bought them from farmers at a price lower than the market rate).

---

731 R. H. Bates, *Markets and States in Tropical Africa. The Political Basis of Agricultural Policies*, Berkeley–Los Angeles 1981, pp. 20–21.

Nkrumah thought that all of these difficulties were temporary – and were the price that had to be paid for building the country's industry and economic (and therefore political) independence. He explained to the citizens of his country:

> It may be true in some instances that our local products cost more, though by no means all of them, and then only in the initial period [...] It is precisely because we were, under colonialism, made the dumping ground of other countries' manufactures and the providers merely of primary products, that we remained backward; and if we were to refrain from building, say, a soap factory simply because we might have to raise the price of soap to the community, we should be doing a disservice to the country.[732]

At the beginning of the 1960s, local products were protected in Ghana by a ban on the import of competing products. Local factories thus had no incentive either to produce in large quantities, or to offer goods that were cheap or high in quality: they were guaranteed a profit and could calmly maintain that all the needs of the population were being met – in the end, after all, everything they produced found a buyer.

Nkrumah believed that industrialization at any cost was a necessary step in the building of socialism, and therefore on the path to independence and prosperity. In the introduction to his autobiography, he wrote:

> The ideology of my Party may be formulated as follows: no race, no people, no nation can exist freely and be respected at home and abroad without political freedom. Once this freedom is gained, a greater task comes into view. All dependent territories are backward in education, in agriculture and industry. The economic independence that should follow and maintain political independence demands every effort from the people, a total mobilisation of brain and manpower resources. What other countries have taken three hundred years or more to achieve, a once dependent territory must try to accomplish in a generation if it is to survive. Unless it is, as it were, "jet-propelled", it will lag behind and thus risk everything for which it has fought. Capitalism is too complicated a system for a newly independent nation. Hence the need for a socialistic society.[733]

Nkrumah had several reasons for rejecting capitalism, besides the fact it was "too complicated." He judged that the problems that had plagued the former colonies were created by capitalism, and therefore could not be resolved by it. Furthermore, capitalism led to an unequal distribution of goods, and created a highly unstable economy – because it was driven by profit and not the good of society, which was to be the main goal of socialism.[734]

---

732 Quoted in R. H. Bates, *Markets and States...*, p. 73.

733 K. Nkrumah, *Autobiography*, x.

734 A. Biney, *The Political and Social Thought...*, p. 106.

His vision of socialism, however, lacked coherence. He never presented it in a systematic, lucid way. One thing is for certain: African socialism would be a socialism of community, not of class struggle. In it, the state would play a central role, planning development and running the largest investments. Nkrumah was nonetheless not hostile to private capital, though he did feel ambivalence toward it: on the one hand, he courted Western businessmen and sought help from Western governments in the construction of his largest industrial project, the building of dams on the Volta River. On the other hand, the Ghanan leader considered Western capital – including development aid – to be a tool that helped the West consolidate its domination over other countries.

Western capital thus carried with it threats. In 1962, Krobo Eduesi, minister of industry in Nkrumah's government, boasted:

> Since December last year, Ghana has for the first time decided to exercise one of the weapons of economic sovereignty—import control! So long as this weapon is carefully and wisely yielded, our young and infant industries which are facing ruthless competition from long established and giant monopoly industries overseas, will be protected from dumping.[735]

In explaining his political philosophy, Nkrumah wrote that the forces of neocolonialism were too powerful for one nation to stand up against – hence the need for collective action by all Africans. The worse things became in Ghana, the more its prime minister would speak of the need for pan-African economic planning.[736]

In April 1961, in the face of mounting problems with inflation and supplying goods, Nkrumah declared that the goals of his party – full employment, home construction and the building of industry – should be the task of the "whole nation," which should devote itself to working together to accomplish these tasks. "How are we to achieve this goal within the shortest possible time?, he asked. "Socialism is the only pattern that can within the shortest possible time bring the good life to the people."

In order to build socialism, they had to first build up industry, invest in farming equipment and electrify the country. "Hence my preoccupation with the Volta River Project and other schemes that will provide water power both for electricity and irrigation of regions that are starved of water at certain periods

---

735 K. Akonor, *Africa and IMF…*, p. 20.

736 K. Botwe-Asamoah, *Kwame Nkrumah's Politico-Cultural Thought and Policies. An African-Centered Paradigm For the Second Phase of the African Revolution*, New York–London 2005, p. 20.

of the year." Planning was now to enter a new stage, as previous efforts had been disappointing. "Our planning hitherto has been largely piecemeal and unpurposeful. It has not been linked in an organised manner". Nkrumah complained of chaos and the waste of "precious funds" and "technical staff." His party was to be "the pivot of our economic planning".

This enterprise as a whole demanded the "consultation and participation of the people," as a result of which Ghana was to become "the truest kind of democracy that has ever functioned". Here, Nkrumah did not explain exactly what he had in mind.[737]

Any criticism of the prime minister's vision was rejected. Polish economist Ignacy Sachs recalled a conference in Ghana in the 1960s, at which he stated that the proposed rate of growth in the plan then in effect was unrealistic. He was then told by the head of planning to never forget that "for we Africans only the best in the world is good enough."[738]

Nkrumah's response to growing economic problems was to rule with an iron hand. In 1964 he declared himself president for life, and Ghana a one-party state. He created a host of organizations designed to mobilize support, such as the PVA (Party Vanguard Activists). He was also becoming increasingly disconnected from the lives of ordinary people. In 1965 inflation and shortages of flour caused the price of bread to rise from half a crown to five shillings (whereas the average wage of a worker in Accra was six shillings). Nkrumah was not even aware of this development. When Hyman M. Basner, a South African journalist and political émigré from South Africa visited Nkrumaha in the presidential palace in October 1965, he brought him two loaves of bread. The news that they cost five shillings apiece and were filled with air came as a shock to Nkrumah. He blamed the rise in prices on corrupt officials at the centralized state wholesaler, who were selling expensive imported flour to bakeries. The problem remained unresolved, however.[739] After an attempt on the Nkrumah's life, the prisons began to fill up with his political opponents. Joseph Kwame Danquah, the leader's main rival in previous democratic elections, was imprisoned twice. The second time he was chained to the floor of his cell, starved and refused medical treatment. When he died, an official statement gave the cause as heart failure. Nkrumah ostentatiously plunged himself into mourning and travelled to Danquah's native village, where he stood over the deceased's grave in quiet reflection.

---

737 A. Biney, *The Political and Social Thought of Kwame Nkrumah*, Houndmills–New York 2011, p. 103.

738 M. Kula, "Swój do swego… po co?", *Studia migracyjne – Przegląd polonijny*, 2009, p. 2.

739 A. Biney, *The Political and Social Thought…*, p. 97.

The country's financial situation was a catastrophe. Wasteful spending on investments was compounded by a drastic fall in the price of cocoa, which despite Nkrumah's efforts was still the country's main source of foreign currency. In 1958 the price of a tonne of cocoa on the London stock market was 977 USD, while in 1965 it had fallen to barely 400 USD. An ambitious spending programme had brought with it an enormous deficit, paid for from currency reserves – until they ran out. Nkrumah's final development plan did not bring the happiness it had promised. It remained only on paper and, ultimately, no attempt was even made to implement it.

Nevertheless, in January 1966 the construction of the dams on the Volta River was completed. Nkrumah personally flipped the switch – and electricity flowed from the new power station into the heart of the country.[740] By now his government was deeply unpopular: inflation had spun out of control, shops were empty, and Ghana lacked foreign currency to import medicines and spare parts. In February, Nkrumah was removed from power by a military coup. Crushed and humiliated, the prophet of the African renaissance died six years later in exile. His great investment project had become a hostage to Western interests: profits from the dams on the Volta flowed mainly into the pockets of Western investors.

The example of Ghana speaks volumes not only because it reveals the defects of African-style socialism. The lack of coherence in Nkrumah's ideology was typical of many African regimes. Elements of it were repeated, however, throughout the developing world. It was believed everywhere that the development of industry promoted independence; that a policy of import substitution, or a conscious limiting of imports and replacing foreign products with domestic ones was called for; that the state should steer development, even building its own industrial enterprises, since no one else would do it, and these were the motor of growth.

The brutal political economy that formed the background of such a programme was also shared by many countries. African, Arab or Latin American leaders did not control their societies the way Stalin or Mao did; they did not rule giant countries in isolation from the world or have a comparable apparatus of coercion at their disposal. The foundation of Nkrumah and other post-colonial leaders' power was a coalition of various local interests, whose demands had to be met if these leaders were to maintain their hold on power. They were also forced to consider social discontent.

---

740 K. Botwe-Asamoah, *Kwame Nkrumah's Politico-Cultural Thought…*, p. 116.

The paradox of these systems was that in the name of development and prosperity, the heaviest burdens were placed on the shoulders of the poorest.[741] In the case of Ghana, these were the farmers who produced cocoa. Even before independence, Nkrumah's government had been given control of the Ghana Cocoa Marketing Board – a company created in 1947 with a monopoly on the purchase of cocoa in Ghana and its sale on the world market. It was originally created to guarantee farmers stable cocoa prices – compensating them for oscillations in prices from funds it accumulated during periods of high prices. For Nkrumah, the Cocoa Marketing Board became the main source of funds for financing his industrial programme. Purchase prices were set lower than on global markets, and the surplus was seized by the state. The company also quickly grew into a gigantic state-operated Moloch, employing tens of thousands of people, who were also charged with, among other things, supplying farmers with fertilizer and fungicidal agents, and helping them improve production. There was only one thing it did not do – pay workers a decent wage.

Governments in many African countries obtained money by similar means: for example, in Tanzania in the years 1971–1976, farmers received from one fifth to one half of the market price for their products.[742] Of 28 African countries studied by the World Bank in 1994, fully half of them tightly controlled the food market and agricultural products according to this model.[743] It was the same with cotton production in Chad and Benin, coffee in Burundi, peanuts in Niger, and coffee and cocoa in Sierra Leone. In Togo in the 1970s, producers' income fell by almost half over just a few years, though world prices were rising at that time.[744]

In the absence of a domestic middle class, the backbone of support for African governments came from government workers. The government did not have sufficient funds to pay them a decent wage – and therefore it purchased this group's support (or at least acceptance) by regulating the prices of basic foodstuffs, on which Africans spent most of their income. It thus had a double motivation for controlling agricultural production.

In many countries, attempts were made to organize state-run farms, but these culminated in catastrophe, as they did in the USSR and other countries of the

741 This mechanism was described in the classic works of economists Robert H. Bates and Benno J. Ndulu.

742 R. H. Bates, *Markets and States…*, p. 39.

743 R. H. Bates, "Domestic interests and control regimes", in *The Political Economy of Economic Growth in Africa, 1960–2000*, vol. 1, ed. B. J. Ndulu, et al., Cambridge–New York 2008, p. 178.

744 Ibid., p. 183.

socialist bloc. In Ghana, they began to be organized in 1962. Four years later there were 135, employing a total of 20,8000 workers. Hundreds of tractors were imported for use on them. State farms received 90% of the budget for agricultural development. Nonetheless, they were very badly managed, and were obliged to sell food at below market prices. As a result, their losses were enormous: in 1971 their annual revenue did not even cover a month's costs.[745]

State enterprises were also inefficient because they served as a means for providing employment to masses of people. A commission studying the activity of the Cocoa Marketing Board in Ghana after the fall of Nkrumah noted that one of the local branches employed a dance group, football players, and actors and actresses, not to mention many other workers who could hardly be called essential. "The CMB's area of operation … embraces activities and involves a staff which would have appeared absurd only ten years ago," the authors of the report commented.[746]

In order to cope with a decline in agricultural production and simultaneously maintain low food prices on the market, governments not only imported food, but created complex systems of subsidies and incentives for their own farmers. In Ghana the government covered a third of the price of corn seed and three quarters of the price of rice seed. In Nigeria the government tried raising its own type of corn – better adapted to local conditions (unsuccessfully) and offered farmers credit at interest rates 5% lower than the market demanded. In Kenya and Zambia, governments subsidized part of the cost of research into new strains of corn. In Ghana a special bank was created to loans to farmers at interest rates no higher than 6%, thus considerably lower than the rate of inflation. That bank, however, only demanded repayment of two thirds of its loans; the rest amounted to a subsidy. The main problem with these loans was that they were primarily given to individuals with political connections. It was equally difficult to obtaining government-allocated fertilizer, which only in theory belonged to everyone. Allocations were always a reward for political supporters.[747]

Support for local industry proceeded in a similar fashion. The most important and most frequently employed mechanism was controlling the import of competing goods. In Kenya in the years 1965–1972, the government acceded to 90% of the requests from local and foreign companies asking for protection from competition by raising customs tariffs, limiting import licenses, and lowering the duty on raw

745 R. H. Bates, *Markets and States…*, op. cit., pp. 46–47.
746 Ibid., p. 27.
747 Ibid., p. 53.

materials brought in from abroad.[748] In Kenya, the Committee for the Protection of Industry oversaw requests for import licenses: importing paints or varnishes from abroad required the prior consent of the local manufacturers' association. The manufacturers of hundreds of different categories of goods, from car batteries to burlap bags, were protected in a similar fashion. If the committee found that the imported article was also produced in the country, it had the right to deny licensing to the importer, and it used that right without hesitation. Because the industrial sector was very small in most African countries, and a given article was not produced by more than a few companies, this policy promoted concentration and division of the market – naturally at the expense of the consumer. Thus, de facto monopolies were created, which had no motivation to keep prices low and quality high. Manufacturers found it more worthwhile to fight for their profits in government offices than on the market. Foreign investors, too, were often guaranteed a de facto monopoly if they built a factory in the country. For example, the Kenyan government gave the British Leyland company *de facto* exclusive rights to automobile assembly, and Firestone – to tire production. In the same country, *de facto* monopolies existed in petroleum and food processing, and in the production of cement, matches, sugar, building materials and textiles.[749]

The system was thus logical: the rhetoric of self-sufficiency and development went hand-in-hand with looking after local interests, whether these were a manufacturers' group or urban supporters of the government. Territorially dispersed and uneducated, farmers were incapable of overthrowing those in power, so it was easiest to burden them with the costs of buying support from those groups on which the government depended for its power. Farmers protested using the only method available to them – either bribing officials, or selling their goods on the black market, or, if all else fails, limiting production. In Nigeria, agricultural production fell by 2% in the decade after independence, while in Ghana it rose by 0.3% and then decreased in the 1970s by 3.1%.[750]

The most dramatic course of action chosen was the attempt to control farmers in Tanzania. For the country's socialist president, Julius Nyerere, the matter was literally one of life and death. When the country (then, before it merged with Zanzibar, called Tanganika) gained independence, half a million of its inhabitants were saved from dying of hunger only by food aid. At that time, Nyerere said:

748 Ibid., p. 64.
749 Ibid., p. 68.
750 R. Betts, *Decolonization…*, op. cit., p. 71.

> Poverty, ignorance and disease must be overcome before we can really establish in this country the sort of society we have been dreaming of. These obstacles are not small ones, they are more difficult to overcome than any alien government. From now on we are fighting not man, but nature.[751]

The first two Tanzanian economic plans – first a three-year plan 1961–1964), followed by a five-year plan (1964–1969) – did not lead to a breakthrough. Nyerere was struggling with a classic problem of underdevelopment: he did not have the means to finance the development of industry, which he believed to be the key to breaking out of poverty. Agriculture presented an additional challenge. How to change poor farmers into farmers producing large yields of commercial crops for foreign markets?

In 1956, before the end of the colonial era, the mission statement of the World Bank called for radical social transformation: the world of traditional villages needed to be destroyed, in order for quick new cultivation methods to be introduced. The author of a report prepared by the Bank wrote:

> The Mission concludes that quicker progress toward these ends is likely to be made, within the limitations of the resources available for government action, by planned settlement of empty areas.… When people move to new areas, they are likely to be more prepared for and receptive of change than when they remain in their familiar surroundings. And where people are under pressure to move or see the advantage of doing so, they can be required to abide by rules and to adopt new practices as a condition of receiving new land.[752]

Two types of new settlements were anticipated. In the first type, the government would provide farmers with land and would help them cultivate their fields. The second was a form of trade cooperative, in which the government also provided machines, fertilizer, and advice, and in return received part of the profits from the largest (as the plan optimistically assumed) harvests. The authors were not dismayed by the spectacular failure of the programme for peanut cultivation in Tanzania during the colonial period. Even tractors built from Sherman tanks were unable to cope with Tanzanian soil and weather: a plan made in the abstract did not take real conditions into account in the least. The preliminary study for the project took just two weeks and was conducted from the air.[753]

---

751 Quoted in J. Iliffe, *A Modern History of Tanganyika*, Cambridge 1994, p. 576.

752 Quoted in M. Jennings, *Surrogates of the State: NGOs, Development, and Ujamaa in Tanzania*, Bloomfield 2008, p. 41.

753 J. C. Scott, *Seeing Like State: How Certain Schemes to Improve the Human Condition Have Failed*, New Haven 1998, p. 229.

Nyerere's government quickly accepted an essentially colonial resettlement plan. The Five-Year Development Programme (1964–1969) was supposed to produce 69 modern model villages. The establishment of one village was supposed to cost 150,000 British pounds. The residents were to be carefully selected, and the government was to lend them money to settle and begin cultivation, and to provide qualified managers to run the village. The entire project was to cost 12 million pounds, or 13% of the state's entire budget allocated for development investment.[754] It turned out to be a complete failure: ministries could not agree among themselves on issues, plans remained on paper, and the building of the villages started very late – not until 1965. When construction of the 23 villages finally began, a mere 3,642 farmers were persuaded to settle in them. Contrary to plans, none of the new villages had a pharmacy or a school, and only two had reliable sources of water.

Nyerere was close to the ideal of an African politician: an incorruptible, widely respected advocate for the poorest, with an aversion to violence. The socialism he imagined was community-based in character: the state was the owner of most of the means of production, it levelled incomes and provided most social services. In a pamphlet entitled "Ujamaa" on the fundamentals of African socialism, Nyerere painted an idyllic picture of a traditional, community-based Africa: socialism was to mean a return to traditional values, but in modern conditions. The word in "ujamaa" itself can be translated as "family" or "brotherhood": it implied respect for the other, community property and the obligation to work.[755] As a Polish economist of the time observed, from the point of view of the Polish People's Republic, "we would not have called that socialism."[756] Nyere explained that the concept of "ujamaa":

> describes our socialism. It is opposed to capitalism, which seeks to build a happy society on the basis of the exploitation of man by man; and it is equally opposed to doctrinaire socialism which seeks to build its happy society on a philosophy of inevitable conflict between man and man. We, in Africa, have no more need of being "converted" to socialism than we have of being "taught" democracy. Both are rooted in our own past--in the

754 M. Jennings, *Surrogates of the State…*, p. 42.

755 G. Kitching, *Development and Underdevelopment in Historical Perspective. Populism, Nationalism and Industrialization*, London 2011, pp. 64–65.

756 S. Chodak, J. Kleer, *Socjalizm i modernizacja w „czarnej" Afryce*, Warszawa 1967, p. 14.

traditional society which produced us. Modern African socialism can draw from its traditional heritage the recognition of "society" as an extension of the basic family unit.[757]

Paternalism and autocracy were inscribed in this vision of society as a large, traditional family. Frustrated by economic stagnation and his lack of success in building industry, Nyerere evolved over the years towards a vision of development in which growth moved to the background and what mattered most was equalizing incomes and building what he imagined to be the traditional African sense of community. (Proof that equality was a typical feature of traditional African society was supposed to be the fact, as he argued in "Ujamaa," that it had had no millionaires.) Nyerere gradually grew more radical. In 1967, he announced the "Arusha Declaration," in which he drafted his vision of a socialist, agrarian Utopia. He was at that time greatly impressed by Mao's China, where he had visited some show communes, as well as Israeli kibbutzes. Economic constraints were also a factor: the country had proven too poor to invest in industry, and since poor villagers represented 97% of its residents, socialism could not be achieved without them. In his declaration, Nyerere enumerated the following conditions for development (a) intelligence, b) hard work, and c) good leadership, and insisted on self-sufficiency: foreign aid and investment created dependency.

> There are various forms of exploitation. We must not forget that people who live in towns can possibly become the exploiters of those who live in the rural areas. All our big hospitals are in towns and they benefit only a small section of the people of Tanzania. Yet if we had built them with loans from outside Tanzania, it is the overseas sale of the peasants' produce which provides the foreign exchanges for repayment. Those who do not get the benefit of the hospital thus carry the major responsibility for paying for them.[758]

Nyerere was right to the extent that in most "backward" countries, including those in Africa, poor farmers subsidized city populations in this way. He did not have any idea about how to change this, however. He decided to back a huge, ambitious programme of forced resettlements into new, rationally designed villages (called "ujamaa" of course), in which farmers were to cultivate land together, overseen by state experts. Ten years later, in 1977, over 3 million people had been resettled, and their old houses demolished.[759] Because people did not want to move themselves, Nyerere, frustrated by the plan's slow realization, announced in September 1973

757 J. Nyerere, "Ujamaa. Basis of African Socialism", *Journal of Pan African Studies*, 1987, vol. 1 no. 1, p. 1.

758 J. Nyerere, Arusha Declaration, quoted from: http://www.marxists.org/subject/africa/nyerere/1967/arusha-declaration.htm.

759 M. Jennings, *Surrogates of the State…*, p. 48.

that moving was compulsory.[760] The operation was conducted by the army. The planning and founding of a new village lasted one day – which meant in practice that people were abandoned in empty space. The promised infrastructure and help were, of course, non-existent – the new, communal forms of farming were supposed to be sufficient. On the other hand, the state did prescribe in detail what to sow and harvest, in keeping with the plan proceeding from the top.

An official carrying out Operation Planned Villages (as it was named, military fashion) in the Shinyanga district in 1974 summed it up by calling the operation a matter of compulsion – since Tanzania could not wait passively while the majority of residents lived a "dead life" in the countryside.[761]

Thus, traditional life was seen as "dead life": only a modern life was real life. Public services – access to healthcare, education, food aid – were available only to the inhabitants of the new villages. Villagers were settled along roads so that it would be easier to control them, and villages were designed not according to rules of efficiency, but following a modernist, geometric aesthetic that officials associated with modernity and efficiency.[762]

Instead of African communities, the "Ujamaa" programme created a centralized, authoritarian state which had little to do with equality – and in practice was run by urban, bureaucratic elites who also had the most comfortable lives in it.[763] Tanzania was a *de facto* one-party state by 1965. Nyerere observed then that British-style democracy had become redundant:

> Now my argument is that a two-party system can be justified only when the parties are divided over some fundamental issue … If, on the other hand, you have a two-party system where the difference between the parties are not fundamental, then you immediately reduce politics to the level of a football match. A football match may, of course, attract some very able players; it may also be entertaining; but it is still only a game, and only the most ardent fans (which are not usually the most intelligent) take the game very seriously. This, in fact, is not unlike what has happened in many of the so-called democratic countries today, where some of the most intelligent members of society have become disgusted by the hypocrisy of the party games called politics, and take no interest in them.[764]

---

760 I. G. Shivji, "The village in Mwalimu's thought and political practice", in *The Legacy of Nyerere*, eds. C. Chachage, A. Cassam, Kampala 2010, p. 123.

761 Quoted in J. C. Scott, *Seeing Like State*…, p. 234.

762 Ibid., p. 237

763 N. van de Walle, *African Economies and the Politics of Permanent Crisis 1979–1999*, Cambridge 2001, p. 57.

764 A. Eckert, "Julius Nyerere, Tanzanian Elites, and the Project of African Socialism", [in:] *Elites and Decolonization in the Twentieth Century*, eds. J. Dulffer, M. Frey, pp. 228–229.

TANU (the Tanzanian African National Union), Nyerere's party, systematically liquidated the remains of the embryonic democracy inherited from the British, as well as the traditional system of rule. The country was in crisis, and political campaigns did not help: as "Ujamaa" progressed, Tanzania was besieged with catastrophic hunger, and agricultural production fell instead of rising. Over 60% of the new villages were organized in quasi-desert areas, not suited to regular cultivation. In the years 1973–1974, the country needed gigantic food imports: according to Nyerere himself, a cow could have been bought for each Tanzanian family with the money spent.[765]

When Nyerere left office in 1985, Tanzania, after 24 years of experimentation, was as poor as it had been on the day it gained independence. It was not a typical case, however – not only because its leader had abandoned dreams of industrialization (though he did so only because he had no choice), but also because he stepped down from office voluntarily. Over the three decades following independence, there were over 75 coups d'état in the post-colonial world. In Ghana itself, there were three from 1966 to 1972 alone.

The political economy of African post-colonial countries was logical and coherent, but a crucial element was missing: a significant rise in the standard of living. Though African countries saw a considerable rise in the 1960s and 1970s, in many of them, the economy could not keep up with the growing population. Though over the course of 40 years of independence the countries of sub-Saharan Africa made progress – per capita income was 40% higher in 2000 than in 1960 – and average life expectancy and access to education markedly improved, the other parts of the developing world saw significantly greater improvements. In the end, the gap between Africans' incomes and those of the inhabitants of developing countries in Latin America and Asia grew by a third between 1960 and 2000.[766]

2. Socialism is more than mere logic

India, the largest of the post-colonial countries, also strove for a home-grown version of socialism. Unlike African countries, India not only had its own industrial tradition and highly qualified specialists in many areas, but had been

765 J. C. Scott, *Seeing Like State…*, p. 239.

766 B. J. Ndulu, S. A. O'Connell, "Policy Plus: African Growth Performance, 1960–2000", [in:] *The Political Economy of Economic Growth in Africa, 1960–2000*, vol. 1, eds. B. J. Ndulu, et al., Cambridge–New York 2008, p. 5.

discussing the issue of how to emerge from poverty and backwardness for several decades.

This was the main subject of the writings and thought of the outstanding Indian colonial-era economist Mahadeva Govinda Ranade, who died in 1901. In the 1890s, Ranade had written:

> We need only walk through our streets, and study the most superficial aspects of our economic situation and the fact forces itself upon us that we are a people of little resources. Many millions among us scarcely earn a couple of annas a day. Many millions more are always underfed, and live on the borderland of famine and slow death, into which the failure of a single monsoon precipitates them[767].

Ranade had an ambivalent attitude toward British rule over India: on the one hand, he thought it perpetuated the country's poverty; on the other, he believed that contact with the West had torn India out of a centuries-long lethargy. As Ranade himself has written, the German Friedrich List was the Western economist to whom he was most indebted.[768] (List inspired a great many economists from countries on the periphery; we shall return to him presently.) Like many intellectuals from the developing world, Ranade had a less than stellar opinion of his compatriots:

> The characteristics of our social life are the prevalence of status over contract, of combination over competition. Our habits of mind are conservative to a fault. Labour is cheap and plentiful, but unsteady, unthrifty, and unskilled. Capital is sacarce, immobile, and unenterprising […] Agriculture is the chief support of nearly whole population, and this agriculture is carried on under conditions of uncertain rainfall. Commerce and manufactures on a large scale but recent importations […] Our laws and institutions favour a low standard of life, and encourage sub-division and not concentration of wealth. The religious ideals of life condemn the ardent pursuit of wealth as a mistake to be avoided as far as possible […] To these must be added the economical drain of wealth and talents, which foreign subjugation has entailed on the country.[769]

The prescription for ending underdevelopment was supposed to be industrialization – brought about primarily using the country's own strength and by means of its own capital. Ranade wrote that the latter did not really amount to much, but if it could be concentrated in a few, decisive hands, it should suffice. Hostility toward foreign, especially British, capital, was in fact typical of

767 Quoted in A. K. Dasgupta, *A History of Indian Economic Thought*, London–New York 2002, p. 88. The greater part of the book is devoted to a discussion of Ranade's views.

768 J. Adams, "The Institutional Economics of Mahadev Govind Ranade", *Journal of Economic Issues*, vol. 5, 1971.

769 Quoted in J. Adams, *The Institutional Economics…*, op. cit.

all nineteenth-century Indian nationalists: they saw it as a lever of exploitation, rather than of development.[770] The country should invest in secular education and not restrict the import of western technical expertise and machines. "When factories and mills on a small or large scale were set up all over the land, the present paralysis would give way to a play of energies," the economist wrote.[771] Ranade was open to foreign trade on the condition that India would export goods and import technologies. He considered the main obstacle to the development of industry to be the absence of native capital, which in turn was caused by a lack of incentives to save. (In addition, savings were locked up in precious metals and not invested.) Because Indians lacked experience in modern business, and local businessmen were not able to conduct business on an adequately large scale, the state should look after investment. In 1890 Ranade said:

> We can well count upon the assistance of the State in regulating our Cooperative efforts by helping us to form Deposit and Finance Banks, and facilitating recoveries of advances made by them, by encouraging New Industries with Guarantees or Subsidies, or loans at low interest, by pioneering the way to new Enterprises, and by affording facilities for Emigration and Immigration, and establishing Technical Institutes and buying more largely the Stores they require here and, in many cases, by producing their own Stores.[772]

Ranade did not set any protectionist goals, although they were applied in the countries that India was to be modelled on – Germany, France, and the United States. He did not touch on this theme at all, perhaps – as one specialist in his thought suspects – because India was a British colony and to do so was unthinkable from a political perspective.[773]

Gandhi, the founder and father of the Indian nation, was by comparison with Ranade (and many other representatives of the elites) a hopeless romantic and radical dreamer. Towards the end of the 1920s, Gandhi's colleague and successor, Nehru, was fascinated by Soviet economic planning and development of industry: "The Soviets have put magic into the word [planning]," he is said to have said in 1933.[774] As for Gandhi, he had an aversion to planning: he even told a group of Indian communists once that they wanted to turn India into the USSR, and that this was pathetic because it showed they lacked respect for the culture of

---

770 B. Chandra, *India's Struggle for Independence: 1857–1947*, London 1989, p. 94.
771 Quoted in A. K. Dasgupta, *A History of Indian Economic Thought*, p. 91.
772 Quoted in Ibid., p. 94.
773 Ibid., p. 98.
774 S. Ghose, *Jawaharlal Nehru, A Biography*, Bombay 1993, p. 232.

their own country.[775] He believed that India was moving toward industrialization, modernization, and a strong state, whereas his ideal India was a land of farmers living in traditional villages – self-sufficient and living modestly, though without hunger. "The whole planning is a waste of effort. But he (Nehru) cannot be satisfied with anything that is not big," Gandhi wrote in a private letter.[776] In his programmatic, visioanry book *Hind Swaraj*, published in 1909, he wrote that India's civilization had no equal:

> I believe, that the civilization India has evolved is not to be beaten in the world. Nothing can equal the seeds sown by our ancestors [...] Many thrust their advice upon India, and she remains steady. This is her beauty: it is the sheet-anchor of our hope [...] India, as so many writers have shown, has nothing to learn from anybody else, and this is as it should be. We notice that the mind is a restless bird; the more it gets the more it wants, and still remains unsatisfied. The more we indulge our passions the more unbridled they become. Our ancestors, therefore, set a limit to our indulgences. They saw that happiness was largely a mental condition. A man is not necessarily happy because he is rich, or unhappy because he is poor. The rich are often seen to be unhappy, the poor to be happy. Millions will always remain poor. Observing all this, our ancestors dissuaded us from luxuries and pleasures [...] It was not that we did not know how to invent machinery, but our forefathers knew that, if we set our hearts after such things, we would become slaves and lose our moral fiber."[777]

Gandhi was opposed to large cities and industry. He saw them as sources of contamination. He dreamed of an India in which people lived modestly and avoided rivalry over material goods. He thought that the advent of modern civilization had brought with it thieves and plunderers, sin and prostitution. Nehru believed that poverty could be rooted out and that planning and the development of industry represented the only road in that direction. His concession to the master consisted in admitting that traditional crafts – for Gandhi, the foundation of the economy – would have their place in the new India.

In 1938, nearly 10 years before independence, the Congress Party created a National Planning Committee. Nehru became its chairman. Nehru was thinking of socialism, thought it had to be a different socialism from the Soviet kind – and at first, for tactical reasons, he preferred not to talk about it. In 1939, he wrote in a letter to one of the Committee members:

---

775 D. Yergin, J. Stanislaw, *The Commanding Heights. The Battle for the World Economy*, New York 2002, p. 53.

776 S. Ghose, *Jawaharlal Nehru...*, op. cit., p. 232.

777 M. Gandhi, *Hind Swaraj or Indian Home Rule*, http://www.soilandhealth.org/03sov/0303critic/hind%20swaraj.pdf

If we start with the dictum that only under socialism there can be planning, we frighten people and irritate the ignorant. If, on the other hand, we think of planning apart from socialism and thus inevitably arrive at some form of socialism, that is a logical process which will convert many who are weary of words and slogans[778].

In 1940 Nehru was arrested by the British and the committee's work came to a standstill. The idea, however, remained active: a group of influential Bombay industrialists led by J. R. D. Tata, head of the largest family business conglomerate in India, wrote its own economic plan in 1944, anticipating the state government's support for industrialization. The magnates of business naturally did not want socialism, but they did want a modern, industrialized nation that protected its indigenous capitalists – and they thought such a plan was the only solution.

Gandhi's opposition remained firm to the end. When in October 1945 the British released Nehru and other Party Congress leaders, he wrote a list to Nehru in which he clarified that he had not relinquished his vision for the Indian economy – unplanned, rural, and based on traditional crafts.

... people will have to live in villages, not in towns; in huts, not in palaces Crores of people will never be able to live at peace with each other in towns and palaces. They will ... resort to both violence and untruth.

Nehru replied:

The question before us is not of truth versus untruth or non-violence versus violence. ... I do not understand why a village should necessarily embody truth and non-violence. A village, normally speaking, is backward intellectually and culturally and no progress can be made from a backward environment. Narrow-minded people are much more likely to be untruthful and violent ...[779]

"The world has changed", such was the announcement the young idealist made to the old. When Gandhi was murdered in January 1948, India was moving in the direction designated by Nehru. The socialism he had imagined was a peculiar mixture of concern for the idealized masses, inherited from Gandhi, belief in self-sufficiency (typical of many leaders of post-colonial countries), a mistrust of Western capital and modern faith in "scientific" methods of planning.[780] Nehru was not opposed to native capital, but considered it weak and lacking mobility, certainly not sufficient for the "great push forward."

The Indian system of planning arose gradually from 1948 to 1952. The Planning Commission, founded in 1950 and chaired by Nehru himself, had the

778 S. Ghose, *Jawaharlal Nehru...*, op. cit., p. 233.

779 Ibid., p. 234.

780 S. Tharoor, *Nehru. The Invention of India*, New York 2003, p. 175.

deciding vote in all economic affairs. In Nehru's vision, three sectors would co-exist in India – the state sector, encompassing key branches of industry (such as energy, steel and transportation); the sector regulated by the state (most big business) and the sector operating on free market principles (most small enterprises). Growth and development would be dependent on large public investments. Planning was less detailed than in countries in the orbit of the USSR, but more detailed than in the West at that time – with detailed tables of "raw materials" and "products" for particular branches of industry. "The idea of planning and a planned society," Nehru observed in the early 1940s, "is accepted now in varying degrees by almost everyone." (In the following passage, with his typical distaste for radicalism, he warned against haste, the use of violence and serving the interests of a narrow group of industrialists: planning only made sense when it was conducted in the common interest.)[781]

Atop this carefully constructed machine for state planning stood, not a trained economist, but a physicist and statistician: Prasanta Chandra Mahlanobis. He had formulated an image of the economy using the exact sciences, in which everything could be described using a detailed system of equations and statistics. The first plan merely assembled various projects developed during the colonial era, but it placed little emphasis on industrialization. Two-thirds of expenditures were marked for farming, energy, transportation and education. In 1952, the First Community Development Programme was declared; its aims included the building of roads, schools, and community centres in rural areas. Socialism was recognized as the official state (and Party Congress) ideology two years later, though Nehru was quick to stipulate that this did not mean total nationalization, the confiscation of property, or class struggle, but merely a preference for state industry, equality and social harmony. Planning began in earnest with the Second Five-Year Plan (1956–61). State automobile factories, steelworks, airlines, and even a line of hotels were established.[782] The Indian leader's philosophy was an intriguing mixture of Marxist ideas, Gandhian thought and Western liberalism; he was more a poet than a dogmatist and systematizer.[783] He was certainly opposed to dictatorship and violence. He valued the achievements of the USSR, but was happiest with Lenin's NEP, which had left a great deal of room for the free market. "The price paid for rapid industrialization," he said in 1956, "has been terrific in some socialist countries. I am certain that no country with any kind of

---

781 J. Nehru, *The Discovery of India*, Oxford 1994, p. 501.

782 J. N. Bhagwati, P. Desai, *India: Planning for Industrialization. Industrialization and Trade Policies since 1951*, Oxford 1970, p. 127.

783 S. Ghose, *Jawaharlal Nehru*, 240

parliamentary democracy can possibly pay it. [...] But even a dictator cannot go too far without the consent of the people."[784]

The second plan did, however, assume accelerated industrialization based to a great extent on the Soviet model. It planned to double the amount spent on investment in the first plan, and placed an emphasis on the production of steel and machines and technologically advanced products: India was to cease being primarily a provider of raw materials to the West, and thereby finally achieve real independence.

Following the logic of this model, Nehru considered heavy industry, particularly steel, to have the highest importance for the country's future. In 1953 he said:

> One thing is clear to me: that if we do not develop heavy industry here, then we either eliminate all modern things such as railways, airplanes and guns, as these things cannot be manufactured in small-scale industry, or else import them. But to import them from abroad is to be the slaves of foreign countries. Whenever these countries wished they could stop sending these things, bringing our work to a halt; we would thus remain slaves.[785]

Mahlanobis, the chief planner, was the author of a growth model that in practice was identical to the one developed in the USSR by Feldman in the 1920s (there is no evidence that he knew of Feldman's work). Mahlanobis's model likewise postulated that the secret of growth lay in investments and the accumulation of capital, and he proposed a similar transaction: it was worth tightening one's belt and investing now, in order to gather fruits in the form of higher consumption in the future. First and foremost, the government ought to invest in the production of "the means of production." Heavy industry naturally was to have priority.

The implementation of these plans, however, met with obstacles from the very start: floods and droughts in 1956 and 1957 forced the country to import food on a large scale, and the import of machines for newly constructed factories was unbelievably expensive, and ate into the country's modest foreign currency reserves. India had to ask for assistance from the World Bank and the United States. By 1958, all that remained of the original plans were investments in energy and three massive steelworks, built by the British, Russians and Germans, respectively.[786]

---

784 Ibid., p. 244.

785 quoted in A. Panagariya, *India. The Emerging Giant*, New York 2008, p. 25.

786 S. Ghose, *Jawaharlal Nehru*, op. cit., p. 247.

The first two five-year plans could be declared successful: national income rose by 42%, and per capita income by 16%. Farm production had risen by half, and industrial production almost two times over. All of this was not enough, however: prosperity remained a distant dream.

During the second plan, due to the government's need for foreign currency for investment, it limited imports and introduced a system of licensing for foreign trade. This also had an ideological purpose, in that it encouraged self-sufficiency.

Nationalization was not considered, but the private sector needed to be subordinated to the planners' aims. This was achieved by means of a complicated system of licensing and regulations, which had been quickly expanding since 1951. The government developed a detailed catalogue of types of businesses; each new investment required its permission. Theoretically, enterprises employing fewer than 50 persons (if they used machines) or 100 persons (if they did not) were exempted, but in practice the government required permission for each businessman attempting to expand his activities.[787] The law had given officials enormous power – not only could they in certain circumstances take control of enterprises, but they could also control prices and distribution in certain trades. In the 1950s, the bureaucracy rarely used this power to its advantage; later, however, the system stiffened and expanded. By the 1960s, before issuing permission to import raw materials or machines, officials expected an exact description of the production technology and machinery used, and they could refuse permission if they concluded that what was to be imported could be purchased domestically (even if at a higher price).

In the 1950s, the administration was still functioning efficiently, the number of cases it oversaw was small, and its procedures were not riddled with corruption. In the subsequent decade, all of this gradually changed: officials took decisions in an arbitrary manner and became susceptible to lobbying. Lobbying got the most results when it was carried out by large companies, who also had the greatest interest in restricting the activities of their foreign competitors.[788] In issuing licenses, officials also failed to analyze the economic rationality of the enterprise.[789]

As a result, economic growth slowed, the third five-year plan was not executed, and the economy plunged into stagnation. From 1964 to 1970 at least six extensive government reports were issued placing blame for the worsening situation squarely on the system of licensing. Reforms nonetheless went nowhere,

787 A. Panagariya, *India. The Emerging…*, op. cit., p. 35.

788 Ibid., p. 40.

789 Ajit K. Dasgupta, *A History of Indian …*, op cit., p. 171.

since the power of the rooted interests in the bureaucracy and big business was too great. The world's largest post-colonial country closed its borders to the world and plunged into economic lethargy, crushed by the gigantic weight of a corrupt and inefficient bureaucracy. India did not endure disasters comparable with those experienced by Mao's China, but its economic results were no better.

3. Open veins of Latin America

In the countries of Latin America, too, there was a widespread sense that the West was dealing the cards on world markets. It was true that they had gained their independence in the early nineteenth century, but a hundred years later they still felt like pariahs in the international order and were keenly aware of how their post-colonial heritage burdened them.

In the early 1970s, Eduardo Galeano, a Uruguayan left-wing journalist and intellectual imprisoned by the military dictatorship in that country, wrote the following about Latin America:

> The region has been condemned to sell primary products to keep foreign factories humming; and it happens that those products are mostly exported by strong consortiums with international connections, which have the necessary world-market relations to place their products under the most convenient conditions – the most convenient *for them*, suiting the interest of buyer countries: that is the to say, *at the lowest prices*. In international markets there is a virtual monopoly of demand for raw materials and of supply of industrial products, while suppliers of basic products, who are also buyers of finished goods, operate separately. The former, grouped around, and dominated by, the United States – which consumes almost as much as all the rest of the world – are strong; the latter are isolated and weak: the oppressed competing against the oppressed. The so-called free play of supply and demand in the so-called international market does not exist; the reality is a dictatorship of one group over the other, always for the benefit of the developed capitalist countries.[790]

Galeano entitled his book *Open Veins of Latin America*. It was from these "open veins" that the exploited continent's wealth and raw materials flowed in the direction of the centres of world business. There – in Washington, New York, London, Paris, Amsterdam and Hamburg, in the quiet of offices and amidst the clamour of stock market floors, the Europeans and American set world prices, and Latinos had no choice but to submit to them. As a result, they were producing more and more, but were able to buy less and less. "What Latin America sells gets constantly cheaper," Galeano wrote, "and – also in relative terms – what it buys gets

---

790 E. Galeano, *Open Veins of Latin America*, New York 1997, pp. 237–238

constantly dearer." He calculated that in 1954 Uruguay could buy a Ford tractor for the equivalent of 22 young bulls; 20 years later it had to sell twice as many.[791]

A perceived reliance on foreign capital and structural trade dependence on the West for the past 30 years had led politicians and economists in Latin America to the same conclusion as the rest of the developing world: it was necessary to build up domestic industry, whose products would replace imported goods and bring much-desired independence. All of the elements typical of economic doctrines in post-colonial countries took shape in a unified theory in Latin America. Nationalistic and emancipatory ideology and economic analysis both led these leaders to the same conclusion.

The starting point was the feeling of their growing backwardness in relation to Europe and the United States. This belief was not unfounded. In 1700 the level of income in the Spanish and Portuguese colonies in Latin America was the same as in the British colonies in North America: their paths of development began to visibly diverge about a hundred years later.

Currently accepted theories explain the low economic growth in the Latin countries primarily in terms of the difference between the social structures of the British and Spanish colonies.[792] While the former were settled mainly by free people of equal status, with relatively small differences in property among them, enormous inequalities in the division of property, knowledge and power weighed heavily on the countries of Latin America from the first days of their independence. For the small groups of European settlers ruling masses of subjugated Indians and slaves brought from Africa it was relatively easy to create institutions that ensured power and property for the elite, but it hampered economic development because they were based on the unequal distribution of existing goods more than on the creation of a new production base. A second explanation also stresses the legacy of the colonial past: decades of violence, upheavals and instability in Latin America following independence had caused the continent to develop slowly in the nineteenth century, when the United States began to outpace it. That period also witnessed an emerging international structural division between developed and industrial countries, on the one hand, and backward agricultural ones on the other, which determined that in the twentieth century,

---

791 Ibid., p. 238.

792 A classic exposition of this theory can be found in S. Engerman, K. Sokoloff, "Institutional and Non-Institutional Explanations of Economic Differences", NBER Working Paper no. w9989, September 2003; and in K. Sokoloff, S. Engerman, "History Lessons. Institutions, Factor Endowments, and Paths of Development in the New World", *Journal of Economic Perspectives*, 2000, vol. 14, no. 3.

the divide between North and South America in terms of economic development became irremediably fixed. In the decades following independence, Latin America developed economically, though more slowly than Western countries (particularly the United States); it kept pace with them in the years 1860–1938 and began to fall back again in the postwar period, with the brief exception of the 1970s. Though Latin America had periods of rapid growth – especially the years 1880–1914, and again in the years 1938–1980, only in the 1970s decreased its distance from the countries of the West.[793]

Yet beyond these numbers – which show slow but systematic growth – we see development that was colonial and incomplete in nature: islands of modernity were surrounded by an almost feudal economy dominated by large landowners who produced tobacco, coffee and sugar for global markets. They ruled masses of poor people who were deprived of any prospects for a better life, whose language and skin colour were often different, and who lived in very primitive conditions.

A good example of such change is Mexico during the era of the dictator Porfirio Diaz (1876–1910). The numbers unambiguously show that the country was developing: the population rose by 1.4% yearly (to 25.2 million in 1910), and economic growth amounted to 2.7% annually. Foreign trade increased almost four-fold, driven by exports of cotton and raw materials. The railway network increased from 666 km in 1876 to 24,560 in 1910, and the production of sugar increased five-fold. The discovery of oil began a great boom: by 1911, Mexico had become the third biggest oil producer in the world. Its GDP rose from 435 million pesos in 1877 to 1,184 million in 1910, doubling on a per capita basis.

However, beyond these indicators lay an economy that was semi-colonial in its structure. Foreign capital controlled 90% of the 80 largest enterprises, including nine of the top ten. 80% of textile production was in the hands of the French, while oil drilling was carried out almost exclusively by companies backed by British capital. In banking, over 94% of capital belonged to foreign banks. Americans invested the most in Mexico's economy during the reign of Diaz – over 1 billion dollars (not adjusting for inflation) – more than Mexico's entire domestic capitalist class. Americans controlled 80% of the mining and owned tens of millions of hectares of land, and the U.S. received three quarters of Mexico's exports.

793 L. Prados de la Escosura, "When Did Latin America Fall Behind?", [in:] *The Decline of Latin American Economies Growth, Institutions, and Crises*, eds. S. Edwards, G. Esquivel, G. Marquez, Chicago–London 2007, p. 15 ff.; the article also offers a survey of the literature on this subject.

Even the railways were built in such a way as to facilitate the delivery of goods to the U.S.[794]

The profits from this growth went largely into foreign hands. At the same time, Mexican peasants were losing their land to plantation owners who raised sugar for export. According to one estimate, 90% of the residents of Mexico's central provinces had no land. The production of food for the local market was being supplanted by production for export, while food in cities was growing more expensive. In 1908 the purchasing power of a typical income in the cities was the same as it had been a century earlier.[795]

Mexico's situation was typical of that in most Latin American countries.[796] For many Latinos, it was clear that the sources of these problems were structural in nature, and slow, unevenly distributed economic growth in conditions of dependence could not solve them. The West's economic domination was accompanied by political dependence. The American ambassador was the most important person in local politics and often decided who would wield power. Protests against foreign domination were combined with the belief that it was structurally tied to economic underdevelopment, poverty and the exclusion of the majority.[797]

This was the context in which economic efforts to overcome backwardness were being discussed in Latin America. A structural change was necessary, and such a change – so went the view shared by all intellectuals in the developing world concerned about modernization and development – would not occur automatically. It had to be achieved through a conscious, collective effort.

During his trial after the unsuccessful attack on the Moncada Barracks in 1953, Fidel Castro, the revolutionary fighting to overthrow the Cuban dictatorship, made his famous speech in which he expressed the feelings of many educated Latinos. "History will absolve me," he said, justifying his decision to take up arms:

> What is inconceivable is that there should be men going to bed hungry while an inch of land remains unsown; what is inconceivable is that there should be children who die without medical care; that thirty percent of our campesinos cannot sign their names and ninety-nine percent don't know the history of Cuba; that most families in our countryside should be living in worse conditions than the Indians Columbus found when he

794 J. Foran, *Taking Power. On the Origins of Third World Revolutions*, Cambridge–New York 2005, p. 35.

795 Ibid., p. 36.

796 Perhaps with the exception of Argentina, where the standard of living was closest to that of Western countries.

797 H. Szlajfer, *Droga na skróty: nacjonalizm gospodarczy w Ameryce Łacińskiej i Europie Środkowej w epoce pierwszej globalizacji*, Warszawa 2005, p. 19 ff.

> discovered the most beautiful land human eyes had ever seen [...] Cuba continues to be a factory producing raw materials. Sugar is exported to import candles; leather exported to import shoes; iron exported to import plows.[798]

The answer to this injustice was to be a new policy of economic nationalism, which declared that economic independence from foreign countries must go hand-in-hand with changes in the social structure (toward a more egalitarian one) and the economic structure (toward industrialization).

This was an expansion of a considerably older idea. One of the founding fathers of the United States, Alexander Hamilton, had expressed the view in 1791 that deliberate restrictions on imports would encourage development of the country's domestic industry.[799] A few years later, in 1800, Johann Gottlieb Fichte gave fuller expression to the same idea in his treatise *The Closed Commercial State.*[800] Fichte wrote that for the purpose of maintaining the peace, nations should be isolated from each other. His treatise was a disinterested, analytical and consistent apologia for national collectivism. It was overlooked and forgotten in the liberal age of the nineteenth century, but was rediscovered in Germany during the First World War, when it had become isolated from the world by the allied blockade.[801]

Fichte's state was egalitarian: all citizens are to be "comfortably and warmly clothed" before anyone is able to wear beautiful clothes. The national economy would be entirely planned by the government, which would decide what was to be produced and in what quantities, at what prices good would be sold, and who their buyers would be. The bureaucracy controlled everything: the number of craftsmen allowed in a particular trade was recorded in special registers, and officials ensured that this number was not exceeded. Since the government had to control the supply of goods on the market, it also had to control foreign trade. Fichte wrote:

> The state is obliged to guarantee for all its citizens, through law and compulsion, the state of affairs that results from this balance of commerce. Yet it cannot do this if there is any person able to influence this balance who does not stand under the state's law and command. [...] All commerce with foreigners must be forbidden to its subjects and rendered impossible. It is not necessary to prove that there is absolutely no place

---

798 Quoted in: J. Foran, *Taking Power*, op. cit. p. 61.

799 A. Hamilton, *Report on the Subject of Manufactures*, Philadelphia 1828 (sixth edition).

800 J. G. Fichte, *The Closed Commercial State: Perpetual Peace and Commercial Society from Rousseau to Fichte*, Princeton 2011.

801 On the reception of Fichte, see M. A. Heilperin, *Studies in Economic Nationalism, Publications de L'Institut Universitaire de Hautes Etudes Internationales no. 35*, Geneve–Paris 1960, pp. 83–84.

for commerce between the subjects and foreigners in the system of trade set forth. The government should be able to count on a certain quantity of goods entering into trade, in order that it may always guarantee its subject the continuing enjoyment of his accustomed needs. How will it achieve this vis-a-vis a foreigner, since indeed in cannot determine the prices that he must pay in his country to live and to purchase raw materials? [...] It should fix and guarantee the price of goods. [...] The government should guarantee to its subjects the sale of his produce or manufactured goods and the fitting price at which they are sold. How can the government do this if its subject should sell to foreign countries whose relation to the goods of the government's subject the government is able neither to oversee nor to regulate?[802]

The German philosopher captures here in its pure form the conflict that would plague all planned economies. None of them, even the hermetically sealed USSR under Stalin or China under Mao, could manage without engaging in trade with foreign countries. The unpredictability of global markets continually clashed with the plan and introduced confusion and an element of uncertainty into what, to the planners at least, had seemed like rational calculations.

Fichte was also opposed to exports, perceiving in them a potential threat to the political stability of the government. It is difficult to build industry when one is dependent on foreign markets, he argued, since demand there is unstable and unpredictable, and its potential collapse, leading to the bankruptcy of export-oriented businesses, could provoke a crisis and discontent in society. Thus, according to Fichte, a simple choice has to be made between a "rational and well-organized state" and foreign trade. In a rational state, ordinary citizens cannot trade directly with foreigners.[803] Fichte knew that limiting foreign trade by imposing taxes and special restrictions on it would initially breed discontent among the public, who would think that this would adversely affect their quality of life. Citizens nonetheless had to reconcile themselves to this policy, as it was a rational measure, and in the long term would serve the common interest. First, foreign trade had to be nationalized. Next the government needed to gradually reduce and eliminate it. (Limiting ordinary citizens' freedom to travel was also a further logical step: they simply had no need to travel if they were not performing artists or scholars.)

Only a nation that is free of dependence on foreign countries – and industrialized, because it produces everything to meet its own needs – can develop in an unhindered and safe manner. This was the same conclusion reached by the most well-known nineteenth century theoretician of economic nationalism, the German economist Friedrich List. In his *National System of Political Economy*

---

802 J. G. Fichte, *The Closed Commercial State*, Albany 2012, p. 107

803 M. A. Heilperin, *Studies...*, op. cit. p. 86.

(published in Germany in 1841, and in the United States, where List worked for many years as a journalist, in 1856), he was severely critical of then-dominant liberal ideas on open borders and free trade.[804] List had no doubts that nations producing industrial goods had an advantage over agricultural countries in commercial exchange. He had a prescription for the latter, however: isolation – whether established through withdrawal from trade or through war – would, once transitional difficulties passed, stimulate development. On the stagnation in trade caused by war, he wrote:

> While, however, the manufacturer (especially if he belongs to a nation powerful at sea, and carrying on extensive commerce) readily finds compensation from the agriculturists of his own country, or from those of other accessible agricultural countries, the inhabitant of purely agricultural country suffers doubly through this interruption of intercourse. The market for his agricultural products will fail him entirely, and he will consequently lose the means of paying for those manufactured goods which have become necessaries to him owing to previously existing trade; his power both of production and consumption will be diminished. If, however, one agricultural nation whose production and consumption are thus diminished by war has already made considerable advances in population, civilisation, and agriculture, manufactures and factories will spring up in it in consequence of the interruption of international commerce by war. War acts on it like a prohibitive tariff system."[805]

If after such a war-related interruption, List wrote, an agricultural country returns to the old rules of trade, its young industry will fail because it is unable to compete with more powerful and more experienced industrialized countries. A system of prohibitive tariffs was therefore necessary, one that would protect native producers, even at the cost of temporarily lowering the standard of living for those purchasing imported goods. A responsible government should explain to its citizens that they had to tighten their belts now in order to have a better life in the future.

It was no coincidence that List was popular in the nineteenth century in both the United States and in Germany, rising industrial powers that were protecting their markets with high tariffs against competition from British industry, which was more advanced. The lessons learned during the war were taken to heart in Latin America. Economists and politicians there had noticed, and remembered well, that industry developed most rapidly during world wars, when imports from the West were limited.

---

804 K. Tribe, *Strategies of Economic Order. German Economic Discourse 1750–1950*, Cambridge 1995, p. 33 ff.

805 F. List, *National System of Political Economy*, vol. 2, New York 2006, p. 79.

In 1948, riding a wave of postwar optimism and concern for the poorest countries' development, the UN created the Economic Commission for Latin America (ECLA). In 1950, Raúl Prébisch, an economist from Buenos Aires trained in the neoclassical tradition, became its second executive director. Prébisch had grown up in a country that at least until the 1920s could pass for an example of liberalism's economic successes. According to David Ricardo's classical theory of comparative advantage, Argentina was making incredible gains and developing at an impressive pace, exporting what it could produce most cheaply, especially grain and meat, to Western countries (chiefly Great Britain), and importing machines and consumer goods in exchange. After a few decades of economic prosperity, Argentina in the 1920s was one of the world's richest countries, and in terms of per capita GDP surpassed both Canada and Australia. In the 1920s, however, problems began to appear: the prices of Argentina's main export products fell, and the country lapsed into stagnation. The reason for this lay in external conditions. The British market was beginning to shrink, and the new global economic hegemon, the United States, had plenty of its own grain and beef, and therefore did not need what Argentina had to offer.

These changes in trade relations coincided with the Great Depression of the 1930s, which caused a global decline in prices. To make things worse, agricultural products dropped in price significantly faster than industrial ones. According to Prébisch's calculations, in 1933 Argentina had to increase its sales of goods on global markets by as much as 73% in order to import the same amount from abroad as it had in the mid-1920s (itself not a prosperous time).[806]

Around 1937, Prebisch and his colleagues in the Central Bank of Argentina (where he then worked) developed a theory that explained the relative collapse in prices on agricultural products. Industrial production was flexible: it decreased together with a fall in demand. Prices obviously fell as well, but slowly and very predictably. At the same time, in agricultural markets, the supply was determined by farmers, many of whom had very small fields that were planted every year. Since supply was less flexible, the price would fall faster if demand collapsed.

Agricultural countries were thus naturally, his conclusion went, in a worse situation in relation to global markets. Furthermore, there were good reasons to think that their situation was also subject to constant deterioration regardless of whether the economy thrived or crashed. In 1949 the UN published a report in which its experts stated unambiguously that the prices of farm products had systematically

---

806 J. M. Cypher, J. L. Dietz, *The Process of Economic Development*, Abingdon–New York 2009, p. 170 ff.

fallen on global markets since the nineteenth century.[807] Naturally this had to have a bad influence on exporter countries' development, since it meant they had less money for investment and imports.[808]

To support his theory, Prébisch cited statistical studies made by an economist working for the UN, Hans W. Singer. In them he found the argument clearly laid out: the poverty of agricultural countries was caused by their structure of production. "The principle of specialization along the lines of static comparative advantages has never been generally accepted in the underdeveloped countries, and not even generally intellectually accepted in the industrialized countries themselves," Singer wrote.

> In the economic life of a country and in its economic history, a most important element is the mechanism by which "one thing leads to another," and the most important contribution of an industry is not its immediate product (as is perforce assumed by economists and statisticians) and not even its effects on other industries and immediate social benefits [...] but perhaps even further its effect on the general level of education, skill, way of life, inventiveness, habits, store of technology, creation of new demand, etc. And this is perhaps precisely the reason why manufacturing industries are so universally desired by underdeveloped countries; namely, that they provide the growing points for increased technical knowledge, urban education, the dynamism and resilience that goes with urban civilization [...].[809]

Such industries could only be built by importing machinery, and that, Singer demonstrated, was impossible, due to the worsening terms of trade between agricultural and industrial countries: the former were producing ever increasing quantities of goods, but earning less and less, a claim the economist supported with detailed statistical studies.

He may have been correct – the dispute over whether he really was correct continued over the next several decades, and involved very sophisticated discussions about the methodology used to gather economic statistics.[810] This argument continues today and remains unresolved, though a recent survey of 24 studies

---

807 *Relative Prices of Exports and Imports of Under-developed Countries: A Study of Post-war Terms of Trade Between Under-developed and Industrialized Countries*, New York 1949, p. 13.

808 Ibid., p. 126.

809 H. W. Singer, "The Distribution of Gains between Investing and Borrowing Countries", *The American Economic Review*, 1950 vol. 40, no. 2.

810 The debate is summarized in, e.g. P. Sarkar, "The Singer-Prebisch Hypothesis: A Statistical Evaluation", *Cambridge Journal of Economics*, 1986, no. 10; see also H. W. Singer, "The Terms of Trade Controversy" [in:] *Pioneers in Development*, ed. G. Meier, D. Seers, Oxford 1984, pp. 275–303.

published in the years 1984–2005 points to a decreasing trend in prices for agricultural products on global markets (it was found in 19 out of the 24 studies).[811]

In the late 1940s and early 1950s, Singer explained the deteriorating situation faced by exporters of agricultural products in terms of differences between agricultural and industrial countries in terms of their social structure and the mechanisms guiding their domestic politics: whereas in agricultural countries a rise in productivity simply translated into increased production (and not higher wages), in industrial countries unions and politicians fought to ensure that higher productivity translated into higher pay – and not necessarily lower product prices.

Such considerations led Prébisch and his colleagues at ECLA to a highly rational conclusion: the only road leading out of backwardness was industrialization, and this had to be tied to changes in the country's economic and social structure. The economies of Latin American countries needed to be reoriented toward the export of industrial products and domestic consumption. Initially, ECLA therefore recommended a strategy of import substitution: replacing imported products with domestically produced ones by means of high tariffs, controlling trade and supporting investments in those branches of industry that promised/assured the fastest growth. The process had to begin with basic consumer goods, before including more complex and advanced ones. The new industrial culture would also increase agricultural productivity, bringing in new technologies and better-educated workers.

In such circumstances, economic planning was crucial. Years later, Prébisch reminisced:

> The structural changes inherent in industrialization require rationality and foresight in government policy and investment in infrastructure to accelerate growth, to obtain the proper relation of industry with agriculture and other activities, and to reduce the external vulnerability of the economy. These were strong reasons for planning. Another important one was the need to intensify the rate of internal capital accumulation through proper incentives and other policy measures. International financial resources were to complement and enhance a country's capacity to save, while changes in the structure of trade were necessary to use these savings for capital goods imports. Planning should help obtain these resources and accomplish the latter objective. Planning was

811 J. A. Ocampo, M. A. Parra, "The Continuing Relevance of the Terms of Trade and Industrialization Debates" [in:] *Ideas, Policies and Economic Development in the Americas*, ed. E. P. Caldentey, M. Vernengo, London 2007, 157 ff.

compatible with the market and private initiative. [...] But it did not necessarily require detailed state investment, except in infrastructure and development promotion.[812]

Though the belief in the structural dependency of underdeveloped capitalist countries on the West was widespread from the 1950s to the 1970s, there was a difference of opinion as to whether the development of dependent countries was possible – and if so, whether it would demand radical solutions.

Exponents of the theory of dependency– Raúl Prébisch, Paul Baran, Celso Furtado, Fernando Enrique Cardoso, and André Gunder Frank – included economists, sociologists and political scientists, Marxists and non-Marxists; some believed in the need for revolution, others believed that breaking free of the circle of dependence could take place without such an upheaval. They were united in their choice not to analyze the economic development of particular countries in isolation, but to examine global capitalism as a system in which there was a lack of equality, with positions of privilege and marginal positions.[813] Andre Gunder Frank was a determinist: he wrote that backward countries (contrary to what Marx had once believed) were not simply at an earlier stage on the road to prosperity and industrial power: their place in the structure of global trade condemned them to a subordinate place, to a misformed social and economic structure. In his classic book *Capitalism and Underdevelopment in Latin America*, published in 1967, he found confirmation for this theory in the history of Chile and Brazil. Violence was the source of their economic dependence: the "capitalist metro-satellite relationship between Europe and Latin America," Frank wrote, "was established by force of arms," with the former condemning its former colonies to being merely suppliers of raw materials and capital and keeping a close eye on them to ensure – if necessary by means of military force – that they did not try to change their position.[814] The unorthodox Marxist Paul A. Baran was pessimistic: according to him, local elites in underdeveloped countries had allied themselves with international capitalists, sacrificing long-term growth in their own countries in the name of short-term profits. The system by which latifundia and plantations grew crops for export was coherent and logical, and it could not be expected to undergo spontaneous transformation. Interests, lifestyle and social contacts united the elites of underdeveloped countries and the centre of

812 R. Prebisch, "Five Stages in My Thinking on Development", in *Pioneers in Development*, p. 180.

813 P. Franko, *The Puzzle of Latin American economic development*, Lanham–Plymouth 2007, pp. 57–58.

814 A. G. Frank, *Capitalism and Underdevelopment in Latin America: Historical Studies of Chile and Brazil*, London 1967, p. 21.

the system: without a shift in power and a social upheaval (here Frank and Baran agreed) improving the situation of the millions who were shut out/excluded by this system was unthinkable.[815] These theorists, who admitted to drawing inspiration from Lenin's theory of imperialism, deviated from it in a significant way. For Lenin, imperialism was merely one of the phases in the development of capitalism – development that necessarily occurs following a defined path. Countries of the periphery and dependent territories played a role in this system, first assisting in the primary accumulation of capital, then acting as a means of late capitalism's "escape" from the contradictions plaguing it: the exploitation of imperial possessions allowed capitalists to protect themselves from the rise of competition that could hinder the growth of their companies.[816] For Lenin, just as for Marx, capitalism nonetheless remained the motor of history: once a country entered onto the path of development, it could no longer veer from it.

Since the publication of Baran's book *The Political Economy of Growth* in 1957, it had become clear to many Marxists and Marxist-leaning intellectuals in peripheral countries that no Third World country could change its position in the global system of capitalism and emerge from its state of economic dependence by natural means. This view had already begun to appear in Soviet writings in the 1920s. By the 1960s, it had become obvious to many Marxists that the bourgeoisie of the underdeveloped countries was unwilling to bear the burden of industrialization, because it was too deeply integrated with the global capitalist system and had no interest in changing it. The declaration of the first conference of the Organization for Latin American Solidarity (OLAS) in 1967 explained this structural shortcoming of the Latin American bourgeoisie in the following terms:

> It would be absurd to suppose that ... the so-called Latin American bourgeoisie is capable of developing a political line independent ... of imperialism, in defence of the interests and aspirations of the nation. The contradiction within which it is objectively trapped is, by its nature, insuperable.[817]

---

815 P. A. Baran, *On the Political Economy of Backwardness*, Manchester School, no. 1, 1952, reprinted and quoted in: *The Political Economy of Development*, ed. C. Wilber, K. P. Jameson, New York 1973.

816 G. Palma, "Dependency: A Formal Theory of Underdevelopment or a Methodology for the Analysis of Concrete Situations of Underdevelopment?", *World Development*, 1978, vol. 2 no. 6, especially p. 885 ff.

817 Quoted in D. Booth, "Andre Gunder Frank: An Introduction and Appreciation", [in:] *Beyond Sociology of Development. Economy and Society in Latin America and Africa*, eds. I. Oxaal, T. Barnett, D. Booth, Oxon–New York 2011, pp. 5–66.

This view of the structural sources of underdevelopment quickly became orthodoxy, and remained so until at least the early 1980s. The countries of Latin America would not develop on their own – the process demanded, if not revolution, then at least, as ECLA had stated, "deliberate direction of the process of import substitution industrialization through the use of planning."[818]

Some prominent theorists of dependency tried to play an active role in enacting structural change. The Brazilian Celso Furtado stayed in Europe after serving in the army in World War II and wrote a doctoral thesis in economics at the Sorbonne; in 1949, he began working with Prébisch as an economist at ECLA. In 1957–58, he spent a year at Cambridge, where he befriended two distinguished Keynesians, Joan Robinson and Nicholas Kaldor. After his return to Brazil in 1959 he wrote the classic book *The Economic Growth of Brazil*, in which he analyzed the causes of his country's underdevelopment from a broad historical perspective. Brazil, he wrote, had been driven by an "outward impulse" in colonial times, which had shaped its social and economic structure. Furtado did not believe (unlike W. A. Lewis) in the possibility of absorbing masses of people from rural areas into urban-based industry: the sector was too small, and moreover, was using modern, imported technologies that did not require large numbers of unspecialized workers. A legacy of colonialism was extensive social stratification – in Brazil only about 10% of the population, the elites and middle classes, were consumers of industrial products, so local manufacturers had little surplus market for their goods and could not expand their businesses.

After returning to Brazil, Furtado also began a political career: he became the head of BNDES, a state bank that financed large, development-oriented industrial and infrastructural investments, and shortly afterward became Minister of Planning and was responsible for the recently announced "Triennial Plan" (Por. Plano Trienal) for development. He also founded SUDENE – a government agency devoted to eliminating the cultural and economic divide separating the Brazil's poor north from the its more affluent south (the difference between the average income of a farmer in the north and of a resident of São Paulo was greater in the 1950s than the difference in income between a resident of São Paulo and the average citizen of Western Europe).

Furtado emigrated from Brazil after a military coup in 1964 backed and financed by the CIA – among the reasons for the coup was the fact that the gov-

818 R. Capriles, M. de Gonzalo, "Economic and Business History in Venezuela", [in:] *Business History in Latin America: The Experience of Seven Countries*, Liverpool 1999, p. 160.

ernment was trying to limit the export of foreign (mainly American) companies' profits and nationalize oil refineries (also controlled by Americans). In the years 1965–1985 Furtado worked as a professor at the Sorbonne; after the return to democratically elected governments in the 1980s he was appointed ambassador and Minister of Culture. Furtado, the author of 30 books that were translated into 15 languages and sold two million copies, was always a proponent of industrialization, but he perceived the problems it created (above all, an increase in inequality – its benefits were enjoyed by the top few percent of society). With the passage of time and his increasing engagement in practical political matters, he became less and less radical.

Another eminent intellectual, the sociologist Fernando Henrique Cardoso, was eventually elected President of Brazil. Before becoming a patron of liberal reforms in his country (he held office from 1995 to 2002) he was an incisive critic of the social structure of Latin American societies, demonstrating how Brazil's "enclave economy"– consisting of modern export-oriented sectors of the economy – bolstered a alliance between the latifundists and native bourgeoisie and thus impeded development.[819] Unlike the most pessimistic attitude of the *dependistas*, Cardoso believed that development (even feeble and fragmentary "dependent development") was still possible, even within the existing international division of labor.[820]

> The political sphere of social behavior necessarily influences the form of the development process. Thus, in a global interpretation of development, arguments based solely on market incentives and reactions do not suffice to explain industrialization and the economic process. Such incentives or mechanisms to defend the economy can only begin an industrialization process; its continuation requires changes favorable to development in the international market, and, still more essential, elements favorable to a broader measure of autonomy within the socio-political game of the developing countries.[821]

Industrialization could not, therefore – if it were to be carried out in a healthy manner, fostering long-term development and leading to true independence – be subordinated to the market: it must be implemented by the state and not according to the criterion of profit. It should be subordinated to changes in the social structure: its purpose was to be transformational, not purely economic

819 F. Henrique Cardoso, E. Faletto, *Dependency and Development in Latin America*, Berkeley–Los Angeles 1979, pp. 75–76.

820 G. Rist, *The History of Development. From Western Origins to Global Faith*, London 2006, pp. 116–117.

821 F. Henrique Cardoso, E. Faletto, *Dependency and Development in Latin America...*, Op. cit., pp. 19–20.

(according to theorists of dependence, no such thing as "pure economics" exists; for Marxists the idea had always been a bourgeois fiction).

In practice, the countries of Latin America had been pursuing a policy of import substitution long before Prébisch and his colleagues from ECLA developed a theoretical basis for it. This had been a reaction to the Great Depression of the 1930s, which had caused a sudden collapse in Western demand for agricultural products and raw materials. In Chile in the years 1929–1932, GDP decreased by almost 40%, and the level of imports and exports fell correspondingly by 78% and 84%. The situation further deteriorated, as it did in Poland at the time due to the government's stubborn adherence to the gold standard, making Chilean exports less competitive. Prices for its two main export products, brass and saltpetre, fell on international markets by 60–70%. Recovery from the collapse took a long time: GDP did not return to its pre-Depression level until 1938, and in per capita terms remained lower (due to population growth).[822] Chilean elites of every political stripe drew a very simple conclusion from this economic disaster – liberalism had outlived its day, capitalism had disappointed them, and the country in the future should avoid being dependent on exports and exposed to such external shocks.

At the other end of Latin America, in Mexico, the government of President Lazaro Cardenas announced a "Six-Year Plan" in 1934 that included agrarian reform and support the development of Mexican industry. Over the course of his six years in power, Cardenas distributed 18.8 million hectares of latifundia (more than during the previous 20 years, in which a less radical version of reform had been enacted), created the state-run *Nacional Financiera* bank to provide credit for investment in industry, and in 1938 nationalized the oil industry. The state made gigantic investments in infrastructure: the roadways increased seven-fold.[823] In December 1940, Mexico officially pronounced industrialization to be the main goal of its economic policy, and gradually closed its borders to imports of foreign goods.

Most Latin American nations went through a similar evolution. A policy of import substitution might also have seemed to Latin American intellectuals and politicians to be the only rational choice because they simply saw no alternative. Leaving the market to its own devices appeared particularly naïve. That would require at the very least the ability to trade with the U.S. on equal terms, and suc-

---

822 P. Meller, *Un siglo de economia politica chilena 1890–1990*, Ed. Andres Bello, Barcelona–Buenos Aires–Mexico–Santiago 1998, pp. 47–48.

823 J. C. Moreno-Bird, J. Ros, *Development and Growth in the Mexican Economy*, Oxford–New York 2009, pp. 87–88.

cessive administrations in Washington made no secret of the fact that this was not in their interest.

In the 1930s, the Roosevelt administration adopted what it called a "good neighbour" policy toward Latin America, dictating disadvantageous bilateral trade deals and intervening repeatedly in the domestic politics of Latin American countries. The U.S. provided its neighbours to the south with military and economic aid – not in order to support growth, but to consolidate its domination in the western hemisphere, a policy that was spoken and written about openly in Washington. During the Second World War the United States promised – in an attempt to win the support of Latin American governments – to actively support the development and diversification of their economies. After 1945, Truman nevertheless refused to organize a pan-American economic conference and quickly dashed all hopes of a Marshall Plan for Latin America. Brazil, for example, was outright refused a one million dollar loan that it had sought.

The U.S. government immediately cancelled the wartime price regulations that had led to a quick rise in the prices for goods imported to Latin America from the north. However, long-term contracts signed during the war for imports of raw materials and agricultural goods were not renegotiated, so the countries of Latin America had to sell their export products at low wartime prices. This cost them the colossal (at that time) sum of three million dollars, i.e., the majority of the trade surplus accumulated during their "wartime prosperity". In response to protests, the U.S. government replied that it had sacrificed lives and money defending the entire hemisphere from totalitarianism.[824]

In the postwar decades, Latin American hopes for obtaining assistance from the U.S. for economic development were revealed to have been misplaced. Washington's policies were now dictated by the fear of communism, of which the progressive radicalization of the Cuban revolution was seen as a harbinger – and Cuba was one of the wealthiest and most developed nations in the region, with a standard of living comparable to that of the countries of southern Europe. On 13 March 1961 President Kennedy announced the creation of the "Alliance for Progress," which he declared would be a "vast cooperative effort, unparalleled in magnitude and nobility of purpose, to satisfy the basic needs of Latin American people for homes, work and land, health and schools".[825] In August 1961 at an intergovernmental conference in Punta del Este in Uruguay, Secretary of State

824 S. G. Rabe, *Eisenhower & Latin America. The Foreign Policy of Anti-Communism*, Chapel Hill–London 1988, pp. 11–16.

825 S. G. Rabe, *The Most Dangerous Area in the World. John F. Kennedy Confronts Communist Revolution in Latin America*, Chapel Hill–London 1999, p. 2.

C. Douglas Dillon assured the representatives of Latin American governments that they could count on 20 billion dollars of private and public capital from the U.S. over the course of the next decade. Together with 80 billion dollars in investments from domestic sources, this was to guarantee real economic growth of 2.5% per capita annually, that is, twice the rate of the 1950s.

In practice, however, the U. S. did not back up its promises with action. In exchange for economic aid, the Kennedy administration expected full political cooperation, and interests tied to American exporters blocked reform projects in those countries that undertook them. In the two countries that were supposed to demonstrate the successes of the "Alliance," Venezuela and Chile, the project ended in complete failure. Chile, which had fallen into economic stagnation – its per capita growth in the 1950s did not exceed 1% annually – received over one billion dollars in aid over the following decade, the largest amount per capita in all of Latin America. This money linked the U.S. to the unpopular right-wing President Jorge Alessandri (1958–1964), and was largely designed to keep him in power. Without success: the Americans had to spend hundreds of thousands of dollars more and use the CIA to guarantee the victory of a right-wing candidate in the 1964 election. The U.S. similarly intervened in Brazil's elections.[826] The "Alliance for Progress" proved to be a disaster – it neither accomplished its intended political goals, nor did it help Latin America achieve modernization and economic growth.

In contrast, a national industrial policy based on import substitution seemed for a long time to bring impressive successes. From the 1920s to the 1940s, countries with higher tariffs developed faster than those with more open economies, and until the 1970s the level of trade barriers did not have an obvious connection to growth.[827] For two decades, the average rate of growth in Latin America exceeded 6% annually.[828]

Brazil initiated an active industrial policy in the 1940s, and Chile and Venezuela in the 1950s.[829] Between 1958 and 1967, half of public investment expenditures were invested in the steel industry, making Brazil into a self-sufficient producer of

---

826 S. G. Rabe, *The Most Dangerous Area…*, op. cit., pp. 113–114.

827 A. Vamvakidis, "How Robust is the Growth-Openness Connection? Historical Evidence", *Journal of Economic Growth*, 2002, no. 7.; M. A. Clemens, "Why did the Tariff-Growth Correlation Change after 1950?", *Journal of Economic Growth*, 2004, no. 9.

828 S. Edwards, S. Teitel, "Introduction to Growth, Reform, and Adjustment: Latin America's Trade and Macroeconomic Policies in the 1970s and 1980s", *Economic Development and Cultural Change*, 1986, vol. 34, no. 3.

829 L. C. Bresser Pereira, *Economia Brasileira: Uma Introdução Crítica*, Editora 34, São Paulo 1998, p. 51.

steel.[830] Domestic production of automobiles followed. The public sector began to mushroom. In the 1960s, the number of state enterprises rose to more than 700, mostly in large, capital-intensive industries, such as energy, metallurgy and the chemical industry. In 1979, state companies in Brazil represented just 7% of all companies, while 50% of capital investments were concentrated in them.[831]

Even the poorest countries, such as Bolivia, tried to implement an industrial policy. When a revolution broke out 1952, the country was completely controlled by three large tin mining companies. Although they were owned by Bolivians, they were treated by Bolivian law as foreign companies and sent most of their profits abroad.[832] Before the revolution, the three mining companies provided the country with 95% of its foreign currency and over half of the government's budget.[833] When the National-Revolutionary Movement (Span. Movimiento Nacional Revolucionario, or MNR), supported by the middle class and the trade unions, took power, it nationalized the mining companies and introduced agrarian reform, stripping landowners of power. It also attempted to accelerate economic growth by following the prescriptions then popular, that is, supporting industrialization by means of tariffs and subsidies. In 1964, a pro-American military dictatorship took control of the country, opening the country to foreign loans and investments and eliminating industrial subsidies.[834] As it turned out, the mountainous, land-locked and sparsely populated country (population 4.6 million in 1970) was unable to attract foreign investment outside of the mining industry, and the policies dictated by the International Monetary Fund and the World Bank placed greater emphasis on stability and protecting the interests of foreign capital than on the development of local industry. In practice, the Bolivian government was too weak to impose its own investment priorities on foreign investors, and too poor to finance major projects on its own. However, opening the economy to foreign capital and carrying out the recommendations

830 Alice H. Amsden, *Escape from Empire. The Developing World's Journey Through Heaven and Hell*, Cambridge–London 2007, p. 89.

831 J. Kochanowicz, "Reforming Weak States and Deficient Bureaucracies", [in:] *Intricate Links: Democratization and Market Reforms in Latin America and Eastern Europe*, ed. J. M. Nelson, Washington 1994, p. 209.

832 M. Kula, *Anatomia rewolucji narodowej: Boliwia w XX wieku*, Warszawa 1999, p. 37 ff.

833 S. Eckstein, F. Hagopian, "The Limits of Industrialization in the Less Developed World: Bolivia", *Economic Development and Cultural Change*, vol. 32, no. 1, 1983.

834 J. Dunkerley, *Rebellion in the Veins. Political Struggle in Bolivia 1952–1982*, London 1984, particularly p. 163 ff.

of international financial institutions did not help – toward the end of the 1970s Bolivia was one of the poorest countries in Latin America.

The weakness of government bureaucracies and their susceptibility to pressure groups had posed a problem for import substitution policies from the outset. The new industrial sectors – gigantic steelworks and chemical factories, refineries and automobile plants – were considerably less productive than those of their Western competitors, and thus required constant protection. A side effect of such protectionism was overly high exchange rates for Latin American currencies, which discouraged exports.[835] For this reason, basic consumer goods were significantly more expensive in most Latin American countries than in developed countries. In Chile in the 1960s, a bicycle cost four times as much as in the United States, small transistor radios cost three times as much as in Europe, and a small electric heater was nearly twice as expensive as on the international market. High tariffs on many components needed for the production of various industrial products had a similar effect.[836]

Supporters of this import substitution strategy believed it should be used in a limited way. The economist Albert O. Hirschman – one of its advocates – wrote that it should meet three basic conditions. Firstly, customs protections and subsidies should be temporary and reduced over time. Secondly, they should not be too high – they were meant to force manufacturers to be more productive, not incline them to behave imprudently. Third, only certain branches of industry should be protected – ideally those that, in keeping with the doctrine of "unbalanced development," would "pull" along with them the development of the largest number of local sectors of industry.

These conditions were not fulfilled, primarily for political reasons. It did not take much time for lobbyists for a particular industry's to persuade politicians that their industry was the one that deserved protection. Customs regulations in Latin America spanned thousands of pages and included thousands of products in a complicated system of licenses, tariffs and exceptions.

In Chile – to stay with that example – not only did bicycles and radios cost several times more than they did in developed countries: local products were also much lower in quality. Shoes quickly fell apart, and electric equipment simply stopped working. Customs barriers had reached a surrealistic level: the duty on

---

835 S. Edwards, "Forty Years of Latin America's Economic Development: From the Alliance for Progress to the Washington Consensus", NBER working paper 15190, July 2009.

836 V. Bulmer-Thomas, *The Economic History of Latin America Since* Independence, Cambridge–New York 2003 p. 275 ff.

car tires was 125%, on drills – 75%, on heaters – 244%, on electric motors – 162%, on radios – 340%, on vacuum cleaners – 85%, on refrigerators – 136%. In the mid-1960s the Chilean government also required importers to make a deposit equal to 10,000%(!) of the imported product at the central bank before their goods could pass through customs. Because customs procedures were lengthy, and the annual inflation rate had risen to above 30%, keeping money in an interest-free account further raised the cost of imported goods. In Mexico, tariffs on consumer goods – from textiles to tobacco, shoes, soap, paper and cars – ranged from 57% to 141%.[837] In the 1970s, over 70% of imports to Mexico required licensing.[838] The average customs duty amounted to 131% in Argentina, 168% in Brazil, 138% in Chile, 112% in Colombia and 61% in Mexico.[839]

The political economy of Latin American industrialization programmes differed in a significant way from the African model, though it, too, was supported by an alliance between urban population groups – the national bourgeoisie, the bureaucratic middle class and urban workers. These groups were the primary short-term beneficiaries of programmes to develop the domestic market, the government's protectionist policies and public investments. The most privileged were the middle and working classes. The middle class gained additional jobs in government offices and state enterprises, better access to education, and increased power for the bureaucracies in which they were employed. Workers received protection from their trade unions, influence over national policy, and social welfare benefits. As in Africa, the Latin American *pacto social* operated at the expense of the rural population and the urban poor, to whom it offered nothing. Although the need for foodstuffs grew in cities, rural areas remained underdeveloped and underinvested – the overwhelming majority of funds were designated for the development of industry. Social welfare legislation privileged the relatively small group of urban residents who were formally employed – at the cost of slum dwellers, who were mainly employed in the informal sector.[840] As a result, economic growth was unevenly distributed, the gap between the poor and rich grew, and Latin American politics – built on

837 G. Esquivel, G. Marquez, "Economic Effects of Closing the Economy: The Mexican Experience", [in:] *The Decline of Latin American Economies Growth, Institutions, and Crises*, eds. S. Edwards, G. Esquivel, G. Marquez, Chicago–London 2007.

838 N. Lustig, *Mexico: The Remaking of an Economy*, Washington 1998, p. 14.

839 S. Edwards, *Forty Years of Latin America's Economic Development…*, op. cit.

840 E. Cardoso, A. Helwege, "Populism, Profligacy and Redistribution", [in:] *The Macroeconomics of Populism in Latin America*, ed. R. Dornbusch, S. Edwards, pp. 61–62.

this social coalition – remained permanently unstable. Social inequality increased people's susceptibility to political radicalization.[841]

This dynamic was not just typical for Latin American countries. Throughout most of the developing world, development policy was guided by a strikingly similar logic, both in economic and political terms. Efforts at industrialization through import substitution were also made in Pakistan, Turkey and Thailand.[842] Economic planning was implemented in Turkey, Syria, Egypt, Iran, Indonesia and Taiwan. Nationalization of major enterprises, prohibitive tariffs on imports and the construction of the largest dam in Africa were key ingredients in Nasser's "Arab socialism" in Egypt – which nevertheless diverged clearly from the Soviet model, as did the policies of Nehru, Nyerere, Nkrumah and most other leaders in the post-colonial world.[843] All of these regimes tried to maintain power through the support of a nationalistically-oriented middle class, which was fairly closely tied to the government and dependent on it. All were also marked by permanent instability, which revealed itself when the mechanisms created by domestic policies hindered growth. Public spending helped buy support, as long as it could continue to be increased. When the system exhausted itself, a crisis occurred.

Space here does not allow for a discussion of all of those projects, which differed from one another significantly in terms of the scope, level of radicalism, scale of nationalization, and extent of government control over the economy. Their common elements, however, should be noted. All were based on the belief that the nation-state was the mainspring of economic development. All postulated that capitalism in its Western version was a game with marked cards in which the West always won. All were deeply distrustful of outsiders, particularly the West, but they were also – despite rhetoric underscoring the brotherhood of all colonial nations and the community of the "non-aligned world" – wary of their neighbours. The trade barriers erected by the countries of Africa and Latin America protected them not only from Western imports, but also from those of neighbouring countries. All of these projects were also marked by hostility towards foreign capital. Even when it was needed and efforts were being made to encourage investment, it was treated with mistrust, considered a tool of imperialism and neocolonial

---

841 A. Przeworski, C. Curvale, "Does Politics Explain the Economic Gap between the United States and Latin America?" [in:] *Falling Behind. Explaining the Development Gap Between Latin America and the United States*, ed. F. Fukuyama, Oxford–New York 2008, p. 100.

842 Cf. *Economic Transition in the Middle East*, ed. H. Handoussa, Cairo, 2000.

843 J. Gordon, *Nasser. Hero of the Arab Nation*, Oxford 2006, pp. 70–76.

domination (such fears were not necessarily irrational, as we see from the story of the "Alliance for Progress" and U.S. investment in Latin America).

All of these undertakings would have been impossible without faith in the rationality and effectiveness of government bureaucracies, in whom more trust was placed than in market forces – and again, for good reason, since local capitalism did not appear to offer any hope for development. Economic liberals were not only small in number, but were also generally considered to be what Galeano called "ideologists of impotence."[844]

All of these visions assumed that the rate of accumulation and investment could be increased through local efforts. In practice, this meant draining money from the poorest members of society, usually farmers, and in many cases, also from the consumers of the expensive and low-quality goods produced by local industry.[845] The grim irony of this situation is, nonetheless, only visible from a distance: at the time this was universally believed to be the price of development, as there was no other path. These policies were not as ineffective as their neoliberal critics often claimed in the 1970s and 80s: they assured at least two decades of high economic growth and brought at least a partial structural transformation to many countries of the "Third World." But only the countries of Asia managed to make the leap into modernity once and for all.

844 E. Galeano, *Open Veins…*, op. cit., p. 3.

845 R. K. Sah, J. E. Stiglitz, *Peasants Versus City-Dwellers. Taxation and the Burden of Economic Development*, Oxford–New York 1992, p. 17 ff.

They have absolutely no will to work. The men squat in their white clothes smoking on their long pipes and dream of the past, never thinking of the present nor hoping for the future.
Japanese colonial administrator Nitobe Inazō speaking about Koreans, "A Decaying Nation", 1906[846]

Chapter 7. Small dragons

Korea and Taiwan, 1945–1980

1. Export or death[847]

On the night of 8–9 July 1853, Lieutenant John Duer, commander of the USS *Mississippi*, watched as a "brilliant orange and blue meteor" flew across the sky over the fleet of American warships moored in Tokyo Bay. In his log, he wrote that he took this as a good omen. His dangerous expedition would end in success.[848]

The commander of the fleet, Commodore Matthew Perry, had just delivered a proposal for a trade agreement to a representative of the Japanese imperial government. The Japanese rejected the proposal, but Perry offered to leave them time to consider it further. He would return in a year's time for a definitive reply.

In actuality, this was an ultimatum from the West to the closed Asian country. Japan had been in self-imposed isolation since the mid-seventeenth century, allowing only very limited and strictly controlled trade with the outside world through the port of Nagasaki. Europeans were treated as a fifth column. They were a source of contamination that must not be allowed to spread, and a necessary evil that had to be kept from putting down roots. One of the conditions laid down by Japanese authorities for Portuguese merchants since the 1630s was a prohibition on European women residing in trade colonies – with the only exception being professional prostitutes.[849] Japan rulers were committed to maintaining domestic tranquillity and harmony, which they tended to believe contact

846 Quoted in A. Dudden, *Japan's Colonization of Korea. Discourse and Power*, Honolulu 2005, p. 134.

847 Japanese slogan from the 1950s.

848 D. G. Wittner, *Commodore Matthew Perry and the Perry Expedition to Japan*, New York 2005, p. 80.

849 L. M. Cullen, *A History of Japan, 1582–1941. Internal and External Worlds*, Cambridge–New York 2003, pp. 36–37.

with strangers could only upset. No one, or almost no one, among the Japanese wanted to open up to the outside world, writes historian Louis M. Cullen.[850]

When in 1854 a U.S. fleet of nine ships returned for an official response, Japanese politicians had a strategy of their own prepared. They were well aware of Europe's military superiority – Perry's fleet alone had more cannons than the coastal batteries around the capital – and, of course, they knew that almost all of Asia had already be subjected to European domination. They decided therefore to play for time and to acquiesce as little as possible. The treaty ultimately signed in 1858 – which at the request of the Japanese included the possibility of renegotiation after 14 years – was meant to serve one goal: to maintain the country's independence, giving up to the foreigners as little as possible, and using this time to modernize the army so that it would be capable of resisting future foreign aggression.[851] The Meiji Restoration that followed also had this as its main purpose.

One of the gifts Perry had brought for the emperor was a working miniature steam train, intended to demonstrate the power of American industry.[852] The message conveyed to the Japanese was not necessarily the one the sender had intended: Japan needed to modernize if it wanted to maintain its independence.

The country began to open up to the West at an impressive rate, but it did so in a carefully controlled manner. By the 1860s, Japanese students were attending universities in America and Europe, and soon after, working in their factories and shipyards. The country had a lot of catching up to do. The debut of this future industrial power in international trade was disappointing. Japan's pavilion at the International Exhibition in London in 1862 was described by the press as being "such a ramshackle assortment of artefacts that it looked just like an old antique shop." "I could not bear to look", noted one of the Japanese students living in London at the time.[853]

The attitude of the Japanese towards Europeans, like many non-European peoples, was a mixture of awe, fear and disgust. The Meiji Restoration introduced European patterns to things big and small. Ito Hirobumi, the primary author of the 1889 Constitution, was so impressed by German Imperial Chancellor Bismarck that he even held his cigar the same way Bismarck did in photographs.

---

850 L. M. Cullen, *A History of Japan…*, op. cit., p. 97 and 177.

851 L. M. Cullen, *A History of Japan…*, op. cit., p. 178.

852 D. G. Wittner, *Commodore Matthew Perry…* op. cit., p. 85.

853 A. Cobbing, *The Japanese Discovery of Victorian Britain. Early Travel Encounters in the Far West*, Richmond 1998, p. 95.

British ambassador Sir Harry Parkes' Victorian sideburns were imitated by many of the leading politicians of the Meiji, with limited success.[854]

Forty years after Commodore Perry's visit, Japan already had its own constitution, parliament, aristocratic titles, newspapers and centralized administration based on European models. Gone were the old feudal domains, replaced by prefectures under the authority of the central government. As late as the 1860s, Marx could write in the *New York Herald Tribune* that the island nation was a model example of feudalism. By the 1890s, the Chinese diplomat Huang Chun-Hsien in his letters from Tokyo was already calling Japan an example of modern centralization.

Given the scale and depth of change it involved, the Meiji Restoration encountered surprisingly little resistance. The well-known researcher of Asian economies Robert Wade has written about the difference between "hard" and "soft" states, seeing in this distinction the foundations for economic success. A "hard" state shapes society in accordance with the needs of the ruling bureaucracy. "Soft" states act according to dictates resulting from the plays for power of various social interests. The United States is a "soft country; Japan, Korea and Taiwan are "hard" countries.[855]

The Japanese state was definitively "hard". For the Japanese, the best school for modern living was the army, which itself was also a primary target of modernization efforts. The establishment of an army based on conscription, in accordance with decrees, laws and regulations modelled on the German, British and French systems, was a landmark event in the history Japan's path to modernity.[856] Its slogan was "a soldier is a model for society". Various social institutions – from schools and hospitals to factory dormitories – were organized according to military models. Marches, salutes, military uniforms and short haircuts were introduced in schools. This new social order was evident in the country's classrooms, where emphasis was placed on "cleanliness" and "order". In dormitories, the rigour maintained was on par with that of military barracks. In 1886, teachers began to be trained according to a military regime, "military-style" physical education was adopted, and students were under observation day and night by supervisors and upperclassmen. Meticulous rules governed every aspect of life: in the barracks where prospective teachers lived, no more than 10 people were allowed to a room, with each resident being assigned three shelves with an exact

---

854 M. B. Jansen, *The Making of Modern Japan*, Cambridge–London 2000, p. 335.

855 R. Wade, *Governing the Market. Economic Theory and the Role of Government in East Asian Industrialization,* Princeton 1990, p. 337.

856 N. Akira, "The Social Order of Modern Japan", [in:] *The Political Economy of Japanese Society, vol. 1, The State or the Market?*, Oxford–New York 1997, p. 199 ff.

length of three *shaku* (90.9 cm); regulations defined where and exactly how too fold one's uniform, underwear, shoes and belt. After five years of such training, teachers brought these models to their schools. Similar rules were in force in factory dormitories. The Education Order of 1872 warned young, mostly teenage workers: "Whether outside or inside, deport yourselves prudently, and never disregard proper feminine manners. Take care never to violate the rules against joking, singing vulgar popular songs, speaking in a loud voice, and removing clothes. Both body and clothing must be kept thoroughly clean."[857] The Education Order of 1872 stated: "in the village, no home without learning; in the home, no person without learning". Society was to be disciplined like an army and be subjected to a military-style system of indoctrination.

Uniformity and standardization were to be part of every aspect of life. In November 1872, the government abolished the old calendar, introducing – in place of 50,000 separate bells regulating the rhythm of the day in 50,000 Japanese villages –standard time and a calendar based on those used in the West. This reform also had a spiritual dimension. A Proclamation by the Governor of Kyoto supplied the reform's ideological rationale:

> The need to value time and work industriously has been frequently proclaimed. It is for this purpose that drums to beat the hours have been set up in every school, that the solar calendar is now being adopted and the time system revised, and that all districts throughout the country must keep the same time. People should keep time all the more seriously than ever:
>
> 1. Take care not to be late in disregard of time commitments to others, or to do such things as waste time in idle talk or disturb the work of others.
> 2. To avoid differences in working hours caused by long and short days, carpenters and other day labourers are urged to contract for wages based on working from a certain time in the morning to a certain time in the afternoon, without regard for the time of sunrise and sunset.
> 3. With the abolishing of the old calendar, all sales of publications such as astrological explanations of karma surrounding past, present, and future lives, and compatibility between men and women, must absolutely stop.
> 4. Furthermore, telling ghost stories is prohibited by law. In order to develop talent and wisdom and not fall into barbarism, evil customs of the past, including telling ghost stories to frighten and quiet crying children, are prohibited by the clear laws mentioned above, which warn against telling or listening to falsehoods.[858]

All of these measures to promote modernization were imposed from above by the imperial bureaucracy. In the West, the introduction of an official standard

857 Ibid., p. 199.
858 Ibid., p. 202.

time had been dictated by the need to coordinate domestic and international railway, shipping and telegraph systems. In Japan, this order was reversed: in an effort to modernize, the state began developing all of these systems, but it first standardized time. Prior to the adoption in April 1876 of an hourly work schedule in factory administration, such a means of measuring time had never been used in Japan. This change, too, was introduced by bureaucratic *fiat*. All modern institutions – barracks, hospitals, prisons, railways and government offices – became schools of punctuality based on a top-down system of order.[859] The main features of the Meiji Restoration – nationalism, an economy viewed as a collective strategic project, almost military in nature, subordinated to collective interests (rather than those of particular businessmen or individual citizens), a powerful bureaucracy, carefully selected imports of technology (including management techniques), and a highly self-disciplined society – would all later become features of the Japanese model, which was emulated by neighbouring East Asian countries.

Yet prior to the Meiji Restoration, the Japanese economy had not been stagnant: economic growth had been pronounced since the eighteenth century. Rice harvests and the number of labourers employed by farmers rose, technical innovations were introduced (although none on the level of the steam engine), new textile factories opened and books devoted to new farming techniques appeared. Meanwhile, the population grew slowly: between the 1721 and 1846 censuses, which historians consider to be accurate, the population increased by only three percent.

Although this increase was very similar to what Western Europe experienced before the industrial revolution (at least since the mid-seventeenth century.), it is unlikely that when Commodore Perry's fleet made its diplomatic visit, Japan's per capita income was as high as England's a century earlier.[860] Some historians think that industrialization might have taken place on its own and without contact with the West, and that domestic trade had a greater impact on its development than state intervention; however, this is not the dominant view.[861] Yet there is no doubt that this growth provided Japan with the means to build its own industry: the level of education among the population increased, but its business enterprises grew larger and more complex.

---

859 Ibid., p. 204.

860 T. C. Smith, *Native Sources of Japanese Industrialization, 1750–1920,* Berkeley–Los Angeles 1989, p. 16.

861 Cf. e.g. S. Tsunoyama, "Sino-Japanese Trade and Japanese Industrialization", [in:] *Japanese Industrialization and the Asian Economy*, eds. A. J. H. Latham, H. Kawakatsu, London–New York 1994, p. 194 ff.

Compared to the West, Japan around 1900 was still a poor and underdeveloped country. The distance separating them was particularly pronounced in heavy industry and machine building, and in the length of their railway lines. The first steam locomotive was not produced in Japan until 1893, and the first battleship not until 1910. The hand of government was visible in almost every major industrial project in the form of subsidies, protective tariffs and loans. The first big steel mill – Yawata – was founded by the state in 1895 through a resolution of the parliament, and it was subsidized generously for several years before it became profitable. The First World War brought the first real boom: the Japanese started exporting textiles on a large scale, and industrial production rose by 72 percent in the years 1914–1919.[862] Isolation from European competition brought even greater benefits to Japan than to the countries of Latin America. The government invested heavily in infrastructure: by 1930, 90 percent of houses in Japan had electric light, which was a much higher proportion than in most Western European countries.[863] The main beneficiary of the country's modern industrial production, however, continued to be the army.[864]

This project as a whole was never guided by a uniform and consistent ideology. The Japanese borrowed certain ideas from Western thought – "productive forces" from Marx, "innovation" and "management of demand" from Keynes, and the idea of "total war" from German political thought – but they did so selectively and always placed them in a Japanese context. The Great Depression was key to the emergence of Japanese economic thinking: as in most peripheral countries, the collapse of the liberal agenda led Japan to a search for its own national path to prosperity and power. The country's main priorities became national security – which, according to Japanese politicians, required that the country arm itself – and industrial self-sufficiency (self-sufficiency in terms of raw materials was unthinkable for an overcrowded and small island country, hence the need for expansion). Industrial policy was caught up in the cult of production. The economy was a strategic undertaking for the entire nation: the state needed to oversee it.

Japanese regulations during this period were subordinated to three main principles. The first was *sangyō kōzō*, that is, building an optimal industrial structure through government policy; "optimal" here meant one whereby Japan would achieve the best possible position in terms of world trade. The second keyword,

---

862 L. M. Cullen, *A History of Japan…*, op. cit., p. 250.

863 K. Smith, *A Time of Crisis: Japan, the Great Depression and Rural Revitalization*, Cambridge 2001, p. 23.

864 H. Oshima, "Review: Accelerated Growth: Japan's Experience", *Economic Development and Cultural Change*, 1970, vol. 19, no. 1, p. 114.

kado kyōsō, meant restricting competition in order to concentrate resources effectively in selected industries, and maintaining controlled order in economic growth. The third principle, *seisansei*, meant rejecting profit as the most important criterion in management. Companies were to sacrifice short-term profits in order to assure themselves an obedient and loyal workforce dedicated to raising productivity.[865] This of course did not mean that unions were tolerated: the State remained hostile to the idea of workers self-organizing.

Key industries were carefully nurtured. Even those that remained private were often in practice creations of the state. A good example of this is provided by the automotive industry. Investment in the industry began in 1907 when the Japanese army became interested in acquiring motor vehicles. The first subsidies for domestic production were enacted into law 1918. These however proved ineffective: it was still cheaper to import mass-produced American cars. Ford soon opened a Model A assembly plant in Yokohama, which turned out 20,000 vehicles a year. General Motors assembled a similar number of cars in Japan, mainly using parts produced in the U.S. As a result, the first Japanese manufacturers – Hakuyosha, Miyata Seisakujyo and Orient Jidousha Seizou – failed because they could not compete with American mass production.

In the 1930s, the government decided that the import of automotive parts was negatively affecting the balance of trade, as well as making an important manufacturing sector increasingly dependent on the outside world. In 1936, the Automobile Manufacturing Enterprise Law was passed, which required manufacturers to obtain a government license if they wanted to produce more than 3000 vehicles a year. This license could only be granted to Japanese companies. Each licensed company received a five-year exemption from taxes and duties on imports of machinery, but in return had to agree to obey the orders of government officials (this is stated in the law). Nissan and Toyota were the first companies to receive such a license. At the same time, the government ordered the Americans to cut back on production and raised tariffs on imported cars to 70 percent. As a result, local automobile production increased from almost from zero to 35,000 in 1939, while imports dropped to zero. Before the outbreak of the Second World War, Japan was able to produce domestically nearly all the automobiles it needed – and most importantly, the trucks required by the army.[866]

---

865 B. Gao, *Economic Ideology and Japanese Industrial Policy. Developmentalism from 1931 to 1965*, Cambridge 2002, p. 14.

866 K. Togo, "Infant Industry Protection Policy Reconsidered: The Case of the Automobile Industry in Japan", [in:] *Miraculous Growth and Stagnation in Post-War Japan*, eds. K. Hamada, K. Otsuka, G. Ranis, K. Togo, New York 2011, pp. 16–17.

This was an almost textbook example of both protecting a nascent national industry and of import substitution. It was also successful, unlike many such projects in Latin America, and brought long-term benefits: Toyota and Nissan are today among the largest car manufacturers in the world.

During the Great Depression and wartime mobilization new systems for maintaining control over industry were developed – including compulsory state-controlled producers' associations, which decided not only on the levels, composition and methods of production, but also on the terms, prices and timing of transactions; it also had the authority to set the level of profits, dividends and bonuses.[867] Companies remained private, but the economy was managed by the State beyond just the strategic level, with its bureaucracy exercising deep-reaching control.

This style of managing industrialization was accompanied by the ideology of "technological patriotism", which arose in the 1930s, and made advancements in technology and organizational efficiency national political objectives. In Japanese propaganda, the engineer was a soldier in service to the empire. Belief in the superiority of the "Japanese spirit" and "Japanese blood" were among the elements constituting Japan's imperial ideology. However, a second important foundation was the belief that the Japanese had a special predisposition for success in science, technology and the organization of production. This superiority was defined narrowly – it applied not to those in the basic and social sciences, but to engineers and technical experts, whose work led to advancements in production. Japan needed to be independent from the West, and it could achieve this by emancipating itself from technical thinking and technology imported from the West. The "New Order for Science-Technology" proclaimed in Asia by the imperial government during the war treated Japan as a centre for scientific research and production, while the surrounding countries – primarily occupied Manchuria – were to provide the centre with resources and, if needed, a workforce.[868]

Japan's defeat in the war and its occupation by the U.S. led to a transformation in this model, but not to the abandonment of its primary objectives. In the 1940s, the Americans dismantled the *zaibatsu* – the powerful family-based conglomerates that dominated industry and commerce – separating ownership of the companies from their management. In practice, however, the changes were primarily political and ideological. Japan had been demilitarized, but the struggle

867 B. Gao, *Economic Ideology...* op. cit., p. 26.

868 H. Mizuno, *Science for the Empire. Scientific Nationalism in Modern Japan*, Stanford 2009, p. 43 ff.

for national survival and independence continued, moving from the battlefield to the realm of international trade and production. Until at least the mid-1960s, Japan's postwar leadership cadre had been shaped during the prewar years, which were dominated by a quasi-fascist cult of unity and productivism. The "religion of export" was an attempt to build national power using non-military methods. A popular slogan in the 1950s was "export or die".

The economy remained a collective, strategic effort. Although Japan had lost the war, Prime Minister Shigeru Yoshida maintained that a "defeated nation, by analyzing and exploiting the shifting relations among world powers, could contain the damage incurred in defeat and instead could win the peace".[869] Yoshida's strategic plan envisaged an alliance with the United States, which, in exchange for political and military support, would provide Japan with economic aid and military protection, while it concentrated its resources on building its economic might.

The Americans were also eager to see the economic rebirth of Japan: the U.S. needed an ally in the fight against communism in Asia, but given its hegemony in world trade and position as the world's largest exporter, it was not afraid of competition. The diplomat George F. Kennan, who was an adviser to Truman and one of the fathers of the doctrine of containment, mainly emphasised the need for the U.S. to maintain control over the supply of raw materials to the islands, thereby giving it veto power over Japanese policy.[870] The liberalization of the Japanese economy under the 1949 "Dodge Line" imposed by the occupiers was likewise limited in scale. It abolished state control over the distribution and pricing of raw materials for production and replaced direct control of credit with indirect control. It freed up market forces, but the state still professed the principle of "limited competition". The American market remained open to its allies. The Korean War (1950–1953) provided a powerful impulse for growth: from July 1950 to February 1951, the U.S. Army ordered over 7,000 trucks from Japanese companies, for a total of $ 13 million, which put the country's automotive industry on its feet.[871] U.S. military spending accounted for almost 40 percent of

869 B. Gao, *Economic Ideology…*, op. cit., p. 29.

870 B. Cumings, "The Origins and Development of the Northeast Asian Political Economy: Industrial Sectors, Product Cycles and Political Consequences", [in:] *The Political Economy of the New Asian Industralism*, ed. F. C. Deyo, Ithaca 1987, p. 61.

871 C. Johnson, *MITI and the Japanese Miracle: Growth of Industrial Policy: 1925–1975*, Stanford 1983, p. 200.

foreign exchange inflows in the mid-1950s. Growth skyrocketed: for two decades Japan grew at nearly 10 percent annually, and national income doubled.[872]

Control over this economic miracle was exercised by the MITI, the Ministry of Industry and Foreign Trade. It was the heart and quintessence of the Japanese technocracy. In a statement issued in the 1980s, a few years before the collapse of the Japanese miracle, in his classic book on the MITI, American economist Chalmers Johnson described the mechanism by which this unique institution operated.

The MITI had a number of tools at is disposal, ranging from preferential loans to the ability to forgive taxes. The most powerful of these tools, however, were the close ties between the bureaucracy and business. The *amakudari* (Jap. descent from heaven) system, for example, assured government bureaucrats positions on the supervisory boards of strategic enterprises. The government controlled the economy through a complex system of licenses, incentives and permits: companies that employed former officials had, of course, better access to these. Johnson did not think of this as "corruption", but merely as an adaptive mechanism; in contrast to the situation in countries ruled by oligarchies in Latin America, this system favoured production. The highest-ranking positions in the *amakudari* system – held by former MITI deputy ministers – were always in strategic export sectors. Satō Kiichiro, president of Mitsui Bank in the 1960s, noted that "during and after the war, … Japan's economy was controlled until it has become second nature with us to uphold a planned, controlled economy."[873]

The nation state remained the primary focus of discussion about economic matters: promoting its interests and importance were an overriding concern. During discussions about trade liberalization in the late 1950s and 1960s, a high MITI official, the director of the Office of Entrepreneurship Sahashi Shigeru said:

> There was the National General Mobilization Law, the state was bestowed with great power to mobilize everything for the purpose of war by coercion and in the form of top-down. In order to make Japan the first class country among the first class countries, the national general mobilization is still needed today, though its format may differ from the wartime. Without the national general mobilization to consolidate the intelligence and power of the whole nation, people will assert and do whatever as they like and consequently Japan can accomplish nothing.[874]

872 F. G. Adams, L. R. Klein, Y. Kumasaka, A. Shinozaki, *Accelerating Japan's Economic Growth. Resolving Japan's Growth Controversy*, London–New York 2008, p. 9.

873 C. Johnson, *MITI and the Japanese Miracle…*, op. cit., p. 71.

874 Quoted in B. Gao, *Economic Ideology…*, op. cit., p. 43.

2. A decaying nation

For decades there were no signs that other Asian nations were capable of moving quickly onto the path laid out by Japan. The reputation of other Asian nations in the West was similar to that enjoyed by the Chinese in the nineteenth century: they were widely seen as lazy, dirty, rotten, rooted in the past and unable to adapt to the discipline of modern times. During the Russo-Japanese War in 1905, the American journalist and specialist on Russia and Asia, George Kennan (a distant cousin of Truman's advisor) wrote about the Koreans:

> They are not only unattractive and unsympathetic to a Westerner who feels no spiritual interest in them, but they appear more and more to be lazy, dirty, unscrupulous, dishonest, incredibly ignorant, and wholly lacking in the self-respect that comes from a consciousness of individual power and worth. They are not undeveloped savages; they are the rotten product of a decayed Oriental civilization[875].

This opinion was a commonly held one at the time. Kennan had no doubt that the civilizational superiority of the Japanese justified their domination over Korea. Another American traveller, Professor George T. Ladd, after his visit to Korea in 1907 said, "[t]he Koreans are the most untrustworthy and lacking in manly virtues of any people I have ever come in contact with". He complained about their lack of manly virtues, cruelty and character, which was worthy, in his opinion, of contempt.[876]

By the 1970s, however, there was talk in the West about the "four little dragons" – South Korea, Taiwan, Singapore and Hong Kong – which had copied/imitated/borrowed the Japanese model of growth and successfully adapted it to local conditions. But while Hong Kong and Singapore were small city-states, and could easily be regarded as unique examples of a civilizational "jump", South Korea and Taiwan were larger parts of ancient Asian empires, and their fate seemed to prove that the success and growth enjoyed by Japan could be repeated. First Japan, then the "four dragons", managed to do what economics textbooks – which had gradually become increasingly neo-classical since the 1970s – considered impossible: enact a policy of import substitution and protecting domestic industry that led to rapid growth in the economic, which did not get bogged down by an inefficiency bureaucracy and political corruption.

Korea's industrialization had already begun in earnest in the 1930s, during colonial times. In 1931, Japan abolished a law prohibiting the building of plants in

875 Quoted in A. J. Brown, *The Mastery of the Far East: The Story of Korea's Transformation and Japan's Rise to Supremacy*, New York 1919, p. 45.

876 Quoted in A. J. Brown, *The Mastery*... op. cit., p. 45.

the colonies that might compete with Japanese enterprises; the Japanese *zaibatsu* (Jap. financial clique) responded by building power plants, textile mills and cement plants in Korea. In 1939, large factories (employing more than 200 workers) made up only one percent of the businesses in Korea, but accounted for two-thirds of industrial production. Korea, however, remained significantly behind Japan: in 1930 just 0.75 percent of the population were industrial workers, while in Japan the proportion was 3.5 times higher. In 1940, the value of Korea's industrial output matched its agricultural production, which for a country that remained backward and dependent, testified to its rapid development.[877] The boards of directors and technicians were mainly Japanese – on the eve of the war there were nearly 100,000 Japanese in Korea – but as Japan began occupying huge expanses of Asia, many had to be replaced by Koreans, allowing them to gain valuable experience. The Japanese Korea quickly dismantled Korea's feudal institutions and built the beginnings of a modern infrastructure, including roads, ports and power lines. They also carried out land reform and built a bureaucracy modelled on Japan's whose tentacles reached even the smallest village.[878]

Despite this, South Korea was still a very poor country. A decade after the war, which completely destroyed both the north and south of the country, the GDP per capita amounted to approximately 80 dollars a year, while in Ghana it was 200 dollars, and in Argentina 3700 dollars.[879]

Despite massive postwar aid from the U.S. – reaching up to 15 percent of GDP and 80 percent of foreign currency revenue – growth took off only after a military coup by a group of officers in 1961, headed by Park Chung Hee. His twenty years in power turned out to be one of the biggest economic success stories in the history of humankind.

Just 100 days after taking power, the junta announced its first five-year development plan. In two books written shortly after the coup – *Our Nation's Path* and *Country, Revolution and I* (the author's ego suited his ambitions) – Park Chung Hee laid out the foundations for his economic policies. There was no talk yet of exports, but two elements were borrowed from other development projects and

---

877 A. Amsden, *The Rise of "The Rest": Challenges to the West from Late-Industrializing Economies*, Oxford–New York 2004, pp. 101–102.

878 A. Amsden, *Asia's Next Giant. South Korea and Late Industrialization*, Oxford–New York 1989, p. 34.

879 K. Mahbubani, "From Confucius to Kennedy. Principles of East Asian Governance", [in:] *East Asian Visions. Perspectives on Economic Development*, eds. I. Gill, Y. Huang, H. Kharas, The International Bank for Reconstruction and Development / The World Bank and The Institute of Policy Studies 2007, p. 197.

clearly inspired by Japan's success – a focus on large companies (production on a larger scale was more economical, just as large economic organizations were considered more efficient) and long-term planning. Park wrote:

> One of the essential characteristics of a modern economy is its strong tendency towards centralization. Mammoth enterprise – considered indispensable at the moment to our country – plays not only a decisive role in the economic development and elevation of living standards, but further, brings about changes in the structure of society and the economy [...] Where the appalling power of mammoth enterprise is concerned, only with private profit under a self-assumed assertion of contribution to national development, there is no free competition [...] Therefore, the key problems facing a free economic policy are coordination and supervisory guidance, by the state, of mammoth economic strength.[880]

Planning was modelled after that in communist countries. Park believed in the power of motivation, which generates profits, and rational (that is, controlled by the state) competition:

> The economic planning or long-range development program must not be allowed to stifle creativity or spontaneity of private enterprise. The overall national development program may necessitate, for the rational operation of the economy, reluctantly imposed administrative controls over the regional relocation of various industries and planning for investment.[881]

In the Korean dictator's next book, *Country, Revolution and I*, there were as many numbers, and descriptions of new plants and investment projects as in the speeches of communist leaders. There were also plenty of examples of how the dictator envisioned rational state planning. His premises were usually fairly simple and not the result of painstaking economic analysis. The shipbuilding industry must be a priority, Park said, because "Korea is surrounded on three sides by the sea", which "the previous government seemed to have been unaware of for the past ten years.[882]

Park was a student of the Japanese system of military education. After his death, the Japanese ambassador praised him as "the last soldier of Imperial Japan".[883] During the war, he had spent two years at a school for army officers in Manchuria,

880 C. H. Park, *Our Nation's Path: Ideology of Social Reconstruction*, Seoul 1962, pp. 228–229

881 C. H. Park, *Our Nation's Path...*, op. cit. pp. 224–225.

882 C. H. Park, *Country, Revolution and I*, Seoul 1970, p. 80.

883 C. Moon, B. Jun, "Modernization Strategy: Ideas and Influences", [in:] *The Park Chung Hee Era. The Transformation of South Korea*, eds. B. Kim, E. F. Vogel, Cambridge–London 2011, p. 117.

and then another two at the prestigious Imperial Japanese Army Academy. He was proud of this and emphasized that it had taught him discipline, loyalty and leadership skills. This education shaped his worldview: among his most important characteristics, he listed his sensitivity to detail, precision, determination and readiness to sacrifice for the nation. His militaristic and nationalistic intellectual orientation was taken straight from Japan during the 1930s and 1940s.

The dictator spent his nights reading books on history, and his favourite was *The Economic History of Japan*. He was an outstanding expert on the Meiji Restoration in Japan. His revolution was to be comparable to the accomplishments of Sun Yat-sen in China, Atatürk in Turkey, and Nasser in Egypt. "These were all holy projects aimed at resurrecting and building up their peoples", he wrote.[884] He consciously incorporated the most important slogans from the Meiji Restoration into his modernization project: *fukoku kyōhei* (Eng. rich nation, strong army) and *shokusan kōgyō* (Eng. industrial development, literally "production promotion").[885] According to Park, the secret to the success of his reforms lay in his elevating to power a new modernizing elite, and his tearing down the old power structures (interested in the benefits of power, not development). The army and industrial production should be under the close oversight of an elite, nationalistically oriented bureaucracy. The South Korean state, like Japan, called for "production promotion, exports, and construction", promoted "construction on the one hand and national defense on the other," and praised "frugality, hard work, and saving."[886]

The success of the Meiji Restoration was not, according to the dictator, the result of economic policy in the strict sense. Park himself did not have much to say about the promotion of exports or the role of the exchange rate. He saw development as a function of the relationship between the state and the social classes, and of ideology.[887] He wrote:

1. The Meiji reform had as its ideological basis a nationalistic patriotism.
2. Thereby they succeeded in Japanizing foreign thoughts that came in volume, and guarding the reform tasks undergoing then-repeated domestic ordeals from foreign invasion.

884 C. H. Park, *Country, Revolution and I*, op. cit. p. 137.

885 R. J. Samuels, *Rich Nation, Strong Army. National Security and the Technological Transformation of Japan*, Ithaca–New York 1994, p. 37.

886 C. Moon, B. Jun, "Modernization Strategy…", op. cit., p. 118.

887 A. Amsden, *Asia's Next Giant…*, op. cit., p. 51.

3. By eliminating the influence of feudal lords and directly connecting the emperor with the energetic middle class, a progressive atmosphere to overcome feudalism was created.
4. Millionaires who promoted the reform were allowed to enter the central stage, both politically and economically, thus encouraging national capitalism. An imperial system was thus established with the emperor at the apex of the pyramid of political and economic forces, and with the nobility serving as elder statesmen of the nation.[888]

Admiration for Japan did not clash with a dislike and distrust of the former colonial power – and this was no paradox. Like many nationalist modernizers, Park intended to base his program on the middle class – businessmen and officials – who were interested in economic growth, not just (like the old feudal elite) in maintaining their income and social position at the price of national backwardness. His program, like the Japanese program, also had its roots in a national obsession with power and external threats. Prosperity and wealth were not values in themselves: they served a different objective, which was increasing the nation's power and importance.

Also typical of the era – and certainly already clear to the reader of this book – was the dictator's conviction that heavy industry and the chemical industry could ensure South Korea's independence and lead it out of backwardness. Park once told his minister of trade and industry that the power that allowed Japan to start a war in the Pacific came from its large steelworks, and that Japan could produce tanks, guns and warships because it had steelworks.[889] Believing in the importance of steel – like many third-world modernizers, from Stalin and Mao to Nehru and Minc – Park made the building of a giant steel conglomerate a priority project in his development plan. Construction began in 1962, and was carried out in spite of the objections of experts from the United States and the World Bank, who regularly pointed out to the government that it had no chance of turning a profit (the facility was saved by exports). In the late 1960s, the dictator's interests shifted toward the chemical industry, which also became a base for a huge export success in the 1970s.

The dictator's original intuitions were, like in the case of Latin America, to follow a policy of import substitution and independence from foreign trade. Efforts were also made to put this into practice in Taiwan in 1958–1959. In both cases, these attempts failed. It quickly became clear that the domestic market in both countries was too small to sustain large-scale enterprises (large-scale production

888 C. H. Park, *Country, Revolution and I*, op. cit., p. 120.
889 C. Moon, B. Jun, "Modernization Strategy…", op. cit., p. 118.

lowered costs).[890] They also moved away from a policy of import substitution for political reasons: politicians in Asian countries feared the formation of political interests that would seek to close markets to competition and enrich themselves on state subsidies, and thus, feared the emergence of social forces that would threaten their power. In the early 1960s, both South Korea and Taiwan began major reforms intended to promote exports. They devalued their currencies to lower the prices of their exports on world markets, began a multi-year program to lower protective tariffs in order to motivate industrialists to increase competitiveness, introduced a system of tax exemptions and loan guarantees to encourage exports, began subsidizing transport and set up special export zones. The state also created export consortiums, forcing many smaller local firms to use one of several specialized trade centres.

Nationalism, state control, and Japanese colonial reign linked the fates of Korea and Taiwan. When the remnants of Chiang Kai-shek's army evacuated to Taiwan along with thousands of officials and businessmen who feared communist repression, they had taken with them under escort by the American fleet the lion's share of the state treasury – then worth 330 million dollars – and numerous artworks. They also carried with them a much more valuable lesson: political success is based on economic success. China's Kuomintang government lost its legitimacy to rule as the result of corruption, hyperinflation and a lack of real ideas about a way out of economic stagnation. This could all happen again. Already in the 1950s, agrarian reform was being carried out in Taiwan, through which the Kuomintang won the support of local farmers. American economic assistance and the opening of the US market to exports from Taiwan helped the development of local industry – first in areas that required intensive and arduous physical labour.[891] There were of course differences between the models of growth in the two countries: while in Taiwan the backbone of the economy was small and medium-sized companies which exported with the help of state-owned commercial centres, the Korean dictatorship supported the development of large industrial and trade conglomerates. Park believed that only large, powerful companies could cope with international markets and ensure an adequate level of innovation.

The fate of the Korean *chaebol* and their investment decisions provided an illustration of the role played by cooperative relations between industries during a

---

890 Jason P. Abbott, *Developmentalism and Dependency in Southeast Asia. The Case of the Automotive Industry*, London–New York 2003, p. 44.

891 X. Song, *Between Civic and Ethnic. The Transformation of Taiwanese Nationalist Ideologies 1895–2000*, Brussels 2009, p. 138 ff.

"big push" – as Rosenstein-Rodan and Hirschman had imagined them a decade earlier. The son of the founder of the LG Group and its second president recalled that in 1985:

> My father and I started a cosmetic cream factory in the late 1940s. At the time, no company could supply us with plastic caps of adequate quality for cream Jars, so we had to start a plastic business. Plastic caps alone were not sufficient to run the plastic-molding plant, so we added combs, toothbrushes, and soap boxes. This plastics business also led us to manufacture electrical and electronic products and telecommunication equipment. The plastics business also took us into oil refining which needed a tanker-shipping company. The oil refining company alone was paying an insurance premium amounting to more than half the total revenue of the then largest insurance company in Korea. Thus, an insurance company was started. This natural step-by-step evolution through related businesses resulted in the Lucky-Goldstar group as we see it today. For the future, we will base our growth primarily on chemicals, energy, and electronics. O u r chemical business will continue to expand toward fine chemicals and genetic engineering while the electronics business will grow in the direction of semiconductor manufacturing, fiber optic telecommunications, and eventually, satellite telecommunications.[892]

Korean *chaebol* were private, but closely integrated with the state through a network of personal relationships and common interests. The most important business decisions were often taken at the dictator's residence. The relations between the President and the *chaebol* were complex and mutual: Korea's leader and business elite needed each other. Chung Hee Park thought that the big conglomerates would help him achieve his political goal – "rich nation, strong army" – while the heads of *chaebol* treated him as a guarantee of their safety and success in business.[893] GDP growth in South Korea and Taiwan were identical – and in the years 1950–1980 averaged 5.7 percent per capita per year. This impressive performance – the best in the history of modern economic growth – was accompanied by substantial social changes: a move away from agriculture towards industry; a significant reduction in social inequality, mortality and unemployment; rapid growth in labour productivity, education levels and life expectancy.[894] The "dragons" had managed to do what they had not done when they reached Latin America, Africa and most of Asia.

892 Quoted in A. Amsden, *Asia's Next Giant…*, op. cit., p. 126.

893 E. Kim, G.-S. Park, "The Chaebol", [in:] *The Park Chung Hee Era. The Transformation of South Korea*, eds. B. Kim, E. F. Vogel, Cambridge–London 2011, p. 267.

894 H. T. Oshima, "The Transition from an Agricultural to an Industrial Economy in East Asia", *Economic Development and Cultural Change*, 1986, vol. 34, no. 4.

3. Success in spite of rule/against the rules

In 1993, the World Bank issued a famous report on the "economic miracle" in East Asia, in which it described in enthusiastic words the gigantic civilizational success of several countries on the continent.[895] It did so without enthusiasm: Japanese sponsors had forced conservative bank officials to prepare the report, recognizing/seeing this as a condition for further financing.[896]

Bank President Lewis T. Preston wrote in the Introduction:

> The authors conclude that rapid growth in each economy was primarily due to the application of a set of common, market-friendly economic policies, leading to both higher accumulation and better allocation of resources. While this conclusion is not strikingly new, it reinforces other research that has stressed the essential need for developing economies to get the policy fundamentals right.[897]

This advice of the President of the World Bank was the motto behind the structural economic transformations being carried out in developing countries – including those in post-communist Eastern Europe – in the 1980s and 1990s. In the case of Asian countries, writes Chalmers Johnson, this was "deliberately misleading": Japan, Korea and Taiwan owed their success precisely due to the fact that they did not put liberal prescriptions into practice.[898] Those that they did – like South Korea in the 1950s – paid for this with a slow growth rate.

The World Bank president admitted, somewhat reluctantly, that government intervention could sometimes work:

> The report also breaks some new ground. It concludes that in some economies, mainly those in Northeast Asia, some selective interventions contributed to growth, and it advances our understanding of the conditions required for interventions to succeed.[899]

The liberal politician believed that Asian interventionism succeeded only due to the fact that – firstly – it removed obstacles to the proper functioning of markets; second – it took place in the context of a "fundamentally good policy"; and, third, that its success depended on the ability of the government to create

---

895 *The East Asian Miracle. Economic Growth and Public Policy*, Washington–New York 1993.

896 C. Johnson, "The Developmental State: Odyssey of a Concept", [in:] *The Developmental State,* ed. M. Woo-Cumings, Ithaca–London 1999, p. 35.

897 *The East Asian Miracle…*, op. cit., p. vi.

898 C. Johnson, "The Developmental State…", op. cit., p. 36.

899 *The East Asian Miracle…*, op. cit., p. vi.

"economic competition", that is, to support those companies that had been most competitive, not just those that were politically important.

This was an illusion: the only example of liberal success in Asia was provided by small Hong Kong, and even that required a creative reinterpretation of an active policy of the local authorities. According to the dominant belief among specialists on growth in Asia, growth was due to the driving force of the state. Japan developed in a way that "flagrantly flouting all received principles of capitalist rationality", wrote Economist Ronald Philip Dore in 1986.[900]

Japan, Korea and Taiwan applied a set of political ideas for growth, which had much in common with those they tried to put into practice in Latin American countries. The list is long – protective tariffs, trade licenses and taxes, loans and grants, state planning of industrial growth, reducing competition and maintaining artificially high levels of investment in relation to GDP. All of this took place at the expense of workers who earned relatively little and paid a higher price for locally produced goods, but in return received a promise of a quick increase in the standard of living in the future. However, while growth in Latin America collapsed in the 1970s, Asian countries continued to develop rapidly: they were evidently doing something better. "In other countries – in Turkey and India, for example – subsidies have been dispensed primarily as giveaways", says Alice H. Amsden, one of the most prominent researchers of the history of Asian economies. The key to success in Japan, South Korea and Taiwan was discipline, which the State imposed on businesses and employees. Its roots are essentially cultural and historical in character: a meritocracy in the civil service, militarism, a lack of natural resources and a hyperactive student movement that was monitoring politicians during the dictatorship.[901] Elsewhere Amsden writes about the role of experience in manufacturing – the earlier it began (as in the case of Korea and Taiwan, which were colonies of Japan), the faster the subsequent growth.[902] Another historian of Asia's success, Robert Wade wrote about the difference between a "hard" and "soft" state – which was mentioned earlier in the chapter.

Many researchers of the Asian "miracle" emphasize the blurring of the opposition between the state and the market, the role of nationalism and a sense of danger, and a clear rejection of the neoclassical economy as inconsistent with a vision of the economy and society not as a sum of individual interests, but as a harmonious whole. Neoclassical economics sees the economy as a natural

900 R. P. Dore, *Flexible Rigidities. Industrial Policy and Structural Adjustment in the Japanese Economy 1970–1980,* Stanford 1986, p. 18.

901 A. Amsden, *Asia's Next Giant…*, op. cit., p. vi.

902 A. Amsden, *The Rise of "The Rest"…*, op. cit., p. 101 ff.

system that is controlled by the invisible hand of the market, which always seeks a balance between supply and demand. The Japanese, and behind them the elite of South Korea and Taiwan, consider the economy as a system that plastycznie submits to the will of man. Programmes for industrialization were always, above all, projects for social change, and not strictly just economic calculations.[903]

The main component of the Asian success was not so much the adoption of appropriate economic policies, understood as technical solutions on the issues of taxes, duties or subsidies, but in the ideology consistently professed by the elite. Political decisions such as deliberately undervaluing the exchange rate in order to facilitate exports, which, according to Dani Rodrik, contributed much to growth in Asia, were mainly the result of ideology and political power plays within Asian societies and less a matter of technocratic calculation.[904]

Asian authors often emphasize the importance of "Asian values", such as hard work, thrift and perseverance, as well as education, dedication and selflessness elites – who think most of all about the good of the country, and not about their own pockets and the benefits of power. Kishore Mahbubani, a Singapore diplomat and one of the Asia's most famous political scientists, writes:

> Why did East Asian elites perform better than many of their Latin American counterparts? Any attempt to give a full answer to this question will reveal the complexity of the East Asian story. Culture is certainly part of the explanation. Since the days of Confucius, the ethical fabric of East Asian societies has been laced with the belief that obligation to society is an integral part of being an ethical person. But a similar strain occurs in other societies, including Christian and Muslim societies [...] This willingness to learn Western best practices and to adapt and apply them may thus be the key distinguishing feature of East Asian elites. In theory, these elites might have been afraid of losing their cultural identity in trying to copy the West. In practice, they retained their deep cultural confidence that they could learn from the West and not lose their souls. Hence, both the capacity to learn and the confidence to accept Western best practices are central elements of the East Asian narrative.[905]

In response to the question why did Asian elites fare better than the elites in Latin America, Mahbubani has two answers: the Confucian heritage ("Since the days of Confucius, the ethical fabric of East Asian societies has been laced with

---

903 B. Gao, *Economic Ideology...*, op. cit., p. 48.

904 D. Rodrik, *The Real Exchange Rate and Economic Growth: Theory and Evidence*, July 2007, http://www.cid.harvard.edu/neudc07/docs/neudc07_s1_p04_rodrik.pdf

905 K. Mahbubani, *From Confucius to Kennedy...*, op. cit., p. 190.

the belief that obligation to society is an integral part of being an ethical person.") and a tendency to follow the "best practices of the West".[906]

Less idealistic authors usually emphasize the complex political economy of East Asian societies. Economic growth was from this perspective a side effect, although perhaps the most important one. South Korea's state promoted growth: it supplied public goods, such as security and education, and built an infrastructure conducive to investment. "But [...] this was not necessarily intentional," writes David Kang. "Corruption was rampant in Korea, and the state intervened in the way it did because its doing so was in the interests of a small group of business and political elites."[907]

Kang examines the divergent trajectories of the two Asian countries – Korea and the Philippines – of which the latter have long been richer and seemed fated to success. World Bank Report from 1957 stipulated a repeat of the success of Japan.[908] In 1955, per capita GDP in the Philippines was twice as high as that in Korea. Countries razed in 1970 in 1985 South Korea was already five times richer.[909]

Both countries were thoroughly corrupt, and the links between government and the business remained very close. South Korean state also took decisions to support various business ventures because, because businessmen had good political connections, not because it is particularly deserving of support for economic reasons. These two countries differed, however, the political dynamics. In Korea, the influence of political and economic elites balanced each other and the whole system gained legitimacy through economic growth. In the Philippines – first surviving episode democratic, then a long dictatorship of Ferdinand Marcos – the situation was different: first the state was weak and vulnerable to pressure from various interest groups, and later – under the dictatorship – has become so strong that the ruling could with impunity and without enforce restrictions and steal a large part of domestic capital. There also had to remain in power, hold an investment in education or infrastructure. Kang came to the conclusion that not all corruption is harmful for growth "if the transfer of wealth is from businessmen to politicians and results in productive investments, a nation may even benefit".[910]

906 Ibid.

907 D. C. Kang, *Crony Capitalism. Corruption and Development in South Korea and the Philippines*, Cambridge 2004, p. 6.

908 D. C. Kang, *Crony Capitalism...*, op. cit., p. 181.

909 Ibid., p. 40.

910 Ibid., p. 184. The literature on the relationship between corruption and economic growth is quite extensive. Cf., e.g. P. Bardhan, "Corruption and Development: A Review of Issues", *Journal of Economic Literature*, 1997, no. 35; M. Khan, "The Efficiency

Whatever the causes of the Asian success, both his politics and ideology are the most distant from liberal laissez-faire. In the 1970s this lesson, however, was completely forgotten – or at least ignored. The world has lost faith in the fact that the state can be leveraged development and believed in the power of the free market mover.

Implications of Corruption", *Journal of International Development*, 1996, vol. 8, no. 5; A. Shleifer, R. Vishney, "Corruption", *Quarterly Journal of Economics*, 1993, no. 108.

Chapter 8

Truly important and significant hypotheses will be found to have "assumptions" that are wildly inaccurate descriptive representations of reality, and, in general, the more significant the theory, the more unrealistic the assumptions (in this sense).
Milton Friedman, 1953[911]

"Until 1973 or thereabouts it was easy to be an optimist."
Economist Robert Solow on the loss of faith in state intervention in the economy during the 1970s.

1. Malaise

Elites in peripheral countries believed for a number of reasons that the state could serve as a lever to pull their homelands out of backwardness and allow them to escape their peripheral status. Contributing to this belief was the experience of the Great Depression in the 1930s and the presumed success of planned economies (especially in the USSR), as well as economic theory, which had allotted the state a vital role in stimulating economic growth.

In the 1970s, elites in the poorest countries (now called "developing countries), economists involved in development, and international institutions providing aid to these countries, all quickly began to lose faith in the state and socialism. They now began placing their faith in the market, free trade and the free flow of capital. A number of factors led to this transformation: but its spiritual, intellectual and institutional roots can be traced back, like in the 1930s, to the West. Now, like then, the new ideology for promoting growth in developing countries had been born at the desks of Western intellectuals and in the universities and think-tanks of the world's core states.

It is impossible to identify the exact date this process began. Its political starting point was the visible failure in the early 1970s of the Keynesian model for growth in the United States and Western Europe. But historian Kamran Dadkhah points to an even earlier date – 15 August 1971 – when U.S. President Richard

911 M. Friedman, "The Methodology of Positive Economics", [in:] *Essays in Positive Economics*, Chicago 1966, p. 14.

Nixon proclaimed that the fight against rising inflation had become the main goal of economic policy.[912] In his announcement, Nixon said:

> One of the cruelest legacies of the artificial prosperity produced by war is inflation. Inflation robs every American, every one of you. The 20 million who are retired and living on fixed incomes – they are particularly hard hit. Homemakers find it harder than ever to balance the family budget. […] The time has come for decisive action – action that will break the vicious circle of spiraling prices and costs.[913]

Nixon imposed a 10 percent duty on imports, announced cuts in public spending and taxes, and suspended the convertibility of the dollar into gold, which he claimed was to protect the U.S. currency against attacks by speculators.

Keynesian economic policies assumed that increasing public spending would stimulate demand and help maintain full employment. The price for stimulating this demand was moderate inflation.[914] An inverse relationship was thus believed to exist between the level of unemployment and inflation: a drop in inflation was supposed to lead to a rise in unemployment. In 1970, belief in this correlation began to waver, as unemployment and inflation rose in tandem – from three to six percent. Under the threat of strike, on 1 August 1970, the United Steelworks of America negotiated a three-year contract that included a 30 percent increase in wages. On 2 August, the United Transportation Union ended a long and economically costly strike after winning a wage increase totalling 42 percent over the course of a 42-month collective agreement.[915]

Nixon's decision also meant in practice the dismantling of the monetary system established under the Bretton Woods Agreement in 1944, which had linked global currencies through a fixed exchange rate pegged to the dollar. Bretton Woods had ensured Western countries stable exchange rates during more than two decades of postwar economic growth.[916] In the early 1970s, the United States began to record a trade deficit for the first time in its twentieth-century history.

---

912 K. Dadkhah, *Evolution of Macroeconomic Theory and Policy*, Berlin–Heidelberg 2009, p. 117 ff.

913 Quoted in *Public Papers of the Presidents of the United States, Richard Nixon, 1971*, General Services Administration, National Archives and Records Service, Office of the Federal Register, Washington 1972, p. 888.

914 E. K. Hunt, M. Lautzenheiser, *History of Economic Thought. A Critical Perspective*, Armonk 2011, p. 465.

915 K. Dadkhah, *Evolution of Macroeconomic Theory…*, op. cit., p. 119.

916 M. D. Bordo, *The Bretton Woods International Monetary System: An Historical Overview*, NBER Working Paper no. 4033, March 1993, http://www.nber.org/papers/w4033, reprinted in *A Retrospective on the Bretton Woods System*, eds. M. D. Bordo,

Currency devaluation under the Bretton Woods system was practically impossible. The price of gold rose, causing an outflow of gold (exchangeable for dollars at a fixed rate) from the U.S. The American move eventually led to a system of free-floating exchange rates, set by the market.[917]

The backdrop to these extraordinary decisions by Nixon was an economic recession in the U.S. (which ended in November 1970.) and upcoming Presidential elections. Economist Milton Friedman, who would soon gain fame as one of the main architects of the move away from Keynesianism in the 1970s, later recalled:

> I had a session with Nixon sometime in 1970 … in which he wanted me to urge Arthur [Burns, FED chairman] to increase the money supply more rapidly [laughter] and I said to the President, "Do you really want to do that? The only effect of that will be to leave you with a larger inflation if you do get reelected." And he said, "Well, we'll worry about that after we get reelected." Typical. So there's no doubt what Nixon's pleasure was.[918]

Nixon won the election. On the matter of inflation, however, Friedman had been right.

A prominent economist, Robert Solow, recalled twenty years later that until 1973 "it was easy to be an optimist". In West Germany and the U.K., the unemployment rate remained at 1–3 percent, while inflation was "tolerable" in the range of 2–3.5 percent annually.[919] However, tensions in the U.K.'s economy had been growing since the early 1970s: for example, in 1972 miners won large pay rises from the conservative government, but more than a million people were unemployed. In 1973, the U.K. trade deficit exceeded one billion pounds. Paradoxically, writes historian Kenneth R. Hoover, the Keynesian notion that the government should perform a regulatory role in the economy led the public to blame it for the country's economic problems, regardless of their actual cause.[920]

B. Eichengreen, Chicago 1993, pp. 3–98; and B. Eichengreen, *Global Imbalances and the Lessons of Bretton Woods*, NBER Working Paper no. 10497, May 2004.

917 A. Rose, *A Stable International Monetary System Emerges: Bretton Woods*. NBER Working Paper no. 12711; J. Mills, *A Critical History of Economics*, Houndmills–New York 2002, p. 31.

918 Interview with Milton Friedman from 2 May 2000, [in:] *Inside the Economist's Mind. Conversations with Eminent Economists*, eds. P. A. Samuelson, W. A. Barnett, Malden–Oxford 2007, p. 116.

919 R. Solow, "Did Policy Errors of the 1960s Sow the Seeds of Trouble in the 1970s?", [in:] *The Legacy of the Golden Age. The 1960s and Their Economic Consequences*, eds. A. Cairncross, F. Cairncross, London–New York 2003, p. 159.

920 K. R. Hoover, *Economics as Ideology. Keynes, Laski, Hayek and the Creation of Contemporary Politics*, Lanham–Oxford 2003, p. 200.

A surge in oil prices in 1973 set off by political events, in particular, the Arab-Israeli war, was a critical turning point. From that time onward, the West suffered a dramatic – in comparison with previous decades – deceleration in economic growth.[921] Productivity in the major economies of the West slowed by half, while the inflation rate increased – exceeding 11 percent in the U.S. and 24 percent in the U.K. in 1974. Western countries would never return to the low unemployment levels of the 1960s.

Robert Solow looked for the genesis of the crisis and of "stagflation" – low growth combined with inflation – in the 1970s, not so much in the "oil shock" as in the policies of successive U.S. administrations during the previous decade. At the beginning of the 1960s, the economists employed in the Kennedy administration estimated that by stimulating demand, the unemployment rate in the U.S. could be reduced to 4 percent – and that any drop below that threshold carried the risk of inflation spiralling out of control.[922] "Later research has tended to conclude that 4 per cent was half a percentage point (or maybe a bit more) too low," wrote Solow. Meanwhile, massive spending on the war in Vietnam helped push the U.S. unemployment rate down to 3.5 percent in 1969. Solow commented:

> Instead, the prosecution of the war in Vietnam was allowed to drive the unemployment rate to 3.8 per cent in 1966 and 1967, and then down to 3.5 per cent in 1969. This was not a result of miscalculation or inattention. It was straight politics. The war was becoming unpopular; protests and demonstrations were frequent and visible. Those who favoured the active prosecution of the war feared that a decision to finance the war by taxation would merely emphasize its costs and bring normally conservative elements of the population into opposition. Congress might have substituted cutbacks in Mr Johnson's domestic programmes. Inflation seemed the preferable alternative.[923]

In retrospect, Solow placed blame for the troubles of the 1970s on a sudden drop in productivity in Western countries – which had grown at an unprecedented pace for almost three decades after the war.[924]"It made stagflation harder to deal with. The point I have in mind is easiest to see in connection with the adverse supply shock. One way or another the consequent loss of real income had to be shared out," wrote Solow.[925] Lower growth in productivity growth made macroeconomic

921 M. Olson, "The Productivity Slowdown, the Oil Shocks, and the Real Cycle", *Journal of Economic Perspectives*, 1988, vol. 2 no. 4.; W. Nordhaus, *Retrospective on the 1970s Productivity Slowdown*, NBER Working Paper no. 10950, December 2004.

922 R. Solow, "Did Policy Errors...", op. cit., p. 163.

923 Ibid.

924 Cf. W. Nordhaus, *Retrospective on the 1970s...*, op. cit.

925 R. Solow, "Did Policy Errors...", op. cit., p. 170.

policy much more difficult to execute, and meant that old solutions would no longer work: keeping inflation in check, for example, would require a much deeper recession, with higher unemployment than in previous downturns. Yet, while a lower rate of growth in productivity was clearly visible looking back 20 years later, Solow wrote in 1992, in the 1970s it had been easier to place blame on misguided macroeconomic policy.

The potential of the State to act as an engine of economic growth seemed to have exhausted itself in the Eastern bloc, as well: in the West it was no secret that economic growth had slowed markedly in the Soviet Union since the mid-1960s, and that the entire socialist bloc was increasingly lagging behind in terms of technology.

2. The revolution of the neoliberals

Very important changes had been taking place since the late 1960s in economic theory, as well, and this could be seen on several levels. It had evolved both in terms of its methods – moving towards mathematical models – and its object of interest. Alternatives to faith in state intervention, planning and Keynesian "stimuli" had been under development since the 1950s in conservative think-tanks and by a few lonely economists, mainly those associated with the University of Chicago.

At the beginning, they were completely marginalized. As the famous American intellectual and literary critic Lionel Trilling wrote in 1950, "nowadays there are no conservative or reactionary ideas in general circulation."[926]

In 1950, Friedrich August von Hayek was given a position as a professor on the Committee on Social Thought at the University of Chicago, where he remained until 1962 (he had been rejected by the Economics Department, and his salary was paid by a private sponsor, the Kansas-based Volker Fund).[927] He was the author of a book published in 1944, *The Road to Serfdom*, a passionate defence of political and economic freedom in its classical liberal sense.[928] In the book, Hayek rejected economic planning not only as irrational and inefficient, but also contrary to the principle of human freedom, and leading – step by step – to the political enslavement of the nation's citizens (although he distinguished between

926 L. Trilling. *The Liberal Imagination*. New York 2008 [1950], p. xv.

927 J. Burns, *Goddess of the Market. Ayn Rand and the American Right*, Oxford–New York 2009, p. 103–104.

928 F. A. von Hayek, *The Road to Serfdom. Text and Documents. The Definitive Edition*, ed. B. Caldwell, Chicago–London 2007 [1944].

"good" from "bad" planning without specifying exactly what this meant). In a highly emotional diatribe against "collectivism", Hayek wrote:

> What is called economic power, while it can be an instrument of coercion, is, in the hands of private individuals, never exclusive or complete control, never power over the whole life of a person. But centralized as an instrument of political power it creates a degree of dependence scarcely distinguishable from slavery.[929]

The book was noticed, but received without enthusiasm.[930] It was rejected by several publishers, and no one expected it would become a best seller.[931] Keynes read it on the way to the conference in Bretton Woods, where he would act as one of the chief architects of the postwar economic order, and wrote to Hayek that it was a "grand book": "I morally and philosophically find myself in agreement with virtually the whole of it". At the same time, he added, some state intervention in economic life was necessary:

> You admit here and there that it is a question of knowing where to draw the line. You agree that the line has to be drawn somewhere, and the logical extreme is not possible. But you give us no guidance whatever as to where to draw it.[932]

Hayek could not be fooled by such complements. Keynes, he said years later, still "believed that he was fundamentally still a classical English liberal and wasn't quite aware of how far he had moved away from it. His basic ideas were still those of individual freedom. He did not think systematically enough to see the conflicts. He was, in a sense, corrupted by political necessity."[933]

Hayek had great success as publicist with an abridged version of his book published in 1947 by the highly popular American magazine *Reader's Digest* in an edition of one million copies.[934] One of its readers was Anthony Fisher, a young war veteran who, having made a fortune raising chickens after the war, founded

---

929 Ibid., p. 116.

930 Cf. B. Caldwell, "Introduction", [in:] F. A. von Hayek, *The Road to Serfdom*, op. cit., pp. 1–22; M. Lane, "The Genesis and Reception of The Road to Serfdom", [in:] *Hayek: A Collaborative Biography. Part 1 Influences, from Mises to Bartley*, ed. R. Leeson, Houndmills–New York 2013. pp. 43–60.

931 K. Phillips-Fein, *Invisible Hands. Conservative Movement from the New Deal to Reagan*, New York 2009, p. 41.

932 Quoted in F. A. Hayek, *The Road to Serfdom*..., op. cit., pp. 23–24.

933 Interview with Thomas W. Hazlett from 1977 originally published in *The Reason*, July 1992, http://reason.com/archives/1992/07/01/the-road-from-serfdom.

934 K. R. Hoover, *Economics as Ideology*..., op. cit., p. 202.

in 1955 an economic think-tank, the Institute of Economic Affairs.[935] Its task was to promote free-market ideas.[936] Thanks to such sponsors, in the 1970s, there was already a whole network of similar institutions in the U.S., including the Foundation for Economic Education (involved in reforming the teaching of economics in secondary schools and universities to reflect the values of classical liberalism), the American Enterprise Institute, the Cato Foundation and the Heritage Foundation, which provided economic and social analysis and played an active role in shaping public opinion.[937]

In 1947, Hayek was one of the main organizers of a conference in the village of Mont Pelerin, not far from the town of Vevey, Switzerland, where 39 intellectuals, mainly economists, but also philosophers and historians (among them were Karl Popper, Ludwig von Mises and Milton Friedman) established an association dedicated to the resurrection of neoliberal economic ideas and reintroducing them into political discourse.[938] Four economists participating in the first meeting would late receive the Nobel Prize – Hayek, Milton Friedman, George Stigler and Maurice Allais. The participants prepared an ideological manifesto in which they wrote:

> The central values of civilization are in danger. Over large stretches of the earth's surface the essential conditions of human dignity and freedom have already disappeared. In others they are under constant menace from the development of current tendencies of policy. The position of the individual and the voluntary group are progressively undermined by extensions of arbitrary power.[939]

"The importance of that meeting", Milton Friedman later recalled, "was that it showed us that we were not alone."[940]

Hayek's ideas – that the market's spontaneous order was always better than a seemingly rational plan, and that behind the noble ideals of socialism and redistribution in fact lay oppression and misery, which led to his claim of "the

---

935 Cf. *Think Tanks & Civil Societies. Catalysts for Ideas and Action*, eds. J. G. McGann, R. K. Weaver, New Brunswick 2009, p. 112 ff.

936 R. E. Backhouse, *The Puzzle of Modern Economics. Science or Ideology?*, Cambridge–New York 2010, pp. 140–141.

937 K. R. Hoover, *Economics as Ideology…*, op. cit., pp. 206–207.

938 G. L. Schneider, *The Conservative Century. From Reaction to Revolution*, Lanham–New York 2009, p. 42.

939 D. T. Critchlow, *The Conservative Ascendancy: How the GOP Right Made Political History*, Cambridge, Mass. 2007, p. 16.

940 G. H. Nash, *The Conservative Intellectual Movement in America Since 1945*, Wilmington 2006, p. 34.

fundamental immorality of all egalitarianism"[941] – continued to circulate on the American right. One passionate reader of his work was Barry Goldwater, the radically conservative candidate for U.S. president in 1964, who lost the election, but whose campaign became the organizational nucleus of the modern American right. In 1974, Hayek received the Nobel Prize in economics. Although he shared it with an economist with leftist views, Gunnar Myrdal, it was a sign of the changing spirit of the times. Also in 1974 Conservative British politician Margaret Thatcher founded in the U.K. the Centre for Policy Studies, a think-tank dedicated to the popularization of extreme neoliberal views.[942]

Another great figure in the neoliberal, free-market revolution against the state's involvement in the economy was Milton Friedman, an economist from Chicago (he received the Nobel Prize in 1976.). Friedman was not only the author of a new theory on the causes of inflation – which in his view had always been a political phenomenon induced by an excessive money supply, and thus *de facto* a product of government – but also an ideologue of neoliberalism: his 1962 book *Capitalism and Freedom* also drew attention on the marketplace of ideas, although it received a number of critical reviews.[943] Over the years, nearly half a million copies were sold. In his Introduction to the 1982 edition, he noted that "the change in the climate of opinion" that had taken place mainly during the 1970s had been "produced by experience, not by theory or philosophy":

> Russia and China, once the great hopes of the intellectual classes, had clearly gone sour. Great Britian, whose Fabian socialism exercised a dominant influence on American intellectuals, was in deep trouble. Closer to home, the intellectuals, always devotees of big government and by wide majorities supporters of the national Democratic party, had been disillusioned by the Vietnam War, particularly the role played by Presidents Kennedy and Johnson. Many of the great reform programs – such guidons of the past as welfare, public housing, support of trade unions, integration of schools, federal aid to education, affirmative action – were turning to ashes. As with the rest of the population, their pocketbooks were being hit with inflation and high taxes. These phenomena, not the persuasiveness of the ideas expressed in books dealing with principles, explain the transition from the overwhelming defeat of Barry Goldwater in 1964 to the overwhelming victory of Ronald Reagan in 1980 – two men with essentially the same program and the same message.[944]

941 F. A. von Hayek, *New Studies in Philosophy: Politics, Economics and the History of Ideas*, London 1978, p. 157.

942 K. R. Hoover, *Economics as Ideology…*, op. cit., p. 208.

943 W. Ruger, J. Meadowcroft, *Milton Friedman*, London 2011, p. 173.

944 M. Friedman, *Capitalism and Freedom*, Chicago–London 2002, p. xiii.

In the writings of Hayek and Friedman, moral and political arguments against state intervention in the economy intertwined with economics. Democracy, wrote Friedman, was inseparable from private property and the free market. The decade of crisis in the 1970s provided fertile ground for this message: neoliberalism seemed to offer a real political alternative to current policies, which had evidently exhausted their potential. In *Capitalism and Freedom*, among those things the government should not be involved in, Friedman enumerated agricultural subsidies, import tariffs and export restrictions, production controls, setting a minimum wage, regulating companies (banks, in particular), subsidised housing, pensions and disability pensions, licenses to conduct economic activity, and consumption during peacetime and running national parks. "This list is far from comprehensive", he added in conclusion.[945] Only the natural order of market forces was compatible with prosperity, democracy and freedom.

In 1950, while working in Paris as a consultant for the American agency responsible for administering the Marshall Plan, Friedman wrote a memorandum in which he recommended abandoning the system of fixed exchange rates established six years earlier at Bretton Woods (devised in part by Keynes, who himself had lost a fortune trading currencies in the 1920s). Friedman wrote that the fear of "speculators" was completely irrational: "People who argue that speculation is generally destabilising seldom realize that this is largely equivalent to saying that speculators lose money, since speculation can be destabilising in general only if speculators sell when currency is low in price and buy when it is high." As he put it years later, "It just seemed to me sensible that the only way you could make money was by buying low and sellinh high, and not the other way around. And if that's the case, then people who destabilize the market lose their shirt, and so they aren't going to be around for long."[946]

This argument was presented without any empirical evidence: to Friedman it was obvious that the market, left to its own means, would return to a state of equilibrium, and was an effective economic instrument.

Friedman's contribution to the neoliberal revolution of the 1970s went far beyond his ideological writings and monetary theory of inflation and market fluctuations (laid out in the 1960s in a monumental work co-written with Anna Schwartz, *Monetary History of the United States, 1857–1960*).[947]

---

945 Ibid., pp. 35–36

946 J. Fox, *The Myth of the Rational Market: A History of Risk, Reward, and Delusion on Wall Street*, New York 2009, pp. 92–93.

947 M. Friedman, A. Schwartz, *A Monetary History of the United States, 1867–1960*, Princeton 1963.

In a lecture delivered at the 80th annual meeting of the American Economic Association on 29 December 1967,[948] Friedman questioned the "permanant trade-off" between inflation and unemployment – an idea that had provided the justification for Keynesian economic ideas. Following the statistical surveys conducted by the New Zealand economist William A. Phillips, the results of which were published in 1958, it had been generally accepted that lower inflation was accompanied by higher unemployment, and this mechanism had come to be considered in both the U.S. and the U.K. as a scientifically established economic constant (represented by the so-called Phillips curve).[949] Friedman introduced the concept of a "natural rate of unemployment", characteristic for a given economy. Those steering economic policy could not know the real natural rate of unemployment, and any attempt to bring the unemployment rate below its natural level stimulated inflationary expectations. (This did not mean that political decisions had no influence on it: e.g., establishing a higher minimum wage raised the natural rate of unemployment because it no longer paid to hire the least productive workers).

Friedman's message had a very practical political moral. Politicians could control the nominal money supply. Their control over the real economy however was in practice very limited and could easily do more harm than good. Friedman said that monetary authorities could not use their control of the money supply to control "real" phenomena– "the real rate of interest, the rate of unemployment, the level of real national income, the real quantity of money, the rate of growth of real national income, or the rare of growth of the real quantity of money."[950] Economic theory told Friedman the same thing as his moral and political convictions.[951]

Another economist, Edmund S. Phelps, arrived at very similar conclusions to Friedman's at about the same time.[952] More important than his strictly economic theories – which neither politicians nor the journalists who shaped public opinion necessarily understood – were his political conclusions. These were expressed

948 M. Friedman, "The Role of Monetary Policy", *The American Economic Review*, vol. 58, no. 1, March 1968.

949 A. W. Phillips, "The Relation Between Unemployment and the Rate of Change of Money Wage Rates in the United Kingdom, 1861–1957", *Economica*, vol. 25, no. 100, November 1958.

950 M. Friedman, "The Role of Monetary Policy...", op. cit.

951 M. De Vroey, "Getting Rid of Keynes? A Reflection on the Recent History of Macroeconomics", [in:] *Keynes's General Theory After Seventy Years*, eds. R. W. Dimand, R. A. Mundell, A. Vercelli, Houndmills–New York 2010, p. 172.

952 E. S. Phelps, "Money-Wage Dynamics and Labor-Market Equilibrium", *Journal of Political Economy*, vol. 76, no. 4, 1968.

using the same language economists were beginning to use to talk about the economy. In his memoirs, Phelps uses such phrases as "the economy can be blown off the natural path it has been following" or "the natural rate of unemployment."[953]

Natural in economics meant what the market determines without state intervention. The latter is thus *unnatural*. This was the language of a new and promising radical break with the economic orthodoxy of the 1960s.

Unemployment was not caused by a lack of jobs, but was the result of decisions made by individuals; in an article from a collection edited by Phelps, the authors echo his claims, defining the unemployed as individuals "who regard the wage rates at which they could currently be employed as temporarily low, and who therefore choose to wait or search for improved conditions rather than invest in moving or changing their occupation".[954] People were unemployed because they found the working conditions available to them unattractive – unemployment was thus a matter of matching pay expectations to the realities of the labour market. Unemployment therefore did not result from a lack of demand for labour – all the unemployed could find jobs if they agreed to lower earnings.[955]

Another turning point in the evolution of economics was the theory of rational expectations formulated by Robert Lucas in 1972.[956] Not only did he assume that unemployment was the result of a mismatch of expectations between the unemployed and the labour market, he developed this idea into theory in which such mismatches were the result of false expectations: if everyone could correctly predict the future, supply and demand in markets would remain in balance, and a state of full employment would be reached. The cause of fluctuations in employment, according to his model, were the unpredictable policies (especially monetary policies) of the state, because they caused rational market players to make mistakes in their forecasts – thus creating short-term fluctuations in

---

953 E. S. Phelps, *Recollections of My Past Research in Economics. Speech on the Award of an Honorary Professorship*, Beijing Technology and Business University, Beijing, 1 June 2005, http://www.columbia.edu/~esp2/BeijingTechAndBusUniversity2005D4.pdf.

954 Lucas, R. E. and L. A. Rapping, "Real Wages, Unemployment, and Inflation", [in:] *Microeconomic Foundations of Employment and Inflation Theory*, eds. E. Phelps, et al., New York 1970, p. 285. Cf. also R. Leeson, *The Eclipse of Keynesianism: The Political Economy of the Chicago Counter-Revolution*, Houndmills–New York 2000; R. Leeson, "The Political Economy of the Inflation-Unemployment Trade-Off", *History of Political Economy*, vol. 29, no. 1, 1997.

955 R. E. Backhouse, *The Puzzle of Modern Economics…*, op. cit., pp. 130–131.

956 R. E. Lucas, "Expectations and the Neutrality of Money", *Journal of Economic Theory*, vol. 4, no. 2, 1972.

production and employment. Lucas' theory provided a much stronger argument against state intervention in the economy than the writings of Friedman and the monetarists.[957] Lucas, a former student of Friedman's, was aware of this. "For many of us, the shock wave of Friedman's libertarian-conservative ideas forced a rethinking of our whole social philosophy," he later recalled: "I tried to hold on to my New Deal politics, and remember voting for Kennedy in 1960 … But however we voted, Friedman's students came away with the sense that we had acquired a powerful apparatus for thinking about economic and social questions."[958]

In the new perspective of the 1970s, inflation acted on the economy like a stimulant whose effect was only temporary. Later, expectations of inflation are incorporated into the calculations of marketplace participants. In practice, Keynesian "stimuli" worked like a drug – increasing doses were need to achieve the desired effect, and its costs, in the form of inflation, rose.

In the late 1960s, the belief grew among a group of economists associated with the University of Chicago that the market was not only an instrument efficient, but a perfect one. Eugene Fama formulated a definition of an efficient market in relation to stock exchanges and equity prices: a "weak" understanding of market efficiencies meant that an investor could not attain a higher rate of profit than the average for the overall market based on an analysis of past trends; "semi-strong" efficiency meant that an investor could not beat the market based on publicly available information; "strong" efficiency meant that the market was so perfect that even investors with access to inside corporate information would not be able to outsmart it. Many economists from Chicago – including Fama – acknowledged this hypothesis, at least in its weakest form.[959] The market represented collective, distributed wisdom that reacted instantly and adjusted perfectly to every swing in supply and demand; any state intervention in this mechanism was only a feeble attempt at manipulation, doomed to failure and by necessity harmful.

In 1974, Robert Barro added another argument to the already hefty arsenal available to opponents of state intervention in the economy, formulating a theory called "Ricardian equivalence".[960] The government, it said, could borrow to stimulate the economy, but rational investors knew that at some point it would have to repay this debt, and this repayment would require higher taxes in the future. According to the theory of rational expectations, the owners of capital would then

957 R. E. Backhouse, *The Puzzle of Modern Economics…*, op. cit., p. 131.

958 Quoted in J. Fox, *The Myth of the Rational Market…*, op. cit., p. 94.

959 J. Fox, *The Myth of the Rational Market…*, op. cit., p. 101.

960 R. Barro, "Are Government Bonds Net Wealth?", *Journal of Political Economy*, no. 82, 1974.

invest in government bonds. The level of savings corresponded to the level of public debt. In this way, public spending "crowded out" private investment from the economy, and so the level of demand in the economy remained the same. This meant that government spending could not increase demand. In the case of an open economy open to capital flows from abroad, the mechanism worked similarly: repayment of debt required the sale of public assets to foreign investors, thereby reducing the revenue base of the government in the future and raising the prospect of future tax increases. The government could increase the deficit to stimulate the economy, but this would only be an illusion, and an expensive one at that ("the presence of government transaction costs implies that the net-wealth effect of government bonds would actually be negative," Barro wrote).[961]

Economic orthodoxy had changed. In 1978, Robert Lucas and Thomas Sargent were already writing of "the spectacular failure of the Keynsian models", which was unable, in their opinion, the anticipate the stagflation of the 1970s:

> That these predictions were wildly incorrect, and that the doctrine on which they were based is fundamentally flawed, are now simple matters of fact, involving no novelties in economic theory. The task which faces contemporary students of the business cycle is that of sorting through the wreckage, determining which features of that remarkable intellectual event called the Keynesian Revolution can be put to good use, and which others must be discarded.[962]

3. Disillusionment with the Leviathan

The 1970s also brought increasing use of the market as a model – based on a vision of a society consisting of rational and calculating individuals, concerned primarily with benefitting themselves – rather than social phenomena. A pioneer in this field was Gary Becker (who, like Phelps, and Lucas, received a Nobel Prize in economics).[963] Since the 1950s, he had been applying standard economic techniques to problems that were previously on the margins of interest in the discipline. Becker described e.g., the attitude of people towards the education system in the same way that companies invested in machines – education was an "investment

961 R. J. Barrow, "Are Government Bonds Net Wealth", Journal of Political Economy, vol. 82, no. 6, 1974, p. 1097.

962 R. E. Lucas, T. J. Sargent, "After Keynesian Macroeconomics", [in:] *Rational Expectations and Econometric Practice*, vol. 2, eds. R. E. Lucas, T. J. Sargent, Minneapolis 1981, p. 295.

963 Becker in 1992, Lucas in 1995, Phelps in 2006.

in human capital".[964] Later he took up issues that had generally tended to interest sociologists – the issues of discrimination, marriage, divorce, and crime.[965] In a widely-discussed essay about crime, he suggested that "a useful theory of criminal behavior can dispense with special theories of anomie, psychological inadequacies, or inheritance of special traits and simply extend the economist's usual analysis of choice."[966] Man was a rational individual calculating profits, risks and loss: crime in Becker's view was the result of rational – if not necessarily conscious – analysis.

In around 1960, several economists, in particular Mancur Olson, Gordon Tullock and James Buchanan, took up decision-making issues outside of the market – in a wide sphere of social behaviour that included, among others things, politics, including the behaviour of the bureaucracy, elections and lobbying.[967] In the 1970s, public choice theory became an integral part of economics and had a huge impact on economic policy, because it often dealt with situations in which the government failed, because politicians and bureaucrats themselves acted primarily as individuals focused on individual economic advantage.[968]

In terms of peripheral and the poorest countries – known in the 1970s under the current nomenclature as "developing countries" – economic analyses of their mechanisms of power were essentially reports on corruption and increasing social differences between young elites and the rest of society. Government was apparently not a vehicle for growth, but merely a burden – very often, if not always. Since the state was the source of pensions and inefficiencies, it needed to reduce its impact on the economy as much as possible.

Since the early 1970s, the literature on "power to pensions" and corruption was rapidly growing. While in the 1950s, the phenomenon of mismanagement

---

964 G. S. Becker, "Investment in Human Capital: A Theoretical Analysis", *Journal of Political Economy*, vol. 70, no. 5, October 1962; cf. also G. S. Becker, *Human Capital: A Theoretical and Empirical Analysis, with Special Reference to Education*, Chicago 1983.

965 Cf., e.g. G. S. Becker, *The Economics of Discrimination*, Chicago 1971; G. S. Becker, *The Economic Approach to Human Behavior*, Chicago 1976; G. S. Becker, H. G. Lewis, "On the Interaction between the Quantity and Quality of Children", *Journal of Political Economy*, vol. 81, no. 2, 1973; G. S. Becker, *A Treatise on the Family*, Cambridge 1981.

966 G. S. Becker, "Crime and Punishment: An Economic Approach", [in:] *Essays in the Economics of Crime and Punishment*, ed. G. S. Becker, Minneapolis 1974, p. 2

967 Cf. *Teoria wyboru publicznego. Wstęp do ekonomicznej analizy polityki*, ed. J. Wilkin, Warszawa 2005; L. Filipowicz, K. Opawski, "Teoria wyboru publicznego: wybrane koncepcje badawcze", *Ekonomista*, no. 3, 1992; *Elementy teorii wyboru społecznego*, ed. G. Lissowski, Warszawa 2001.

968 Cf. Mancur Olson and Ronald Wintrobe's analysis of Stalinist dictatorship in Chapter 3.

was given in practice no place in models of growth, it now assumed a dominant position.

A classic example of such an analysis was a very influential article by Anne O. Krueger of the American Economic Review in June 1974.[969] Analysing, among other things, the examples of India and Turkey, Krueger evaluated the negative impact of restrictions on international trade on overall well-being. "The restrictions give rise to rents of a variety of forms, and people often compete for rents," she wrote. The main source of inefficiency and costs to society for Krueger was the discrepancy between the private and social cost of various activities. The state was responsible for causing this division, e.g., by issuing import licenses from which well-connected business executives profited, while the rest of the population was forced to pay more for goods. Trade restrictions led to corruption, smuggling and the creation of a black market; all of these phenomena were profitable for those who took part in them, but they reduced the overall level of prosperity. Moreover, Krueger argued that the more the state intervened in the economy, the greater opportunity to obtain state benefits – legally and illegally – and the greater the overall losses: e.g., import licenses specifying the exact amount of goods that could be imported are much more costly from a social point of view than high tariffs.

The scepticism about the government's role in the economy that had a lead role in this new theory and the sense of disappointment caused by the crisis resulted in new policy recommendations for peripheral countries. The turning point was a seminar in Houston, Texas, which took place on 3–5 February 1977. The participants were eminent economists actively involved in development.[970] The atmosphere was sombre. There was a widespread feeling of disappointment in the achievements of the past three decades. Albert O. Hirschman enumerated the failures of development policy: growing social inequality, a lack of progress in the fight against poverty, overwhelming incompetence in the UN bodies charged with supporting development.

> There are also the terrible facts of mass slaughter, expulsion of ethnic minorities (often entrepreneurial and therefore hated) and political opponents, imprisonment wihtout trial, torture and other violations of basic human rights, and the $370 billion spent on armaments, compared with $17 billion on net concessional transfers (in 1975).[971]

---

969 A. O. Krueger, "The Political Economy of the Rent-Seeking Society", *The American Economic Review*, vol. 64, no. 3, June 1974.

970 *Toward a New Strategy for Development: a Rothko Chapel Colloquium*, ed. A. O. Hirschman, Oxford 1979.

971 Ibid., p. 46.

The paper also contained a comprehensive list under the telling title "discarded ideas." The ideas about how to achieve rapid economic development that had dominated in previous decades, Hirschman argued, had arisen in the wake of the perceived success of the Marshall Plan in Western Europe (and the success of planned economies). "The problem of development is, however, fundamentally different from the problem of reconstructing war-damaged advanced economies", he wrote.[972] Among the "discarded ideas" he included prioritizing industrialization and infrastructure, central economic planning, and the notion that the key to economic growth was high savings and investment rates. He noted: "It was found, however, that capital accounted for only a relatively small portion of growth, and that growth was not synonymous with development."[973]

Thinking based on "foreign trade pessimism" was unjustified as was the belief that rapid increases in production indicated an increase in prosperity. The elites in developing countries underestimated the negative impact of rapid population growth and environmental devastation, and perceived Western aid from a very narrow perspective – as a source of capital and technology. Meanwhile, they should have been learning from developed countries how to conduct effective educational, monetary, regional, employment and trade policies. Hirschman said:

> Policies were dominated by the reaction to colonialism. The governments of many newly independent states wanted to do what the colonial powers had neglected to do. This reinforced the desire for planning, for industrialization and for import substitution. It also fed the desire, after the achievement of political independence, for economic self-sufficiency. Latin American countries, which had been independent for a long time, felt that economic independence, which did not follow from political independence, was elusive.[974]

Moreover, international institutions such as the World Bank and the UN had overlooked the failures of this former strategy. The emphasis on the development of industrial production was abandoned in favour of an aim that seemed much less ambitious, namely ensuring a minimum level of existence in the poorest countries for millions of starving paupers, who were growing in numbers. Hopes for a "leap into modernity" and the structural modernization of society had turned out to be merely pipe dreams. More and more attention was now being paid to research on corruption and the informal sector.[975] The world of the periphery had changed,

---

972 Ibid.

973 Ibid.

974 Ibid., p. 47.

975 E. Thornbecke, "The Evolution of the Development Doctrine, 1950–2005", [in:] *Advancing Development. Core Themes in Global Economics*, eds. G. Mavrotas, A. Shorrocks, Houndmills–New York 2007, p. 11.

but by no means in the direction suggested by the classical theory of modernization: its societies were not becoming more like those of the developed West in either structural or political terms.

The optimism of the 1960s gave way to pessimism. The Western world was in crisis, and tested and proven prescriptions for economic growth had ceased to provide results. Fears about population pressures, environmental destruction and the depletion of natural resources – which began to be voiced after the oil crisis in 1973 – were grounded in books like *The Population Bomb*, published by Paul Erlich in 1968, and a report released in 1972 by the Club of Rome that had been prepared by a group of Western intellectuals.[976] It contained a description of the results of a computer simulation, which included five "trends of global concern": "accelerating industrialization, rapid population growth, widespread malnutrition, depletion of nonrenewable resources, and a deteriorating environment."[977] The report foresaw reaching "the limits to growth [...] within the next one hundred years" and predicted that the result would be a "sudden and uncontrollable decline in both population and industrial capacity."[978] It was not only the future that filled the authors with fear: some feared industrial civilization was on the brink of collapse as a result of the current global crisis, which they wrote represented a "complex of problems troubling men of all nations: poverty in the midst of plenty; degradation of the environment; loss of faith in institutions; uncontrolled urban spread; insecurity of employment, alienation of youth; rejection of traditional values; and inflation and other monetary and economic disruptions."[979]

From this perspective, even the successes of development in recent decades did not seem convincing. The American economist Hollis Chenery wrote in a book published by the World Bank in 1974:

> It is now clear that more than a decade of rapid growth in underdeveloped countries has been of little or no benefit to perhaps a third of their population ... Paradoxically, while growth policies have succeeded beyond the expectations of the first development decade, the very idea of aggregate growth as a social objective has increasingly been called into question.[980]

---

976 P. R. Erlich, *Population Bomb*, London 1971; D. H. Meadows, et al., *The Limits to Growth*, Penguin Books, New York 1972.

977 D. H. Meadows, et al., *Limits to Growth*, op. cit., p. 21.

978 Ibid., p. 23.

979 Ibid., p. 10.

980 Quoted in R. E. Wood, *From Marshall Plan to Debt Crisis. Foreign Aid and Development Choices in the World Economy,* Berkeley–Los Angeles 1986, p. 197.

Although the economic goal of the United Nations' "decade of development" – annual GDP growth exceeding 5 percent – had been achieved in many developing countries, this was accompanied by a sense of disappointment and the realization that prosperity remained a distant prospect, and that the price for this growth had been rising inequality. In 1971, Mahbub ul Haq, an expert at the World Bank, wrote:

> In Pakistan, which increased a healthy growth rate during the 1960s, unemployment increased, real wages in the industrial sector declined by one third, per capita income disparity between East and West Pakistan nearly doubled, and concentratiosn of industrial wealth became an explosive economic and political issue. And in 1968, while the international world was still applauding Pakistan as a model of development, the system exploded – not only for political reasons, but for economic unrest. Brazil has recently achieved a growth rate close to 7 percent, but continuing maldistribution of income continues to threaten the very fabric of its society.[981]

Similar reflections were the order of the day. Soon, the World Bank felt compelled to declare that it "at no time embraced W. W. Rostow's stage theory of development and the 'takeoff into self-sustained growth.'"[982] The death of modernization theory was thus officially announced. It joined the repertoire of "discarded ideas."

The 1970s brought another important experiment in social policy. In September 1973, a military coup in Chile overthrew the democratically elected government of President Salvador Allende and replaced it with a military dictatorship led by a junta headed by Augusto Pinochet.

After the coup, a group of young Chilean economists trained at the University of Chicago, known as the "Chicago boys", carried out a free-market revolution – necessitated by the inflation and economic chaos into which the country had been plunged toward the end of Allende's rule.[983] In 1955, Theodore W. Schulz, then Chair of Economics at the University of Chicago, travelled to Chile and signed an agreement with the Universidad Católica de Chile in Santiago for a select group of students to do postgraduate study in Chicago. Between 1955 and 1963 some 30 young Chileans took advantage of this opportunity, and were imbued with the ideas of Friedman and Hayek. Another result of this agreement was the creation of the Centro de Investigaciones Económicas, a research institute that regularly hosted visiting professors from Chicago. In the late 1960s, the alumni of both institutions began teaching economics in Chile. In 1968, they founded a private

981 Quoted in Ibid., p. 198.

982 Ibid., op. cit., p. 199.

983 P. E. Sigmund, *The Overthrow of Allende and the Politics of Chile*, Pittsburgh 1980, p. 283.

think-tank, Centro de Estudios Socio-Económicos, in which, among other things, they wrote a radical neoliberal electoral programme for Jorge Alessandri, the candidate of the Chilean right in the 1970 presidential election.[984]

The entire project, writes historian Juan Gabriel Valdés, was a carefully planned transfer of new political ideas to a peripheral country.[985] Chile was supposed to be, as the project administrators from Chicago wrote in one report, a "laboratory" for creating a process that would make it possible to change the dominant thinking on the economy in the societies of peripheral countries.[986] From their perspective, poverty and backwardness in Chile were the result of bad political decisions, as was the inflation that plagued the country. All that was required to deal with them was to unleash the forces of the free market and entrepreneurship.

The new government carried out a radical privatization of businesses previously nationalized by Allende and lowered import tariffs. It also established a fixed exchange rate pegged to the dollar. This shock therapy was meant to set in motion a radical Darwinian cleansing of the economy of inefficient companies. Under no circumstances would the State bail out failing companies. The right to strike was also drastically limited and labour unions dissolved (workers could organize only at the factory level). In addition, private individuals and businesses could borrow as much money as they wanted money from wherever they chose, including from abroad – this was their own business and responsibility. After a deep recession which lasted until 1976, Chile's economy began to grow rapidly, with the average annual GDP growth rate exceeding 7.2 percent.[987] Inflation fell (although it still exceeded 30 percent in 1980), and real wages grew at a rate of 9 percent annually.[988]

Two apostles of neoliberalism – Hayek and Friedman – supported Pinochet's reforms, although they distanced themselves from the crimes of his regime, which was extremely repressive.[989] The irony of the situation in which neoliberal

---

984 P. Silva, *In the Name of Reason. Technocrats and Politics in Chile*, University Park 2008, pp. 148–149.

985 J. G. Valdés, *Pinochet's Economists: The Chicago School of Economics in Chile*, Cambridge 1995, pp. 127–128.

986 Ibid., p. 130.

987 Ibid., p. 27.

988 P. Meller, *Un Siglo de Economia Política Chilena (1890–1990)*, Santiago 1998, pp. 196–198.

989 Cf. A. Rouquié, "The Military in Latin American Politics Since 1930", [in:] *Latin America. Politics and Society since 1930*, ed. L. Bethell, Cambridge–New York 1998, pp. 170–171.

economic principles were put into practice by a dictatorship that had to answer for the deaths of at least several thousand people seemed to long remain unnoticed by them.[990] Under the pressure of propaganda about this "economic miracle" it was also easy to overlook the rapidly widening social divisions.[991] While in 1969, the top 20 percent of society received 43.2 percent of total earnings, in 1978 this number had reached 58.2 percent.[992] Soon the pension system was changed (Chileans were to set aside money individually for retirement in private accounts) and a system of vouchers was introduced for educational services (in place of a system of free public education).[993]

Friedman met with Pinochet in 1975 to advise him on economic matters. Hayek admired Pinochet's Chile so much that he decided to hold a meeting of his Mont Pelerin Society in Viña del Mar, the seaside resort where the coup against Allende had been planned.[994]

In 1978, Friedman wrote a famous letter to the *London Times*, in which he argued that "I have not been able to find a single person even in much maligned Chile, who did not agree that personal freedom was much greater under Pinocheta than it had been under Allende."[995]

Later, Friedman added in a letter to *Newsweek* that "despite my sharp disagreement with the authoritarian political system in Chile, I do not regard it as an evil for an economist to render technical economic advice to the Chilean government". He did so, he said "to help end the plague of inflation," which was just as much an act of humanitarian aid as a doctor helping to fight an epidemic.[996]

The economic miracle turned out to be short-lived. In 1982, Chile was plunged once again into crisis. The global recession caused the price of the country's main export commodity – copper – to fall by a third. The resulting foreign trade deficit proved untenable at the peso's fixed exchange rate (the decision to maintain the

---

990 L. H. Oppenheim, *Politics in Chile. Democracy, Authoritarianism and the Search for Development*, Boulder 1999, p. 141.

991 V. Valdivia Ortiz de Zárate, *El Golpe Después Del Golpe: Leigh vs. Pinochet: Chile 1960–1980*, Santiago 2003, p. 136.

992 L. H. Oppenheim, *Politics in Chile...*, op. cit., p. 147.

993 S. Haggard, R. R. Kaufman, *Development, Democracy and Welfare States. Latin America, East Asia and Eastern Europe*, Princeton–Oxford 2008, p. 108.

994 C. Robin, *The Reactionary Mind. Conservatism from Edmund Burke to Sarah Palin*, Oxford–New York 2011, p. 74.

995 L. Manzetti, *Neoliberalism, Accountability, and Reform Failures in Emerging Markets*, University Park 2009, p. 250.

996 M. Friedman, R. D. Friedman, *Two Lucky People. Memoirs*, Chicago 1998, p. 596.

fixed exchange rate was later seen as a serious mistake and the main cause of the crisis). Households which had taken out huge loans during the consumer boom and were now unable to pay them back. In 1983, GDP fell by 15 percent, industrial production declined by 20 percent, and unemployment reached 30 percent. Private financial institutions suffered losses that on average exceeded capital reserves by two-fold.[997] The government was forced to take over so many banks that people began calling the period "the Chicago road to socialism".[998] Friedman wrote then that the regime would be unable to cope with the economy until it also provided its citizens with political freedom.

Yet the negative consequences of the neoliberal reforms long remained in the shadow of the obvious economic successes of the Pinochet government. Perhaps they had to go unnoticed, just as it was easy in the 1930s and 1940s to ignore the high social costs of planned economies, and in the 1960s to rave about the achievements of Mao's China.

Only incorrigible idealists on the left still believed in the efficacy of a state-run economy. Well-known economist Joan Robinson, whose theoretical writings were considered to be within the Keynesian mainstream, was just ending her fascination with Maoism. She wrote in a book review on the economic successes of communist North Korea: "Obviously, sooner or later the country must be reunited by absorbing the South into socialism."[999]

The "climate of opinion" (in the words of Milton Friedman) or "structure of feeling" (in the words of the literary critic Raymond Williams) had changed, and with this change in attitudes, came changes in policy.[1000] In 1979, Margaret Thatcher won the elections in the U.K. under the banner of a return to a "true" free-market and reducing the power of the unions. In 1980, conservative neoliberal Ronald Reagan was elected U.S. President. Yet, even earlier, the Carter administration had begun deregulating many sectors of the U.S. economy, and the fight against inflation had become a priority – even at the cost of recession and unemployment.[1001] In 1979, the Islamic revolution of Ayatollah Khomeini overthrew the authoritarian and secular government of the Shah in Iran, which

---

997 J. G. Valdés, *Pinochet's Economists…*, op. cit., p. 29. Cf. also P. O'Brien, J. Roddick, *Chile: The Pinochet Decade: The Rise and Fall of the Chicago Boys*, New York 1983.

998 D. Yergin, J. Stanislaw, *Commanding Heights…*, op. cit., p. 240.

999 M. S. Turner, *Joan Robinson and the Americans*, Armonk 1989, p. 92.

1000 J. Higgins, *Raymond Williams: Literature, Marxism and Cultural Materialism*, Abingdon–New York 1999, p. 37.

1001 W. C. Biven, *Jimmy Carter's Economy. Policy in the Age of Limits*, Chapel Hill–London 2002, p. 237 ff.

had long been the model for modernization in the Middle East.[1002] In 1979, Senegal was the first country in Africa to receive a bail-out loan from the World Bank and the International Monetary Fund – and under their pressure began a program of structural reforms in the spirit of neoliberalism.[1003] Since the late 1970s, Poland had been in continual crisis, deepened further by the Solidarity revolution, which exposed the weaknesses of its socialist-style planned economy and the illusory nature of Gierek's "economic miracle".

The 1970s in fact brought a challenge to the entire modernist vision of the world – from architecture to industrial policy. State economic planning had been a product of the same era as the geometrical, rationally planned modern blocks of flats built in "housing factories" that were now becoming a thing of the past. In a famous essay written in 1977, historian and architecture critic Charles Jencks assigns a place and date for this "death of modernism": "Modern Architecture died in St. Louis, Missouri on July 15, 1972 at 3.32 p.m. (or thereabouts) when the infamous Pruitt-Igoe scheme, or rather several of its slab blocks, were given the final coup de grace by dynamite [...] Boom, boom, boom."[1004]

The housing estate about which he was writing had been rejected by its residents and become a nest of crime and pathology; devastated and abandoned – it was ultimately blown up.

The idea that you could schedule people's lives rationally and centrally – including what they would eat, where they would live, what their professional and family life would be like from cradle to grave – proved to be a utopia. The geometrically planned state-run villages in Tanzania were no less a failure than Pruitt-Igoe in St. Louis. But at least they could be dismantled without the use of dynamite.

1002 Cf. e.g. *The Making of Modern Iran. State and Society under Riza Shah, 1921–1941*, ed. S. Cronin, London–New York 2003.

1003 N. van de Walle, *African Economies and the Politics of Permanent Crisis, 1979–1999*, Cambridge–New York 2001, p. 1.

1004 C. Jencks, *The Story of Post-Modernism*, Chichester 2011, p. 27.

Chapter 9. Conclusion

The politics of growth: 1943–1980

1. The search for an ideal type

The eminent historian Witold Kula once wrote that past economic decisions often appear incomprehensible and clearly absurd in retrospect. Commenting on the research of another historian, Tadeusz Korzon, Kula wrote:

> [Tadeusz] Korzon, in exploring the history of the factories founded by magnates in Poland in the eighteenth century, found he was unable to explain them using modern, rational categories. Everything about them, starting with their "poor" location, seemed absurd. He thus turned to explanations based on the "unprofessionalism" of the feudal lords who founded them. But if we introduce into our analysis an eighteenth-century category that was no longer part of the calculations made by businesses in Korzon's times, namely the distinction between cash and non-cash expenses in a feudal economy, the problem can be explained according to internally consistent criteria. How many of the elements that determined human behaviour in Poland in the eighteenth century are we unaware of?[1005]

Korzon, wrote Kula, simply accepted that all business enterprises were established to earn profits. But this was an ahistorical assumption. Prince Karol Radziwiłł, (1734–1790), for example, founded the famous Slutsk belt factory for political reasons, as well: he gave the belts as gifts during the Confederation of Radom in order to win over supporters, and used them to reward his allies and show off his wealth and splendour.

Concepts about economic growth that were widely held in peripheral countries in the postwar period are presented today in an equally ahistorical manner. From the perspective of the neoliberal economic thinking and writing that has dominated since the 1980s, earlier ideas seem to be wrong, absurd and incomprehensible, and are often explained as being merely products of ideology.[1006] Here are just two of many such examples. In a booklet entitled "The Economy", historian Wojciech Roszkowski describes the "rise and fall of the command system" as primarily an attempt to realise a communist utopia that was doomed from the

1005 W. Kula, *Rozważania o historii*, PWN, Warszawa 1958, p. 90.

1006 Cf. e.g. W. Roszkowski, *Gospodraka. Wzrost i upadek systemu nakazowo-rozdzielczego*, Warszawa 2008; L. Balcerowicz, *Systemy gospodarcze*, Warszawa 1989; W. Kuczyński, *Po wielkim skoku*, Warszawa 2012 (in particular, the Introduction by L. Balcerowicz).

outset to failure and led to tragic results. A much broader perspective is taken by journalists Daniel Yergin and Joseph Stanislaw, whose book *The Commanding Heights: The Battle for the World Economy* is an attempt to describe the intellectual and political sources of the free market's return to favour in the 1970s and 1980s. The popularity of economic planning and state intervention in the economy is for them a historical mistake, though perhaps an understandable one in light of the circumstances – including the Great Depression and the popularity of Keynesian economic theory – but also something that was finally overcome.[1007]

The thesis of the present book is different: it attempts to show the rational nature of the political ideologies underpinning efforts to achieve economic growth in underdeveloped countries. It also attempts to show the theoretical and historical contexts in which economic decisions were taken that today may seem absurd and incomprehensible, but which at the time were considered, even by experts, natural, rational and innovative. It therefore represents an attempt to show the historicity of this project.

It is difficult to reduce to a single model the wide variety of ideas about the economy found in peripheral countries after 1945. The means used to attempt to achieve accelerated development, however, had many common features. Thus, although there were many of them, it is worth trying to describe an ideal type (as defined by Max Weber) from among these political and economic strategies.

They can generally be divided into three main spheres – the goals and values pursued; the political and economic techniques rulers had at their disposal to achieve them; and finally, the political calculations that both allowed them to build a social base for their power and that limited their room for manoeuvre. All of these spheres were organically linked. Many modern scholars of political thought, most of whom adhere to rational choice theory, would most likely accept that ideology is the mainstay of political power and provides the only justification for it. From this perspective, what counts most are the group interests of the elites; discourse is merely a product of these interests. Theory and practice went hand in hand, and it is impossible to prove the former preceded the latter. In Latin American countries, for example, a policy of import substitution had been in place since the 1920s, before economic theory provided a justification for it.

The model rhetoric for accelerated development included several commonly occurring views and arguments, which were expressed with different levels of intensity and in different configurations. The starting point was a critique of capitalism – if not capitalism in its Western European form, then that form with

---

1007 D. Yergin, J. Stanislaw, *Commanding Heights…* op. cit.

which the modernizing elites in peripheral countries were dealing with at the time. Here is a summary of these main arguments:

- The Great Depression demonstrated the limits of the opportunities for growth in free-market capitalism.
- The Great Depression also tangibly and painfully showed poor and agricultural countries their double dependence on the West – as a source of capital and as a market for locally produced goods. After the experience of the Great Depression, becoming independent from both one and the other became an obvious priority. Western capital markets started to become available to poor countries on a wide scale only in the 1970s. Before this time, the West could not be counted on as a source of capital (a painful fact many countries became aware of – among them Poland – during the interwar period): capital flowed in and out of countries according to its own dictates and was invested in export-oriented sectors such as mining, which often perpetuated an economic structure that was undesirable from the point of view of the modernizing elite. Global markets were equally capricious, and a fall in prices of a major export commodity – for example, cocoa in Ghana or coal in Poland – created problems for to the entire country (and its government).
- Peripheral capitalism was not conducive to growth: it did not assure an adequate rate of capital accumulation and investment. It was also inextricably linked to an anachronistic, semi-feudal social structure, which acted as a brake on development. The small surplus that that these very poor societies could generate was consumed by the traditional (and often ethnically foreign) elite or exported abroad, where it provided additional capital for foreign investors.
- Criticism of capitalism was generally associated with economic nationalism and social radicalism. Capitalism brought poverty and misery to the masses, and wealth to a small elite (often linked by family and financially ties to the former colonial powers or the USA). The fear of foreign economic and political domination increased the feeling of a need for mobilization. The fear of external threats – whether from neo-colonialism or an armed invasion – was common in modernization projects such as Stalinist industrialization, the Great Leap Forward in China, and Nkrumah's economic programme. This was an important reason why industrialization also had a strategic and military dimension, and why economic interests were often deliberately subordinated to an imagined or real strengthening of the power of the state. It was also a reason for haste. For example, in 1929 the Soviet Political Bureau

expected a Western invasion within five years.[1008] The stakes for success in programmes for industrialization included their very survival. Extreme situations demanded – as many have said – radical methods.

- The last argument was that an accelerated programme of development was attainable, and its supporters provided as positive, or so they thought, examples: Fascist Italy and Germany (before World War II), the USSR and Japan. Imitation was never total: even South Korea's Park Chung Hee, despite being in awe of the Japanese model, did not seek to duplicate it. The examples cited above serve to show that a "leap into modernity" in a short time was possible; it merely required a mobilising of resources.

This is not a description of reality at that time, only a summary of the arguments made then. It shows that from this perspective, economic development was always primarily a social and political endeavour, not an economic one *per se*. It also had a clearly outlined objective: emancipation from foreign tutelage and influence, a strengthening of the country's military power, or at least a strengthening of its international position and the legitimacy of the power elites who had undertaken this great task. It also aimed to transform the country's social structure and introduce modern technologies. Economic calculations and raising the country's standard of living were usually left in the background, although they remained important, at least on the level of rhetoric. Business was to serve social objectives and not merely earn profits. Economic growth was only part of a wider modernization project. The standard of living of citizens was an important long-term objective, but if it had to be sacrificed in the short term, it was necessary to do so – for the sake of a better future. This was an essential element of Feldman's the growth model in the USSR, of the practice of the Chinese Communists, and of Nkrumah's and Gomulka's programmes for industrialization. Since the country lacked capital and the West could not be counted on for help, it was necessary to acquire it in the only place it could be found, in the shallow pockets of the citizens. In poor agriculture countries, this always meant the peasants or farmers – both in the case of Stalin's Russia and in Nkrumah's Ghana. Although the level of violence of the two regimes (and their effectiveness) was incomparable, they shared similar ideas in regard to capital accumulation.

The general guidelines for economic policy grew out of these premises. The list of tools governments had at their disposal to move their countries onto a path of rapid growth was extensive:

1008 Cf. A. Erlich, *The Soviet Industrialization Debate*, op. cit., p. 28.

- Nationalization and direct investment in industry by the state. From the perspective of the time, a number of arguments spoke in favour of the state taking ownership of its largest enterprises. National assets would come under control of the national government: profits would flow into the national treasury, not into the pockets of foreigners, and could be used to support further domestic investments. The nationalization of oil production in Mexico in 1938. – one of many such examples – was seen as a great national triumph over the power of the West, and the crowning moment of the revolution.[1009] "Nationalization" of the economy could vary greatly in scope. It could take the form of the government acquiring private companies that were struggling – as in Poland before 1939. It might only apply to key industries, such as energy, transport and heavy industry. Outside of countries like China, the Soviet Union and the socialist bloc countries, the state usually allowed a degree of market freedom: but even if it did not formally become the owner, it took the company under its supervision (more about the forms this took below).
- Changing the social structure of the country – and unseating the traditional elites – it was necessary to institute agrarian reform and divide up old feudal estates among the peasantry. This was not merely an act of historical justice. The rulers wanted in this way to gain the support of the peasants, to break the influence of the former elite, and expand the markets for local industry.
- Changes in the structure of agriculture served to accelerate accumulation: a commonly used mechanism was instituting a state monopoly on the purchase of agricultural products and setting prices at a level at which the state received the bulk of the surplus.
- Economic planning was universally accepted and recommended by international institutions. this took many forms, which differed in scope and the means of control – from the extreme methods of the command economy in place during the height of Stalinist modernization, by which companies had to fulfil dozens of targets designated by the chief planner, to planning by means of indicators which determined investment and production objectives for both state and private companies.
- The state assuming control of credit policy. This could involve the nationalization of part or all of the banking system, or even setting up a bank to finance development projects (such as BNDSA in Brazil).

1009 Cf. e.g. T. Rosenberg, "Latin America's Magical Liberalism", [in] *Politics and Social Change in Latin America: Still a Distinct Tradition?*, eds. H. J. Wiarda, M. MacLeish Mott, Westport–London 2003, p. 210.

- The State taking control of foreign trade and treating it as a tool of development policy. This especially concerned customs duties, import permits and the promotion of imports; the primary focus was the importation of capital goods at the expense of consumer goods and the import of technology. The state also controlled exchange transactions, manipulating exchange rates in accordance with policy objectives. Monopolies were also often established on the exports of goods from the country, which had to go through state-owned commercial centres (in any event, companies were given strong incentives to make use of them).
- The state placed controls on prices and wages in the economy; it tried to manage the domestic market and ensure access to basic consumer goods – especially food – at low prices. This included centralization and nationalization of at least a portion of wholesale trade and a system of subsidies for the production of basic consumer goods.
- The state tried to carry out a revolution in how people lived – it sometimes altered the calendar and often changed family law; it prohibited traditional clothing, and tried to liquidate the old feudal or tribal power structures and replace them with its own modern administration. This was accompanied by the expansion of the formal education system, initially, at the primary level.

This required centralising power in the hands of the modernizing elite and providing it with greater control over social life. The forms this took could be more or less repressive – from Asian dictatorships and Latin American populism, to the total state of Mao and Stalin. Authoritarianism, however, was a common feature of most economic projects to make a "great leap forward", and ideology provided a justification for it: the governing authorities had to fulfil their historical mission, act as the vanguard of the proletariat, or had a mission to defend the new nation from foreign domination. A characteristic feature of this discourse was haste: there was no time for party politics and discussions, the time for action was now.

Very different regimes were assumed within this wide range of instruments of power – from the mild authoritarianism of Nkrumah to Mao's totalitarian state. Most of them built up their political base of support from people employed by the state – the army, and officials and employees of the formal sector in urban areas. They were the ones who primarily benefited from the low prices of agricultural commodities. It was upon them, not the scattered and poor peasants or farmers, on which the government's survival depended. The city was modernity: in the city was industry, in which the state invested. Even Nyerere's agricultural policy in Tanzania – carried out under the slogan of "villagization" – assumed a significant transfer of resources from the countryside to the cities. In Nyerere's

model villages, the state defined in minute detail what the settlers would grow, and purchased their crops (or at least intended to do so, because in practice the result was often quite different).

2. Ruritania: the case of Central Europe

Various models of state-inspired growth can be included within this broad ideal type.

Imagine a poor, agricultural country – let's call it Ruritania – making use of the best traditions in political science.[1010] Let it be in Central Europe, because it was for this region that Rosenstein-Rodan formulated his theory of accelerated growth in a classic article in 1943. It is the year 1945, or perhaps 1948. In Ruritania, a group of resilient young intellectuals come to power, many of whom were educated in the West. They have read and appreciate Marx, even if they do not think of themselves as Marxists. They are clearly nationalistic in their attitudes. Their aim is to overcome centuries of backwardness in their country, while also attaining international recognition and strengthening the country, whose legitimacy rests on the promise of modernity and national emancipation.

Young intellectuals affiliated with the Democratic People's Peasant-Workers Party of Ruritania (DPPWPR) are in full control of the country. More than 70 perent of Ruritanians work the land; the people are poor and uneducated (not counting a handful of landowners), and industry – where it exists – is in foreign hands. The main export commodities of Ruritania are raw materials and food – mainly coal and grain, because Ruritania lies in Central Europe.

Ruritaniaė main problem, say foreign economists (whose views are confirmed by the few Ruritanians who have dabbled in economics at Western universities) is the low rate of investment. Ruritania allots only five to six percent of its GDP to investment; this often does not result in growth, because the money is used to support the mining industry and build small food-processing plants. Given this situation, the country is doomed to stagnation.

Additional capital is required in order to change the situation. In better times, this could be obtained from abroad. But presently, in the wake of the Great Depression, this in unlikely. In addition, foreign capital brings with it foreign influence – often from powerful enemies of the nation – from which Ruritania earlier

1010 Cf. e.g. E. Gellner, *Nations and Nationalism,* Ithaca 2006, p. 58 ff.; L. von Mises, *Theory of Money and Credit*, 2009, s. 442 ff.; R. Klitgaard, *Controlling Corruption*, Berkeley–Los Angeles 1988, p. 6 ff.; the name comes from two novels written by Anthony Hope in the 1890s, the best known of which is *The Prisoner of Zenda* (1894).

liberated itself. Bringing in capital from outside on the scale required is therefore impossible; international capital markets are still in their infancy, and even if they were more open, such a move would be politically unthinkable (remember, this is taking place in the 1940s).

Ruritania must therefore increase its rate of accumulation by means of its own domestic resources. Economists propose a solution. Lower the standard of living of Ruritanians – temporarily! – and use the surplus for investment.

Of course, initially, the former elites can be forced to return what they have taken. This is easy, and moreover, historically justified. It is a great act of social justice (which Ruritanians could read, for example, in the writings of the renowned Polish economist Oskar Lange). Land needs to be distributed to the peasants, and foreign capitalist landlords expelled. DPPWPR builds a political base among nationalistically-minded Ruritanians, and is popular, but this does not solve the problem of accumulation. The elites consume conspicuously, but this is a small part of overall GDP.

So there are two ways to raise capital.

The first is the nationalization of industries – particularly mining, which produces for export. Coal mines in Ruritania become the property of the state, which sets the wages of the miners at a low level, and exports the coal abroad.

And what if Ruritania does not have such riches? Then the only source of capital would be the countryside, which is home to 70 percent of Ruritanians.

Here, the DPPWPR has a few instruments available.

First, the least drastic means is a state purchasing monopoly. Private intermediaries can be eliminated and prices for Ruritanian cocoa or corn set below market value. Food is then exported, and the resulting surplus invested. But it soon turns out that the peasants are selfish and stubborn and their selfish interests blinds them to scale of the national project. It turns out that they do not want to sell what they produce so cheaply. Agricultural production stops increasing. The government of Ruritania then seizes upon another means: it introduces quotas and compulsory deliveries. A political propaganda campaign in the countryside accompanies this policy, and heavy fines are imposed on recalcitrant farmers.

When this does not work, the DPPWPR turns to another method: collectivization. Peasants are grouped together in cooperatives that are placed under state control. The government will now direct production. Economists suggest that this offers a major advantage: larger farms that can produce more efficiently. Dividing the land into small parcels landowners made sense in the preceding stage of development, when the party was fighting for popularity; now it needs to change this policy. After several years of turmoil, thanks to the blood, sweat and tears of Ruritanians, the party manages to increase the rate of accumulation: it now reaches 20 percent. Questions still remain: who is to invest? And in what?

The first question is obvious: the state has to invest. In the wake of the Great Depression, Ruritanian elites associate the market with chaos and irrationality. Besides they believe that capitalism has kept Ruritania in a state of backwardness. In this system, Ruritania was a peripheral country, which merely provided raw materials to the western centre. Capitalists invest only in what brings them profits – and this is not necessarily consistent with the country's long-term interests. State investments must be planned (even the UN encouraged the establishment of a planning committee!) and calculated over a period of years. No taking chances! Nothing can be left to fate: these issues are too important for the country to allow this. Ruritania has ahead of it a long march towards a prosperous future.

But what to invest in? What will bring the largest increase in production in the shorted possible time? The answer: steel mills and power plants, the chemical and machinery industries. First we produce the means of production, and later we will be able to develop light industry easily and economically, and target production to meet needs of the population.

This choice also has significant political advantages. First of all, it increases Ruritania's military potential, and thus increases the security of the DPPWPR government. This is important because the DPPWPR elites are convinced they are threatened by domestic and foreign enemies. Secondly, it will free the country of the need for costly imports. Ruritanian economists have calculated that an hour of work in industry is worth as much as 6 to 10 hours of work by a villager in the field. This is why every imported machine requires a major effort to export, and is thus a huge burden on the countryside. The sooner we produce our own machines, the faster the standard of living in rural areas will rise, and Ruritanians (who are now underfed because the country needs to export food) will be able to live better.

An open question is whether nationalization should affect all of industry, or only the largest factories, and finally, should the state builds large factories itself or in cooperation with domestic capital. This depends on the political situation. Imposing controls on trade makes sense if market prices are high and inflation is eating into peoples' incomes. In this case, the nationalization of trade should be considered, or, at least in part, in order to give the ruling elite a chance to catch its breath. In addition, the DPPWPR sincerely believes that shortages are not due to its politics, but a conspiracy on the part of speculators.

Now we can clearly see a third – and necessary – part of the Ruritanian strategy: the State must take full control of foreign exchange, capital flows and foreign trade. The DPPWPR cannot afford to have Ruritanians wasting badly needed hard currency, in order to, for example, import cars or luxury consumer goods. We need to state this clearly: "We cannot afford this" (According to Czesław Bobrowski, Władysław Gomułka often said this). Moreover, government policies would lead to capital flight abroad – we need to prevent this in advance, because capitalists think only about their own interests, and are generally held in contempt.

Increasing investment at the expense of lower consumption; government control over agriculture, industry and planning; control over foreign trade – these are the three pillars of the development model that the party proudly calls "Ruritanian socialism". It is labelled Ruritanian in order to emphasize that this is a unique, home-grown achievement, not a copy of someone else's ideas, even of those countries with whom Ruritania maintains a brotherly friendship.

How did things turn out in Ruritania? In the 1970s, shortly after the oil crisis, the country fell into stagnation, and then plunged into recession. For years, disgruntled Ruritanians demanded changes. To remedy the situation, after a long period of political crisis, Ruritania had to enlist the help of the International Monetary Fund and the World Bank in order to save itself from bankruptcy. A condition of the aid, however, was the implementation of a programme of free market reforms, prepared with the help of foreign experts, including privatization, trade liberalization and an opening up to foreign capital.

But this is a completely different story.

Bibliography

Abbott J. P., *Developmentalism and Dependency in Southeast Asia. The Case of the Automotive Industry*, London – New York 2003.

Abelhauser W., *Germany: guns, butter and economic miracles*, [in:] *The Economics of World War II*, red. M. Harrison, Cambridge 2000.

Abu-Lughod J. L., *Before European* Hegemony, New York – Oxford 1989.

Acemoglu D., *Introduction to Modern Economic Growth*, Princeton 2008, s. 1060 i n. lub F. Crouzet, *The History of the European Economy, 1000–2000*, Charlottesville – London 2001.

Acemoglu D., J. Robinson, *Economic Origins of Dictatorship and Democracy*, Cambridge 2006.

Acemoglu D., J. Robinson, *Why Nations Fail: The Origins of Power, Prosperity, and Poverty*, New York 2012.

Acemoglu D., J. Robinson, *Why Nations Fail. The Origins of Power, Prosperity, and Poverty*, New York 2012.

Acemoglu D., S. Johnson, J. A. Robinson, *Institutions As the Fundamental Cause Of Long-Run Growth*, [in:] *Handbook of Economic Growth*, red. P. Aghion, S. N. Durlauf, Amsterdam 2005.

Acemoglu D., S. Johnson, J. Robinson, *The rise of Europe: Atlantic trade, institutional change and economic growth*, "American Economic Review", 2005, no. 2.

Adams B., *Tiny Revolutions in Russia. Twentieth-Century Soviet and Russian History in Anecdotes*, New York – London 2005.

Adams F. G., L. R. Klein, Y. Kumasaka, A. Shinozaki, *Accelerating Japan's Economic Growth. Resolving Japan's Growth Controversy*, London – New York 2008.

Adams J., *The Institutional Economics of Mahadev Govind Ranade*, "Journal of Economic Issues", 1971, v. 5, no. 2.

Adelman I., *Confessions of an incurable romantic*, [in:] *Recollections of Eminent Economists*, red. J. A. Kregel, v. 2, Houndmills – London 1989.

Adelman I., Economic Growth and Social Equity in Developing Countries, Stanford 1973.

Akira N., *The social order of modern Japan*, [in:] *The Political Economy of Japanese Society, v. 1: The State or the Market?*, Oxford – New York 1997.

Akonor K., *Africa and IMF Conditionality. The Unevenness of Compliance*, New York – London 2006.

Alasheev S., *Informal relations in the Soviet system of production* [in:] *Management and Industry in Russia, Formal and Informal Relations in the Period of Transition*, red. S. Clarke, Edward Elgar, Aldershot – Brookfield 1995.

Aldcroft D. H., *Europe's Third World. The European Periphery in the Interwar Years*, Aldershot – Burlington 2006.

Allen L., *The Global Financial System, 1750–2000*, London 2001.

Allen R. C., *Engel's Pause: Pessimist's Guide to the British Industrial Revolution*, University of Oxford Department of Economics Discussion Paper 315, kwiecień 2007.

Allen R. C., *Farm to Factory: A Reinterpretation of the Soviet Industrial Revolution*, Princeton 2003.

Allen R. C., *Real wages in Europe and Asia: A first look at the long-term patterns*, [in:] *Living Standards in the Past. New Perspectives on Well-Being in Asia and Europe*, red. R. Allen, v. Bengtsson, M. Dribe, Oxford 2005.

Allen R. C., *The British Industrial Revolution in Global Perspective*, Cambridge 2009.

Amadae S. M., *Rationalizing Capitalist Democracy. The Cold War Origins of Rational Choice Liberalism*, Chicago 2003.

Ambroziewicz J., R. Wiśniowski, *Tam zapomniano o socjalizmie*, „Po Prostu", 1955, no. 39.

Amsden A. H., *Escape from Empire. The Developing World's Jouney Through Heaven and Hell*, Cambridge – London 2007.

Amsden A., *Asia's Next Giant. South Korea and Late Industrialization*, Oxford – New York 1989.

Amsden A., *The Rise of „The Rest": Challenges to the West from Late-Industrializing Economies*, Oxford – New York 2004.

Andors S., *China's Industrial Revolution. Politics, Planning and Management 1949 to the Present*, New York 1977.

Apter D. E., *Nationalism, government, and economic growth*, "Economic Development and Cultural Change", 1959, no. 2.

Arch Getty J., O. V. Naumov, *The Road to Terror. Stalin and the Self-Destruction of the Bolsheviks, 1932–1939*, New Haven – London 1999.

Arch Getty J., *Origins of the Great Purges. The Soviet Communist Party Reconsidered, 1933–1938*, Cambridge 1985.

Archer J. E., *Social Unrest and Popular Protest in England*, Cambridge 2000.

Arndt H. W., *Economic Development: A Semantic History*, "Economic Development and Cultural Change", 1981, no. 3.

Arndt H. W., *Economic Development: the History of an Idea*, Chicago 1987.

Arndt H. W., *The origins of structuralism*, "World Development", 1985, no. 2.

Ascher W., *Bringing in the Future. Strategies for Farsightedness and Sustainability in Developing Countries*, Chicago - London 2009.

Avakov A. A., *Two Thousand Years of Economic Statistics. World Population, GDP and PPP*, New York 2010.

Avineri S., *Karl Marx on Colonialism and Modernization*, Garden City 1968.

Backhouse R. E., *The Puzzle of Modern Economics. Science or Ideology?*, Cambridge - New York 2010.

Bagiński P., K. Czaplicka, J. Szczyński, *Międzynarodowa współpraca na rzecz rozwoju. Ewolucja, stan obecny i perspektywy*, Warszawa 2008.

Bairoch P., *Europe's Gross National Product: 1800–1975*, "Journal of European Economic History", 1976, no. 2.

Bairoch P., M. Levy-Leboyer, *Disparities in Economic Development since the Industrial Revolution*, London 1981.

Bairoch P., *The Economic Development of the Third World since 1900*, London 1975.

Balcerowicz E., *Przetarg planistyczny. Mechanizm i skutki społeczno-gospodarcze*, Warszawa 1990.

Balcerowicz L., *Systemy gospodarcze*, Warszawa 1989.

Bałtowski M., *Gospodarka socjalistyczna w Polsce*, Warszawa 2009.

Banerjee A., E. Duflo, *The Experimental Approach to Development Economics*, "Annual Review of Economics", 2009.

Baran P. A., *Ekonomia polityczna wzrostu*, przeł. J. Grzywicka, Warszawa 1958.

Baran P. A., *On the Political Economy of Backwardness*, "Manchester School", 1952, no. 1.

Baran P. A., *The Political Economy of Development*, red. Ch. Wilber, K. P. Jameson, New York 1973.

Bardhan P., *Corruption and development: a review of issues*, "Journal of Economic Literature", 1997, no. 35.

Barnett V., *A Long Wave Goodbye: Kondrat'ev and the Conjuncture Institute, 1920–28*, "Europe-Asia Studies", 1995, no. 3.

Barro R., *Are government bonds net wealth?*, "Journal of Political Economy", 1974, no. 82.

Barry B., *Senegambia and the Atlantic Slave Trade*, Cambridge 1998.

Bates R. H., *Domestic interests and control regimes*, [in:] *The Political Economy of Economic Growth in Africa, 1960–2000*, v. 1, red. B. J. Ndulu, S. A. O'Connell, R. H. Bates, P. Collier, Ch. C. Soludo, Cambridge – New York 2008.

Bates R. H., *Markets and States in Tropical Africa. The Poltical Basis of Agricultural Policies*, Berkeley – Los Angeles – London 1981.

Bayer J., W. Dziak, *Kilka uwag o chińskim nacjonalizmie*, Warszawa 2010.

Becker G. S., *A Treatise on the Family*, Cambridge 1981.

Becker G. S., *Crime and punishment: an economic approach*, [in:] *Essays in the Economics of Crime and Punishment*, red. G. S. Becker, W. M. Landes, Minneapolis 1974.

Becker G. S., H. G. Lewis, *On the interaction between the quantity and quality of children*, "Journal of Political Economy", 1973, v. 81, no. 2.

Becker G. S., *Human Capital: A Theoretical and Empirical Analysis, with Special Reference to Education*, Chicago 1983.

Becker G. S., *Investment in human capital: a theoretical analysis*, "Journal of Political Economy", 1962, v. 70, no. 5.

Becker G. S., *The Economic Approach to Human Behavior*, Chicago 1976.

Becker G. S., *The Economics of Discrimination*, Chicago 1971.

Beckerman W., *The Economist as Modern Missionary*, "Economic Journal", 1961, no. 261.

Beckles H., *Freeing slavery. Gender paradigms in the social history of Caribbean slavery*, [in:] *Slavery, Freedom and Gender, The Dynamics of Caribbean Society*, red. B. Moore, B. W. Higman, C. Campbell, P. Bryan, Barbados – Jamaica – Trinidad and Tobago 2003.

Beksiak J., v. Gruszecki, U. Grzelońska, J. Papuzińska, D. Żochowski, *Polska gospodarka w XX wieku. Eseje historyczno-ekonomiczne*, Łódź 2003.

Belova E., P. R., Gregory, *Dictator, loyal, and opportunistic agents: the Soviet archives on creating the Soviet economic system*, "Public Choice", 2002, no. 113.

Bénétrix A. S., K. H. O'Rourke, J. G. Williamson, *The Spread of Manufacturing to the Periphery 1870–2007: Eight Stylized Facts*, IIIS Discussion Paper no. 401, czerwiec 2012.

Berend I. T., *Central and Eastern Europe 1944–1993. Detour from the Periphery to the Periphery*, Cambridge – New York 1996.

Berg E. J., *Socialism and economic development in Tropical Africa*, [in:] *Comparative Economic Systems*, red. J. S. Prybyla, New York 1969.

Berg M., *The Age of Manufactures, 1700–1820. Industry, Innovation and Work in Britain*, London – New York 2004.

Bergère M.-C., *Sun Yat-Sen*, Stanford 1998.

Bergson A., *The Real National Income of Soviet Russia since 1929*, Cambridge 1961.

Berliner J. S., *The Innovation Decision in Soviet Industry*, Cambridge 1976.

Bernadzikiewicz T., *Przerosty etatyzmu. Uwagi o gospodarce państwowej w Polsce*, Warszawa 1935.

Bernstein W. J., *The Birth of Plenty. How the Prosperity of the Modern World Was Created*, New York 2010.

Bessel R., *Mobilization and demobilization in Germany, 1916–1919*, [in:] *State, Society and Mobilization in Europe during the First World War*, red. J. Horne, Cambridge 2002.

Bettelheim Ch., *Cultural Revolution and Industrial Organization in China. Changes in Management and the Division of Labor*, New York – London 1974.

Bettelheim Ch., *Great Leap Backward*, [in:] N. G. Burton, Ch. Bettelheim, *China since Mao*, New York – London 1978.

Betts R., *Decolonization*, New York – London 2004.

Beveridge W., *Social Insurance and Allied Services*, London 1942.

Bhagwati J. N., P. Desai, *India: Planning for Industrialization: Industrialization and Trade Policies since 1951*, Oxford 1970.

Bielschowsky R., *Celso Furtado's contribution to structuralism and their relevance today*, "ECLAC Review", 2006, no. 88.

Biney A., *The legacy of Kwame Nkrumah in retrospect*, "Journal of Pan African Studies", 2008, v. 2, no. 3.

Biney A., *The Political and Social Thought of Kwame Nkrumah*, Houndmills – New York 2011.

Biven W. C., *Jimmy Carter's Economy. Policy in the Age of Limits*, Chapel Hill – London 2002.

Blackwell W. J., *The Beginnings of Russian Industrialization, 1800–1860*, Princeton 1968.

Bobrowski Cz., *Planowanie gospodarcze. Problemy podstawowe*, Warszawa 1965.

Bobrowski Cz., *Wspomnienia ze stulecia*, Lublin 1985.

Bocheński A., *Rzecz o psychice narodu polskiego*, Warszawa 1972.

Boettke P. J., *The Political Economy of Soviet Socialism*, v. 8, London – New York 2001.

Boldizzoni F., *Means and Ends. The Idea of Capital in the West, 1500–1970*, Houndmills – New York 2008.

Booth D., *Andre Gunder Frank: an introduction and appreciation*, [in:] *Beyond Sociology of Development. Economy and Society in Latin America and Africa*, red. I. Oxaal, v. Barnett, D. Booth, Oxford – New York 2011.

Bordo M. D., *The Bretton Woods International Monetary System: An Historical Overview*, [in:] *A Retrospective on the Bretton Woods System*, red. M. D. Bordo, B. Eichengreen, Chicago 1993.

Borsch S. J., *The Black Death in Egypt and England*, Austin 2005.

Bosker M., E. Buringh, J. L. Van Zanden, *From Baghdad to London. The Dynamics of Urban Growth in Europe and the Arab World, 800–1800*, Utrecht University/IISH working paper, 2008.

Botwe-Asamoah K., *Kwame Nkrumah's Politico-Cultural Thought and Policies. An African-Centered Paradigm For the Second Phase of the African Revolution*, New York – London 2005.

Boulton J., *„Turned into the street with my children destitute of every thing": the payment of rent and the London poor, 1600–1850*, [in:] *Accomodating Poverty. The Housing and Living Arrangements of the English Poor, c. 1600–1850*, red. J. McEwan, P. Sharpe, Houndmills – New York 2011.

Bowen H. V., *The Business of Empire. The East India Company and Imperial Britain, 1756–1833*, New York 2006.

Bowman A., A. Wilson, *Quantyfying the Roman economy: integration, growth, decline?*, [in:] *Quantyfying the Roman Economy. Methods and Problems*, red. A. Bowman, A. Wilson, Oxford 2009.

Boyce R., *The Great Interwar Crisis and the Collapse of* Globalization, London – New York 2009.

Bożyk P., *Marzenia i rzeczywistość, czyli anatomia polskiego kryzysu*, Warszawa 1983.

Bradford DeLong J., *Slouching Towards Utopia. Economic History of the World in the Long Twentieth Century, 1870–2010* (w przygotowaniu).

Bramall Ch., *Chinese Economic Development*, London – New York 2009.

Brautigam D., *The Dragon's Gift. The Real Story of China in Africa*, Oxford – New York 2009.

Bresser Pereira L. C., *Economia Brasileira: Uma Introdução Crítica*, São Paulo 1998.

Brindley E. F., *Individualism in Early China. Human Agency and the Self in Thought and Politics*, Honolulu 2010.

Broadberry S., A. Klein, *Aggregate and per capita GDP in Europe, 1870–2000: continental, regional and national data with changing boundaries*, 27 października 2011.

Broadberry S., B. Gupta, *The early modern great divergence: wages, prices and economic development in Europe and Asia, 1500–1800*, "Economic History Review", 2006, no. 1.

Broadbridge S. A., *Aspects of economic and social policy in Japan 1868–1945*, [in:] *The Cambridge Economic History of Europe*, v. 8, *The Industrial Economies: The Development of Economic and Social Policies*, red. P. Mathias, S. Pollard, Cambridge 1989.

Brofenbrenner M., [recenzja R. Nurkse, *Problems of Capital Formation in Underdeveloped Countries*], "Journal of Political Economy", 1954, no. 2.

Brovkin V., *Russia After Lenin. Politics, Culture and Society 1921–1929*, London – New York 2005.

Brown A. J., *The Mastery of the Far East: The Story of Korea's Transformation and Japan's Rise to Supremacy*, New York 1919.

Brus W., *Ogólne problemy funkcjonowania gospodarki socjalistycznej*, Warszawa 1961.

Brus W., *System jugosłowiański z bliska*, „Życie Gospodarcze", no. 1, 7 stycznia 1957.

Brus W., *Zmora reformowania socjalistycznego systemu ekonomicznego*, „Teoria Ekonomii. Prace i Materiały", 1997, no. 4.

Bucharin N., *Ekonomika okresu przejściowego*, Warszawa 1990.

Bulmer-Thomas V., *The Economic History of Latin America Since Independence*, Cambridge – New York 2003.

Burchardt J., *Paradise Lost. Rural Idyll and Social Change since 1800*, London – New York 2002.

Burke E., *The Works of Edmund Burke with a Memoir*, v. 1, New York 1834.

Burnard T., *Mastery, Tyranny and Desire. Thomas Thistlewood and his Slaves in the Anglo-Jamaican World*, Chapel Hill – London 2004.

Burnard T., *The planter class*, [in:] *The Routledge History of Slavery*, red. G. Heuman, v. Burnard, London – New York 2011.

Burns J., *Godess of the Market. Ayn Rand and the American Right*, Oxford – New York 2009.

Capriles R., M. de Gonzalo, *Economic and business history in Venezuela*, [in:] *Business History in Latin America: The Experience of Seven Countries*, Liverpool 1999.

Cardoso E., A. Helwege, *Populism, profligacy and redistribution*, [in:] *The Macroeconomics of Populism in Latin America*, red. R. Dornbusch, S. Edwards, Chicago 1991.

Carr E. H., *The Bolshevik Revolution 1917–1923*, Harmondsworth 1972.

Carr E. H., *The Soviet Impact on the Western World*, Londyn 1946.

Chai J. C. H., K. C. Roi, *Economic Reform in China and India*, Cheltenham – Northampton 2006.

Chakravarty S., *Paul Rosenstein-Rodan: an appreciation*, „World Development", 1983, no. 1.

Chandra B., *India's Struggle for Independence: 1857–1947*, London 1989, s. 94.

Chaney E., *Tolerance, Religious Competition and the Rise and Fall of Muslim Science*, working paper, Harvard University, listopad 2008.

Chang J., J. Halliday, *Mao. The Unknown Story*, New York 2005; wyd. pol. *Mao*, przeł. P. Amsterdamski, Warszawa 2007.

Chatterjee P., *Nationalist Thought and the Colonial World*, London 1993.

Chen Y., *Transition and Development in China. Towards Shared Growth*, Farnham – Burlington 2009.

Chichren Lin C., *The reinstatement of economics in China today*, „The China Quarterly", 1981, no. 85.

Chirot D., *The Origins of Backwardness in Eastern Europe: Economics and Politics From the Middle Ages Until the Early Twentieth Century*, Berkeley – Los Angeles – Oxford 1991.

Chodak Sz., J. Kleer, *Socjalizm i modernizacja w „czarnej" Afryce*, Warszawa 1967.

Chumiński J., *Strukturalne uwarunkowania nieefektywności gospodarki socjalistycznej*, [in:] *Modernizacja czy pozorna modernizacja. Społeczno-ekonomiczny bilans PRL 1944–1989*, red. J. Chumiński, Wrocław 2010.

CIA's Analysis of the Soviet Union, 1947–1991, red. G. K. Haines, R. E. Leggett, Washington 2001.

Clark C., *Development economics: the early years*, [in:] *Pioneers in Development*, red. G. M. Meier, D. Seers, Washington 1984.

Clark G., *Farewell to Alms, A Brief Economic History of the World*, Princeton – Oxford 2007.

Clark G., *Why isn't the whole world developed? Lessons from the cotton mills*, „Journal of Economic History", 1987, no. 1.

Clemens M. A., *Why did the tariff-growth correlation change after 1950?*, „Journal of Economic Growth", 2004, no. 9.

Cobbing A., *The Japanese Discovery of Victorian Britain. Early Travel Encounters in the Far West*, Richmond 1998.

Cohen S., *Bukharin and the Bolshevik Revolution. A Political Biography, 1888–1938*, Oxford – New York – Toronto – Melbourne 1980.

Conquest J., *The Harvest of Sorrow. Soviet Collectivization and the Terror Famine*, New York 1986.

Conquest R., *The Great Terror: Reassessment*, Edmonton 1990; wyd. pol. *Wielki Terror*, przeł. W. Jeżewski, Warszawa 1997.

Constantine S., *The Making of British Colonial Development Policy, 1914–1940*, London 2005.

Critchlow D. T., *The Conservative Ascendancy: How the GOP Right Made Political History*, Princeton 2007.

Croll E., *From Heaven to Earth. Images and Experiences of Development in China*, London – New York 1994.

Crouzet F., *Capital Formation in the Industrial Revolution*, London 1972.

Cullen L. M., *A History of Japan, 1582–1941. Internal and External Worlds*, Cambridge – New York 2003.

Cumings B., *The origins and development of the Northeast Asian political economy: industrial sectors, product cycles and political consequences*, [in:] *The Political Economy of the New Asian Industralism*, red. F. C. Deyo, Ithaca 1987.

Cummings B., *Korea's Place in the Sun: A Modern History*, New York 2005.

Curtis M., *The Asiatic mode of production and Oriental despotism*, [in:] *Marxism: The Inner Dialogues*, red. M. Curtis, New Brunswick 1997.

Cypher J. M., J. L. Dietz, *The Process of Economic Development*, Abingdon – New York 2009.

Cypher J. M., J. L. Dietz, *The Process of Economic Development*, London – New York 2009.

Dadkhah K., *Evolution of Macroeconomic Theory and Policy*, Berlin – Heidelberg 2009.

Dale G., *Karl Polanyi: The Limits of the Market*, Cambridge – Malden 2010.

Dasgupta A. K., *A History of Indian Economic Thought*, London – New York 2002.

David W. L., *The Conversation of Economic Development. Historical Voices, Interpretations, and Reality*, Armonk 1997.

Davies R. W., *Grain, class, and politics during NEP: The Politburo meeting of December 10, 1925*, [in:] *The Lost Politburo Transcripts. From Collective Rule to Stalin's Dictatorship*, red. P. R. Gregory, N. Nalmark, New Haven – London 2008.

Davies R. W., S. G. Wheatcroft, *The Years of Hunger: Soviet Agriculture, 1931–1933*, New York 2002.

Davies R. W., *Stalin as economic policy-maker: Soviet agriculture, 1931–1936*, [in:] *Stalin. A New History*, red. S. Davies, J. Harris, Cambridge 2005.

Davies S., *Popular Opinion in Stalin's Russia*, Cambridge 1997.

Davis B. J., *Home Fires Burning. Food, Politics and Everyday Life in World War I Berlin*, Chapel Hill – London 2000.

Davis D. B., *Inhuman Bondage. The Rise and Fall of Slavery in the New World*, Oxford 2006.

De Vroey M., *Getting rid of Keynes? A reflection on the recent history of macroeconomics*, [in:] *Keynes's General Theory After Seventy Years*, red. R. W. Dimand, R. A. Mundell, A. Vercelli, Houndmills – New York 2010.

DeLong B., B. Eichengreen, *The Marshall Plan: History's Most Successful Structural Adjustment Program*, National Bureau of Economic Research Working Paper no. 3899, 1991.

DeLong J. B., *Hopeless Unemployment*, Project Syndicate, 1 sierpnia 2012, http://www.project-syndicate.org/commentary/hopeless-unemployment, dostęp 30 sierpnia 2012.

Deng G., *The Premodern Chinese Economy. Structural Equilibrium And Capitalist Sterility*, London – New York 1999.

Dernberger R. F., *The People's Republic of China at 50: the economy*, [in:] *The People's Republic of China After 50 Years*, red. R. L. Edmonds, Oxford – New York 2000.

Dernberger R., *Radical ideology and economic development in China: the Cultural Revolution and its impact on the economy*, „Asian Survey", 1972, v. 12, no. 12.

Dikötter F., *Mao's Great Famine. The History of China's Most Devastating Catastrophe, 1958–62*, London – Berlin – New York 2010.

Dirks N. B., *The Scandal of Empire. India and the Creation of Imperial Britain*, Cambridge – London 2006.

Dobb M., *Political Economy and Capitalism*, London 1950.

Doboszyński A., *Gospodarka narodowa*, Wrocław 2004.

Dobroczyński M., *Charakter chińskiej odrębności*, „Athenaeum", 2006, no. 16.

Domar J. D., *Szkice z teorii wzrostu gospodarczego*, przeł. L. Niżyński, Warszawa 1962.

Dore R. P., *Flexible Rigidities. Industrial Policy and Structural Adjustment in the Japanese Economy, 1970–1980*, Stanford 1986.

Drozdowski M., *Polityka gospodarcza rządu polskiego 1936–1939*, Warszawa 1963.

Duda S., *Liberalizm a etatyzm: dyskusja o gospodarczej roli państwa w drugiej Rzeczypospolitej*, „Rzeszowskie Zeszyty Naukowe: Prawo – Ekonomia", 1997, v. 22.

Dudden A., *Japan's Colonization of Korea. Discourse and Power*, Honolulu 2005.

Dunin-Wąsowicz K., *Polski ruch socjalistyczny 1939–1945*, Warszawa 1993.

Dunkerley J., *Rebellion in the Veins. Political Struggle in Bolivia, 1952–1982*, London 1984.

Dwilewicz Ł., *Reformy Bolesława Jaszczuka i polityka gospodarcza ekipy gierkowskiej – zwrot i ciągłość*, [in:] *Dekada Gierka. Wnioski dla obecnego okresu modernizacji Polski*, red. K. Rybiński, Warszawa 2011.

Dziak W., J. Bayer, *Mao: zwycięstwa, nadzieje, klęski*, Warszawa 2007.

Dziewulski K., *Spór o etatyzm: 1919–1939*, Warszawa 1981.

Easterlin R. A., *Why isn't the whole world developed?*, „The Journal of Economic History", 1981, no. 1.

Easterly W., *Development doesn't require big government*, „The Wall Street Journal", 3 października 2008.

Easterly W., R. Levine, *The European Origins of Economic Development*, NBER Working Paper 18162, czerwiec 2012.

Eastman L. E., *Seeds of Destruction. Nationalist China in War and Revolution, 1937–1949*, Stanford 1984.

Eatwell J., M. Milgate, *The Fall and Rise of Keynesian Economics*, Oxford 2011.

Eckert A., *Julius Nyerere, Tanzanian elites, and the project of African socialism*, [in:] *Elites and Decolonization in the Twentieth Century*, red. J. Dulffer, M. Frey, London 2011.

Eckstein A., *China's Economic Revolution*, London – New York 1978.

Eckstein S., F. Hagopian, *The limits of industrialization in the less developed world: Bolivia*, „Economic Development and Cultural Change", 1983, v. 32, no. 1.

Economic Transition in the Middle East, red. H. Handoussa, Cairo 2000.

Edwards S., *Forty Years of Latin America's Economic Development: From the Alliance for Progress to the Washington Consensus*, NBER working paper 15190, lipiec 2009.

Edwards S., S. Teitel, *Introduction to growth, reform, and adjustment: Latin America's trade and macroeconomic Policies in the 1970s and 1980s*, „Economic Development and Cultural Change", 1986, v. 34, no. 3.

Egan D., M. A. Egan, *Joseph Stalin. An Annotated Bibliography of English-Language Periodical Literature to 2005*, Lanham – Toronto – Plymouth 2007.

Eichengreen B., *Global Imbalances and the Lessons of Bretton Woods*, NBER Working Paper no. 10497, maj 2004.

Eichengreen B., *The European Economy since 1945. Coordinated Capitalism and Beyond*, Princeton 2007 – Oxford 2007.

Elementy teorii wyboru społecznego, red. G. Lissowski, Warszawa 2001.

Eltis D., S. D. Behrendt, D. Richardson, H. S. Klein, *The Trans-Atlantic Slave Trade: A Database on CD-Rom*, New York 1999.

Engerman S., K. Sokoloff, *Institutional and Non-Institutional Explanations of Economic Differences*, NBER Working Paper no. 9989, wrzesień 2003.

Erlich A., *Preobrazhenski and the economics of Soviet industrialization*, „The Quarterly Journal of Economics", 1950, v. 64, no. 1.

Erlich A., *The Soviet Industrialization Debate, 1924–1928*, Cambridge 1960.

Erlich P. R., *Population Bomb*, London 1971.

Esquivel G., G. Marquez, *Economic effects of closing the economy: the Mexican experience*, [in:] *The Decline of Latin American Economies Growth, Institutions, and Crises*, red. S. Edwards, G. Esquivel, G. Marquez, Chicago – London 2007.

Farber S., *The Origins of the Cuban Revolution Reconsidered*, Chapel Hill 2006.

Fay P. W., *The Opium War 1840–1842*, Chapel Hill 1997.

Fei J. C. H., A. C. Chiang, *Maximum-speed development through austerity*, [in:] *The Theory and Design of Economic Development*, red. I. Adelman i E. Thorbecke, Baltimore 1969.

Feigon L., *Mao: A Reinterpretation*, Chicago 2002.

Feinstein Ch. H., P. Temin, G. Toniolo, *International economic organization: banking, finance, and trade in Europe between the wars*, [in:] *Banking, Currency, and Finance in Europe between the Wars*, red. Ch. H. Feinstein, Oxford 1995.

Feinstein Ch., *Pessimism perpetuated: real wages and the standard of living in Britain during and after the Industrial Revolution*, „Journal of Economic History" 1998, no. 58.

Feldman G., *Przyczynek do teorii tempa wzrostu dochodu narodowego*, „Studia Ekonomiczne", 1963, v. 10.

Fenby J., *Modern China. The Fall and Rise of a Great Power*, New York 2008.

Ferguson N., *Civilization. The West and the Rest*, New York 2011.

Feuerwerker A., *Economic trends, 1912–1949*, [in:] *The Cambridge History of China*, v. 12: *Republican China, 1912–1949*, cz. 1, Cambridge 1983.

Fichte J. G., *Zamknięte państwo handlowe*, przeł. J. Nowotniak, [in:] idem, *Zamknięte państwo handlowe i inne pisma*, Warszawa 1996.

Filipowicz L., K. Opawski, *Teoria wyboru publicznego: wybrane koncepcje badawcze*, „Ekonomista", 1992, no. 3.

Filtzer D., *Soviet Worker and Late Stalinism*, Cambridge 2004.

Filtzer D., *Soviet Workers and De-Stalinization: The Consolidation of the Modern System of Soviet Production Relations, 1953–1964*, New York 1992.

Filtzer D., *Soviet Workers and Stalinist Industrialization: The Formation of Modern Soviet Production Relations, 1928–1941*, London 1986.

Findlay R., K. O'Rourke, *Power and Plenty. Trade, War, and the World Economy in the Second Millenium*, Princeton – Oxford 2007.

Fisher J. R., *The Economic Aspects of Spanish Imperialism in America, 1492–1810*, Liverpool 1997.

Fisman R., E. Miguel, *Economic Gangsters. Corruption, Violence and the Poverty of Nations*, Princeton – Oxford 2008.

Fitzpatrick S., *Education and Social Mobility in the Soviet Union*, Cambridge 2002.

Fitzpatrick S., *Everyday Stalinism. Ordinary Life in Extraordinary Times: Soviet Russia in the 1930s*, Oxford 2000, s. 46; wyd. pol. *Życie codzienne pod rządami Stalina. Rosja radziecka w latach trzydziestych XX wieku*, tłum. J. Gilewicz, Kraków 2012.

Fitzpatrick S., *Stalin's Revolution*, Oxford 2008.

Fogel R. W., *An Overview of the Changing Body: Health, Nutrition and Human Development in the Western World since 1700*, NBER Working Paper 16938, kwiecień 2011, http://www.nber.org/papers/w16938.

Fogel R., *The Escape from Hunger and Premature Death, 1700–2100*, Cambridge 2004.

Foran J., *Taking Power. On the Origins of Third World Revolutions*, Cambridge – New York 2005.

Foster J., *Class Struggle and the Industrial Revolution*, London 2005.

Fox J., *The Myth of the Rational Market: A History of Risk, Reward, and Delusion on Wall Street*, New York 2009.

Francisco R. A., B. A. Laird, R. D. Laird, *The Political Economy of Collectivized Agriculture: A Comparative Study of Communist and Non-Communist Systems*, New York 1979.

Frankel H. S., *United Nations Primer for Development*, „Quarterly Journal of Economics", 1952, no. 3.

Franko P., *The Puzzle of Latin American Economic Development*, Lanham – Plymouth 2007.

Friedman B. N., *Industrial Evolution*, „The New York Times", 9 grudnia 2007.

Friedman M., *A Memorandum to the Government of India*, 1955.

Friedman M., A. Schwartz, *A Monetary History of the United States, 1867–1960*, Princeton 1963.

Friedman M., *Capitalism and Freedom*, Chicago – London 2002.

Friedman M., R. D. Friedman, *Two Lucky People. Memoirs*, Chicago 1998.

Friedman M., *The Methodology of Positive Economics*, [in:] idem, *Essays in Positive Economics*, Chicago 1966.

Friedman M., *The role of monetary policy*, „American Economic Review", 1968, v. 58, no. 1.

Friedmann J., *China's Urban Transition*, Minneapolis – London 2005.

Friszke A., *O kształt niepodległej*, Warszawa 1989.

Fung E. S. K., *The Intellectual Foundations of Chinese Modernity. Cultural and Political Thought in the Republican Era*, New York 2010.

Fürst J., *Stalin's Last Generation. Soviet Post-War Youth and the Emergence of Mature Socialism*, Oxford 2010.

Galeano E., *Otwarte żyły Ameryki Łacińskiej*, przeł. I. Majchrzakowa, W. Majchrzak, Kraków 1983.

Galor O., D. N. Weil, *Population, technology and growth: from the Malthusian regime to the demographic transition and beyond*, „American Economic Review", 2000, no. 4.

Gandhi M., *Hind Swaraj or Indian Home Rule*, http://www.soilandhealth.org/03sov/0303critic/hind%20swaraj.pdf.

Gao B., *Economic Ideology and Japanese Industrial Policy. Developmentalism from 1931 to 1965*, Cambridge 2002.

Gao M., *The Battle for China's Past. Mao and the Cultural Revolution*, London – Ann Arbor 2008.

Garczyński S., *Anatomia Rzeczypospolitey Polskiey. Synom Oyczyzny ku przestrodze y poprawie. Mianowicie, o sposobach: zamnożenia Polskę ludem pospolitym, konserwowania dziatwy wieiskiey przez niedostatek y niewygody marnie ginącey, y wprowadzenia handlow y manufaktur zagranicznych. Dawniey spisana, z Przydatkami teraz wydana*, Warszawa[?] 1753.

Gaskell P., *The Manufacturing Population of England. Its Moral, Social and Physical Conditions, and the Changes which Have Arisen from the Use of Steam Machinery; with an Examination of Infant Labour*, London 1833.

Gelber H. G., *Opium, Soldiers and Evangelicals. Britain's 1840–1842 War with China, and its Aftermath*, Houndmills – New York 2004.

Gellner E., *Nations and Nationalism*, Ithaca 2006; wyd. pol. *Narody i nacjonalizm*, przeł. v. Hołówka, Warszawa 1991.

Gerschenkron A., [recenzja A. Nove, *Was Stalin Really Necessary? Some Problems of Soviet Political Economy*], „The Economic History Review", 1965, v. 17, no. 3.

Gerschenkron A., *Economic Backwardness in Historical Perspective*, New Heaven – London 1951.

Ghose S., *Jawaharlal Nehru, A Biography*, Bombay 1993.

Giertych J., *O wyjście z kryzysu*, Warszawa 1938.

Gill G., *The Origins of the Stalinist Political System*, Cambridge – New York 2002.

Gilman N., *Mandarins of the Future. Modernization Theory in Cold War America*, Baltimore 2003.

Gittings J., *The Changing Face of China. From Mao to Market*, Oxford 2006.

Göcek F., *East Encounters West. France and the Ottoman Empire in the Eighteenth Century*, New York – Oxford 1987.

Goh E., *Constructing the U.S. Rapprochement with China, 1961–1974. From „Red Menace" to „Tacit Ally"*, Cambridge 2005.

Goldstone J., *Why Europe? The Rise of the West in World History, 1500–1850*, New York 2009.

Goldsworthy V., *Inventing Ruritania: The Imperialism of the Imagination*, New Haven 1998.

Gołębiowski J. W., *Sprawa nacjonalizacji przemysłu i odbudowy gospodarki narodowej w programach ważniejszych stronnictw politycznych podczas II Wojny Światowej*, [in:] *Wojna i okupacja na ziemiach polskich*, red. W. Góra, Warszawa 1984.

Gołębiowski J., *Sektor państwowy w gospodarce Polski międzywojennej*, Warszawa 1985.

Gołębiowski Ł, *Lud Polski. Jego zwyczaje, zabobony*, Warszawa 1830.

Gomułka W., *Pamiętniki*, v. 1, red. A. Werblan, Warszawa 1994.

Good D. F., *The state and economic development in Central and Eastern Europe*, [in:] *Nation, State and the Economy in History*, red. A. Teichova, H. Matis, Cambridge – New York 2003.

Goodman D. S. G., *Deng Xiaoping and the Chinese Revolution. A Political Biography*, London – New York 1994.

Gordon J., *Nasser. Hero of the Arab Nation*, Oxford 2006.

Górski J., *Polska myśl ekonomiczna a rozwój gospodarczy 1807–1830. Studia nad początkami teorii zacofania gospodarczego*, Warszawa 1963.

Grabski S., *Ku lepszej Polsce*, Warszawa 1938.

Granick D., *Job Rights in the Soviet Union: Their Consequences*, Cambridge 1987.

Gregory P. R., *An introduction to the economics of the Gulag*, [in:] *The Economics of Forced Labor. The Soviet Gulag*, red. P. R. Gregory, V. Lazarev, Stanford 2003.

Gregory P. R., J. Sailors, *The Soviet Union during the Great Depression: the autarky model*, [in:] *The World Economy and National Economies in the Interwar Slump*, red. v. Balderston, New York 2003.

Gregory P. R., *Terror By Quota: State Security from Lenin to Stalin (An Archival Study)*, New Haven - London 2009.

Gregory P. R., *The Political Economy of Stalinism*, Cambridge 2003.

Gregory P., *Restructuring the Soviet Economic Bureaucracy*, New York 1990.

Gunder Frank A., *Capitalism and Underdevelopment in Latin America: Historical Studies of Chile and Brazil*, London 1971.

Gungwu W., *Anglo-Chinese Encounters since 1800. War, Trade, Science, and Governance*, Cambridge - New York 2003.

Guo R., *How the Chinese Economy Works*, Houndmills - London 2009.

Guthrie D., *China and Globalization. The Social, Economic and Political Transformation of Chinese Society*, New York - London 2009.

Hagen J. M., V. W. Ruttan, *Development policy under Eisenhower and Kennedy*, „Economic Development Center Bulletin" 87-10, University of Minnesota, listopad 1987.

Haggard S., R. R. Kaufman, *Development, Democracy and Welfare States. Latin America, East Asia and Eastern Europe*, Princeton - Oxford 2008.

Hall D., *In Miserable Slavery. Thomas Thistlewood in Jamaica, 1750–1786*, Barbados - Jamaica - Trinidad and Tobago 1999.

Hamilton A., *Report on the Subject of Manufactures*, wyd. 6, Philadelphia 1828.

Hanes III W. T., F. Sanello, *The Opium Wars. The Addiction of One Empire and the Corruption of Another*, Naperville 2002.

Hardt Ł., *Problem realistyczności założeń w teorii ekonomii*, „Ekonomista", 2012, no. 1.

Harley C. K., *Reassessing the Industrial Revolution: a macro view*, [in:] *The British Industrial Revolution. An Economic Perspective*, red. J. Mokyr, Boulder - Oxford 1999.

Harrison M., *Communism and Economic Modernization*, Centre for Competitive Advantage in the Global Economy, University of Warwick, working paper no. 92, 2012.

Harrison M., *Economic growth and slowdown*, [in:] *Brezhnev Reconsidered*, red. E. Bacon, M. Sandle, Houndmills - New York 2002.

Harrison M., *Prices in the Politburo, 1927: market equilibrium versus the use of force*, [in:] *The Lost Politburo Transcripts. From Collective Rule to Stalin's Dictatorship*, red. P. R. Gregory, N. Nalmark, New Haven - London 2008.

Harrison M., *Soviet Planning in Peace and War, 1938–1945*, Cambridge 2002.

Hatcher J., J. Bailey, *Modelling the Middle Ages. The History and Theory of England's Economic Development*, Oxford 2001.

Hatziprokopiou M., K. Velentzas, *Preobrazhensky and the theory of economic development*, [in:] *The Canon in the History of Economics: Critical Essays*, red. M. Psalidopoulos, London 2000.

Hayek F. A. von, *Droga do zniewolenia*, przeł. K. Gurba i in., Kraków 1999.

Hayek F. A. von, *New Studies in Philosophy: Politics, Economics and the History of Ideas*, London 1978.

Hayek F. A. von, *The Road to Serfdom. Text and Documents. The Devinitive Edition*, red. B. Caldwell, Chicago - London 2007.

Hayek F. A. von, *The Use of Knowledge in Society*, „American Economic Review", 1945, v. 25, no. 4.

Heilperin M. A., *Studies in Economic Nationalism*, Geneve - Paris 1960, Publications de L'Institut Universitaire de Hautes Etudes Internationales no. 35.

Henderson W. O., *Walther Rathenau. A pioneer of the planned economy*, „The Economic History Review. New Series", 1951, v. 4, no. 1.

Henrique Cardoso F., E. Faletto, *Dependency and Development in Latin America*, Berkeley - Los Angeles 1979; wyd. pol. *Zależność a rozwój w Ameryce Łacińskiej: próba interpretacji socjologicznej*, przeł. H. Siewierski, Z. Jakubowska, Warszawa 2008.

Higgins J., *Raymond Williams: Literature, Marxism and Cultural Materialism*, Abingdon - New York 1999.

Higgs R., *Depression, War and Cold War. Studies in Political Economy*, Oxford 2006.

Higman B. W., *Plantation Jamaica 1750–1850. Capital and Control in a Colonial Economy*, Jamaica - Barbados - Trinidad and Tobago 2008.

Hilton B., *A Mad, Bad, and Dangerous People? England, 1783–1846*, Oxford 2006.

Hirschman A. O., *A dissenter's confession*, [in:] *Pioneers in Development*, red. G. Meier, D. Seers, Oxford 1984.

Hirschman A. O., *The Strategy of Economic Development, Westview Press*, Boulder - London 1958.

Hochschild A., *Duch króla Leopolda*, przeł. P. Tarczyński, Warszawa 2012.

Hogan M. J., *The Marshall Plan. America, Britain and the Reconstruction of Western Europe*, Cambridge 1987.

Holzer J., *Europa zimnej wojny*, Kraków 2012.

Honeyman K., *Child Workers in England, 1780–1820*, Aldershot – Burlington 2007.

Hoover K. R., *Economics as Ideology. Keynes, Laski, Hayek and the Creation of Contemporary Politics*, Lanham – Oxford 2003.

Horlings E., *Pre-industrial economic growth and the transition to an industrial economy*, [in:] *Early Modern Capitalism. Economic and Social Change in Europe, 1400–1800*, red. M. Prak, London – New York 2010.

Horn J., *The Path Not Taken. French Industrialization in the Age of Revolution, 1750–1830*, Cambridge – London 2006.

Horowitz I. L., *Three Worlds of Development. The Theory and Practics of International Stratification*, New York 1966.

Horvitz L. A., Ch. Catherwood, *Encyclopedia of War Crimes and Genocide*, New York 2009.

Humphries, *Childhood and child labour in the British Industrial Revolution*, „Economic History Review", 2012 (w druku).

Hung Mo P., *Lessons from the history of Imperial China*, [in:] *Political Competition, Innovation and Growth in the History of Asian Civilizations*, red. P. Bernholz, R. Vaubel, Cheltenham – Northampton 2004.

Hunt E. K., M. Lautzenheiser, *History of Economic Thought. A Critical Perspective*, Armonk 2011.

Hunt Tooley T., *The Hindenburg program of 1916: a central experiment in wartime planning*, „The Quarterly Journal of Austrian Economics", 1999, v. 2, no. 2.

Iliffe J., *A Modern History of Tanganyika*, Cambridge 1994.

Ingrao B., G. Israël, *The Invisible Hand: Economic Equilibrium in the History of Science*, Cambridge 1990.

Inikori J., *Africans and the Industrial Revolution in England: A Study in International Trade and Economic Development*, Cambridge 2002.

Inikori J., *Transatlantic slavery and economic development in the Atlantic world, West Africa, 1450–1850*, [in:] *The Cambridge World History of Slavery*, v. 3, red. D. Eltis, S. L. Engerman, Cambridge 2011.

Inside the Economist's Mind. Conversations with Eminent Economists, red. P. A. Samuelson, W. A. Barnett, Malden – Oxford 2007.

Ip H., *Intellectuals in Revolutionary China, 1921–1949. Leaders, Heroes and Sophisticates*, London – New York 2005.

Jacob W., *Report on the Trade in Foreign Corn: And on the Agriculture of the North of Europe*, London 1826.

Janos A. C., *East Central Europe in the Modern World. The Politics of the Borderlands from Pre- to Postcommunism*, Stanford 2000.

Janowski M., *Inteligencja wobec wyzwań nowoczesności. Dylematy ideowe polskiej demokracji liberalnej w Galicji w latach 1889–1914*, Warszawa 1996.

Janowski M., *Narodziny inteligencji, 1750–1831*, Warszawa 2008.

Jansen M. B., *The Making of Modern Japan*, Cambridge – London 2000.

Janta-Połczyński A., *W głąb Z.S.R.R.*, Warszawa 1933.

Janus P., *W nurcie polskiego etatyzmu. Stefan Starzyński i Pierwsza Brygada Gospodarcza 1926–1932*, Kraków 2009.

Jarosz A., J. Kaliński, A. Zawistowski, *Bibliografia historii gospodarczej Polski w latach 1944–1989*, Warszawa 2003.

Jarosz D., *Polityka władz komunistycznych w Polsce w latach 1948–1956 a chłopi*, Warszawa 1998.

Jarosz J., v. Wolsza, *Komisja Specjalna do Walki z Nadużyciami i Szkodnictwem Gospodarczym 1945–1954*, Warszawa 1995.

Jedlicki J., *Jakiej cywilizacji Polacy potrzebują*, Warszawa 2002.

Jedlicki J., *Nieudana próba kapitalistycznej industrializacji: analiza państwowego gospodarstwa przemysłowego w Krolestwie Polskim XIX w.*, Warszawa 1964.

Jedlicki J., *Świat zwyrodniały. Lęki i wyroki krytyków nowoczesności*, Warszawa 2000.

Jencks Ch., *The Story of Post-Modernism*, Chichester 2011.

Jennings M., *Surrogates of the State: NGOs, Development, and Ujamaa in Tanzania*, Bloomfield 2008.

Jha R., *Macroeconomics for Developing Countries*, London – New York 2003.

Jian Ch., *Mao's China and the Cold War*, Chapel Hill – London 2001.

Johnson Ch., *MITI and the Japanese Miracle: Growth of Industrial Policy, 1925–1975*, Stanford 1983.

Johnson Ch., *The developmental state: odyssey of a concept*, [in:] *The Developmental State*, red. M. Woo-Cumings, Ithaca – London 1999.

Johnson K. A., *Women, the Family and Peasant Revolution in China*, Chicago – London 1983.

Jolly R., *UN Contributions to Development Thinking and Practice*, Bloomington 2004.

Jones Ch. I., *Was an Industrial Revolution inevitable? Economic growth over the very long run*, "Advances in Macroeconomics", 2001, no. 2.

Jones D. M., *The Image of China in Western Social and Political Thought*, Houndmills – New York 2001.

Judt T., *Powojnie. Historia Europy po 1945 roku*, przeł. R. Bałtord, Poznań 2011.

Kaczmarek v. T., *Kto kieruje globalizacją? Think-tanki – kuźnie nowych idei*, Warszawa 2011.

Kalecki M., *Dzieła*, v. 4: *Socjalizm. Wzrost gospodarczy i efektywność inwestycji*, Warszawa 1984.

Kaliński J., *Bitwa o handel 1947–1948*, Warszawa 1970.

Kaliński J., *Gospodarka Polski w latach 1944–1989. Przemiany strukturalne*, Warszawa 1995.

Kaliński J., *Plan Odbudowy Gospodarczej (1947–1949)*, [in:] *Czesław Bobrowski – mistrz ekonomii stosowanej*, red. M. Kulowa, Warszawa 2004.

Kaliński J., *Pomoc czy wyzysk? Stosunki gospodarcze między Polską i ZSRR*, [in:] *Białe plamy – czarne plamy. Sprawy trudne w relacjach polsko-rosyjskich (1918–2008)*, red. A. D. Rotfeld, A. W. Torkunow, Warszawa 2010.

Kaliński J., *Przyspieszenia wzrostu w dziejach gospodarczych Polski*, [in:] *Między zacofaniem i modernizacją. Społeczno-gospodarcze problemy ziem polskich na przestrzeni wieków*, red. E. Kościk, v. Głowiński, Wrocław 2009.

Kaliński J., Z. Landau, *Gospodarka Polski XX wieku*, Warszawa 2003.

Kaliński J., *Zarządzanie gospodarką*, [in:] *PZPR jako machina władzy*, red. D. Stola, K. Persak, Warszawa 2012.

Kamermans J. A., *Materieele cultuur in de Krimpenerwaard in de zeventiende en achttiende eeuw*, Wageningen 1999.

Kamieński H., *Filozofia ekonomii materialnej ludzkiego społeczeństwa*, Warszawa 1959.

Kang D. C., *Crony Capitalism. Corruption and Development in South Korea and the Phillipines*, Cambridge 2004.

Kaple D. A., *Dream of a Red Factory. Legacy of High Stalinism in China*, New York -Oxford 1994.

Kaufman A., *The origin of „the politcal economy of socialism"*, „Soviet Studies", 1953, no. 3.

Keesing D. B., *Economic lessons from China*, „Journal of Development Economics", 1975, no. 2.

Khan Khattak S. K., *Islam and the Victorians. Nineteenth Century Perceptions of Muslim Practices and Beliefs*, London – New York 2008.

Khan M., *The efficiency implications of corruption*, „Journal of International Development", 1996, v. 8, no. 5.

Khlevniuk O., *The Economy of the OGPU, NKVD, and MVD of the USSR, 1930–1953*, [in:] *The Economics of Forced Labor. The Soviet Gulag*, red. P. R. Gregory, V. Lazarev, Stanford 2003.

Khomiakov-Andreev G., *Bitter Waters. Life and Work in Stalin's Russia*, Boulder 1997.

Killick T., *Development Economics in Action*, New York 1978.

Kim E., G.-S. Park, *The chaebol*, [in:] *The Park Chung Hee Era. The Transformation of South Korea*, red. B. Kim, E. F. Vogel, Cambridge - London 2011.

King S., *The Residential and Familial Arrangements of English Pauper Letter Writers, 1800–40s*, [in:] *Accomodating Poverty. The Housing and Living Arrangements of the English Poor, c. 1600–1850*, red. J. McEwan, P. Sharpe, Houndmills - New York 2011.

Kirby W., *Engineering China. Birth of the developmental state, 1928–1937*, [in:] *Becoming Chinese. Passages to Modernity and Beyond*, red. W.-H. Yeh, Berkeley - London 2000.

Kisielewski S., *Dzienniki*, Warszawa 1996.

Kisielewski S., *Dzienniki*, Warszawa 2001.

Kitching G., *Development and Underdevelopment in Historical Perspective. Populism, Nationalism and Industrialization*, London 2011.

Klein N., *Doktryna szoku*, przeł. H. Jankowska i in., Warszawa 2008.

Klitgaard R., *Controlling Corruption*, Berkeley - Los Angeles 1991.

Kloc K., *Rady robotnicze w przedsiębiorstwie samorządnym w Polsce w latach 1956–58*, Lublin 1984.

Kochanowicz J., *Could a Polish noble became an entrepreneur? Mentality, market and capital*, [in:] idem, *Backwardness and Modernization. Poland and Eastern Europe in the 16th–20th Centuries*, Aldershot 2006.

Kochanowicz J., *Początki planowania w Polsce po II wojnie światowej w perspektywie porównawczej*, [in:] *Ekonomia i ekonomiści w czasach przełomu*, red. E. Mączyńska, J. Wilkin, Warszawa 2010.

Kochanowicz J., *Polska w epoce nowoczesnego wzrostu gospodarczego*, [in:] *Modernizacja Polski: Struktury, agencje. instytucje*, red. W. Morawski, Warszawa 2010.

Kochanowicz J., *Reforming weak states and deficient bureaucracies*, [in:] *Intricate Links: Democratization and Market Reforms in Latin America and Eastern Europe*, red. J. M. Nelson, Washington 1994.

Kochanowicz J., *The Polish economy and the evolution of dependency*, [in:] *The Origins of Backwardness in Eastern Europe: Economics and Politics From the Middle Ages Until the Early Twentieth Century*, red. D. Chirot, Berkeley - Los Angeles - Oxford 1991.

Kochanowicz J., *Wprowadzenie*, [in:] L. von Mises, *Kalkulacja ekonomiczna w socjalizmie*, przeł. J. Jabłecki, Warszawa, 2011.

Koepke N., J. Baten, *The biological standard of living in Europe during the last two millennia*, „European Review of Economic History", 2005, no. 1.

Kofman J., *Nacjonalizm gospodarczy – szansa czy bariera rozwoju. Przypadek Europy Środkowo-Wschodniej w okresie międzywojennym*, Warszawa 1992.

Kohli A., *State-Directed Development: Politcal Power and Industrialization in the Global Periphery*, Cambridge 2004.

Kołakowski L., *Główne nurty marksizmu*, v. 1–3, wyd. 7, Warszawa 2009.

Kornai J., *Niedobór w gospodarce*, przeł. U. Grzelońska, Z. Wiankowska, Warszawa 1985.

Kornai J., *Siła idei. Zapiski z intelektualnej podróży*, przeł. J. Okuniewski. S. Szymański, Warszawa 2008.

Kornai J., *The Socialist System. The Political Economy of Communism*, Oxford 1992.

Koryś P., *The state as an entrepreneur: reorientation of the economic policy of the Republic of Poland in late 1930s and the developing of state capitalism*, niepublikowany maszynopis.

Kostro K., *Biografia naukowa Friedricha A. von Hayeka w setną rocznicę urodzin*, „Ekonomista", 1999, no. 1–2.

Kostro K., *Hayek kontra socjalizm: debata socjalistyczna a rozwój teorii społeczno-ekonomicznych Friedricha Augusta von Hayeka*, Warszawa 2001.

Kotkin S., *Magnetic Mountain. Stalinism as the Civilization*, Berkeley – Los Angeles 1997.

Kotowicz-Jawor J., *Presja inwestycyjna w latach siedemdziesiątych*, Warszawa 1983.

Kowalik T., *Michał Kalecki a pierwsze reformy gospodarcze w Polsce*, „Nauka Polska", 1989, no. 2.

Kowalik T., *Spory o ustrój społeczno-gospodarczy w Polsce, lata 1944–1948*, Warszawa 2006.

Kremer M., *Population growth and technological change: one million B.C. to 1990*, „Quarterly Journal of Economics", 1993, no. 3.

Krueger A. O., *The political economy of the rent-seeking society*, „American Economic Review", 1974, v. 64, no. 3.

Krugman P., *Capitalism's Mysterious Triumph* (1997), http://web.mit.edu/krugman/www/ (dostęp 2 października 2009).

Krugman P., *The Fall and Rise of Development Economics*, [in:] *Rethinking the Development Experience. Essays Provoked by the Work of Albert O. Hirschman*, red. L. Rodwin, D. Schon, Washington 1994.

Krzywicka K., *Latynoamerykanizm – w poszukiwaniu tożsamości regionalnej w Ameryce Łacińskiej*, [in:] *Ideologie, doktryny i ruchy narodowe. Wybrane problemy*, red. S. Stępień, Lublin 2006.

Kuczyński W., *Po wielkim skoku*, Warszawa 2012.

Kueh Y. Y., *China's New Industrialization Strategy. Was Chairman Mao Really Necessary?*, Cheltenham – Northampton 2008.

Kula M., *Anatomia rewolucji narodowej: Boliwia w XX wieku*, Warszawa 1999.

Kula M., *Swój do swego… po co?*, „Studia Migracyjne – Przegląd Polonijny", 2009, no. 2.

Kula W., *Przywilej społeczny a postęp gospodarczy*, „Przegląd Socjologiczny", 1947, z. 1–4.

Kula W., *Rozważania o historii*, Warszawa 1958.

Kula W., *Szkice o manufakturach*, v. 1, Warszawa 1956.

Kuran T., *Institutional causes of economic underdevelopment in the Middle East: a historical perspective*, [in:] *Institutional Change and Economic Behaviour*, red. J. Kornai, L. Maytyas, G. Roland, Houndmills – New York 2008.

Kuran T., *Islam and Mammon: the Economic Predicaments of Islamism*, Princeton 2005.

Kuran T., *The Long Divergence: How Islamic Law Held Back the Middle East*, Princeton 2010.

Kuznets P. W., *An East Asian model of economic development: Japan, Taiwan, and South Korea*, „Economic Development and Cultural Change", 1988, no. 3.

Kuznets S., *Growth and income inequality*, „American Economic Review", 1955, no. 1.

Kwiatkowski E., *Dysproporcje. Rzecz o Polsce przeszłej i obecnej*, opr. A. Garlicki, Warszawa 1989.

Kydland F. E., E. C. Prescott, *Time to build and aggregate fluctuations*, „Econometrica", 1982, no. 6.

Kynaston D., *Austerity Britain, 1945–51*, London – Berlin – New York 2007.

Lacey J., *Keep From All Thoughtful Men. How U.S. Economists Won World War II*, Annapolis 2011.

Lam T., *A Passion for Facts. Social Surveys and the Construction of the Chinese Nation-State 1900–1949*, Berkeley – London 2011.

Landau L., *Gospodarka światowa. Produkcja i dochód społeczny w liczbach*, [in:] idem, *Wybór pism*, Warszawa 1957.

Landau L., *Płace w Polsce w związku z rozwojem gospodarczym*, [in:] idem, *Wybór pism*, Warszawa 1957.

Landau Z., *Etapy rozwoju Polski Ludowej*, „Przegląd Historyczny", 1987, no. 2.

Landau Z., J. Tomaszewski, *Gospodarka Polski międzywojennej 1918–1939*, v. 4: *Lata interwencjonizmu państwowego 1936–1939*, Warszawa 1989.

Landau Z., *Kwiatkowskiego wizja gospodarki polskiej*, „Zeszyty Naukowe Uczelni Warszawskiej im. Marii Skłodowskiej-Curie", 2011, no. 33.

Landau Z., *National income in historical research (on material from the period of the interwar Poland)*, „Acta Poloniae Historica", 1976, no. 33.

Landau Z., W. Roszkowski, *Polityka gospodarcza II RP i PRL*, Warszawa 1995.

Landes D., *Bogactwo i nędza narodów. Dlaczego jedni są tak bogaci, a inni tak ubodzy?*, przeł. H. Jankowska, Warszawa 2005.

Lange O., *Dlaczego kapitalizm nie potrafi rozwiązać problemu krajów gospodarczo zacofanych*, [in:] idem, *Dzieła*, v. 1, Warszawa 1973.

Lange O., *Gospodarcze podstawy demokracji w Polsce*, [in:] idem, *Dzieła*, v. 2, Warszawa 1973.

Lange O., *Maszyna licząca i rynek*, [in:] idem, *O socjalizmie i gospodarce socjalistycznej*, Warszawa 1966.

Lange O., *On the Economic Theory of Socialism*, „The Review of Economic Studies", 1936, no. 1; 1937, no. 2.

Lange O., *On the Economic Theory of Socialism*, Minneapolis 1938; wyd. pol. *O ekonomicznej teorii socjalizmu*, [in:] idem, *Dzieła*, v. 2, Warszawa 1972.

Late Stalinist Russia. Society Between Reconstruction and Reinvention, red. J. Fürst, London – New York 2006.

Latham M. E., *Modernization as Ideology. American Social Science and „Nation Building" in the Kennedy Era*, Chapel Hill 2000.

Leeson R., *The Eclipse of Keynesianism: The Political Economy of the Chicago Counter-Revolution*, Houndmills – New York 2000.

Leeson R., *The political economy of the inflation-unemployment trade-off*, "History of Political Economy", 1997, v. 29, no. 1.

Leibenstein H., *Rozwój i zacofanie gospodarcze. Studia z teorii rozwoju gospodarczego*, przeł. E. Vielrose, Warszawa 1963.

Lenoe M., *Closer to the Masses. Stalinist Culture, Social Revolution, and Soviet Newspapers*, Cambridge – London 2004.

Lerner D., J. S. Coleman, *Modernisation*, [in:] *International Encyclopedia of Social Sciences*, New York 1968.

Lerner D., *The Passing of Traditional Society. Modernizing the Middle East*, Glencoe 1958.

Leszczyński A., *Sprawy do załatwienia. Listy do „Po Prostu" 1955–1957*, Warszawa 2000.

Levy D. M., S. J. Peart, *Soviet Growth and American Textbooks*, SSRN research paper, 3 grudnia 2009, http://ssrn.com/abstract=1517983

Lewin M., *Lenin's Last Struggle*, Ann Arbor 2005.

Lewin M., *The Making of the Soviet System*, New York 1994.

Lewis A. W., *Development economics in the 1950s*, [in:] *Pioneers in Development*, red. G. M. Meier, D. Seers, Washington 1984.

Lewis A. W., *United Nations Primer for Development: Comment*, „Quarterly Journal of Economics", 1953, no. 2.

Lewis W. A., *Economic development with unlimited supplies of labour*, „The Manchester School", 1954, no. 2.

Lipiński E., *Historia powszechnej myśli ekonomicznej do roku 1870*, Warszawa 1968.

List F., *National System of Political Economy*, v. 2, New York 2006.

Lockman Z., *Contending Visions of the Middle East. The History and Politics of Orientalism*, Cambridge – New York 2004.

Love J. L., *Crafting the Third World. Theorizing Underdevelopment in Rumania and Brazil*, Stanford 1996.

Love J. L., *The roots of unequal exchange: Mihail Manoilescu and the debate of the 1930s*, [in:] *Ragnar Nurkse (1907–2007). Classical Development Economics and its Relevance for Today*, red. R. Kattel, J. A. Kregel, E. S. Reinert, London – New York 2011.

Lovell D. W., *From Marx to Lenin. An Evaluation of Marx's Responsibility for Soviet Authoritarianism*, Cambridge 1984.

Low D. A., *Fabrication of Empire. The British and the Uganda Kingdoms 1890–1902*, Cambridge 2009.

López J., M. Assous, *Michal Kalecki*, Houndmills – New York 2010; wyd. pol. *Michał Kalecki*, przeł. A. Szeworski, Warszawa 2011.

Lucas R. E., *Expectations and the neutrality of money*, „Journal of Economic Theory", 1972, v. 4, no. 2.

Lucas R. E., v. J. Sargent, *After Keynesian macroeconomics*, [in:] *Rational Expectations and Econometric Practice*, v. 2, red. R. E. Lucas, v. J. Sargent, Minneapolis 1981.

Lucas R. E., *Understanding business cycles*, „Carnegie-Rochester Conference Series on Public Policy", 1977, no. 5.

Lustig N., *Mexico: The Remaking of an Economy*, Washington 1998.

Lutze v. D., *China's Inevitable Revolution. Rethinking America's Loss to the Communists*, Houndmills – New York 2007.

Łapa M., *Modernizacja państwa. Polska polityka gospodarcza 1926–1929*, Łódź 2002.

Łukawer E., *Spór o racjonalność gospodarki socjalistycznej. Z historii problemu*, Kraków 2005.

MacFarquhar R., M. Schoenhals, *Mao's Last Revolution*, Cambridge – London 2006.

MacGilvray E., *The Invention of Market Freedom*, Cambridge 2011.

Maddison A., *Chinese Economic Performance in the Long Run, 960–2030 AD*, Paris 2007.

Maddison A., *Growth and Interaction in the World Economy. The Roots of Modernity*, Washington 2005.

Maddison A., *The West and the rest in the world economy, 1000–2030: Maddisonian and Malthusian interpretations*, „World Economics", 2008, no. 4.

Maddison A., *The World Economy*, v. 1: *A Millenial Perspective*, v. 2: *Historical Statistics*, Paris 2006.

Mahbubani K., *From Confucius to Kennedy. Principles of East Asian governance*, [in:] *East Asian Visions. Perspectives on Economic Development*, red. I. Gill, Y. Huang, H. Kharas, Washington – Singapore 2007, s. 197.

Maisels Ch. K., *The Emergence of Civilization, From Hunting and Gathering to Agriculture, Cities, and the State in the Near East*, London – New York 1993.

Makowski K., *Świat według Mao Zedonga: doktrynalne podstawy chińskiej polityki zagranicznej (1949–1976)*, Toruń 2006.

Malenbaum W., *Modern economic growth in India and China. The comparison revisited, 1950–1980*, „Economic Development and Cultural Change", 1982, v. 31, no. 1.

Malinowski M. J., *Ideologie afrykańskie 1945–1985*, Wrocław 1986.

Malthus T., *An Essay on the Principle of Population, as It Affects the Future Improvement of Society, with Remarks on the Speculations of Mr. Godwin, M. Condorcet, and Other Writers*, London 1798; wyd. pol. *Prawo ludności*, przeł. K. Stein, Warszawa 2003.

Małowist M., *Poland, Russia and Western trade in the fifteenth to the seventeenth centuries*, „Past and Present", 1958, no. 13.

Małowist M., *Problem nierówności rozwoju gospodarczego Europy późnym średniowieczu*, [in:] *Europa i jej ekspansja XVI–XVII w.*, red. H. Zaremska, Warszawa 1993.

Małowist M., *The problem of the inequality of economic development in Europe in the later Middle Ages*, „Economic History Review", 1966, no. 1.

Małowist M., *Wschód a Zachód Europy w XIII–XVII wieku. Konfrontacja struktur społeczno-gospodarczych*, Warszawa 1973.

Mały rocznik statystyczny 1938, Warszawa 1938.

Mandelbaum K., *Industrialization of Backward Areas*, Oxford 1947.

Manning R. T., *The Soviet economic crisis of 1936–1940 and the Great Purges*, [in:] *Stalinist Terror. New Perspectives*, red. J. A. Getty, R. v. Manning, Cambridge 1993.

Manzetti L., *Neoliberalism, Accountability, and Reform Failures in Emerging Markets*, University Park 2009.

Mao Tse-tung, *Jü-kung przesunął góry. Przemówienie wygłoszone przez towarzysza Mao Tse-tunga z okazji zamknięcia VII Zjazdu Komunistycznej Partii Chin (11 czerwca 1945 roku)*, [in:] idem, *Dzieła wybrane*, v. 4, Warszawa 1958.

Mao Tse-Tung, Lin Piao, *Post-Revolutionary Writings*, red. K. Fan, Garden City 1972.

Mao Tse-Tung, *Selected Works*, v. 5, Peking 1977.

Mao Tse-Tung, *Szesnaście wierszy*, Warszawa 1959.

Mao Tse-Tung, *Wojna Chin przeciwko Japonii*, Warszawa 1949.

Mao Zedong, *Comment on suppressing and liquidating contrrevolutionaries*, 8 maja 1951, [in:] *The Writings of Mao Zedong 1949–1976*, red. M. Y. M. Kau, J. K. Leung, M.E. Sharpe, Armonk – London 1986.

Marczewska-Rytko M., *Indyjski Kongres Narodowy w warunkach konsolidowania systemu demokratycznego*, [in:] *Ideologie, doktryny i ruchy narodowe. Wybrane problemy*, red. S. Stępień, Lublin 2006.

Marks K., *Kapitał. Krytyka ekonomii politycznej*, v. 1: *Proces wytwarzania kapitału*, przekł. zbior., Warszawa 1951.

Marks K., *Rządy brytyjskie w Indiach*, [in:] K. Marks, F. Engels, *Dzieła*, v. 9, Warszawa 1965.

Mathurin Mair L., *Women field workers in Jamaica during slavery*, [in:] *Slavery, Freedom and Gender, The Dynamics of Caribbean Society*, red. B. Moore, B. W. Higman, C. Campbell, P. Bryan, Barbados – Jamaica – Trinidad and Tobago 2003.

Mau V., I. Starodubovskaya, *The Challenge of Revolution. Contemporary Russia in Historical Perspective*, Oxford 2003.

Maul D., *Human Rights, Development and Decolonization*, London – New York 2012.

Mazurek M., *Socjalistyczny zakład pracy*, Warszawa 2005.

Mazurek M., *Społeczeństwo kolejki. O doświadczeniach niedoboru 1945–1989*, Warszawa 2010.

Mączak A., *Między Gdańskiem a Sundem*, Warszawa 1972.

Mączak A., *The social distribution of landed property in Poland from the 16th to the 18th century*, [in:] *Third International Conference of Economic History*, v. 1, Paris 1968.

Mączak A., *U źródeł nowożytnej gospodarki europejskiej*, Warszawa 1967.

McCloskey D. N., *The Bourgeois Dignity. Why Economics Can't Explain the Modern World*, Chicago 2010.

Meadows D. H., D. L. Meadows, J. Randers, W. W. Behrens III, *Granice wzrostu*, przeł. W. Rączkowska, S. Rączkowski, Warszawa 1973.

Measures for the Economic Development of Under-Developed Countries. Report by a Group of Experts appointed by the Secretary-General of the United Nations, New York 1951.

Meier G. M., *The formative period*, [in:] *Pioneers in Development*, red. G. M. Meier, D. Seers, Washington 1984.

Meier G. M., *The old generation of development economists and the new*, [in:] *Frontiers Of Development Economics. The Future In Perspective*, red. G. M. Meier, J. E. Stiglitz, New York 2001.

Meisner M., *Mao Zedong. A Political and Intellectual Portrait*, London 2007.

Meller P., *Un siglo de economia politica chilena 1890–1990*, Barcelona – Buenos Aires – Mexico – Santiago 1998.

Memoirs of Nikita Khruschev, Commissar 1918–1945, red. S. Khrushchev, University Park 2005.

Memoriał kierownika Biura Informacji KC WKP(b) Leonida Baranowa oraz instruktorów KC WKP(b) Nikołaja Puchłowa i Władimira Owczarowa „O antymarksistowskiej orientacji w kierownictwie PPR", [in:] *Polska – ZSRR. Struktury podległości. Dokumenty WKP(b) 1944–1949*, red. G. A. Bordiugow, A. Kochański, A. Koseski, G. F. Matwiejew, A. Paczkowski, Warszawa 1995.

Micklethwait J., A. Wooldridge, *The Right Nation. Conservative Power in America*, New York 2004, s. 60.

Mielants E. H., *The Origins of Capitalism and the Rise of the West*, Philadelphia 2007.

Miguel E., M. Kremer, *Worms: Identifying Impacts on Education and Health in the Presence of Treatment Externalities*, „Econometrica", 2004, no. 72.

Mills J., *A Critical History of Economics*, Houndmills – New York 2002.

Miłosz Cz., *Rodzinna Europa*, Warszawa 1990.

Minc B., *Ekonomia polityczna socjalizmu*, Warszawa 1973.

Mironov B., *The burden of grandeur. Physical and economic well-being of the Russian population in the eighteenth century*, [in:] *Living Standards in the Past. New Perspectives on Well-Being in Asia and Europe*, red. R. Allen, v. Bengtsson, M. Dribe, Oxford 2005.

Mises L. von, *Kalkulacja ekonomiczna w socjalizmie*, przeł. J. Jabłecki Warszawa 2011.

Mises L. von, *Theory of Money and Credit*, Auburn 2009.

Mises L. von,, *Socjalizm*, przeł. S. Sękowski, Kraków 2009.

Mitcham Ch. J., *China's Economic Relations with the West and Japan, 1949–79. Grain, Trade and Diplomacy*, London – New York 2005.

Mitter R., *Gorzka rewolucja. Zmagania Chin z nowoczesnym światem*, przeł. v. Białogórska, Warszawa 2008.

Mizuno H., *Science for the Empire. Scientific Nationalism in Modern Japan*, Stanford 2009.

Modernization. The Dynamics of Growth, red. M. Weiner, New York – London 1966.

Mokyr J., *The Enlightened Economy. Britain and Industrial Revolution*, London – New York 2011.

Moon Ch., B. Jun, *Modernization strategy: ideas and influences*, [in:] *The Park Chung Hee Era. The Transformation of South Korea*, red. B. Kim, E. F. Vogel, Cambridge – London 2011.

Morawski W., *Poglądy gospodarcze Władysława Gomułki*, [in:] *Gospodarka i społeczeństwo w czasach PRL-u (1944–1989)*, red. E. Kościk, v. Głowiński, Wrocław 2007.

Moreno-Bird J. C., J. Ros, *Development and Growth in the Mexican Economy*, Oxford – New York 2009.

Morewood S., *The demise of the command economies in the Soviet Union and its outer empire*, [in:] *Economic Disasters of the Twentieth Century*, red. M. J. Olivier, D. H. Aldcroft, Cheltenham – Northampton 2007.

Morikawa H., *Zaibatsu: The Rise and Fall of Family Enterprise Groups in Japan*, Tokyo 1992.

Mrozek B., *Mahatma Gandhi – przywódca Indii*, Warszawa 1977.

Mrozek B., *Nehru*, Warszawa 1974.

Mukasa H., E. Millar, *Uganda's Katikiro in England: Being the Offical Account of His Visit to the Coronation of His Majesty King Edward VII*, London 1904.

Mulcahy R. E., *Readings in Economics from Fortune*, New York 1954.

Müller A., *Przyspieszony wzrost gospodarczy w Polsce w latach 1971–1975*, „Zeszyty Naukowe Uczelni Warszawskiej im. Marii Skłodowskiej-Curie", 2011, no. 33.

Myrdal G., *Teoria ekonomii a kraje gospodarczo nierozwinięte*, przeł. S. Ficowski, Warszawa 1958.

Nabiel E., *Gospodarka wojenna Niemiec, 1914–1918*, Warszawa 1959.

Nadolski M., *Programy przeobrażeń ustrojowych w Polsce komunistów i ugrupowań prokomunistycznych w latach 1941–1948*, [in:] *Elity władzy w Polsce a struktura społeczna w latach 1944–1956*, red. P. Wójcik, Warszawa 1992.

Narojek W., *Społeczeństwo planujące, próba socjologii gospodarki socjalistycznej*, Warszawa 1973.

Nash G. H., *The Conservative Intellectual Movement in America since 1945*, Wilmington 2006.

Ndulu B. J., S. A. O'Connell, *Policy plus: African growth performance, 1960–2000*, [in:] *The Political Economy of Economic Growth in Africa, 1960–2000*, v. 1, red. B. J. Ndulu, S. A. O'Connell, R. H. Bates, P. Collier, Ch. C. Soludo, Cambridge – New York 2008.

Nehru J., *Odkrycie Indii*, przeł. S. Majewski, K. Rapaczyński, Warszawa 1957.

Nehru J., *The Discovery of India*, Oxford 1994.

Nietzsche F., *Poza dobrem i złem*, przeł. G. Pieniążek, Kraków 2005, par. 296.

Nkrumah K., *Autobiography*, New York 1957.

Nobel Lectures. Economic sciences 1969–1980, red. A. Lindbeck, Singapore 1992.

Nordhaus W., *Retrospective on the 1970s Productivity Slowdown*, NBER Working Paper no. 10950, grudzień 2004.

Nove A., *Stalinism and After. The Road to Gorbachev*, London – New York 1992.

Nove A., *Was Stalin Really Necessary? Some Problems of Soviet Political Economy*, New York 1964.

Nunn N., N. Qian, *The Potato's Contribution to Population and Urbanization: Evidence from an Historical Experiment*, National Bureau Of Economic Research Working Paper no. 15157, 2009.

Nunn N., *The long-term effects of Africa's slave trade*, „Quarterly Journal of Economics", 2008, no. 1.

Nurkse R., *Problems of Capital Formation in Underdeveloped Countries*, New York 1961.

Nustad K. G., *The development discourse in the multilateral system*, [in:] *Global Institutions and Development. Framing the world?*, London – New York 2004.

Nyerere J., *Arusha Declaration*, http://www.marxists.org/subject/africa/nyerere/1967/arusha-declaration.htm, dostęp: 14 listopada 2012.

Nyerere J., *Ujamaa. Basis of African socialism*, „Journal of Pan African Studies", 1987, no. 1.

O'Brien P., *European Economic Development: The Contribution of the Periphery*, „The Economic History Review", 1982, no. 1.

O'Brien P., J. Roddick, *Chile: The Pinochet Decade: The Rise and Fall of the Chicago Boys*, New York 1983.

Ocampo J. A., M. A. Parra, *The continuing relevance of the terms of trade and industrialization debates*, [in:] *Ideas, Policies and Economic Development in the Americas*, red. E. P. Caldentey, M. Vernengo, London 2007.

Ogushi A., *The Demise of the Soviet Communist Party*, London – New York 2005.

Olson M., *Dictatorship, Democracy and Development*, „American Poltical Science Review", 1994, no. 3.

Olson M., *Logika działania zbiorowego. Dobra publiczne i teoria grup*, przeł. S. Szymański, Warszawa 2012.

Olson M., *The Productivity Slowdown, the Oil Shocks, and the Real Cycle*, „Journal of Economic Perspectives", 1988, v. 2, no. 4.

Oppenheim L. H., *Politics in Chile. Democracy, Authoritarianism and the Search for Development*, Boulder 1999.

Orłowski W., *Gospodarka polska w ostatnim tysiącleciu*, http://www.nobe.pl/gospodarka-pol-1000.htm.

Orłowski W., *W pogoni za straconym czasem. Wzrost gospodarczy w Europie Środkowo-Wschodniej 1950–2030*, Warszawa 2010.

Oshima H. T., *The transition from an agricultural to an industrial economy in East Asia*, „Economic Development and Cultural Change", 1986, v. 34, no. 4.

Oshima H., *Accelerated Growth: Japan's Experience*, „Economic Development and Cultural Change", 1970, v. 19, no. 1.

Osiatyński J., *Michał Kalecki o gospodarce socjalistycznej*, Warszawa 1983.

Pakenham T., *The Scramble for Africa*, London 2001.

Palma G., *Dependency: A formal theory of underdevelopment or a methodology for the analysis of concrete situations of underdevelopment?*, „World Development" 1978, no. 6.

Palme Dutt R., *Britain's Crisis of Empire*, London 1949.

Palmer C. A., *Africa in the making of the Caribbean*, [in:] *Slavery, Freedom and Gender, The Dynamics of Caribbean Society*, red. B. Moore, B. W. Higman, C. Campbell, P. Bryan, Barbados – Jamaica – Trinidad and Tobago 2003.

Panagariya A., *India. The Emerging Giant*, New York 2008.

Park C. H., *Country, Revolution and I*, Seoul 1970.

Park C. H., *Our Nation's Path: Ideology of Social Reconstruction*, Seoul 1962.

Parrish M., *The Lesser Terror. Soviet State Security, 1939–1953*, Westport – London 1996.

Parthasarathi P., *Agriculture, labour, and the standard of living in eighteenth-century India*, [in:] *Living Standards in the Past. New Perspectives on Well-Being in Asia and Europe*, red. R. Allen, v. Bengtsson, M. Dribe, Oxford 2005.

Paruch W., *Autorytarna formuła legitymizacji władzy w piłsudczykowskiej myśli politycznej – warianty, kontrowersje, poszukiwania*, [in:] *Kryzysy i sposoby ich przezwyciężania w myśli politycznej XX wieku*, red. W. Wojdyło, Toruń 2004.

Paruch W., *Piłsudczykowska koncepcja polityki równowagi (1926–1939). Przesłanki, założenia, składniki, ewolucja*, [in:] *Świat wokół Rzeczypospolitej. Problematyka zagraniczna w polskiej myśli politycznej w pierwszej połowie XX wieku*, red. W. Paruch, K. Trembicka, Lublin 2007.

Paruch W., *Przejawy i ograniczenia liberalizmu w piłsudczykowskiej myśli politycznej (1926–1939)*, [in:] *Polskie zbliżenia z liberalizmem*, red. v. Godlewski, D. Karnowska, Toruń 2006.

Paruch W., *Założenia systemowe antydemokratycznej modernizacji Rzeczypospolitej – rozważania o piłsudczykowskiej myśli politycznej (1926–1939)*, [in:] *Demokracja. Centrum i peryferie. Procesy modernizacyjne państwa w polskiej myśli politycznej XX–XXI wieku*, red. A. Bałaban, J. Faryś, v. Sikorski, P. Słowiński, Szczecin 2008.

Patrikeeff F., *Stalinism, totalitarian society and the politics of perfect control*, [in:] *Redefining Stalinism*, red. H. Shukman, London – Portland 2003.

Pepłowski F., *Słownictwo i frazeologia polskiej publicystyki okresu oświecenia i romantyzmu*, Warszawa 1961.

Perlstein R., *Enemies of state*, „Democracy. A Journal of Ideas", 2011, no. 19.

Phelps E. S., *Money-wage dynamics and labor-market equilibrium*, „Journal of Political Economy", 1968, v. 76, no. 4.

Phelps E. S., *Recollections of My Past Research in Economics. Speech on the Award of an Honorary Professorship*, Beijing Technology and Business University, Pekin, 1 czerwca 2005, http://www.columbia.edu/~esp2/BeijingTechAndBusUniversity2005D4.pdf.

Phillips A. W., *The relation between unemployment and the rate of change of money wage rates in the United Kingdom, 1861–1957*, „Economica", 1958, v. 25, no. 100.

Phillips-Fein K., *Invisible Hands. Conservative Movement from the New Deal to Reagan*, New York 2009.

Pierwsze wydanie polskie pod tytułem *Droga do niewoli* ukazało się w Londynie w 1982 roku.

Pines Y., *The Everlasting Empire: The Political Culture of Ancient China and Its Imperial Legacy*, Cambridge - London 2012.

Pirani S., *The Russian Revolution in Retreat, 1920–24. Soviet Workers and the New Communist Elite*, London - New York 2008.

Plan budowy COP, „Polska Gospodarcza", 1938, no. 40.

Platon, *Prawa*, przeł. M. Maykowska, Warszawa 1960.

Poboży B., *W walce o Polskę Ludową. Wizje przyszłej Polski w myśli politycznej ruchu ludowego w latach 1939–1945*, [in:] *Dylematy historii i polityki. Księga dedykowana profesor Annie Magierskiej*, red. R. Chwedoruk, D. Przastek, Warszawa 2008.

Polanyi K., *Wielka transformacja: polityczne i ekonomiczne źródła naszych czasów*, przeł. M. Zawadzka, Warszawa 2010.

Pollard S., *Factory discipline in the Industrial Revolution*, „The Economic History Review", 1963, no. 2.

Pollock D., D. Kerner, J. L. Love, *Raúl Prébisch on ECLAC's achievements and deficiencies: an unpublished interview*, „Cepal Review", 2001, no. 75.

Pomeranz K., *Standards of living in eighteenth-century China: regional differences, temporal trends, and incomplete evidence*, [in:] *Living Standards in the Past. New Perspectives on Well-Being in Asia and Europe*, red. R. Allen, v. Bengtsson, M. Dribe, Oxford 2005.

Pomeranz K., *The Great Divergence. China, Europe, and the Making of the Modern World Economy*, Princeton 2000.

Ponczek E., *Aksjologiczny wymiar lewicowości w polskiej myśli politycznej w latach II wojny światowej*, [in:] *Polska lewica w XX wieku. Historia - ludzie - idee*, red. v. Ślęzak, M. Śliwa, Kraków 2004.

Popławski B., *Polska szkoła rozwoju - zapomniany paradygmat studiów nad transformacją globalnego południa*, „Kultura Współczesna", 2012, no. 3.

Prados de la Escosura L., *When did Latin America fall behind?*, [in:] *The Decline of Latin American Economies Growth, Institutions, and Crises*, red. S. Edwards, G. Esquivel, G. Marquez, Chicago - London 2007.

Prébisch R., *El desarrollo económico de la América Latina y algunos de sus principales problemas*, „Desarrollo Económico", 1986, no. 103.

Prébisch R., *Five stages in my thinking on development*, [in:] *Pioneers in Development*, red. G. Meier, D. Seers, Oxford 1984.

Prébisch R., *The Economic Development of Latin America and Its Principal Problems*, New York 1950.

Preobrazhensky E. A., *New Economics*, Oxford 1965.

Prieobrażenski J., *Prawo pierwotnej akumulacji socjalistycznej*, przeł. J. Dobieszewski, [in:] *Marksizm XX wieku. Antologia tekstów*, red. J. Dobieszewski, M. J. Siemek, cz. II, Warszawa 1990.

Primi A., *Nurkse and the early Latin American structuralists: a reflection on development theory, industrialization and their relevance today*, [in:] *Ragnar Nurkse (1907–2007). Classical Development Economics and its Relevance for Today*, red. R. Kattel, J. A. Kregel, E. S. Reinert, London – New York 2011.

Programy polskich partii politycznych i ugrupowań partyzanckich lat wojny i okupacji hitlerowskiej, wyb. i red. K. Przybysz, Warszawa 1987.

Przeworski A., C. Curvale, *Does politics explain the economic gap between the United States and Latin America?*, [in:] *Falling Behind. Explaining the Development Gap Between Latin America and the United States*, red. F. Fukuyama, Oxford – New York 2008.

Przybysz K., *Polska myśl polityczna 1939–1945. Zarys problematyki*, Warszawa 2000.

Przybysz K., *Program przeobrażeń politycznych w myśli politycznej Rady Jedności Narodowej oraz opozycji demokratycznej w latach 1945–1947*, [in:] *Elity władzy w Polsce a struktura społeczna w latach 1944–1956*, red. P. Wójcik, Warszawa 1992.

Przybysz K., *U źródeł Trzeciej Rzeczypospolitej. O przyszłości społeczeństwa i państwa w latach 1939–1945*, [in:] *Dylematy historii i polityki. Księga dedykowana profesor Annie Magierskiej*, red. R. Chwedoruk, D. Przastek, Warszawa 2008.

Ptasiński J., *Gomułka – jakiego znałem*, [in:] *Władysław Gomułka we wspomnieniach*, red. B. Szyzdek, Lublin 1989.

Public Papers of the Presidents of the United States, Richard Nixon, 1971, General Services Administration, National Archives and Records Service, Office of the Federal Register, Washington 1972.

Qi S., *Western Literature in China and the Translation of a Nation*, Houndmills – New York 2012.

Rabe S. G., *Eisenhower and Latin America. The Foreign Policy of Anti-Communism*, Chapel Hill – London 1988.

Rabe S. G., *The Most Dangerous Area in the World. John F. Kennedy Confronts Communist Revolution in Latin America*, Chapel Hill – London 1999.

Rada Ekonomiczna przy Radzie Ministrów, *Przegląd bieżącej sytuacji gospodarczej kraju i zadania stojące przed polityką gospodarczą*, Warszawa 1957.

Radzinsky E., *Stalin*, New York 1997.

Rassweiler A., *The Generation of Power. The History of Dneprostroi*, New York – Oxford 1988.

Rawley J., *London, Metropolis of the Slave Trade*, Columbia – London 2003.

Report on the First Results of the Improved Road-Transport Governance (IRTG) Initiative on Interstate Highways, Bamako 2007.

Riskin C., *Feeding China: the experience since 1949*, [in:] *The Political Economy of Hunger*, v. 3, red. J. Drèze, A. Sen, Oxford – New York 2007.

Rist G., *The History of Development. From Western Origins to Global Faith*, London 2006.

Ritschel D., *The Politics of Planning. The Debate on Economic Planning in Britain in the 1930s*, Oxford – New York 1997.

Ritschl A., *The pity of peace: Germany's economy at war, 1914–1918 and beyond*, [in:] *The Economics of World War I*, red. S. Broadberry, M. Harrison, Cambridge 2005.

Robin C., *The Reactionary Mind. Conservatism from Edmund Burke to Sarah Palin*, Oxford – New York 2011.

Robinson G. T., *Rural Russia under the Old Regime*, Berkeley – Los Angeles 1969.

Robinson J., *Economic Management – China 1972*, London 1973.

Rodrik D., *Diagnostics before prescription*, „Journal of Economic Perspectives", 2010, no. 3.

Rodrik D., *The Real Exchange Rate and Economic Growth: Theory and Evidence*, lipiec 2007, http://www.cid.harvard.edu/neudc07/docs/neudc07_s1_p04_rodrik.pdf.

Rogaczewska K., *Myśl ekonomiczna Narodowej Demokracji w kontekście konfliktu liberalizmu i socjalizmu*, [in:] *Narodowa Demokracja XIX–XXI wiek. Dzieje ruchu politycznego*, v. 1, *Koncepcje – ludzie*, Toruń 2012.

Rogaczewska R., *Ekonomiczny wymiar polskiego liberalizmu. Od fizjokratyzmu do szkoły krakowskiej*, Wrocław 2011.

Rose A., *A Stable International Monetary System Emerges: Bretton Woods*. NBER Working Paper No. 12711.

Rosenbaum R. A., *Waking to Danger. Americans and Nazi Germany, 1933–1941*, Santa Barbara – Denver – Oxford 2010.

Rosenberg T., *Latin America's magical liberalism*, [in:] *Politics and Social Change in Latin America: Still a Distinct Tradition?*, red. H. J. Wiarda, M. MacLeish Mott, Boulder 2009.

Rosenstein-Rodan P. N., *Problems of industrialisation of Eastern and South-Eastern Europe*, „The Economic Journal", 1943, no. 210–211.

Rosenstein-Rodan P., *Natura facit saltum: analysis of the disequilibrium growth process*, [in:] *Pioneers in Development*, red. G. M. Meier, D. Seers, Washington 1984.

Rosenstein-Rodan, P., *Uwagi o teorii wielkiego pchnięcia*, „Ekonomista", 1959, no. 2.

Rostow on Growth. A Non-Communist Manifesto, „The Economist", 15 sierpnia 1959 oraz 22 sierpnia 1959.

Rostow W. W., *Concept and Controversy. Sixty Years of Taking Ideas to Market*, Austin 2003.

Rostow W. W., *Politics and the Stages of Growth*, Cambridge 1971.

Rostow W. W., *The Stages of Economic Growth*, Cambridge 1960.

Rostow W. W., *The take-off into self-sustained growth*, „The Economic Journal" 1961, no. 261.

Rostow W. W., *Theorists of Economic Growth from David Hume to the Present*, New York 1992.

Roszkowski W., *Etatyzm przemysłowy w Polsce w latach kryzysu*, „Przegląd Historyczny", 1972, z. 1.

Roszkowski W., *Gospodraka. Wzrost i upadek systemu nakazowo-rozdzielczego*, Warszawa 2008.

Rouquié A., *The military in Latin American politics since 1930*, [in:] *Latin America. Politics and Society since 1930*, red. L. Bethell, Cambridge – New York 1998.

Różański H., *Śladem wspomnień i dokumentów, 1943–1948*, Warszawa 1988.

Rudnicki Sz., *Koncepcje niepodległego państwa w myśli politycznej obozu narodowego*, [in:] *Wizje Polski w myśli politycznej lat I i II wojny światowej*, red. M. Tanty, Warszawa 1990.

Ruger W., J. Meadowcroft, *Milton Friedman*, London 2011.

Rummel R. J., *China's Bloody Century: Genocide and Mass Murder since 1900*, New Brunswick 1991.

Rutland P., *The Politics of Economic Stagnation in the Soviet Union*, Cambridge 1993.

Rychard A., *Władza i gospodarka*, [in:] *Zmierzch socjalizmu państwowego. Szkice z socjologii ekonomicznej*, red. W. Morawski, Warszawa 1994.

Sachs I., *Drogi i manowce świata „B"*, Warszawa 1964.

Sachs W., *The Development Dictionary: A Guide to Knowledge as Power*, London 1992.

Sah R. K., J. E. Stiglitz, *Peasants versus City-Dwellers. Taxation and the Burden of Economic Development*, Oxford – New York 1992.

Samuels R. J., *Rich Nation, Strong Army. National Security and the Technological Transformation of Japan*, Ithaca – New York 1994.

Sarkar P., *The Singer-Prebisch hypothesis: a statistical evaluation*, „Cambridge Journal of Economics", 1986, no. 10.

Schneider G. L., *The Conservative Century. From Reaction to Revolution*, Lanham – New York 2009.

Schram S., *Mao Tse-tung and theory of permanent revolution 1958–69*, „China Quarterly", 1971, no. 46.

Schram S., *The Thought of Mao Tse-Tung*, London 1989.

Schroeder G., *The slowdown in Soviet industry, 1976–1982*, „Soviet Economy", 1985, no. 1.

Schumpeter J., *Capitalism, socialism and democracy*, New York 2003.

Scott J. C., *Seeing Like State: How Certain Schemes to Improve the Human Condition Have Failed*, New Haven 1998.

Scott J., *Behind the Urals. An American Worker in Russia's City of Steel*, opracował i wydał S. Kotkin, Bloomington 1989.

Seers D., *The congruence of Marxism and other neoclassical doctrines*, [in:] *Toward a New Strategy for Development. A Rothko Chapel Colloquium*, New York – Oxford – Toronto – Sydney – Frankfurt – Paris 1979.

Shapiro J., *Mao's War Against Nature. Politics and the Environment in Revolutionary China*, Cambridge – New York 2001.

Shivji I. G., *The village in Mwalimu's thought and political* practice, [in:] *The Legacy of Nyerere*, red. Ch. Chachage, A. Cassam, Kampala 2010.

Shlapentokh V., *A Normal Totalitarian Society. How the Soviet Union Functioned and How It Collapsed*, Armonk – London 2001.

Shleifer A., R. Vishney, *Corruption*, „Quarterly Journal of Economics", 1993, no. 108.

Shore M., *Kosmopolityzm, awangarda i utracona niewinnosć Europy Środkowej*, [in:] eadem, *Nowoczesność jako źródło cierpień*, przeł. M. Sutowski, Warszawa 2012.

Short P., *Mao: A Life*, New York 2000.

Siegelbaum L., A. Sokolov, *Stalinism as a Way of Life*, New Haven – London 2000.

Siegelbaum L., *Soviet State and Society between Revolutions, 1918–1929*, Cambridge 1994.

Siegelbaum L., *Stakhanovism and the Politics of Productivity in the USSR, 1935–1941*, Cambridge 1990.

Sigmund P. E., *The Overthrow of Allende and the Politics of Chile*, Pittsburgh 1980.

Silva P., *In the Name of Reason. Technocrats and Politics in Chile*, University Park 2008.

Singer H. W., *The distribution of gains between investing and borrowing countries*, „American Economic Review", 1950, v. 40, no. 2.

Singer H. W., *The terms of trade controversy*, [in:] *Pioneers in Development*, red. G. Meier, D. Seers, Oxford 1984.

Singer P., *The Life You Can Save. Acting Now to End World Poverty*, Melbourne 2009.

Skidelsky R., *Keynes. Powrót mistrza*, przeł. v. Krzyżanowski, M. Sutowski, Warszawa 2012.

Skieterski S., *Świadomość chłopów okresu kolektywizacji w świetle pamiętników*, „Przegląd Humanistyczny", 1990, no. 4.

Skousen M., *The Making of Modern Economics: The Lives and Ideas of the Great Thinkers*, Armonk 2001.

Skrabalak W., *Polscy socjaliści w XX wieku. Ich rodowody oraz uwarunkowania ich działalności*, Warszawa 2010.

Skrzypek A., *Mechanizmy klientelizmu. Stosunki polsko-radzieckie 1965–1989*, Warszawa 2008.

Slavery and the Rise of the Atlantic System, red. B. Solow, Cambridge 1991.

Słonimski A., *Moja podróż do Rosji*, Warszawa 1997.

Smith A., *Badania nad naturą i przyczynami bogactwa narodów*, v. 1, przeł. S. Wolff, E. Einfeld, Z. Sadowski, Warszawa 2007.

Smith K., *A Time of Crisis: Japan, the Great Depression and Rural Revitalization*, Cambridge 2001.

Smith v. C., *Native Sources of Japanese Industrialization, 1750–1920*, Berkeley – Los Angeles – London 1989.

Smolka S., *Polityka Lubeckiego przed Powstaniem Listopadowym*, v. 1, Warszawa 1983.

Snyder T., *Skrwawione ziemie. Europa między Hitlerem a Stalinem*, przeł. B. Pietrzyk, Warszawa 2011.

Sokoloff K. L., S. L. Engerman, *History lessons…*, dz. cyt.. Zob. też D.

Sokoloff K., S. Engerman, *History lessons. Institutions, factor endowments, and paths of development in the new world*, „Journal of Economic Perspectives", 2000, v. 14, no. 3.

Solow R. M., *Faith, hope and clarity*, [in:] *The Spread of Economic Ideas*, red. D. C. Colander, A. W. Coats, Cambridge 1989, s. 82.

Solow R., *Did policy errors of the 1960s sow the seeds of trouble in the 1970s?*, [in:] *The Legacy of the Golden Age. The 1960s and Their Economic Consequences*, red. A. Cairncross, F. Cairncross, London - New York 2003.

Song X., *Between Civic and Ethnic. The Transformation of Taiwanese Nationalist Ideologies, 1895-2000*, Brussels 2009.

Sosnowska A., *Zrozumieć zacofanie. Spory historyków o Europę Wschodnią 1947-1994*, Warszawa 2004.

Spence J., *The Search for Modern China*, New York - London 1990.

Spojrzenie na Rosję, red. J. Kochanowski, Warszawa 1994.

Sprawy gospodarcze w dokumentach pierwszej „Solidarności", v. 1: *16 sierpnia 1980-30 czerwca 1981*, wyb. i opr. J. Luszniewicz, A. Zawistowski, Warszawa 2008.

Sprenkel O. B. van der, *Max Weber on China*, „History and Theory", 1964, v. 3, no. 3.

Staley E., *World Economic Development: Effects on Advanced Industrial Countries*, New York 1944.

Stalin J., *Dzieła*, v. 12, Warszawa 1951.

Stalin J., *Nowa sytuacja - Nowe zadania budownictwa gospodarczego. Przemówienie wygłoszone na naradzie działaczy gospodarczych 23 czerwca 1931 r.*, [in:] idem, *Dzieła*, v. 13, Warszawa 1951.

Stalin J., *O industrializacji kraju i o prawicowym odchyleniu w WKP(b). Przemówienie na plenum KC WKP(b) 19 listopada 1928 r.*, [in:] idem, *Dzieła*, v. 11, Warszawa 1954.

Stalin J., *Sprawozdanie polityczne KC na XVI Zjeździe WKP(b)*, [in:] idem, *Dzieła*, v. 12, Warszawa 1951.

Stankiewicz T., *Działalność inwestytycjna państwa w Polsce w latach 1945-1947*, Warszawa 1993.

Steckel R. H., R. A. Jensen, *Determinants of Slave and Crew Mortality in the Atlantic Slave Trade*, NBER Working Paper no. 1540, 1985.

Stępień S., *Polska - Europa - świat w myśli politycznej PPS-WRN*, [in:] *Świat wokół Rzeczypospolitej. Problematyka zagraniczna w polskiej myśli politycznej w pierwszej połowie XX wieku*, red. W. Paruch, K. Trembicka, Lublin 2007.

Stites R., *Revolutionary Dreams. Utopian Vision and Experimental Life in the Russian Revolution*, New York - Oxford 1989.

Stola D., *Kraj bez wyjścia. Migracje z Polski 1949-1989*, Warszawa 2012.

Strachan H., *The First World War*, v. 1, Oxford 2001.

Strand D., *An Unfinished Republic. Leading by Word and Deed in Modern China*, Berkeley – London 2011.

Su Y., *Mass killings in the Cultural Revolution: a study of three provinces*, [in:] *The Chinese Cultural Revolution as History*, red. J. W. Esherick, P. G. Pickowicz, A. G. Walter, Stanford 2006.

Summers L. H., *Some skeptical observations on real business cycle theory*, „Federal Reserve Bank of Minneapolis Quarterly Review", 1986, no. 3.

Sutela P., *Soviet economics after Stalin: between orthodoxy and reform*, [in:] *Economics in Russia. Studies in Intellectual* History, red. V. Barnett, J. Zweynert, Aldershot – Burlington 2008.

Swedberg R., *Max Weber and the Idea of Economic Sociology*, Princeton 2000.

Swianiewicz S., *World economic growth and the Soviet challenge*, „The Review of Politics", 1968, no. 4.

Szlajfer H., *Droga na skróty: nacjonalizm gospodarczy w Ameryce Łacińskiej i Europie Środkowej w epoce pierwszej globalizacji*, Warszawa 2005.

Tamedly E. L., *Socialism and International Economic Order*, Caldwell 1969.

Taylor J., *The Generalissimo. Chiang Kai-Shek and the Struggle for Modern China*, Cambridge – London 2009.

Teiwes F. C., *The estabilishment and consolidation of the new regime 1949–1957*, [in:] *The Politics of China. The Eras of Mao and Deng*, red. R. MacFarquhar, Cambridge 1997.

Teiwes F. C., W. Sun, *The End of the Maoist Era. Chinese Politics During the Twilight of the Cultural Revolution, 1972–1976*, Armonk – London 2007.

Teiwes F. C., W. Sun, *The Politics of Agricultural Cooperativization in China. Mao, Deng Zihui, and the „High Tide" of 1955*, Armonk – London 1993.

Temkin G., *Dyskusje o gospodarce socjalistycznej: Marks – Lange – Mises – Hayek*, Warszawa 2011.

Teoria wyboru publicznego. Wstęp do ekonomicznej analizy polityki, red. J. Wilkin, Warszawa 2005.

Tharoor S., *Nehru. The Invention of India*, New York 2003.

The Making of Modern Iran. State and Society under Riza Shah, 1921–1941, red. S. Cronin, London – New York 2003.

The Miracles of Chairman Mao. A Compendium of Devotional Literature, 1966–1970, red. G. Urban, London 1971.

The Origins and Development of Financial Markets and Institutions, red. J. Atack, L. Neal, Cambridge 2009.

The War Against the Peasantry 1927–1930. The Tragedy of the Soviet Countryside, red. L. Viola, V. P. Danilov, N. A. Ivnitskii, D. Kozlov, New Haven - London 2005.

Think Tanks and Civil Societies. Catalysts for Ideas and Action, red. J. G. McGann, R. K. Weaver, New Brunswick 2009.

Thompson E. P., *The Making of the English Working* Class, New York 1963.

Thornbecke E., *The evolution of the development doctrine, 1950–2005*, [in:] *Advancing Development. Core Themes in Global Economics*, red. G. Mavrotas, A. Shorrocks, London - New York 2007.

Tignor R. L., *W. Arthur Lewis and the Birth of Development Economics*, Princeton 2006.

Tikhonov A., *The end of the Gulag*, [in:] *The Economics of Forced Labor. The Soviet Gulag*, red. P. R. Gregory, V. Lazarev, Stanford 2003.

Togo K., *Infant industry protection policy reconsidered: the case of the automobile industry in Japan*, [in:] *Miraculous Growth and Stagnation in Post-War Japan*, red. K. Hamada, K. Otsuka, G. Ranis, K. Togo, New York 2011.

Tomicki J., *Polska Partia Socjalistyczna 1892–1948*, Warszawa 1983.

Tooze A., *The Wages of Destruction. The Making and Breaking of The Nazi Economy*, New York 2008.

Topolski J., *Economic decline in Poland from the sixteenth to the eighteenth centuries*, [in:] *Essays in European Economic History*, red. P. Earle, Oxford 1974.

Topolski J., *Gospodarka polska a europejska w XVI–XVIII wieku*, Poznań 1977.

Topolski J., *Sixteenth century Poland and the turning point in European economic development*, [in:] *A Republic of Nobles. Studies in Polish History to 1864*, red. J. K. Fedorowicz, Cambridge 1982.

Topolski J., *The manorial-serf economy in Central and Eastern Europe in the 16th and 17th centuries*, „Agricultural History", 1974, no. 3.

Toward a New Strategy for Development: a Rothko Chapel Colloquium, red. A. O. Hirschman, Oxford 1979.

Travel Writing 1700–1830. An Anthology, red. E. Bohls, I. Duncan, Oxford 2005.

Trescott P. B., *Henry George, Sun Yat-sen and China: more than land policy was involved*, „The American Journal of Economics and Sociology", 1994, v. 53, no. 3.

Tribe K., *Strategies of Economic Order. German Economic Discourse, 1750–1950*, Cambridge 1995.

Tsoulfidis L., *Competing Schools of Economic Thought*, Heidelberg - London - New York 2010.

Tsui K.-Y., *Forces shaping China's interprovincial inequality*, [in:] *Inequality and Growth in Modern China*, red. G. Wan, Oxford – New York 2008.

Tsunoyama S., *Sino-Japanese trade and Japanese industrialization*, [in:] *Japanese Industrialization and the Asian Economy*, red. A. J. H. Latham, H. Kawakatsu, London – New York 1994.

Turner M. S., *Joan Robinson and the Americans*, Armonk 1989.

Tymiński M., *PZPR i przedsiębiorstwo. Nadzór partyjny nad zakładami przemysłowymi 1956–1970*, Warszawa 2001.

U Thant, *Foreword to the United Nations Development Decade: Proposals for Action, June 1962*, [in:] A. W. Cordier, M. Harrelson, *Public Papers of the Secretaries-General of the United Nations*, v. 6, New York – London 1976.

Ulam A. B., *The Bolsheviks. The Intellectual and Political History of the Triumph of Communism in Russia*, Cambridge – London 1998.

United Nations, *Relative Prices of Exports and Imports of Under-developed Countries: A Study of Post-war Terms of Trade between Under-developed and Industrialized Countries*, New York 1949.

Ustawa o planie 3-letnim, opr. J. Kaliński, Lublin 1981.

Valdés J. G., *Pinochet's Economists: The Chicago School of Economics in Chile*, Cambridge 1995.

Valdivia Ortiz de Zárate V., *El Golpe Después Del Golpe: Leigh vs. Pinochet: Chile 1960–1980*, Santiago 2003.

Vallin J., F. Meslé, S. Adamets, S. Pyrozhkov, *The crisis of the 1930s*, [in:] *Mortality and Causes of Death in 20th-Century Ukraine*, red. F. Meslé, J. Vallin, Dodrecht – Heidelberg – London – New York 2012.

Vamvakidis A., *How robust is the growth-ppenness connection? Historical evidence*, „Journal of Economic Growth", 2002, no. 7.

van de Ven H. J., *War and Nationalism in China, 1925–1945*, London – New York 2003.

van de Walle N., *African Economies and the Politics of Permanent Crisis 1979–1999*, Cambridge 2001.

van de Walle N., *African Economies and the Politics of Permanent Crisis, 1979–1999*, Cambridge – New York 2001.

Vogel E. F., *The Four Little Dragons: The Spread of Industrialization in East Asia*, Cambridge 1991.

Voigtländer N., H.-J. Voth, *Malthusian dynamism and the rise of Europe: make war, not love*, „American Economic Review", 2009, no. 2.

Vonyó T., *Post-war reconstruction and the Golden Age of economic growth*, „European Review of Economic History", 2008, no. 2.

Vonyó T., *Socialist industrialisation or Post-War reconstruction: understanding Hungarian economic growth, 1949–1967*, „Journal of European Economic History", 2010, no. 2.

Vries J. de, *The Industrious Revolution. Consumer Behavior and the Household Economy, 1650 to the Present*, Cambridge 2008.

Wade R., *Governing the Market. Economic Theory and the Role of Government in East Asian Industrialization*, Princeton 1990.

Walder A. G., Y. Su, *The Cultural Revolution in the countryside: scope, timing and human impact*, „The China Quarterly", 2003, no. 173.

Wallerstein I., *Capitalist Agriculture and the Origins of the European World-Economy in the Sixteenth Century*, New York – San Francisco – London 1974.

Wallerstein I., *World system analysis,* [in:] *The Essential Wallerstein*, New York 2000.

Wańkowicz M., *Sztafeta. Książka o polskim pochodzie gospodarczym*, Warszawa 2012.

Wapiński R., *Historia polskiej myśli politycznej XIX i XX wieku*, Gdańsk 1997.

Ward-Perkins B., *The Fall of Rome and the End of Civilization*, Oxford 2005.

Weber M., *The Religion of China*, Detroit 1968.

Weber M., *The Religion of India: the sociology of Hinduism and Buddhism*, Glencoe 1958.

Weil D. N., J. Wilde, *How relevant is Malthus for economic development today?*, „American Economic Review", 2009, no. 2.

Weinar L., *Responsibility and Severe Poverty,* [in:] *Freedom from Poverty as a Human Right. Who Owes What to the Very Poor?*, Oxford – New York 2007.

Weintraub E. R., *How Economics Became a Mathematical Science*, Durham – London 2002.

Weitzman M. L., *Soviet postwar growth and capital-labor substitution*, „American Economic Review", 1970, no. 60.

Welch D., *Germany, Propaganda and Total War, 1914–1918*, New Brunswick 2000.

Wennerlind C., *Casualties of Credit. The English Financial Revolution, 1620–1720*, Cambridge – London 2011.

Westney E., *Imitation and Innovation: The Transfer of Western Organizational Patterns to Meiji Japan*, Cambridge 1987.

Wheatcroft S. G., *The first 35 years of Soviet living standards: secular growth and conjunctural crises in a time of famines*, „Explorations in Economic History", 2009, no. 46.

White H., *Metahistory. Historical Imagination in Nineteenth-Century Europe*, New York 1975.

Wieczorkiewicz P., *Łańcuch śmierci: czystka w Armii Czerwonej 1937–1939*, Warszawa 2001.

Wieczorkiewicz P., *Stalin i generalicja sowiecka w latach 1937–1941: sprawa Tuchaczewskiego i jej konsekwencje*, Warszawa 1993.

Wiktor Z., *Chiny na drodze socjalistycznej modernizacji*, Toruń 2008.

Williams E., *Capitalism and Slavery*, Chapel Hill 1944.

Williams K., *From Pauperism to Poverty*, London 1981.

Wintrobe R., *The Political Economy of Dictatorship*, Cambridge 2000.

Wittner D. G., *Commodore Matthew Perry and the Perry Espedition to Japan*, New York 2005.

Wizje Polski. Programy polityczne lat wojny i okupacji, wstęp, wybór i opracowanie K. Przybysz, Warszawa 1992.

Włudyka T., *„Trzecia droga" w myśli gospodarczej II Rzeczypospolitej: koncepcje Adama Doboszyńskiego*, Kraków 1994.

Wojdyło W., *Koncepcje społeczno-polityczne Stanisława Grabskiego*, Toruń 1993.

Wojdyło W., *Wizja ustroju politycznego państwa w myśli politycznej Stronnictwa Narodowego w drugiej wojnie światowej*, [in:] *Między otwartą a domkniętą myślą polityczną. Szkice o najnowszej refleksji politycznej*, red. R. Bäcker, J. Marszałek-Kawa, Toruń 2006.

Wojdyło W., *Wizja ustroju polityczno-gospodarczego powojennej Polski w projekcjach Komisji Spraw Ustrojowych Rządu Rzeczypospolitej Polskiej na uchodźstwie 1939-1945*, „Athenaeum", 2005, no. 13.

Wolf N., *Should I stay or should I go? Understanding Poland's adherence to gold, 1928–1936*, „Historical Social Research - Historische Sozialforschung", 2007, no. 4.

Wood R. E., *From Marshall Plan to Debt Crisis. Foreign Aid and Development Choices in the World Economy*, Berkeley - Los Angeles 1986.

Woodruff D. M., *The Politburo on gold, industrialization, and the international economy, 1925–1926*, [in:] *The Lost Politburo Transcripts. From Collective Rule to Stalin's Dictatorship*, red. P. R. Gregory, N. Nalmark, New Haven - London 2008.

World Bank, *The East Asian Miracle. Economic Growth and Public Policy*, Washington - New York 1993.

Woronoff J., *West African Wager: Houphouët versus Nkrumah*, Metuchen 1972.

Wójcicki K. W., *Pamiętniki dziecka Warszawy i inne wspomnienia warszawskie*, v. 1, opr. J. W. Gomulicki, Z. Lewinówna, M. Grabowska, Warszawa 1974.

Wójcik S., *Ekonomia społeczna według koncepcji Stanisława Grabskiego*, Lublin 1995.

Wójcik Z., *Historia powszechna XVI–XVII w.*, Warszawa 1991.

Wóycicki A., *Ku ustrojowi korporacyjnemu*, „Przegląd Ekonomiczny", 1938, no. 2, s. 16.

Wrigley E. A., *Energy and the English Industrial Revolution*, Cambridge 2010.

Wrzos K., *Oko w oko z kryzysem: reportaż z podróży po Polsce*, Warszawa 1985.

Wu Y.-L., *Economics, ideology and the Cultural Revolution*, „Asian Survey", 1969, v. 8, no. 3.

Wyczański A., *Czy można porównywać poziom życia gospodarczego krajów w epoce przedstatystycznej?*, [in:] *Badania nad historią gospodarczo-społeczną w Polsce. Problemy i metody*, Warszawa – Poznań 1978.

Wyjątki z dzieł przewodniczącego Mao Tse-Tunga, Wrocław 2005.

Wystąpienie Hilarego Minca na VIII Plenum KC PZPR, 19–21 października 1956 r., „Nowe Drogi", no. 10, październik 1956.

Wywiad z Thomasem W. Hazlettem z 1977 roku, opublikowany w „The Reason", lipiec 1992, http://reason.com/archives/1992/07/01/the-road-from-serfdom.

Yamamura K., *Success Illbegotten? The role of Meiji militarism in Japan's technological progress*, "Journal of Economic History", 1977, no. 1.

Yamamura K., *Zaibatsu, prewar and zaibatsu, postwar*, „Journal of Asian Studies", 1964, no. 4.

Yergin D., J. Stanislaw, *The Commanding Heights: The Battle Between Government and the Marketplace That Is Remaking the Modern World*, New York 1998.

Yik-yi Chu C., *Chinese Communists and Hong Kong Capitalists: 1937–1997*, New York 2010.

Yongming Z., *Nationalism, Identity and state-building. The antidrug crusade in the People's Republic, 1949–1952*, [in:] *Opium Regimes. China, Britain and Japan 1839–1952*, red. v. Brook, B. Tadashi Wakabayashi, Berkeley – Los Angeles – London 2000.

Yung Lee H., *The Politics of the Chinese Cultural Revolution. A Case Study*, Berkeley – Los Angeles – London 1978.

Yusuf S., *Development Economics. Through the Decades*, Washington 2009.

Zachodni spór o socjalizm rynkowy. Wybór tekstów, red. v. Kowalik, Warszawa 1991.

Zagadki wzrostu gospodarczego. Siły napędowe i kryzysy – analiza porównawcza, red. L. Balcerowicz, A. Rzońca, Warszawa 2010.

Zanasi M., *Saving the Nation. Economic Modernity in Republican China*, Chicago – London 2006.

Zanden J. L. van, *Early modern economic growth: a survey of the 67 European economy, 1500–1800*, [in:] *Early Modern Capitalism. Economic and Social Change in Europe, 1400–1800*, red. M. Prak, London – New York 2010.

Zaremba M., *„Bigosowy socjalizm". Dekada Gierka*, [in:] *Polacy wobec PRL. Strategie przystosowawcze*, red. G. Miernik, Kielce 2003.

Zaremba M., *Wielka trwoga. Polska 1944–1947. Ludowa reakcja na kryzys*, Kraków 2012.

Zaremba M., *Zimno, ciepło, gorąco. Nastroje Polaków od „zimy stulecia" do lata '80* (w druku).

Zawistowski A., *Kombinat*, Warszawa – Białystok 2009.

Zweig F., *Pomiędzy dwiema wojnami*, Londyn 1945.

Żarnowski J., *Polska 1918–1939: praca, technika, społeczeństwo*, Warszawa 1992.

Żarnowski J., *Społeczeństwo Drugiej Rzeczypospolitej, 1918–1939*, Warszawa 1973.

Żurawicki S., *Myśl ekonomiczno-polityczna w Polsce okresu międzywojennego*, Warszawa 1970.

Żurawicki S., *Myśl ekonomiczno-polityczna w Polsce okresu międzywojennego*, Warszawa 1970.

Geschichte - Erinnerung - Politik
Posener Studien zur Geschichts-, Kultur- und Politikwissenschaft

Herausgegebenvon Anna Wolff-Powęska und Piotr Forecki

Band 1 Machteld Venken: Stradding the Iron Curtain? Immigrants, Immigrant Organisations, War Memories. 2011.

Band 2 Anna Wolff-Powęska / Piotr Forecki: Der Holocaust in der polnischen Erinnerungskultur. 2012.

Band 3 Marta Grzechnik: Regional Histories and Historical Regions. The Concept of the Baltic Sea Region in Polish and Swedish Historiographies. 2012.

Band 4 Lutz Niethammer: Memory and History. Essays in Contemporary History. 2012.

Band 5 Piotr Forecki: Reconstructing Memory. The Holocaust in Polish Public Debates. 2013.

Band 6 Marek Słoń (ed.): Historical Atlas of Poland in the 2nd Half of the 16th Century. Voivodeships of Cracow, Sandomierz, Lublin, Sieradz, Łęczyca, Rawa, Płock and Mazovia. Volume 1-4. Translated by Agata Staszewska, Editorial Assistance Martha Brożyna. 2014.

Band 7 Maciej Janowski: Birth of the Intelligentsia 1750-1831. A History of the Polish Intelligentsia – Part 1. Edited by Jerzy Jedlicki. Translated by Tristan Korecki. 2014.

Band 8 Jerzy Jedlicki: The Vicious Circle 1832-1864. A History of the Polish Intelligentsia – Part 2. Edited by Jerzy Jedlicki. Translated by Tristan Korecki. 2014.

Band 9 Magdalena Micińska: At the Crossroads 1865-1918. A History of the Polish Intelligentsia – Part 3. Edited by Jerzy Jedlicki. Translated by Tristan Korecki. 2014.

Band 10 Anna Wolff-Powęska: Memory as Burden and Liberation. Germans and their Nazi Past (1945-2010). Translated by Marta Skowrońska. 2015.

Band 11 Thomasz Szarota: On the Threshold of the Holocaust. Anti-Jewish Riots and Pogroms in Occupied Europe. Warsaw – Paris – The Hague – Amsterdam – Antwerp – Kaunas. Translated by Tristan Korecki. 2015.

Band 12 Anna Wolff-Powęska / Piotr Forecki (eds.): World War II and Two Occupations. Dilemmas of Polish Memory. Translated by Marta Skowrońska and Blanka Zahorjanova. 2016.

Band 13 Elżbieta Katarzyna Dzikowska / Agata Handley / Piotr Zawilski (eds.): The Great War. Insights and Perspectives. 2016.

Band 14 Jerzy Jedlicki: A Degenerate World. Translated by Tristan Korecki. Edited by Elena Rozbicka. 2016.

Band 15 Miroslaw Matyja: Zwischen Krieg und Hoffnung. Internierung der 2. polnischen Infanterieschützen-Division in der Schweiz 1940-45. 2016.

Band 16 Adam Leszczyński: Leap into Modernity – Political Economy of Growth on the Periphery, 1943-1980. 2017.

www.peterlang.com

www.ingramcontent.com/pod-product-compliance
Ingram Content Group UK Ltd.
Pitfield, Milton Keynes, MK11 3LW, UK
UKHW041825100926
8556IPUK00002B/19

9 783631 656365